Illegal Online File Sharing, Decision-Analysis, and the Pricing of Digital Goods

Illegal Online File Sharing, Decision-Analysis, and the Pricing of Digital Goods

Michael I. C. Nwogugu

CRC Press
Taylor & Francis Group
Boca Raton London New York

CRC Press is an imprint of the
Taylor & Francis Group, an **informa** business

CRC Press
Taylor & Francis Group
6000 Broken Sound Parkway NW, Suite 300
Boca Raton, FL 33487-2742

First issued in hardback 2017

© 2017 by Taylor & Francis Group, LLC
CRC Press is an imprint of Taylor & Francis Group, an Informa business

No claim to original U.S. Government works

Version Date: 20160901

ISBN-13: 978-1-4987-8393-4 (pbk)
ISBN-13: 978-1-138-42743-3 (hbk)

Library of Congress Cataloging-in-Publication Data

Names: Nwogugu, Michael C. I., author.
Title: Illegal online file sharing, decision-analysis, and the pricing of
digital goods / Michael I.C. Nwogugu.
Description: Boca Raton, FL : CRC Press, 2017. | Includes bibliographical
references and index.
Identifiers: LCCN 2016016054 | ISBN 9781498783934 (alk. paper)
Subjects: LCSH: Internet industry. | Computer file sharing--Economic aspects.
| Computer file sharing--Law and legislation. | Intellectual
property--Economic aspects. | Digital media.
Classification: LCC HD9696.8.A2 N96 2017 | DDC 384.3/3--dc23
LC record available at https://lccn.loc.gov/2016016054

Visit the Taylor & Francis Web site at
http://www.taylorandfrancis.com

and the CRC Press Web site at
http://www.crcpress.com

This book is dedicated to my parents,
Prof. (Dr.) E.I. Nwogugu and Dr. (Ms.) G.N. Nwogugu.

Contents

Author

Michael Nwogugu, CPA (inactive; United States), CMA (inactive; United States), is an author, entrepreneur, and consultant. Mr. Nwogugu has held senior management and board of director positions in companies in the United States and Nigeria in various sectors, including entertainment/Internet/media, automotive, business services, and healthcare. He has completed mergers, acquisitions, reorganizations, joint ventures, and strategic alliances that were collectively worth billions of U.S. dollars. Mr. Nwogugu has advised boards of directors and senior management about sensitive issues such as executive compensation, exemptions from franchising disclosures, labor/employee classifications, tax consequences, complex accounting, cost reduction, transfer pricing, incentive plans, and strategy. He has managed portfolios of commercial real estate and conducted due diligence on large portfolios of commercial mortgages, business loans, and commercial real estate leases. Mr. Nwogugu has written and published articles in international referred journals such as *Managerial Auditing Journal* (Emerald); *International Journal of Law and Management* (Emerald); *Journal of Hedge Funds and Derivatives*; *Applied Mathematics and Computation* (Elsevier); *Journal of International Banking Law and Regulation* (Sweet & Maxwell); *Computer and Telecommunications Law Review* (Thomson Reuters); *Journal of Risk Finance* (Emerald); *Corporate Control and Ownership*; *Discrete Mathematics, Algorithms and Applications* (World Scientific); *International Journal of Mathematics, Game Theory and Algebra* (Nova Publishers); *Banking Law Journal*; *Journal of Bankruptcy Law* (A.S. Pratt & Sons, USA); and *Chaos and Complexity Letters* (Nova Publishers). His articles have been cited as authoritative evidence in court cases in the United States, and he has served as an expert witness in litigation (federal and state courts) and FINRA Arbitration in the United States. Mr. Nwogugu wrote the book titled *Risk in the Global Real Estate Market* (John Wiley & Sons, 2012) and is now completing other books. Mr. Nwogugu earned a BSc (architecture) from the University of Nigeria, Nsukka, a BArch (architecture) from the City University of New York, New York, and an MBA from Columbia University, New York City, New York. He attended Suffolk University (Boston, Massachusetts) Law School's juris doctor degree program for 2 years.

Chapter 1

Introduction*

This book is intended for university professors, PhD researchers in industry (computer science, theoretical economic psychology, and operations research), and PhD-level policy analysts in government. Illegal online file sharing (IOF) has resulted in millions of dollars of losses for many companies and substantial lawsuits by trade groups and entertainment companies.[1] Illegal downloads affect the economics, profitability, and business models of companies in many industries such as entertainment, education, travel, investments/finance, and any business where knowledge has value. In the United States, the Napster case illustrates some of the policy, technological, and economic issues inherent in systems for downloading content. The volume of file sharing continues to grow despite lawsuits and criminal prosecution (by the Recording Industry Association of America and other trade groups), introduction of new digital rights management (DRM) systems and legal content downloading portals. However, video traffic has become a larger component of Internet traffic.

IOF has or can have significant negative economic *multiplier effects* in and across national economies. When IOF occurs, (1) content-production companies and persons lose substantial revenues; (2) as a result, employees of content-production companies are either laid-off or their salaries are reduced, which results in reduced household spending and consumer confidence, and can increase consumer debt; (3) in addition, the content-production companies become less financially stable and have to reduce their investment in content production and/or R&D, all of which results in bad economic news that also has adverse multiplier effects; (4) government spending declines because of both actual and lower anticipated tax revenues, and the government may have to borrow more money to cover budget deficits; (5) consumers become less likely to physically visit retail stores and thus retail revenues and transportation revenues (and government revenues from such activities) are likely to decline; and (6) consumers become more likely to conduct more online searches and to spend more leisure time (and even some work time) on their computers, which increases health risks and associated costs and reduces or can reduce employee productivity. The TERA (2010)[2] study predicted that digital piracy would cause the loss of much as 1.2 million jobs and €240 billion in retail revenues by 2015 if the trend continued. Risen (2013),[3] RIAA (2015),[4] and Scholes (2014)[5] summarized

---

* This chapter contains excerpts from an article that was written by Michael Nwogugu and published as: Nwogugu, M. (2006). Corporate governance and the economics of digital content: Some legal issues. *Computer & Telecommunications Law Review*, 12(1), 5–13.

the extent of the global IOF problem (including multiplier effects), which has not abated. Scholes (2014)[6], Kigerl (2013); Yu (2014); Yoon (2011); Wu and Yang (2013); Wohlers (2012); Hinduja (2012); Dolinski (2012); Coluccio (2013); Chan and Lai (2011); Bateman et al. (2013); Arias and Ellis (2013); and Suzor (2014) made some useful comments about the prevalence of ethical issues and problems inherent in, IOF and software piracy. According to Gavaldà-Mirallesa et al. (2014), BitTorrent (a type of peer-to-peer [P2P] network) alone is used by millions of people each month and accounts for more than one-third of the total worldwide Internet traffic. Peer-to-peer (P2P) Internet traffic represents 40%–70% of overall ISP traffic (the variations are by country, time, and type of Internet traffic).

IOF also causes negative *economic contagion* within and across national economies because when IOF occurs, (1) countries tend to tighten import and trade restrictions against countries where IOF volume is deemed significant; (2) foreign direct investment (in countries that produce substantial legal digital content) can be reduced; (3) the stock prices of international companies (that produce and/or distribute digital content) are negatively affected—many of such companies have international operations; (4) interjurisdictional enforcement *waves* (most often across countries) change the structure of IOF activity in regions in terms of both development and use of IOF software; and (5) the effects of public announcements of enforcement activity on the opportunity costs of IOF activity affect or can affect prices of digital content across countries and the nature of discounts/promotions that are offered by producers/distributors of digital content.

The International Federation of the Phonographic Industry noted in IFPI (2009) that 95% of more than 40 billion files that were used in BitTorrent and Gnutella were used illegally and infringed copyright holders' rights. The number of illegal downloads is much more than legal downloads: (1) according to U.S. newspaper articles, more than 3.6 billion songs are illegally downloaded each month in the United States, and (2) according to the RIAA (a U.S.-based industry trade association), at least 2.6 billion copyrighted files (mostly music) are illegally downloaded each month, and at any given time, more than 5 million online users are sharing an estimated 1 billion files.

IOF is the product (and sometimes the cause) of the continuously changing confluence of, and symbiotic relationships among legal, technological, behavioral, and *industrial organization* factors, which have remained insufficiently analyzed, coordinated, and regulated in many countries. Interdonato and Tagarelli (2015); Adermon and Liang (2014); Stalla-Bourdillon et al. (2014); Sang et al. (2015); and Wu et al. (2014) studied some of these issues. In many countries and jurisdictions, the liability of *intermediaries* remains heavily debated—as discussed in EDRI (2012), Man et al. (2013), Synodinou (2015), Werkers (2011), Edwards (2009), Manta (2011), and Oguer (2011). *Intermediaries* include internet service providers (ISPs), and companies that develop file sharing software, and companies that facilitate third-party file sharing in any manner. IOF has caused and is also a product of *regulatory contagion* within and across countries wherein: (1) industry trade groups in many countries communicate and have been using similar monitoring and enforcement methods; (2) the antipiracy statutes and penalties in some countries (e.g., the United States and the United Kingdom) are conceptually similar in terms of format, procedure, deterrence effects, etc.; and (3) enforcement of antipiracy statutes often requires coordination and cooperation among law enforcement agencies in many countries and they tend to develop and use similar methods—and sponsors/developers of IOF software/systems are familiar with their methods.

Another major issue is the significant unreliability of empirical research methods used in articles that are published in top-ranked psychology and computer science (e.g., human–computer interactions) journals. These defects were discussed in Open Science Collaboration (August 2015), Bohannon (August 2015), Ioannidis (2005), and BEC Crew (August 28, 2015).[7]

P2P traffic is a major security risk for companies and a major bandwidth constraint, and unfortunately, most of the existing solutions function at the server level or at the gateway/

router level. P2P is often disguised as other types of traffic, and P2P traffic bypasses firewalls and proxies. In the analysis of illegal file sharing, the following constraints affect the efficiency of networks/systems: (1) cost of bandwidth; (2) cost of storage capacity; (3) costs of security; (4) network congestion costs; (5) pricing difficulties (determining the exact number of players and the number of times each digital-content file is played); (6) the cost of hardware for playing content (introducing specialized hardware will only increase the final cost of downloading digital content); (7) the form of content that will be transferred (different companies have different file formats); (8) the control of content; and (9) the cost of enforcing intellectual property rights (lawsuits, investigations, staff, etc.).

In many countries, there have been a wide range of antipiracy methods ranging from lawsuits and fines/penalties to shutting down IOF websites and IOF sponsors, to *Hadopi* methods in Europe (which involve monitoring of P2P networks), and to initiatives launched by industry trade associations.[8] Rayna and Barbier (2010), European Publishers Council (2011), Geiger (2007, 2011), Sinha and Mandel (2008), Dimita (2010), Lefranc (2010), Guibault et al. (2007), Strowel (2010), Lovejoy (2011), Meyer and Van Audenhove (2010), and Moiny (2011) discussed some of these antipiracy efforts. It has become obvious that given the civil and criminal penalties in most countries during 2000–2015, lawsuits were not the best solution for combating IOF, primarily because of the substantial transaction costs, reputation effects, weak/low deterrence effects, and the substantial monetary/nonmonetary litigation costs and monitoring costs that are involved. In addition, there is also a *free-loader effect* that distorts antipiracy efforts and is characterized by the following: (1) users may believe that content owners should make such content available after a certain period of time after initial release—probably because the entertainment/ educational value of the digital content is perceived to decline over time, (2) users may believe that the actual cost of creating the content is minimal compared to the price charged for the content and, thus, illegal downloading is justified in order to prevent a perceived rip-off, and (3) users may believe that once the original downloader has paid for the content, he/she has final rights to it and therefore can freely transfer such content to anybody—this is irrespective of the fact that the value of any given content is wholly or partly dependent on the number of people that download or have access to it and the number of times each such person plays such content. This *free-loader effect* is distinct and different from the *free rider problem* in P2P networks, which has been studied and written about (wherein which many P2P users do not contribute their fair share in P2P networks). Shutting down the illegal file sharing websites has the following limitations: (1) it can be applied only to client–server networks that use dedicated websites—the third-generation and fourth-generation P2P networks do not have any identifiable websites and, rather, operate from hard drives of network members; (2) sponsors of such client–server networks and P2P can and do re-create similar new sites once their former websites are shut down; and (3) this method P2P networks can incur substantial monitoring and prosecution costs with low probability of deterrence since sponsors often maintain various similar file sharing websites and can launch new websites.

File sharing in any form compounds pricing of content, because the owner does not know the exact number of users/players and the number of times each user downloads the content. File sharing violates most intellectual property laws and provisions inherent in digital content. Owners of digital content should obtain the full value of their works. Digital content provides a certain level of *utility* or disutility to each consumer. Unfortunately, due to technological limitations and improper business models, most content owners cannot obtain the full value of their digital content. Most digital content is sold using one of the following models: (1) subscription model, in which users pay a fixed periodic fee for the right to download a specific number of file,

(2) pay-per-download model, in which users pay a fixed fee per download, and (3) the free illegal P2P networks. In these models, the consumer has to download content onto a device, and thus has full control of such content, and can subsequently share said content with others illegally. Some companies have attempted to use DRMSs to control/limit sharing of content—however, such systems still result in *leakages* because downloaded content can still be copied.

The omissions in the existing literature on the economics and pricing of digital content include the following:

1. An accurate analysis of the economics and cost structure of digital content within the context of IOF and the legal framework for intellectual property rights.
2. Accurate valuation of digital content within the context of IOF and the existing legal framework for intellectual property rights.
3. Technical solutions to the content-control problem in networks, which consider economic analysis, compliance, and IOF.
4. The dynamics and effects of time within the context of allocation of household resources.
5. The symbiotic effects between network structure and prices of digital content.
6. The effects of the consumers' and content-producers' opportunity costs and regret (e.g., regret-minimizing behavior).

1.1 File Sharing Systems

Several companies have developed systems for digital entertainment—Napster, Mashboxx, StreamCast Networks (Morpheus), Swarm Systems, eXeem, Grokster, and Snocap. However, many of these systems involve P2P networks and are used for illegal file sharing. Many of such companies have been sued in the U.S. courts for IP infringements. Some courts in some countries have imposed criminal and civil sanctions on some of these companies. Other content distribution systems[9] include iPod/iTunes, www.skype.com, Peer Impact, Microsoft, university-based download services (Ruckus Networks, Real Networks Inc., Sea Blue Media LLC, etc.), and F.Y.E.

File sharing systems have evolved from a centralized model (Napster, etc.) to *second-generation* hybrid decentralized systems (Direct Connect Servers, eDonkey, etc.) and *third-generation* and *fourth-generation* wholly decentralized systems (Kazaa, BitTorrent, Videora, etc.) primarily because of lawsuits and criminal prosecution, technological advances, continuing consumer demand, and the low deterrence effects of penalties in many countries. A new type of third-generation system emerged—which is the legal/authorized file sharing systems such as redswoosh (www.redswoosh.com), which were implemented on some university campuses.

1.2 The Law and Illegal File Sharing

Eivazi (2012), Man et al. (2013), Stalla-Bourdillon et al. (2014), Kennedy and Doyle (2007), Synodinou (2015), and Adermon and Liang (2014) analyzed some legal issues inherent in IOF.

1.2.1 Relevant Laws and Critical Developments

There are several critical developments that have been changing the legal, economic, and technological landscape for content control.

U.S. statutes/regulations and court cases are used as examples here because of the following reasons. The United States ranks among the top five countries for bandwidth penetration and consumption. The United States ranks among the top three countries for digital media creation and consumption. The U.S. intellectual property laws are among the most comprehensive and advanced. The United States (both private companies and government agencies) is more active than most countries in enforcing/prosecuting intellectual property laws. Many countries have copied the U.S. intellectual property statutes/regulations. The U.S. Copyright Office handles copyright registration, recording of copyright transfers, and other administrative aspects of copyright law. The U.S. Court of Appeals for the Federal Circuit handles most federal copyright appeals cases.

In many countries, during 2002–2014, there were significant increases in the regulation of the Internet and telecommunication systems, and governments now regulate interconnection fees charged by networks, which in turn affects Internet access prices for consumers and companies. With regard to court cases, the general trend in the United States, Australia, and many countries during 2005–present was that courts tended to enforce IP rights and impose penalties on various persons—individual users, ISPs, and providers/sponsors of illegal P2P software and download sites.

In *MGM v. Grokster*, 545 US 913 (2005), the U.S. Supreme Court ruled on liability for the creation/distribution of P2P systems and file sharing.[10] In the United States, *MGM v. Grokster* remains the controlling case for this issue, although some U.S. federal appeals courts have issued slightly differing interpretations. Other important legal developments in the United States include the AACS encryption key controversy of 2007 and *Flava Works Inc. v. Gunter*—which was an appellate case that analyzed contributory infringement connected to infringing material and social bookmarking. Important legal developments in the EU include *Atari Europe S.A.S.U. v. Rapidshare AG* (court case in Germany) and OiNK's Pink Palace (England). In Singapore, Odex's actions against file sharing marked important changes in enforcement.

Several Australian federal court rulings on liability for creation/distribution of P2P systems and file sharing have remained very influential (see Tamberlin, 2005; Wilcox, 2005). In September 2005, an Australian federal court ruled that Kazaa was liable for copyright infringement, when others use its software, even though Kazaa had posted warnings against copyright infringement on its website.[11] That ruling went beyond the liability standards set in the U.S. Supreme Court's ruling in *MGM vs. Grokster*. However, the ruling was not final.

Artists, owners of content, and entertainment companies may seek alternative means to accommodate illegal P2P file sharing. Some authors/researchers have suggested the creation of a system in which P2P content distribution is modeled like concert revenues and radio licenses—the P2P systems will be free to the public, while such systems collect fees for artists. For example, although radio broadcasts are free to the public, artists are paid when their songs are played, and radio stations achieve this by buying blanket licenses from unions called *performing rights organizations*, which then distribute the fees to artists. Unfortunately, the division of payments among artists is based on statistical sampling and luck. On the Internet, such sampling can be passive and cheap if *audio fingerprinting* is used. Companies like Audible Magic have developed network appliances that recognize millions of songs, and if properly placed, they can produce accurate reports of listening patterns, which will improve the allocation of fees to artists. Thus, P2P systems can conceivably buy licenses from performing rights organizations, and then the unions will pay artists as songs are swapped.

Lack of standardization of digital content remains an issue. Many online stores use their own-brand DRMSs, which limit the types of media players that can be used. Microsoft and

Apple now have their own DRMSs. Sony, Philips, Matsushita, and Samsung developed a common DRMS called the *Marlin Joint Development Association*, which will define basic standards for devices made by these electronics firms. The system enables consumers to enjoy appropriately licensed video and music on any device, independent of how they originally obtained that content. Thus, there is a substantial need for industry-wide standardization of both digital-content formats and DRMSs.

Many companies have launched legal online paid and nonpaid content-subscription services. IOF among university/college students remains a major problem despite the launching of legal file sharing systems within university campuses. Universities are seeking more ways to accommodate or eliminate illegal file sharing. Efforts have ranged from providing guidelines to developing payment systems to partnering with makers/distributors of file sharing systems and file distribution systems. University of Michigan (United States) provided guidelines to its students. Pennsylvania State University (United States) in partnership with Napster offered online music to all its students over the Internet, and Penn State funded the project with its technology budget (Penn State students would be able to download unlimited number of songs on up to three computers, but they would have to pay a 99¢ charge per song or buy an entire album for $9.99 in order to burn them to a CD or transport them to an MP3 player—this was discussed in Wade (2004)). Historically, the *new generation* file sharing systems consume substantial bandwidth, primarily because they are decentralized; and in institutional environments such as universities, that can create substantial costs. According to Wade (2004), during 2002, the *Chronicle of Higher Education* reported that uploading alone from P2P networks accounted for 75% of a university's entire bandwidth capacity.

1.2.1.1 Statutes

Copyright infringement in the United States is governed by several statutes, and Carter and Perry (2004) discussed some of them. The key issues are

1. Whether file sharers, makers of file sharing software, and ISPs are violating criminal/civil copyright laws
2. Whether creators of file sharing software have violated criminal and/or civil copyright laws
3. Whether copyright statutes should be amended to create statutory *secondary liability*, which will make makers/distributors of P2P file sharing systems statutorily liable for actions of people who use their systems
4. Whether special copyright statutes should be created for Internet backbones and ISPs

In the United States, the following relevant federal statutes can be used to prosecute illegal file sharing: the *Copyright Act*, the *Digital Millennium Copyright Act*, the *National Stolen Property Act*, the mail and wire fraud statutes, the *Electronic Communications Privacy Act*, the *Communications Decency Act of 1996*, and the *Internet False Identification Prevention Act of 2000*. A brief summary of some of these laws is as follows:

1. *Copyright Infringement Act and No Electronic Theft Act*: The main elements of these laws are (a) the existence of a valid copyright; (b) infringement by the defendant by reproduction or distribution of the copyrighted work; (c) the defendant acted willfully; and (d) within a 180-day period, the defendant infringed at least 10 copies of one or more copyrighted works with a total retail value of more than $2500. This law applies more directly

to users of file sharing systems as opposed to developers of file sharing software. Applicable defenses under the criminal copyright infringement statute include the *first sale* doctrine and the *fair use* doctrine. Under the first sale doctrine, if someone legally purchases a copy of a copyrighted work, he may freely distribute that particular copy. This defense does not apply to copyright infringement pertaining to digital content and computer software, if sold by licensing agreement (most digital content is sold under licensing agreements that expressly prohibit further distribution). The *fair use* defense requires consideration of four factors: (a) the purpose and character of the use, (b) the nature of the work, (c) the substantive amount of the portion used in relation to the work as a whole, and (d) the effect of the use upon the potential market for the work. The fair use defense is not applicable to file sharing (Barr et al., 2003; Strahilevitz, 2003; Mlcakova and Whitley, 2004; Denegri-Knott and Taylor, 2005).

2. *Digital Millennium Copyright Act*: The Digital Millennium Copyright Act of 1998 (DMCA), the terms of which went fully into effect on October 28, 2000, added Chapter 12 to Title 17 of the U.S. Code. Its purpose is to ban the use of computers and other electronic devices to infringe against copyrights on traditional works. Section 1201 prohibits circumvention of technological measures used to protect copyrighted works. No person may manufacture, import, offer to the public, provide, or otherwise traffic in a technology, product, service, or device that is used to circumvent such technological measures, if one of the following conditions is met: (a) the technology, product, service, or device is primarily designed or produced to circumvent; (b) it has only limited commercial use other than that prohibited by the statute; or (c) it is marketed for use in circumventing. A number of exceptions are available for research and other purposes. Under the DMCA, almost all file sharing systems violate criminal copyright laws (Mlcakova and Whitley, 2004). Section 1202 prohibits interference with the integrity of copyright management information. Section 1202(a) prohibits knowing dissemination of false copyright management information, if done with the intent to induce, enable, facilitate, or conceal copyright infringement, while Section 1202(b) prohibits the intentional removal of copyright management information and the dissemination of works from which the copyright management information has been removed.

3. *National Stolen Property Act*: The National Stolen Property Act 141 (NSPA) prohibits the transportation in interstate commerce of any goods, wares, merchandise, securities, or money valued at $5000 or more and known to be stolen or fraudulently obtained. This statute is applicable to the act of file sharing because perpetrators are in effect engaging in theft.

4. The federal mail and wire fraud statutes prohibit the use of interstate mails or wire communications to further a fraudulent scheme to obtain money or property. One commentator suggests that these statutes would seem to apply to any computer-aided theft involving the use of interstate wire, the mails, or a federally insured bank.

5. The Copyright Act of 1976 (17 U.S.C. Sections 102–110, 121, 412). Copyright Act Sections 502–505.

6. The International Copyright Act of 1891 (United States).

Boyle and Jenkins (2014) lists relevant cases. In summary, both the act of file sharing and the development/distribution of file sharing software are illegal and criminal under current U.S. laws—without regard to whether or not file sharing is *legal* (with consent of author or rights holder) or *illegal*. The applicability of these U.S. laws is somewhat reduced due to the activity thresholds required in order to prosecute people and the required monitoring costs and enforcement costs.

1.2.1.2 Relevant U.S. and Australian Cases

1.2.1.2.1 Problems with *MGM v. Grokster* (U.S. Supreme Court Case)

The main problems that arose from the U.S. Supreme Court's decision in *MGM v. Grokster*, 545 US 913 (2005) are as follows.

The standards for establishing *intent* to promote infringing use by the device-maker are unsettled and vague. The Court did not set very clear standards for establishing intent of the device-maker to encourage perpetrators to share files illegally, but it mentioned acts such as marketing, advertising, customer services, and direct instructions provided to perpetrators as evidence of the device-maker's/distributor's intent to infringe. However, if an individual/entity develops a file sharing system and places it on the Internet, on a website where software is downloaded for free, without any comment or advertising or instructions, people can still use the system for illegal file sharing and cause the same or more economic damage. The Court stated that evidence that the commercial sense of the device-maker's enterprise turns on high-volume use that was infringing would not, by itself, justify an inference of unlawful intent—this holding is grossly insufficient as a basis/standard for determining liability, it effectively weakens copyright protection, and it is a direct contradiction to the Court's other holdings in the case.

The required elements of liability under the *inducement theory* are (1) intent, (2) distribution of device, and (3) evidence of actual infringement by recipients of the device. However, the creator of the illegal file sharing device need not distribute the device—he/she can simply post the device on websites where it can be downloaded for free.

P2P systems also have legal uses in many contexts. The Court did not state conditions under which legal uses of file sharing systems will be permitted. Under the Court's present ruling, ISPs, CD makers, and any maker of any device that can be used to store and/or transmit digital content can be potentially liable for illegal file sharing.

The Court's overall ruling focused only on instances where *MGM v. Grokster* circumstances/conditions exist. The case was an opportunity to address the many varied social and legal issues that arise in different contexts in file sharing. The Court focused excessively on *inducement*. P2P systems can cause substantial economic damage (from copyright infringement) without any *inducement* and without any *knowledge of infringement* (by the creator/distributor of the P2P system) as defined by the Court.

The Court did not sufficiently distinguish *Sony* from *MGM v. Grokster*. The Sony/Betamax doctrine states that makers/distributors of devices used on copying content cannot be held liable for copyright infringement. The Sony/Betamax doctrine (Miles, 2004) is not really applicable to P2P networks and file sharing because of the following factors:

■ Betamax machines do not have the same capacity to cause devastating economic loss within minutes or even seconds, unlike P2P networks that can copy a file to thousands/millions of people all over the world within seconds—hence there is an exponential time multiplier factor in Internet transactions.

■ Betamax involves much more transaction costs that reduce the perpetrator's propensity and capacity to illegally copy content.

■ The potential economic loss and its impact on creativity and incentives to produce content are key considerations.

■ If the Betamax doctrine is applied to P2P systems, then the resulting substantial enforcement costs will preclude effective protection of copyrights—content owners will be forced to identify, investigate, and prosecute individuals.

- Betamax typically involves one-person processes, whereas P2P systems involve multi-person virtual, geographically dispersed interactions—thousands/millions of people interacting simultaneously.
- Betamax is not an Internet-based system.
- The costs involved in copying/sharing files on the Internet (Internet access costs, PC costs) are much lower than the costs of copying content using video recorders.
- Internet-based transactions/interactions are more frequent than copying of content using video recorders.
- People are much more likely to share content through the Internet than by copying such content using video recorders.

In MGM vs. Gokster, the Court did not clearly establish standards for *contributory infringement* and *vicarious infringement*.

The definition of vicarious infringement implies that

1. The device-maker and/or perpetrator must derive some gain from direct infringement in order to be liable, and simultaneously
2. The device-maker (and/or perpetrator) must decline to exercise an affirmative duty to stop or limit infringement

In many instances, the device-makers derive their gain only tangentially and/or indirectly from infringement—as in spyware and adware that are embedded in file sharing systems, and also provide valuable information. The second requirement that pertains to an affirmative *duty to prevent* is impractical because at this time, once the perpetrator has downloaded the file sharing software, the device-maker's capability to stop or limit file sharing is minimal. Even within legal file sharing networks, participants can still share files illegally unless the system permits transfer of only specific files or types of files. Furthermore, individuals/entities that post file sharing software on *free download* websites can cause the same amount of or more economic damage without profiting from the file sharing software—hence the profiteering requirement is of little significance in establishing liability.

The Court did not clearly define contributory *infringement* because it did not make a sufficient distinction between *legal* and *illegal* uses of P2P systems. Unfortunately, P2P systems intended for legal use can also be used for illegal file sharing. The only way to prevent this is to design a P2P system that permits search for and transfer of only a limited number/type of files—but the technology is not yet commercially available. Assuming a company makes a P2P system and markets the system only as a file sharing system for use in only legal purposes but does not in any way state or imply that it can be used for illegal file sharing. A group of individuals can still download/purchase the system and use it for illegal file sharing. Hence, what *MGM v. Grokster* requires is that for any P2P system to be deemed noninfringing, it must inherently contain mechanisms that can distinguish between legal and illegal file sharing, and such mechanisms must be capable of stopping illegal file sharing. This introduces a technological burden that renders all legal file sharing systems illegal.

MGM v. Grokster failed to incorporate and establish liability standards for perhaps the most important element in preventing illegal file sharing—which is the roles of the ISPs, Internet backbones, and web-hosting companies. These entities have the technology and power to curb illegal file sharing.

MGM v. Grokster essentially holds an entity liable for infringing acts committed by others (individuals). This ruling goes against copyright statutes but is in accordance with settled U.S. case law. The issue is that for such *secondary liability* to be effectively enforced, the prosecutors have to provide evidence of intent to infringe, and the Court made contradictory statements about evidentiary standards.

1.2.1.2.2 The Australian Federal Court Cases

There are three Australian federal court cases that have produced rulings that are quite different from *MGM v. Grokster* and imposed varying levels of liability for infringement for various types of entities. Some developments will substantially affect determination of liability for copyright infringement in Australia:

- The Australian/U.S. Free Trade Agreement (FTA) became effective on January 1, 2005; and under the FTA, there are certain *safe harbor provisions* that were incorporated into the Copyright Act, which provides defenses for ISPs if their infrastructure is used for illegal file sharing. The safe harbors cover caching, transmission, hosting, and referencing of infringing content. The safe harbors are conditioned on certain eligibility standards for application.
- In Australia, the proposed ISPs code of conduct that is being developed by the Internet Association of Australia will provide standards for liability for ISPs and web-hosting companies (Buettel, 2010).
- Industry groups have proposed codes of conduct to be implemented by ISPs (Pearce, February 20, 2015).

1.2.1.2.2.1 Universal Music Australia Pty Ltd vs. Sharman License Holdings Ltd.

On September 5, 2005, an Australian federal court issued a decision[12] (see Wilcox, 2005), in which Kazaa was found liable for copyright infringement, even though Kazaa had posted warnings on its website (against illegal file sharing). Kazaa website did not specifically advise users about how to share copyrighted content and did not refer directly to music. Users could share any type of files using the system. In an end-user license agreement, Kazaa's website warned users not to violate copyrights. The Court found that Kazaa had encouraged IOF and that Kazaa had not incorporated any filtering devices in its P2P system that would prevent or reduce illegal file sharing. The Court raised the issue of and imputed *knowledge of infringement* that created a duty to prevent infringement. The Court ordered the defendants to include *non-optional keyword filtering technology* in its P2P system—so that users cannot share certain files listed by record companies and so that only *licensed works* would be shown in the system.[13]

1.2.1.2.2.2 Universal Music Australia vs. Cooper

In a second Australian federal court case (see Tamberlin, 2005),[14] the Court found that a website (www.mp3s4free.net) infringed on copyrights by providing links to websites that had infringing sounds and that Comcen (an ISPA named E-Talk Communications, aka ComCen Internet Services) was liable for copyright infringement by hosting the mp3s4free.net website. This was the first case worldwide in which a court found an ISP and an MP3 website liable for copyright violations (because the ISP allowed its infrastructure to be used to infringe copyrights). The Court also found that the defendant/respondent had violated Section 52 of the Trade Practices Act by making false claims. In the *defendant/ respondent* P2P system, users could download from a central server, although respondent could have disabled the central server. The case raises several issues pertaining to privacy of subscribers (inspection of Internet traffic by ISPs), ISP's duty to copyright holders, duty owed by websites to copyright holders, liability of ISPs for conduct of their subscribers, extend of ISP's duty to incorporate filtering technologies in its infrastructure, etc.

1.2.1.2.2.3 Sony Music Entertainment (Australia) Ltd vs. University of Tasmania

In *Sony Music Entertainment (Australia) Ltd vs. University of Tasmania* (FCA 532, Australia Federal

Court, May 30, 2003), the plaintiffs sued three universities for use of their computer infrastructure for infringing reproduction and communication of MP3 files. See comments in Just, 2003. The suit was mostly procedural (sought discovery) and the plaintiffs sought access to the records, computer servers, CD-ROMs, and back-up tapes of the universities in order to identify the alleged infringers. The Court granted the orders in favor of the plaintiffs but on certain conditions including the preservation of privilege and confidentiality.

1.2.1.2.2.4 *Dallas Buyers Club LLC vs. iiNet Ltd* (2015) FCA 317 (Australia).

In *Dallas Buyers Club LLC vs. iiNet Ltd* (2015) (FCA 317, Australia Federal Court; April 7, 2015), the plaintiffs (Dallas Buyers Club LLC and Voltage Pictures LLC) sued several defendants (iiNet Ltd, Internode Pty Ltd, Amnet Broadband Pty Ltd, Dodo Services Pty Ltd, Adam Internet Pty Ltd, and Wideband Networks Pty Ltd, all of whom were small Australian ISPs) for copyright infringement. The judge ordered the defendant ISPs to provide the names and physical addresses of their customers associated with each of the 4,726 IP addresses (that allegedly engaged in IOF) on the condition that this information will be used only for recovering compensation for copyright infringements and will not otherwise be disclosed without the court's permission. The plaintiffs were to submit to the judge drafts of the letters they intended to send to alleged infringers.

1.3 The Chapters

This section summarizes other chapters of this book.

Chapter 2 discusses human biases, psychological effects, and economic psychology issues inherent in IOF by individuals and institutions—most of which are *higher-order risk preferences* that implicate elements of cognition, perceptions of fairness, value of time, risk aversion, and many other behavioral issues. Illegal file sharing involves various policy, legal, technological, and economic problems that have not yet been resolved even as Internet use continues to grow substantially, and IP rights enforcement efforts are publicized. The lack of efficient methods of controlling downloads of digital content is compounded by suboptimal pricing of digital content. This chapter fills some critical gaps in the existing literature (particularly empirical research in law and economics, criminology, and operations management). Some of these new hypotheses discussed herein cannot be tested using traditional rigorous statistical methods such as regressions because the data do not fit most known distributions and/or the data are likely to vary by age group, profession, household income, family background, geographical location, and other factors, such that it will be unreasonable to make generalizations from regressions and some correlations (hence, surveys and analysis of Internet-usage data may be the most accurate empirical methods). This chapter also introduces new models of illegal file sharing as a production system and uses entirely new approaches (not the traditional operations research methods). Analyzing IOF as production systems facilitates the application of a wide range of techniques in the operations management and operations research literature.

Chapter 3 analyzes the information producer's digital-content strategies in terms of when to produce more content and when to allocate resources to enforcement and prosecution and other factors. An earlier version of this chapter was published as an article in *International Journal of Mathematics, Game Theory & Algebra* in 2009.

Chapter 4 analyzes the risk perception of parties involved in IOF and develops optimal sanctions for IOF under Un-Constrained Transferable Utility and unknown demand. This chapter surveys the extensive literature on enforcement theories from the perspectives of legal enforcement, mathematical models, psychology, politics, and criminology. Illegal file sharing is often complicated by Internet congestion and lax enforcement. Thus, customer experience and firm profitability can be vastly improved by piracy-minimizing and profit-maximizing sanctions that also reduce enforcement costs and monitoring costs. Such optimal sanctions are defined not only in terms of customers' opportunity costs (waiting time, search costs, value of customer's time, etc.) but also in terms of willingness-to-comply with IP laws, expected post-purchase customer nonmonetary utility, customer's wealth and relative wealth, and customer's marginal propensity-to-substitute digital products. These optimal sanctions can also result in lower perceived prices for *high-priority* customers and uniform *quality of service* (QoS) for all customers, all of which are socially more optimal outcomes when different customers place different values on compliance with IP laws. Chapter 4 introduces models of risk perception of information-producing firms that have unknown demand and that sell digital products to customers who have heterogeneous search costs and waiting costs.

Chapter 5 introduces new content-control *protocols* and anti-P2P-file sharing systems that are designed to reduce/eliminate illegal file sharing and improve the control of digital content. An earlier version of this chapter was published as an article in *Computer & Telecommunications Law Review* (Sweet & Maxwell) in 2008.

Chapter 6 addresses the *free rider problem* and *inequality* in Networks—these problems are central elements of the content distributor's challenge of minimizing illegal file sharing while maximizing profits. This chapter also explains why contrary to the existing literature, free riding can be beneficial under some rare circumstances. Thus, customer experience in P2P networks and firm profitability can be vastly improved by either eliminating free riders or by replicating said conditions under which free riding can improve social welfare. This chapter:

1. Introduces new solutions to the free rider problems in networks.
2. Explains why FairTorrent and similar *tit-for-tat* (TFT) P2P systems are not efficient. The information producer modeled herein is not a traditional profit-maximizing entity, but rather is piracy averse, has limited control over the P2P network or client–server network, sells short-lived products, and is most interested in long-term profits. The *free riders* (network members) are generally self-interested, *loss-averse*, and price-sensitive persons who derive mostly nonmonetary utility from consumption of digital content. Free riding can be knowing/voluntary or involuntary. The P2P and client–server networks discussed herein are anonymous legal networks, and thus the effects of actual or potential *coordination* and/or altruism among customers are somewhat limited. IOF within fourth-generation and later P2P computer networks is a major type of nonfinancial systemic risk and operational contagion that adversely affects companies in many industries (education, media/entertainment, travel, healthcare, etc.) and costs them tens of billions of U.S. dollars each year in both lost revenues and enforcement/monitoring costs. There are substantial similarities between *financial networks* (within which systemic risk and financial contagion are propagated) and such illegal file sharing computer networks.

Chapter 7 attempts to resolve some major debates about open-access and marginal cost analysis in the context of pricing digital content and the allocation of enforcement resources. Existing studies of pricing of digital content have not explored the full ramifications of marginal costs and open access. As described in the literature, the *sampling effect* is not entirely correct, and this chapter introduces a more complete definition of the sampling effect. This chapter explains why contrary to some *open-access* theories in the literature, copyright law is necessary—for incentives, for trade (transfer, pledging, sale, documentation) in IP rights, and to preserve social welfare and social order (to reduce crime, torts, and breaches of contracts). This chapter summarily introduces new elements of *marginal cost analysis* (in the pricing of digital content), which can be used for the allocation of resources for the enforcement of IP rights by both government agencies and companies in industry (either individually or by combination of efforts) and for the pricing of digital content in order to reduce illegal file sharing. The new elements are as follows: (1) the marginal cost of digital product substitution (MCDPS), (2) the *marginal cost of cross product substitution* (MCCPS), (3) the *marginal cost of enforcement of IP laws* (MCEIP), (4) the *marginal cost of Internet consumer search* (MCICS), (5) the *marginal cost of physical consumer search* (MCPCS), (6) the *marginal costs of time substitution* (MCTS), (7) the *marginal cost of illegal diffusion* (MCID), and (8) the *marginal cost of channel choice* (MCCC). In many countries, the nature and success of enforcement of laws, and the selection of disputes and offences for prosecution/litigation, and the actual/perceived credibility of *enforcement threats* often depend on the perceived affordability of enforcement costs. This chapter characterizes the right holder's/distributor's marginal costs of producing and distributing/selling one unit of digital content in ways that provide more insight (most articles in the literature do not distinguish between the *marginal cost of production* and the *marginal cost of distribution*). This chapter explains how the present mispricing of digital content contributes to IOF. This chapter critiques theories in several articles such as Benkler (2002) and shows that many of the game theorems in Yoon (2002; *Information Economics & Policy*) are wrong. A few theories in Oyama and Takahashi (2015; *Journal of Economic Theory*) support the author's critique of Yoon (2002). Yoon (2002) completely omitted any analysis of contagion, social networks, or *bilingual games*, whereas significant copyright infringement occurs in P2P networks and in offline social networks. However, the definitions of "q" in Oyama and Takahashi (2015) and the *contagion threshold* in Morris (2000) and Oyama and Takahashi (2015) are wrong. An earlier version of this chapter was published as an article (written by the author) in *Computer & Telecommunications Law Review* during 2006.

Chapter 8 analyzes one of the content distributors' challenge, which is to understand consumer choices in the context of P2P networks and illegal file sharing. Digital piracy is often complicated by anonymous online *coalitions* that thwart enforcement efforts, and lax enforcement, and offline/online coordination by digital pirates. Such coordination is often complex and can be intended or unintended and both observable and unobservable. Thus, customer experience and firm profitability can be improved by developing and implementing new models of choice and stochastic dominance in P2P networks. This chapter critiques *stochastic dominance* models and introduces new models of stochastic dominance of allocations (in network games) that solve some of the problems inherent in *Lorenz dominance* and other forms of stochastic dominance. Such stochastic dominance models incorporate a *prioritization scheme* where the *priority* is defined not only in terms of customers' opportunity costs (waiting time, search costs, etc.) but also in terms of *derivative* behaviors (of individuals and groups), willingness-to-comply with IP laws, prepurchase and post-purchase regret, customer's relative wealth, and customer's *marginal propensity-to-substitute* digital products. The customers (network members) are generally self-interested, *loss-averse*, and price-sensitive persons who derive mostly nonmonetary utility from consumption of digital content. The illegal P2P and client–server networks discussed herein are anonymous legal networks, and thus the effects of actual or potential coordination and/or altruism among customers are somewhat limited.

Chapter 9 analyzes consumer surplus and producer's surplus in the context of pricing of digital content and explains why there cannot be any *equilibrium prices* of digital content in the strict and formal economics sense. This chapter also introduces models of the *enterprise value* of a unit of digital content. The concept of enterprise value can be helpful when making decisions about the allocation of resources for enforcement of IP rights, distribution channels for digital content, the maximum allowable losses from IOF activities, and/or future investment in digital goods. Chapter 9 also critiques *Nash equilibrium* and explains alternative concepts of equilibrium.

Chapter 10 develops three new pricing models for differentiated digital goods in legal P2P and client–server networks. This chapter introduces three new classes of dynamic network games (TU noncooperative client–server networks; noncooperative P2P networks, and cooperative/P2P networks) for which it is possible to calculate the payoffs of individual members/nodes). The chapter introduces three new network allocation mechanisms for sharing the benefits of P2P and client–server networks wherein the mechanism is embedded in the pricing formula that optimizes both consumer welfare and producer/distributor welfare. This chapter develops pricing models that minimize the firm's piracy losses and simultaneously maximize revenue for the information producer under different assumptions regarding customer behavior and utility. This chapter develops models of information-producing firms and content distribution firms that sell differentiated digital products to customers who have heterogeneous online/offline search costs. The conditions for *optimal search* and a *stopping point* in the file sharing network are introduced (and these conditions depart from methods in the literature by not using stochastic calculus, which has been shown to be grossly deficient).

Chapter 11 explains why Shapley value analysis is generally inaccurate for most situations and is not applicable to network access pricing, network cost allocation or benefit allocation, electricity distribution, and the pricing of digital content. Thus, related game theory principles that have been used extensively in developing analytical models for the foregoing types of analysis are inaccurate and inefficient (in the case of Internet networks, the analysis omits illegal file sharing). This chapter has significant implications for academic and industry-oriented research in operations research, electrical engineering, theoretical computer science, and theoretical economics where Shapley value and its variants have been used extensively to develop network allocation and pricing models.

Chapter 12 explains why Stackelberg analysis is inappropriate for most situations and is not applicable to network access pricing, electricity distribution, network cost allocation, and the pricing of digital content (partly because of the constant evolution of networks). The existing literature on network analysis and pricing contains major omissions and gaps, and the effects of IOF on the pricing of network access have been substantially omitted in most literature on network analysis. The chapter has significant implications for academic and industry-oriented research in operations research, electrical engineering, theoretical computer science, and theoretical economics where *Stackelberg analysis* and its variants have been used extensively to develop network access pricing and cost allocation models.

The objectives of Chapter 13 are several: first, to develop a model for network access pricing, which reduces the information producers' losses from copyright infringement and improves social welfare and the efficiency of computer networks. Second, to develop optimal conditions for such pricing scheme, which will incorporate the effects of congestion, social welfare, copyright infringements, evolution of networks, and variations in usage. Third, to analyze some of the main pricing issues and illustrate how the present mispricing of Internet access contributes to network congestion and IOF. Internet network access pricing remains a controversial issue that is of concern to government regulators, consumers, and ISPs, given the growing prevalence of the Internet in daily transactions around the world.

In many chapters of this book, conditions (represented by mathematical equations and/or inequalities) are introduced, under which some hypotheses or events will exist. These conditions are in the nature of one of the following:

■ *Game theory strategies*—similar to the mathematical representation of *supermodularity* and *complementarity* by $\partial^2 f/\partial z_i \partial z_j \geq 0$, for all $i \neq j$, where z_i and z_j are strategies of participants in the action space and each action is chosen from an interval $z_i, z_j \in [a, b]$, and the payoff function ($f(\cdot)$) depends on actions/strategies of two or more types of participants z_i and z_j in the action space ($i = 1,\ldots, n; j = 1,\ldots, n$)
■ *Invariants*—which are used to characterize key elements of groups
■ *Decision elements*—wherein groups of these "conditions" can also be weighted and converted into decision scores for decision-making

Notes

1 See *Hollywood faces new piracy threat*. http://movies.yahoo.com/news/movies.reuters.com/hollywood-faces-new-piracy-threat-reuters.
See *Digital piracy hits the e-book industry*—CNN.com. Available at: http://www.cnn.com/2010/TECH/01/01/ebook.piracy/index.html.
See *Illegal downloading no different from stealing a handbag*. Available at: http://www.guardian.co.uk/media/2010/mar/10/murdoch-illegal-dowloading-stealing-handbag.
See You (October 6, 2014). "A peek inside the Internet's favorite file-sharing network". Science Magazine. Available at: http://www.sciencemag.org/news/2014/10/peek-inside-internets-favorite-file-sharing-network. This article states in part:

> More than a quarter of all Internet traffic belongs to BitTorrent, a file-sharing system that allows users to swap everything from music to movies. Now, for the first time, researchers have revealed a link between a country's economy and the type of files its residents download from BitTorrent. The findings are shedding new light on online behavior and could help law enforcement track down Internet pirates. … By looking at a user's first 100 downloads, the team could predict with 80% accuracy what type of file the user would download next, Duch says. … But what really stood out is that users from the same country displayed a tendency to download the same types of content. After factoring socioeconomic indicators such as a country's gross domestic product per capita and Internet access, analysis showed that users from rich countries such as the United States tended to download more music files, whereas users from poorer countries such as Spain favored movie files. … The data could also be used to evaluate the efficacy of antipiracy policies, he says. … In an unpublished study using the same data, the researchers found that regulations on online downloading tend to produce only short-term effects …

See Gavaldà-Mirallesa, A., Choffnes, D., Otto, J., et. al. (2014). Impact of heterogeneity and socioeconomic factors on individual behavior in decentralized sharing ecosystems. Proceedings of the National Academy of Sciences Of the US (PNAS), 111 (43), 15322–15327. doi: 10.1073/pnas.1309389111.
See Wortham (September 27, 2014). "The Unrepentant Bootlegger". *New York Times*. Available at: http://www.nytimes.com/2014/09/28/technology/the-unrepentant-bootlegger.html?_r=0. This article stated in part:

> …Online piracy is thriving. File-sharing, most of it illegal, still amounts to nearly a quarter of all consumer Internet traffic, according to Cisco Systems' Visual Networking Index. And a recent report from Tru Optik, a media analytics firm, said that nearly 10 billion

movies, television shows and other files, including games and pornography, were downloaded globally in the second quarter of 2014. Tru Optik estimates that about 6 percent of those downloads were legal. ... Congressional efforts, like a proposed Stop Online Piracy Act (or SOPA) introduced in 2011, met with such strident objections from the technology industry that lawmakers backed down. The Copyright Alert System, a voluntary effort by Internet service providers, sends warnings when downloading of copyrighted content is detected, but it is widely considered to be ineffective. Last year, 1.3 million warnings were sent, a fraction of what Tru Optik estimates to be 400 million illegal downloads in the United States each month. The situation has reached an uneasy stasis that pleases no one. Internet advocates say that policing individuals or small-time pirates with outdated laws ignores how ordinary people view entertainment in the real world. And despite its best efforts, the M.P.A.A. has yet to completely extinguish the unauthorized distribution of movies and television shows ...

2 TERA (Paris) (2010).

3 See Risen (2013). This article stated in part:

> ...According to the new study released on Tuesday by British brand protection firm NetNames, approximately 432 (four hundred and thirty two) million unique Internet users worldwide 'explicitly sought' copyright-infringing content during January 2013. In the regions of Europe, North America and Asia-Pacific, the study found that approximately one quarter of Internet users in those regions sought infringing content during January, which increased by ten percent since November 2011. The study was funded by NBC Universal. 'While legitimate services have come along like Netflix, the piracy world hasn't stood still,' ... 'People are infringing all kinds of content, including films, television, music and games. Over 300 (three hundred) million people infringed copyright at least once....

4 RIAA (2015). This article stated in part:

> ...Consider these staggering statistics:
>
> ■ Since peer-to-peer (P2P) file sharing site Napster emerged in 1999, music sales in the United States have dropped by 53%, from $14.6 billion to $7.0 billion in 2013.
> ■ From 2004 through 2009 alone, approximately 30 billion songs were illegally downloaded on file sharing networks.
> ■ NPD reports that only 37% of music acquired by U.S. consumers in 2009 was paid for.
> ■ According to the Information Technology & Innovation Foundation, the digital theft of music, movies, and copyrighted content takes up huge amounts of internet bandwidth—24% globally and 17.5% in the United States.
>
> Digital storage locker downloads constitute 7% of all internet traffic, while 91% of the links found on them were for copyrighted material, and 10% of those links were to music specifically, according to a 2011 Envisional study....

5 See Scholes (2014).

6 Scholes (January 14, 2014) stated in part:

> ...Technicians, editors, producers, hair stylists, and camera operators are just a few of the 2.4 million U.S. employees that make up the entertainment industry, an industry that contributes approximately $80 billion each year to the U.S. economy. And that number is nowhere close to what it should be. It is estimated that 750,000 jobs have been lost due to online piracy... But while the industry struggled to reach a consensus on file types, security, and revenue models, free online file sharing services stepped in to fill the void.

As a result, today seventy percent of online users don't see illegal downloading as a form of 'theft.' In August 2013, Russian web users protested against an anti-piracy law that passed thanks to the Russian government's petitioning platform. Over 1,700 Russian web sites went on strike the day it went into effect, describing the new law as a 'liberty killer,' and demanding for the law to be revoked, as they were accustomed to free films online, including the latest releases. It is not breaking news that pirates want content for free. In fact ninety-five percent of online music downloads are illegal, and the average mobile phone, iPod, or tablet contains $800 (eight hundred US Dollars) worth of pirated content... Today, all content creators, including publishers, production studios, and record labels, suffer from piracy. But it all began with the music industry. Prior to the popular online file sharing service Napster's debut in 1999, global music sales topped $38 billion. But over the course of two years, 60 million active Napster users changed the music industry forever. By the time Napster was shut down, serious damage had been done. As a result, music revenue dropped continuously for the next decade. It was not until 2012 that sales finally went up 3 percent thanks to services like iTunes and Amazon that made buying legal content easier than stealing it. Today, the music industry generates $16.5 billion in revenue, roughly half the amount it did 15 years ago, and only $2.9 billion of that is from digital downloads. The Guardian just recently announced that the number of tracks illegally downloaded in the UK fell by a third this past year, another positive sign for piracy in the music industry. While these are good indications, by no means has piracy been defeated... Although legal content distribution services like Netflix, Crackle, iTunes, Hulu, Amazon, Epix, and Vudu have again made accessing entertainment content legally more convenient, it is estimated that online piracy costs the U.S. economy somewhere around $250 billion per year. When content is illegally taken and distributed, income stops, jobs cannot be supported, and people are left unemployed. There is no question that content piracy has had a negative impact on everyone involved in the entertainment industry and on the overall global economy....

7 BEC Crew (2015). This article stated in part:

> ...A landmark study involving one hundred (100) scientists from around the world has tried to replicate the findings of 270 (two hundred and seventy) recent findings from highly ranked psychology journals and by one measure, only thirty-six percent turned up the same results. That means that for over half the studies, when scientists used the same methodology, they could not come up with the same results... And earlier this year, a separate study found that the prevalence of irreproducible preclinical research exceeds fifty percent, 'resulting in approximately US$28,000,000,000/year (twenty eight billion US dollars) spent on preclinical research that is not reproducible—in the United States alone'....

8 See Hadopi-2—Law 2009-1311 relating to the protection of literary and artistic property on the internet through criminal law (Loi n° 2009-1311 du 28 octobre 2009 relative à la protection pénale de la propriété littéraire et artistique sur internet, 251 Journal Officiel de la République Française [J.O.] [Official Gazette of France], October 29, 2009, p. 18290).
See Directive 2004/48/EC of the European Parliament and of the Council of April 29, 2004 on the enforcement of intellectual property rights.
See Directive 2000/31/EC of the European Parliament and of the Council of June 8, 2000 on certain legal aspects of information society services, in particular electronic commerce, in the Internal Market, OJ L 178, 17.7.2000, pp. 1–16.
See Decision No. 2009-580 DC of June 10, 2009. Available in English from: http://www.conseil-constitutionnel.fr/conseil-constitutionnel/root/bank_mm/anglais/2009_580dc.pdf.
See Anonymous (2011).
See Clayton (2012).

9 See www.weedshare.com; DeCSS-based systems; SunnComm; Viralg; Freenet (http://freenet.source-forge.net); Mercora; various encrypted systems; RealAudio; BitTorrent (see http://www.cs.uiowa.edu/~rbriggs/gt/summary11.doc; http://www.cs.uiowa.edu/~rbriggs/gt/).

10 See *MGM v. Grokster*, 545 US 913 (2005). (See Wilcox, 2005). Also see Tamberlin (2005).

11 See Michel (August 23, 2004). Internet file sharing: The evidence so far and what it means for the future. Available at: http://www.heritage.org/Research/InternetandTechnology/bg1790.cfm.

12 See Wilcox (2005).

13 See Court orders copyright filter on Kazaa. (September 6, 2005). Available at: https://www.theguardian.com/technology/2005/sep/06/business.australia.

14 See Malik (July 14, 2005). Oz ISP, employee and principal held liable for copyright breaches—Money well spent. Available at: http://www.theregister.co.uk/2005/07/14/universal_music_australia_v_cooper/.

Chapter 2

Economic Psychology Issues Inherent in Illegal Online File Sharing by Individuals and Institutions and Illegal Online File Sharing as Production Systems

Illegal online file sharing (IOF) involves substantial psychological issues that implicate elements of cognition, perceptions of fairness, value of time, risk aversion, and many other behavioral issues. The lack of efficient methods of controlling downloads of digital content is compounded by sub-optimal pricing of digital content. This chapter introduces hypothesis of economic psychology factors that directly or indirectly cause IOF and, by doing so, fills some critical gaps in the existing literature (particularly empirical research in psychology, law and economics, criminology, and operations research). More importantly, the theories introduced in this chapter can form the basis for (1) determining whether to handle illegal file sharing as a criminal matter or civil matter and for determining the best forum for such claims (e.g., courts vs. arbitration vs. government administrative agencies); (2) allocation of resources to the investigation and/or prosecution of illegal online file sharing; and (3) the analysis of procedural and substantive due process in the prosecution of illegal file sharing claims in courts and government administrative agencies.

Sang et al. (2015), Cox et al. (2010), Argan et al. (2013), Jambon and Smetana (2012), Borja et al. (2015), and other articles[1] analyzed psychology theories that are relevant.

2.1 Illegal Online File Sharing as a Moneyless Market

IOF is essentially a moneyless market but is not a pure barter market. The IOF market is characterized by the following:

1. Relatively very low transaction costs.
2. Continuous time—trading is done 24 hours per day, each day.
3. Money is not exchanged.
4. The property traded are (a) *personal access rights*—in exchange for the right to make his/her content available to others, the member obtains the right to access other members' content on their computers, and (b) property rights—the right to enjoy digital content.
5. Exchanges are not based on monetary value.
6. Consumer utility has a major impact on the type, frequency, and volume of transactions.
7. There are no *prices* or even shadow prices.
8. The market is relatively transparent. There are readily available data about inventory of digital content.
9. There are substantial knowledge gaps and information gaps among market participants.
10. Market participants have relatively low influence on tastes and consumer choice in the market.
11. The aggregate value of transactions in the market is not a linear function of the size of the market.
12. The market has undefined and continuously evolving geographical boundaries; the market boundary is a function of Internet penetration, leisure time (by geography), and consumer willingness-to-participate (willingness to post digital content for third-party access).
13. The market is illegal, and there are substantial sanctions for participation. Hence, there is a balancing process in which consumers weigh the benefits of participation and the probability of prosecution and sanctions.
14. Activities in this market have a multiplier effect on other parts of the economy—time spent trading, time spent accessing content, psychological effect of content, opportunity costs (lost creativity and productivity), disutility from not finding specific digital content, content-producers' loss of revenues (and resultant layoffs of staff), etc.

2.2 Illegal Online File Sharing Contravenes Most Principles of Search Theory

Research in search theory has attempted to explain the factors that cause or prevent *matching* in markets.

Modern search theory can be categorized into at least five branches of research, which are as follows, and some of which have been influential:

1. The *Diamond–Mortensen–Pissarides* models. These include Mortensen and Pissarides (1994, 1999), Mortensen and Wright (2002), Mortensen (1982), Pissarides (1979), and other articles.[2] The *Diamond–Mortensen–Pissarides* models obviously did not consider the nature of search in different media/contexts such as Internet networks, and the effect of, and search within offline Social Networks.
2. The Koopman (1946, 1980) and Stone (1989, 1992) line of research.
3. Various studies in human–computer interaction that were conducted during the last 15 years—these include but are not limited to the following: Wilson and Schraefel (2010),

Hulleman (2010), Sumita and Zuo (2010), Beck et al. (2010), Becker and Clement (2006), Sonntag (2015), Krajbich et al. (2010), Krajbich and Rangel (2011), and Gopal et al. (2004).

4. Various studies on the criminology of illegal online search—such as Higgins et al. (2006), Kigerl (2013), Yu (2014), Hinduja (2012), Hardy et al. (2013), and Hinduja (2006).

5. The more recent work on consumer search in networks—such as Klampanos and Jose (2012), Wong et al. (2011), Nwogugu (2006/2013), Ciccarelli and Lo Cigno (2011), and Coyle et al. (2009).

6. Research on optimal-search and optimal-stopping, such as Branco et al. (2015), Branco et al. (2012), and Ke et al. (2016) (most of this recent research have used similar approaches and models). Others include Rothschild (1974), Roberts and Weitzman (1981), Moscarini and Smith (2001), Liu and Dukes (2013), and Weitzman (1979).

IOF contravenes most principles of search theory research in that none of the aforementioned approaches has been able to develop models that completely explain all facets of IOF including actual/perceived online/offline transaction costs; psychological effects and biases; psychological contagion in social networks; effects of actual or threatened apprehension and/or prosecution; effects of technology (e.g., decentralized file sharing systems, anonymity and perceived risk of apprehension, transaction costs, choice); and systems/methods of matching in IOF networks.

The Diamond–Mortensen–Pissarides models have been conclusively refuted and contradicted by recent research in search theory. Garcia-Perez (2002) surveyed the literature about equilibrium search models with wage posting. Garcia-Perez (2002) reviewed the basic Burdett and Mortensen (1998) model and explained the main consequences of departing from its two main assumptions—random matching and a linear production function—and showed how the specific modeling of either the production or the matching technology can affect the results regarding the distribution function of offered wages.

The results in Van Denberg and Van Vuuren (2002), Lester (2010), Cooper et al. (2003), Virag (2011), and Shimer and Smith (2000) contradict the Diamond–Mortensen–Pissarides models.

Aoki and Yoshikawa (2009) reviewed Lucas and Prescott (1974) and showed that neoclassical search theory cannot explain the observed pattern of productivity dispersion and that non-self-averaging plays the major role. Aoki and Yoshikawa (2009) noted that empirical observation suggests the presence of disturbing forces that dominate equilibrating forces due to optimizing behavior of economic agents and that it is necessary to seek a new concept of equilibrium different from the standard Walrasian equilibrium in macroeconomics.

Kultti (2000) analyzed a model where buyers and sellers meet randomly, and the meeting probabilities are endogenous and are derived from the basics of the model; and the agents can decide to either search or wait, and the searchers are distributed on the waiters; and prices are determined by bargaining if exactly two agents are matched; and where more than one agent of one type are matched with an agent of another type, there will be an auction. Kultii (2000) found that there are at most, three equilibria, and when the numbers of buyers and sellers differ greatly, it is possible that the equilibrium where the agents on the short side wait is the plausible one.

Chen (2005) noted from Becker's (1973) analysis of the neoclassical marriage market that matching is positive assortative if agent types are complements in household production. Chen (2005) also noted that Shimer and Smith (2000) have shown that this result does not generally extend to markets with search frictions, and they provided additional conditions for the production functions that guarantee assortative matching in these settings. Chen (2005) analyzed the relationship between the Shimer–Smith restrictions and equilibrium matching pattern; and Chen (2005) introduced alternative proofs of their results on assortative matching.

The Diamond–Mortensen–Pissarides models have also been conclusively refuted and contradicted by recent research in information theory. Hulleman (2010) studied tagging in visual search and its results contradict the Diamond–Mortensen–Pissarides models. The Wilson and Schraefel (2010) results contradict the Diamond–Mortensen–Pissarides models. Wilson and Schraefel (2010) noted that despite the many implicit references to the social contexts of search within information seeking and retrieval research, there has been relatively little work that has specifically investigated the additional requirements for collaborative information-seeking interfaces. Wilson and Schraefel (2010) reevaluated an existing analytical inspection framework, designed for individual information seeking, and then applied it to evaluate a recent collaborative information-seeking interface named *SearchTogether*. Wilson and Schraefel (2010) found that the SearchTogether framework (1) can still be applied to collaborative information-seeking interfaces, (2) can successfully produce additional requirements for collaborative information-seeking interfaces, and (3) can successfully model different dynamics of collaborating searchers. Sumita and Zuo (2010) noted that mobile Internet allows ubiquitous information search; and thus, the search times are reduced when mobile access is combined with ordinary PC access. Sumita and Zuo (2010) developed a mathematical model for describing the information search process through the Internet with or without the mobile access and the impact of mobile access on information search completion time and the conversion rate. The Sumita and Zuo (2010) results also contradict the Diamond–Mortensen–Pissarides models.

Hall (2005) and Shimer (2005) stated that the conventional search model of employment dynamics that were developed in Diamond (1982), Mortensen and Pissarides (1994), and Pissarides (1985, 2000) cannot account for cyclical movements in labor market variables within the context of standard real business cycle paradigms. Hall (2005) also stated that while in reality, the labor market slackens substantially in recessions during which workers find it difficult to obtain jobs, the DMP model assumes there is Nash-bargain wage determination and implies that there is stability in the rate of job-finding. Researchers have also noted that the Diamond–Mortensen–Pissarides models for determining wages accommodate too much wage flexibility, which, in turn, dampens the cyclical movements in firms' incentives to hire and to reduce the volatilities of vacancy and unemployment.

The Diamond–Mortensen–Pissarides models have also been conclusively refuted and contradicted by recent research in cognition and vision research. Specifically, Hulleman (2010) notes that several theories and models of visual search assume that inhibitory tagging of items is used to improve the efficiency of the search process by discouraging revisits of previously inspected and rejected items. Hulleman (2010) tested whether search is less efficient when the search display consists of moving items, in four experiments. In the first two experiments, there was no difference between search among static and moving items even though motion conditions were blocked (Experiment 1), or displays contained up to 36 items (Experiment 2). However, in Experiments 3 and 4, where the items used in the search display forced the participants to keep track of individual items, performance dropped when the items moved. Visual search showed a remarkable robustness against motion, which current theories and models of visual search have difficulties to describe. Hulleman (2010) concluded that the results of the experiments indicate that there is a difference between the processes used in easier search and those used in search where items need to be individuated.

Virag (2011) analyzed a model of directed search where the sellers are allowed to post mechanisms with entry fees. Virag (2011) found that regardless of the number of buyers and sellers, the sellers are able to extract all the surplus of the buyers by introducing entry fees and making price schedules positively sloped in the number of buyers arriving to their shops. This is in contrast to results that are achieved for large markets under the assumption that sellers cannot influence the utility of any particular buyer (market utility assumption), in which case buyers obtain strictly positive rents. If there is a bound on the prices or on the entry fees that can be charged, then the equilibrium with full rent extraction does not exist any more, and the market utility assumption is restored for large markets.

Menzio and Shi (2010) developed a general stochastic model of directed search on the job, in which they analyzed a Block Recursive Equilibrium (BRE) where agents' value functions, policy functions, and market tightness do not depend on the distribution of workers over wages and unemployment. Menzio and Shi (2010) formally proved the existence of a BRE under various specifications of workers' preferences and contractual environments, including dynamic contracts and fixed-wage contracts.

Watanabe (2008) studied an (S, s) pricing model in the presence of inflation and price competition in search markets—that is, a model in which consumers' search technologies can influence firms' price setting, price dispersion, and the market structure. Watanabe (2008) found that although price competition among firms is intensified in markets where consumers' search technologies are more efficient, price inflation is, counterintuitively, more likely to increase the monopoly power and stimulate entry of firms in these markets. The Watanabe (2008) model also provides new empirical implications for firms' price setting behaviors.

Peters (1992) compared the performance of three pricing institutions in a decentralized matching model in which random matching occurs. In the first, sellers make public ex ante commitments to trade at prespecified prices before matching occurs. In the second, the buyer and seller engage in an alternating offer bargaining game once a match has occurred. In the third pricing institution, one party is chosen at random to make a take-it-or-leave-it price offer. Peters (1992) found that (1) the steady-state equilibrium with ex ante pricing pareto dominates the steady-state equilibrium with ex post take-it-or-leave-it offers, which in turn pareto dominates the steady-state equilibrium with alternating offers; (2) as the discount factor goes to one, the equilibrium with ex ante pricing generates participation rates that tend toward the pareto efficient level; (3) the ex post pricing institutions generate participation rates that are bounded away from efficient levels; (4) the surplus loss associated with switching from ex ante pricing to take-it-or-leave-it offers is small when the discount factor is close to one; and (5) contrary to many models of decentralized trade, ex post pricing institutions encourage too much search by buyers.

Ernst and Semmler (2010) analyzed global macroeconomic dynamics within the context of when search frictions exist in both labor and capital markets. On the basis of the Merz (1995) macroeconomic model with labor market frictions and capital accumulation, Ernst and Semmler (2010) offer an extension to frictions in capital markets, analogously modeled as a search and matching process and consider exogenous as well as endogenous borrowing constraints while allowing the cost of issuing bonds to change endogenously. Ernst and Semmler (2010) argued that capital market frictions exacerbate and accentuate the interaction between the two markets and magnify the effects of shocks on output, consumption, employment, and welfare; and such interactions of the frictions in labor and capital markets are also shown to give rise to multiple equilibria. On the basis of numerical solution techniques, instead of relying on first- or second-order approximations around a (unique) steady state, Ernst and Semmler (2010) used dynamic programming techniques to compute decision variables and the value function directly and to assess the local and global dynamics of the model.

2.3 Economic, Social, and Psychological Issues That Pertain to Individuals

2.3.1 Existing Literature

Illegal file sharing seems to provide some perceived advantages, utility, and mental stimulus that are not provided by legal purchases from content owners. The relevant literature on the economic psychology of IOF emerged during 2006–2016. *Loss Aversion* has been discussed in the existing literature but not in the context of file sharing. People participate in IOF networks because they are averse to *losing*. In these circumstances, losing is conjectured to be equated to selecting the wrong digital content and/or spending too much time to search for digital content, and/or having to pay for digital content that has uncertain value. This type of loss aversion is complicated by the fact that most digital contents are not sold with dynamic pricing or dynamic prices—there are typically no prices for sampling portions of a unit of digital content.

Rehearsal in online systems has also been discussed in the literature. The issue of regret and sampling of digital content before purchases has been discussed in the literature. Consumers participate in IOF because it greatly reduces the regret inherent in purchasing and using content. Most stores in physical space allow minimal sampling of content, allow only limited product returns, carry relatively lower variety of content, and require more stress/activity/mental effort to view available content. On the contrary, illegal file sharing does not have any of these disadvantages and is free and hence, much more appealing. The declining costs of computer hardware and bandwidth and the growing media capabilities of computers have made the Internet and digital content much more accessible, such that digital experiences are common staples of daily life. The computer and many computerized handheld devices now have many of the functions previously performed by walkmans, cassette players, and other devices. Hence, in today's increasingly digitized environment people are more likely to participate in IOF, compared to 5–15 years ago. The increased volume of human–computer interaction has created certain consequences that exacerbate/increase the propensity to participate in IOF.

Peer motivation effect has been discussed in the literature and illegal file sharing can also be attributed to encouragement and motivation by peers (in social groups) to try the activity. In such cases, the propensity to participate is a function of social networks, education, family background, morality, stress, and beliefs among other factors.

The *authority-deficit effect* has also been discussed in the literature. The absence of a visible police presence in the Internet and absence of electronic tags on information goods (as in physical space) increase consumers' propensity to engage in IOF. These web surfers view the Internet as a distinct world that is much less policed, and hence, much less punitive and more tolerant of criminal misconduct. This thought process increases the propensity to participate in illegal file sharing networks.

The *habit effect* has been discussed in part in the literature and people participate in illegal file sharing as a matter of habit. They can get accustomed to illegally sharing files at specific times of the day, or at specific locations, in specific contexts, and it then becomes part of their social life and routine. The habit effect is supported by the rapid penetration of the Internet in the United States—more than 60% of all households now have access to broadband and more than 70% of the U.S. population aged 18 years or older now have access to broadband at work or at home. Many companies and households have not placed any network restrictions on illegal file sharing sites—hence, availability/access supports the habit.

The *transferred actualization effect* has been tangentially implied in the literature—see Holt and Copes (2010). Illegal file sharing can also be attributed to encouragement and motivation by peers (in social groups) to try the activity. In such cases, the propensity to participate is a function of social networks, peer pressure/motivation, external interaction and influences, utility, and online chat rooms/communities, education, family background, morality, stress, and beliefs. Illegal file sharing is most common in university campuses, offices, and urban areas, all of which are high-population-density, high-interaction, and mental-activity-intensive areas. Thus, illegal file sharing is a way of coping with stress in high-density high-activity areas with diverse populations and is introduced mainly through social circles. IOF can be construed as the execution/actualization of discussions, influences, and group-think that have occurred in physical space but are being manifested in Internet space. Thus, the organic growth of file sharing can be attributed to peer pressure/motivation, external interaction and influences, utility, and online chat rooms/communities.

The *free-products effect* has been discussed in the literature. The advent of the Internet has resulted in numerous types of free promotions and price discounts for products and services. Prices offered on the web are often much lower than prices offered in physical stores. This has created a mentality among web users that the Internet is a bastion and realm of free products and services and deeply discounted prices. This mentality continues to be reinforced by marketing programs and promotions. This mentality can partly account for individuals' propensity to share files and for computer companies' propensity to create file sharing software. Most online search services (Google, Yahoo, etc.) are free. Online file sharing is essentially a form of Internet search. Thus, traditional *free* Internet searches can create a subconscious effect that cause perpetrators to deem illegal file sharing to be comparable to normal/legal *free* Internet searches, and hence acceptable. The process of IOF involves making a decision, sampling content, and revising the decision over time. This process may also create a habit and/or an addiction, depending on the individual's socioeconomic circumstances. In addition to the empirical methods used in, and theory stated in the literature, the following are additional factors for illustrating the free-products/free-search effect: (1) the percentage of participants in illegal file sharing networks that accept free products online or participate in online surveys in exchange for free products within 2–3 different time frames; (2) the weekly changes in the percentage of illegal file sharing network members that are willing to pay discounted prices for digital content and for physical content; (3) a comparison of the numbers of general free online searches and IOF searches conducted by an average consumer within a specific period of time; (4) a comparison of the average price of free products accepted online by file sharing network members over different time frames (weeks, months); (5) a comparison of the changes in the volume of files transferred in IOF networks with the changes in the volume of free products/services distributed online within a specific period of time; and (6) a comparison of the changes in the number of free online searches with the changes in the volume of files transferred in illegal online networks within a specific period.

Asvanund et al. (2004) studied network externalities in P2P networks. Becker and Clement (2006), Hinduja (2006), Jones (2005), Wingrove et al. (2009), and other articles[3] have analyzed compliance by individuals.

Lebowitz (2006), Rob and Waldfogel (2006), Moore and McMullan (2004), and Amiroso and Case (2007) analyzed some of the socioeconomic effects of IOF. Gopal et al. (2004), Amiroso and Case (2007), and Coyle et al. (2009) analyzed the specific decision processes of individuals that participate in IOF. Morris et al. (2009) studied the effect of gender on the propensity to participate in IOF. Higgins et al. (2006, 2008) and Holt and Copes (2010) studied the effects of self-control on individuals' propensity to participate in IOF. Inman and Zeelenberg (2002) analyzed regret and justification in repeat-purchase decisions and switching decisions.

The gaps and omissions in the existing literature are as follows:

1. The studies are not based on any coherent theories of human behavior. Almost all the studies address tangential issues.
2. The empirical studies suffer from the statistical/data-analysis and data-selection problems and issues explained in Dellnitz and Junge (1999), Trafimow (2003), and other articles.[4]
3. The existing literature on IOF does not analyze *moneyless markets*.
4. There has not been any analysis of the perceptions of time with respect to value of time and time–distance relationships.
5. The existing literature erroneously assumes that:
    a. All participants in IOF networks have the same amount of knowledge.
    b. All participants do not experience any regret and experience minimal guilt.
    c. All units of digital content are substitutable—that is, the average human participant's marginal propensity to substitute one unit of digital content for a different unit is usually substantial (compared to other assets/services).

The rest of this section introduces hypotheses and theories of why people participate in illegal file sharing—most of these theories have not been identified or analyzed in the existing file sharing psychology, Internet psychology, and Internet-crime literature.

Most of the biases, behaviors, and *effects* introduced herein are in the nature of higher-order risk preferences and biases—which are *derivative* in nature, wherein one bias/behavior arises partly or solely from or is ancillary to another behavior/bias. Bernard (1926a) distinguished *primary groups* from *derivative groups* and gave specific examples of derivative groups in order of *derivativeness*. Bernard (1926b) distinguished between *primary* and *derivative* attitudes and ideals. Bernard (1936) analyzed conflicts between *primary group attitudes* and *derivative group ideals*. *Hullian theory* in psychology also distinguishes between *direct* and *derivative* human (individual and group) behaviors. Deck and Schlesinger (2014), Noussair et al. (2013), and other articles have analyzed a few higher-order risk preferences.

2.3.2 Hypothesis-1: The Declining Consumer Loyalty Effect

IOF is an indicator of, and a consequence of growing lack of consumer loyalty (which is caused in part by free products and free search), particularly in developed countries, where consumers are bombarded daily with advertisements in trains, buses, elevators, and from radios, TVs, videos, and in almost every aspect of life. The overall impact of these advertising is to reduce consumer loyalty, which ultimately translates into a need to access various types of digital entertainment and an increased propensity to sample new digital content. These result is increased propensity to participate in illegal file sharing networks.

This *declining loyalty effect* is or can be evident in (1) the changes in the percentage of members of IOF networks that are willing to switch among various brands of products at different price points; (2) the percentage of members of IOF networks that have used the same product or service for different time frames (week, quarters, months, etc.); (3) the changes in the percentage of members of IOF networks that are willing to switch brands if given incentives and/or price discounts; and (4) the changes in the composition of digital content downloaded by members of IOF networks.

2.3.3 Hypothesis-2: The Browsing Effect

The *browsing effect*—the increased accessibility of the Internet has made more people to become more likely to browse the Internet as opposed to going to specific websites. Thus, IOF is a direct by-product of this increased propensity to browse the Internet, which arises from increased access to the Internet, increased need for instant gratification, and increased awareness of time management. This theory is supported by the available data—among illegal file sharers, most of the activity is initiated and supported by less than 5% of file sharers.

Some of the consequences of the *browsing effect* and human–computer interaction are dependence; static modes of interaction with others; propensity not to comply with rules/regulations; disregard for disclaimers and *fine print*; desire for online groups and group-based activities; increased propensity to seek out and try the newest web-based contraption; increased propensity to browse; exponentially greater choice of products/services; lower transaction costs; and growth of anonymous web-based systems.

The sheer variety and amount of information available to web surfers can create various sensitivities in consumers and also can numb web surfers and reduces their ability to distinguish good from bad. Most people that participate in illegal file sharing spend considerable amounts of time surfing the web each day. Unlike in the physical world, police presence is minimal in the Internet. Furthermore, the significant mental effort that is required to process information gleaned for many URLs in Internet session and remember such information, and the ease with which the individual changes *frames* essentially reduces the mind's ability to determine what is right or wrong, to assess risk, and to appreciate the value of digital content.

The *browsing effect* is evident in (1) the change in the average duration of consumers' Internet searches during the last 10 years; (2) the changes in the average time spent per session in illegal file sharing networks during the last 5 years; (3) a comparison of the average time spent per session on the Internet for individuals that use PCs, mobile phones, and handheld devices; (4) a comparison of the average time spent per website/URL for individuals that use PCs, mobile phones, and handheld devices; (5) the relationship between the type of Internet access (wireless, narrowband, and broadband), and the number of websites/webpages visited per Internet session, and the average amount of time spent on each webpage; (6) the 10-year historical weekly changes in the percentage of consumers' leisure time that is spent on the Internet, on Internet searches, and on Internet-based entertainment; (7) the relationship between the changes in the average amount of time spent by the average consumer in an Internet session and the changes in the number of members in IOF networks; (8) the percentage of members of IOF networks who spend various amounts of time per Internet session (e.g., an average of v, w, x, y, and z minutes per Internet session) who view IOF as illegal or risky or justified or are not sure of an appropriate classification.

A closely related effect is the *digital games effect*. People are more likely to participate in IOF because the increase in popularity and availability of computer games has substantially changed modern culture and the mindset of people, making them much more prone to participate in online group activities and unregulated activities. In the United States, the computer games sector produces more annual sales revenues than the movie industry. Furthermore, the cost of participation in online digital games (at commercial locations) is relatively low, and this low-participation-cost effect reinforces consumer propensity not to pay for digital content. The digital games proliferation effect is evident in (1) the changes in the percentage of digital games enthusiasts that also participate in IOF during the last 5 years; (2) the weekly changes in the percentage of time that an average consumer devotes to digital games and to IOF; (3) comparison of the changes in the average consumer or household monthly expenditures on digital games, to the perceived and actual monetary values of time spent on illegal file sharing networks, (4) comparison of the *satisfaction* derived from digital games and satisfaction from participation in IOF; and (5) comparison of consumers' definitions of opportunity costs of experiencing digital games and that of participation in IOF.

Illegal file sharing may be an indication of a certain stimulus provided from utility from searching and sampling content in an Internet environment. People do not normally exchange/barter securities (i.e., shares of common stock) or lottery tickets or digital coupons—no meaningful barter market exists for these goods. The barter implicit in OTC financial markets (swaps and derivatives markets) can be explained by economic necessity, perceived/assumed rationality (absence of or relatively lower levels of emotions and attachments), existence of liquid markets that facilitate pricing and hedging, and measurability of values of securities. Thus, there are inherent characteristics of digital content (as a good) that make it amenable to online moneyless exchange, and these include (1) lack of resale value and difficulty in converting downloaded digital content into cash, (2) relatively very low transaction costs, (3) difficulty in establishing true value because digital content has drastically different values to different people, (4) intangible nature of digital content, (5) utility value exceeds its monetary value, (6) emotional value of digital content (emotional attachment), and (7) availability of online communities that create demand for devices such as file sharing networks.

2.3.4 Hypothesis-3: The Deprivation and Exclusion Effect

IOF can be deemed to be a group reaction to various forms of exclusion in physical space and online. Such exclusion could be based on age, sex, marital status, income/wealth, profession, personality, etc. Illegal file sharing is typically free, does not discriminate based on age/location/sex, provides access to communities that have some permanence, reduces class distinctions, and instantly broadens the perpetrator's social networks. All these benefits can be achieved at relatively low costs, with very low social friction (compared to physical space) and with convenience.

The Internet provides substantial choice and variety. This choice is exponentially greater than choice in physical space and is substantially enhanced by the immediacy and instant gratification of the Internet. However, such choice can also create feelings of deprivation: (1) IOF is sometimes a reaction that occurs when people are not able to find specific content on the web or in physical space; (2) IOF is sometimes a reaction to deprivation arising from activities/events in physical space in various aspects of life—relationships, activities, associations, etc.; and (3) IOF becomes a reaction to deprivation among teens arising from parental control and institutional restrictions (schools, universities, etc.).

2.3.5 Hypothesis-4: Reflection/Reassurance Effect

IOF serves as a form of psychological reassurance to perpetrators that there are others who share common and divergent beliefs and tastes. This reassurance is increasingly necessary given the rapid growth in the variety of Internet-based products, systems, games and ideas, increasing globalization, changes in the family structure, and other major changes in modern society. For someone to participate in illegal file sharing (knowing the risks), the person must believe that (1) the other parties in these transactions have the same or worse moral values, (2) the other parties will not report him/her to the government authorities, and (3) the other parties stand to gain as much or more from participation. Thus, given that most people now know that IOF is bad, there is a perceived reflection of the self, and a perceived state of the world (a nonperfect state) in which IOF is feasible.

Implicit in IOF are certain individual expectations and group expectations about criminal prosecution; search costs; utility gained/lost; continued existence of file sharing communities and advances in file sharing technologies (people do not like to engage in short-lived hobbies); cost of switching to another network; peer pressure; morality; Internet communities; distribution of digital content; choice and variety; regret; sampling; and monitoring by and activities of Internet service providers (ISPs). These expectations generate economic utility and, to some extent, minimize regret for individuals and groups and serve as primary motivating factors in IOF.

Some people participate in IOF because it is an expression of an internalized disagreement and protest about the profits that will accrue to the content owner/distributor. These perpetrators believe that since the cost of producing such digital content is low (and subsequent variable/reproduction costs are low), it should be made available to the public for free or at very low cost. Furthermore, perpetrators probably believe that once a consumer has paid for one unit of digital content, then it is equitable for the consumer to do whatever he/she wants with the purchased content (perpetual use rights) including giving away to others (however, this contravenes all copyright laws because copyright laws typically limit rights transferred upon *sale* of digital content). IOF is also a form of *targeted rebellion* against an industry or profession, deemed deficient in some form, or exploitative. This internalized disagreement and protest about prices and fairness is evident in (1) the percentage of perpetrators that believe that prices of online content are fair and that production costs for digital content are low and (2) the percentage of perpetrators that think that payment for digital content or any content should be for perpetual use. The reflection/reassurance effect is different from the *reflection effect* predicted by prospect theory.

2.3.6 Hypothesis-5: Moneyless-Trading Bias

The allure of *moneyless trading* in the United States and in many developed countries has increased during the last 5 years for several reasons: (1) the collapse of the emerging-growth-company sector (NASDAQ) stock market in 2000–2002, (2) the shift of assets from traditional bank accounts to securities accounts, (3) the broadening of the distribution of ages of people that participate in stock markets, (4) the rapid increase in the popularity and volume of investments in securities, and (5) the rapid increase in the global popularity and availability of online games. These factors have created a *trading mentality* that is now affecting other parts of daily life in most developed countries (and in some developing countries).

This *trading mentality* and *moneyless-trading bias* are evident in (1) increases in the volume of activity (trading, webpage listings, ads, email exchanges, etc.) in baseball cards, collectibles, and in auction-website activities; (2) the percentage of retailing websites that offer free products and product promotions; (3) the percentage of time spent on securities market transactions versus IOF networks; and (4) the percentage of time spent on online auctions, online games, and price comparison websites versus IOF networks.

Illegal file sharing represents a form of moneyless trading that is substantially less risky than securities markets. Hence, people are more likely to prefer online purchase to physical purchase.

2.3.7 Hypothesis-6: The Time–Price–Travel Sensitivity Effect

Some people participate in IOF networks in order to greatly reduce search costs, reduce associated psychological distress/effects, and reduce the perceived value of wasted time. Time is typically the main component of the perpetrators' search costs. People are typically willing to commit more time for high reward, high-risk benefits, than to spend money to achieve similar benefits. Other search costs include travel time and expenses, stress, time spent at physical stores, and time/money spent sampling content in physical space. In this context, actualization time is defined as the time it takes to obtain/purchase a desired good/service. The Internet has greatly reduced actualization time, particularly for information goods, and by doing so, has created a demand for even shorter actualization times. Illegal file sharing simply fulfills the need for shorter actualization times and instant gratification—perpetrators can find files faster and do not have to go through the inconvenience of online registration, payment, or searching. One major result is that perpetrators are more likely to have increased time–price sensitivity and increased travel sensitivity due to lower search costs, which is caused by habit (used to achieving low costs for obtaining digital content) and expectations. Note that the time sensitivity, travel sensitivity, and price sensitivity are linked in time and space and occur simultaneously. This increased time–price–distance sensitivity, in turn, causes a higher propensity to participate in IOF networks.

Hence, individuals' sensitivity to absolute time (concepts and perceptions of specific blocks of time), relative time (time spent to achieve an objective through different methods), and dynamic time (the passage of time) is a critical element of the file sharing decision. P2P file sharing software systems substantially alter the time equation for most individuals—P2P systems achieve search objectives in milliseconds. People place different values on various types of time—work time, leisure time, exploration time and search time (not considered leisure). People who are more sensitive to the value of their time will be more likely to participate in illegal file sharing. Thus, time is a key element of the actualization of search in P2P networks. Ariely and Silva (August 2002), Ozmutlu et al. (2003a,b), Diehl et al. (2003), and Bolton et al. (2003) discussed issues pertaining to pricing (but not the *price sensitivity effect*). People participate in IOF networks because they greatly reduce search costs and associated psychological distress/effects. One major result is that perpetrators then have increased price sensitivity due to lower search costs, which is caused by habit (used to achieving low costs for obtaining digital content) and expectations. This increased price sensitivity, in turn, causes a higher propensity to participate in IOF networks. Note that this price sensitivity is both a cause and a *result* of IOF that causes increased volume of illegal file sharing.

The time–price–travel–cost sensitivity can be confirmed by (1) the percentage of consumers that are willing to travel a specific distance to purchase or exchange content within a specific time frame; (2) the changes in the percentage of consumers that purchased both DVDs and computers and handheld devices during the last 5 years; (3) a comparison of individuals that purchased only two of the following—computers, DVDs, handheld devices (iPods, etc.), and mobile phones; and (4) the 5-year historical weekly changes in the percentage of illegal file sharing network members who use wireless devices versus land-based devices.

2.3.8 Hypothesis-7: The Collector Bias

People are more likely to participate in IOF because of a collector bias, which is defined as the consumer's propensity to collect items deemed valuable and to exchange ideas with other collectors, regardless of whether or not the items are obtained illegally (as in IOF). The collector bias has been exacerbated by increasing variety in many aspects of life, increased volume of advertising, increased interest in the stock market, the increasing popularity of auctions of collectibles (especially online auctions), the 'stability' of prices of collectibles, and increased impact of movies and computer games. A distinction is made here between the traditional collector (who buys original CDs/DVDs in original packaging that have true resale value) and the *influenced collector* who simply wants to have a digital library regardless of the resale value. The collectors bias is evident in (1) the changes in the percentage of IOF participants in a network that have digital libraries that contain a minimum threshold number of digital content units; (2) a comparison of the resale values of digital content versus resale values of physical content; and (3) the percentage of illegal file sharing participants that also collect other items such as stamps, cards, etc.

2.3.9 Hypothesis-8: The Favorable Risk–Reward Profile Effect

Consumers participate in IOF because the risk/reward ratio is very favorable. Only a relatively small percentage of IOF perpetrators are cautioned, prosecuted, or fined. In the United States, the penalties for illegal file sharing are relatively low and ineffective. On the other hand, perpetrators pay a fixed fee for Internet access and gain substantial access to substantial digital content. Thus, the risk–reward profile for illegal file sharing is attractive to perpetrators and encourages participation. Individuals with a high risk–reward bias are more likely to participate in illegal file sharing network and to download more files from such networks and to refer their friends to such file sharing networks. The risk–reward bias is evident in (1) the percentage of IOF perpetrators who are arrested or prosecuted or punished, compared to other forms of copyright infringement, (2) the number of ISPs that penalize illegal file sharing perpetrators, and (3) a comparison of the percentage of illegal file sharing perpetrators who believe they may be prosecuted and the same percentage in legal file sharing networks and in physical copyright infringement networks.

2.3.10 Hypothesis-9: Inherent Dislike of an Audience and Profits-Protest

The main *audience* for IOF consists of entertainment companies, entertainment trade groups, entertainment lawyers, educational organizations, entertainers, law enforcement officers, and the judicial system. Thus, people who consistently develop file sharing software (knowing the economically devastating effects it could have) and participate in IOF may have some deep or subconscious dislike/resentment of all or parts of the *audience* for illegal file sharing. For these like-minded people, file sharing becomes a way to participate in a group activity and offend their target audience (Postmes and Brinsting, 2002). Participation in IOF networks may also be a form of protest against the profit-making activities of companies or groups.

2.3.11 Hypothesis-10: The Cost Structure Effect

Apart from concerns about fairness of prices for digital content, perpetrators choose to participate in IOF networks due to concerns about the cost structure implicit in ordinary purchases in physical space and the business models used by *legal* file sharing networks. An individual who purchases content in physical space incurs a certain amount of fixed costs (DVD player, rent, energy costs, time) and variable costs (search costs, transportation costs, cost of DVD, etc.). An individual who uses IOF networks has different fixed costs (computer, bandwidth, time) and variable costs (search costs, time). The file sharing perpetrator's perception of the differences in magnitude of these two classes of costs adjusted for his/her estimated probability of apprehension and prosecution is a major cause of participation in illegal file sharing. The computer has more uses than a DVD player, and computer costs have been declining over the last few years (see Lurie, 2004; Weber et al., 2004).

2.3.12 Hypothesis-11: The Price Sensitivity Effect

Ariely and Silva (August 2002), Ozmutlu et al. (2003a,b), Diehl et al. (2003), and Bolton et al. (2003) discussed issues pertaining to pricing (but not the *price sensitivity effect*). People participate in IOF networks because they greatly reduce search costs and associated psychological distress/effects. One major result is that perpetrators then have increased price sensitivity due to lower search costs, which is caused by habit (used to achieving low costs for obtaining digital content) and expectations. This increased price sensitivity, in turn, causes a higher propensity to participate in IOF networks. Note that this price sensitivity is a *result* of IOF that causes increased volume of illegal file sharing. This price sensitivity effect differs from the time-price-travel effect discussed earlier.

2.3.13 Hypothesis-12: The Regret Effect

Consumers participate in IOF because it greatly reduces the regret inherent in purchasing and using content. Most stores in physical space allow minimal sampling of content, allow only limited product returns, carry relatively lower variety of content, and require more stress/activity/mental effort to view available content. On the contrary, illegal file sharing does not have any of these disadvantages and is free and, hence, much more appealing.

IOF appeals to a more intelligent generation and more informed shoppers who are cost-conscious and time-conscious and seek to derive the highest utility from any efforts in any activity. For such individuals who are searching for digital content, illegal file sharing may provide the highest combinations of effectiveness-utility and regret-minimization compared to any alternative method for obtaining content (the alternatives include physical purchase, a legal file sharing network, legal content download sites, and mail-order). The sources of consumer effectiveness-utility in IOF include community, choice, search and lower search costs, downloading, experiencing content, building a collection, protest, and expectations.

2.3.14 Hypothesis-13: The Expectations Effect

IOF appeals to a more intelligent generation and more informed shoppers who are cost-conscious and time-conscious and seek to derive the highest utility from any efforts in any activity. For such individuals who are searching for digital content, illegal file sharing may provide the highest effectiveness-utility compared to any alternative method for obtaining content (the alternatives include physical purchase, legal file sharing network, legal content download sites, and mail order).

Implicit in IOF are certain individual expectations and group expectations about the following: (1) criminal prosecution; (2) search costs; (3) utility gained/lost; (4) continued existence of file sharing communities and advances in file sharing technologies (people do not like to engage in short-lived hobbies); (5) cost of switching to another network; (6) peer pressure; (7) morality; (8) Internet communities; (9) distribution of digital content; (10) choice and variety; (11) sampling; and (12) monitoring by and activities of ISPs. These expectations generate economic utility/disutility for individuals and groups and serve as primary motivating factors in illegal file sharing.

IOF involves a series of repeat transactions and decisions over a relatively long period of time (compared to one-time purchases of products). Hence, the people who participate in illegal file sharing have a long-term perspective in which they compare the cost savings, probability of prosecution, cost of prosecution, and utility gained from their activities. They typically conclude that over the long run, the total benefits of illegal file sharing outweigh the risks. Indeed, the percentage of illegal file sharing perpetrators who have been prosecuted has been relatively very low. Hence, time horizon in the context of consumer ethics/choice and decision-making is a major determinant of propensity to participate in IOF networks.

This effect/bias is manifested in the following: the average membership tenure of members in IOF networks (compared to that of nonmembers) and/or the changes in the membership tenures of members in IOF networks in other online communities (compared to that of nonmembers).

2.3.15 Hypothesis-14: The Choice-Based Irrationality Effect and Variety-Based Irrationality Effect

IOF is the result of *choice-based irrationality* and *variety-based irrationality*, wherein people can lose control and/or become irrational when faced with substantial choices. Inability to process alternatives, low transaction costs, and low brand loyalty are some elements of these two types of irrationality. Illegal file sharing is a form of social experimentation in an increasingly diverse and information-deluged world, where people constantly seek to test relationships, limits, possibilities, and consequences.

IOF is often positioned and marketed as *normal* activity, whereas it is illegal. Hence, some perpetrators internalize the misguided themes of legality of illegal file sharing networks. This normality effect seems to persist despite publicized prosecutions of illegal file sharing networks and associated perpetrators. The internalization process is reinforced by one or more of the following: relatively low Internet access costs; the favorable risk–reward profile of IOF; lack of enforcement by ISPs; significant similarities between regular free Internet searches and participation in illegal file sharing networks; the relative unsophistication of existing digital rights management systems (DRMSs); ineffective penalties for IOF; and lax government enforcement of copyright laws.

A closely related effect is the *habit effect*. People participate in illegal file sharing as a matter of habit. They can get accustomed to illegal file sharing at specific times of the day or at specific locations in specific contexts, and then it becomes part of their social life and routine. The habit effect is supported by the rapid penetration of the Internet many developed countries where most adults have access to broadband at work or at home. Many companies and households have not placed any network restrictions on illegal file sharing sites—hence, availability/access supports the habit.

2.3.16 Hypothesis-15: Stimuli Effect and Status Effect

Illegal file sharing can be attributed to the mental association of illegal file sharing activities with any of the following:

1. Certain stimuli—such as convenience, relief, increased wealth, beating the system, successful search, pleasure from accessing content, savings in time, reduced search costs, lower stress, community, fellowship, etc. (Ireland, 1994).
2. Certain status—the technologically savvy group, modern and progressive youth, knowledgeable, street-smart, cost-efficient, etc. (Ireland, 1994).

These associations and successful searches in the illegal file sharing networks can greatly increase the individual's propensity to participate in such networks.

2.3.17 Hypothesis-16: The Incomplete Information Effect

The *incomplete information* characteristic inherent in searches for content (digital and nondigital) is a substantial causal factor for participation in IOF. *Incomplete information* refers to dynamic *states* in which the searcher does not have complete/perfect information about various attributes of an experience/product/service and other factors such as the following:

1. Type of nondigital/digital content sought
2. The price of content and its affordability
3. The available alternatives
4. The location of content
5. Search costs
6. The experience of using a P2P file sharing system
7. The experience of the digital content (sometimes, sampling digital content is not enough)

The incomplete information effect involves the development of beliefs based partly on emotions and the updating of such beliefs based on additional information, regret, experiences, cognitive responses to external/internal stimuli, mood changes, and incentives. In the context of searching for digital content for many individuals, illegal file sharing offers perhaps the best means of dealing with incomplete information because it provides the lowest search costs, justification costs, selection costs, and choice-revision costs.

2.3.18 Hypothesis-17: The Transaction-Utility Effect

Illegal file sharing may be an indication of a certain stimulus provided from utility from searching and sampling content in an Internet environment. People do not normally exchange/barter securities (i.e., shares of common stock) or lottery tickets or digital coupons—no meaningful barter market exists for these goods. The barter implicit in OTC financial markets (swaps and derivatives markets) can be explained by economic necessity, perceived/assumed rationality (absence of or relatively lower levels of emotions and attachments), existence of liquid markets that facilitate pricing and hedging, and measurability of values of securities. Thus, there are inherent characteristics of digital content (as a good) that make it amenable to online moneyless exchange, and these include but are not limited to the following: (1) lack of resale value and difficulty in converting downloaded digital content into cash; (2) relatively very low transaction costs; (3) the difficulty in establishing true value because digital content has drastically different values to different people; (4) intangible nature of digital content; (5) utility value exceeds its monetary value; (6) the emotional value of digital content (emotional attachment); and (7) the availability of online communities that create demand for devices such as file sharing networks. The sources of consumer effectiveness-utility in illegal file sharing include community, choice, search and lower search costs, downloading, experiencing content, building a collection, protest, and expectations.

2.4 Economic and Psychological Issues Pertaining to Institutions Associated with IOF

IOF affects the economics, profitability, and business models of companies in many industries such as entertainment, education, travel, investments/finance, and any business where knowledge has value. In the United States, the Napster case illustrated some of the policy, technological, and economic issues inherent in systems for downloading content. Golle et al. (2001) analyzed incentives in file sharing.

The institutions involved in IOF include the following:

1. Government legislators—that enact statutes for regulation of the Internet and intellectual property rights (IPR).
2. Government prosecutors (state, local/municipal, and federal)—that investigate criminal infringement and prosecute misconduct.
3. Software producers—these are individuals or teams of individuals or companies that develop and distribute file sharing software with or without the knowledge/intent that such software will be used for illegal purposes. The knowledge and intent elements are critical in Torts liability and criminal liability.
4. The actual P2P file sharing software (its design and limitations and effects on Internet congestion) and the illegal file sharing virtual markets.
5. Internet service providers: they provide network connections that facilitate illegal file sharing.
6. The courts of law, the penal system, and the penalty system—the judges that adjudicate civil and criminal complaints of infringement. This group also includes the sentencing guidelines for criminal infringement and the penal system (jails, halfway houses, probation systems, etc.).
7. The news media that disseminates information about investigations and prosecutions of illegal file sharing.
8. The trade associations—trade associations in industries whose products are primarily digital content (e.g., financial services, entertainment, education, sports, news)—such as RIAA, which often execute their own investigations and prosecutory actions.

There seems to be certain commonalities among these institutions, some of which are as follows:

1. Knowledge gap—about the functioning and mechanics of P2P systems
2. Lack of understanding of deterrence effects
3. Group think—about how to regulate the Internet

2.4.1 Existing Literature

The existing literature on the psychology of institutions involved in illegal file sharing is scant.

As mentioned herein, *Loss Aversion*, the *Peer Motivation Effect*, and *Rehearsal* have been discussed in the literature. The authority-deficit effect has also been discussed in the literature. The absence of visible police presence in the Internet and absence of electronic tags on information goods (as in physical space) increases consumers' propensity to engage in IOF. These web surfers view the Internet as a distinct world that is much less policed and, hence, much less punitive and more tolerant of criminal misconduct. This thought process increases the propensity to participate in illegal file sharing networks.

The transferred-actualization effect has been indirectly implied in the literature. IOF can be construed as the execution/actualization of discussions, influences, and group-think that have occurred in physical space but are being manifested in Internet space. Thus, the organic growth of IOF can be attributed to peer pressure/motivation, external interaction and influences, utility and online chat rooms/communities.

Pessach (2008) studied *memory institutions*. Johnson et al. (2009) analyzed the requirements for file sharing in organizations. Kleinsteuber (2005) analyzed the roles and weaknesses of the nation-state in the regulation of the Internet. Jenny et al. (2006) surveyed the literature on the psychological factors that affect compliance with rules.

Chi (2008) analyzed some of the socioeconomic effects of illegal file sharing. Nwogugu (2009), Jaisingh (2007), Quiring et al. (2008), Bhattacharjee et al. (2006), Curien and Moreau (2009), Sandulli and Martín-Barbero (2008), Vaccaro and Cohn (2004), Von Lohmann (2004), Zentner (2006), and D'Astous et al. (2005) studied the strategies of information producers that are substantially exposed to IOF. Faulk et al. (2005), U.S. Federal Trade Commission (June 2005), Xiaohe (2006), and Sigismondi (2009) analyzed government policies and public policy issues pertaining to illegal file sharing. Wingrove et al. (2009), Jones (2005), Freeman (2005), Svensson and Larsson (2009), and Yen (May 2009) analyzed various theories of compliance. Gopal et al. (2004), Clement et al. (February 2010), and Amiroso and Case (2007) reviewed behavioral models of digital piracy. Butterfield et al. (2000) analyzed ethics and moral awareness in organizations.

Peters (1992) compared the performance of three pricing institutions in a decentralized matching model in which random matching occurs—which are summarized as follows: (1) sellers make public ex ante commitments to trade at prespecified prices before matching occurs (pricing-1); (2) the buyer and seller engage in an alternating offer bargaining game once a match has occurred (pricing-2); and (3) one party is chosen at random to make a take-it-or-leave-it price offer (pricing-3). Peters (1992) found that pricing-1 dominates pricing-3, which in turn pareto dominates pricing-2. As the discount factor goes to one, the equilibrium with pricing-1 generates participation rates that tend toward the pareto efficient level. Contrary to many models of decentralized trade, ex post pricing institutions encourage too much search by buyers.

There are some gaps and omissions in the existing literature. The empirical studies are not based on any coherent theories of human behavior or organizational dynamics; and almost all the studies address tangential issues. The empirical studies suffer from the statistical/data-analysis and data-selection problems and issues explained in Dellnitz and Junge (1999), Trafimow (2003), and other articles.[4] The existing literature on IOF does not analyze *moneyless markets*.

The following are hypotheses and theories of behavioral factors that are inherent in mechanisms, systems, companies, regulators, and institutions involved in IOF—most of these theories have not been identified or analyzed in the existing file sharing psychology, Internet psychology, and Internet-crime literature.

2.4.2 Hypothesis-1: Profits-Protest Effect

The groups of people that form online P2P networks are essentially forms of virtual organizations. The virtual organizations participate in IOF and software companies develop IOF software because it is a group expression of an internalized disagreement and protest about the profits that will accrue to the content owner/distributor from sales of digital content. These organizations believe that since the cost of producing such digital content is low (and subsequent variable/reproduction costs are low), it should be made available to the public for free or at very low cost. Furthermore, perpetrator organizations probably believe that once a consumer has paid for one unit of digital content, then it is equitable for the consumer to do whatever he/she wants with the purchased content (perpetual use rights) including giving away to others—however, this contravenes all copyright laws, because copyright laws typically limit rights transferred upon *sale* of digital content. IOF is also a form of *targeted rebellion* against an industry or profession, deemed deficient in some form, or exploitative. This internalized disagreement and protest about prices and fairness can be confirmed from the following: (1) the percentage of groups of perpetrator organizations that believe that prices of online content are fair and that production cost for digital content are low and (2) the percentage of perpetrator organizations that think that payment for digital content is proper.

2.4.3 Hypothesis-2: The Information Structure Effect

The groups of people that form online P2P networks are essentially forms of virtual organizations. IOF is the direct and indirect result of the structure of information:

1. Content in digital form—digital format exponentially facilitates the exchange and transfer of content, and boost communication within these virtual organizations.
2. Most file sharing networks use sophisticated search methods that present information and search results in very structured ways that make it much easier to find specific digital content (compared to traditional free online searches). This convenience is a major attractor and cause of participation in IOF networks.
3. Search costs are very low.
4. Regret costs are very low because the consumer can find substitutes quickly and relatively cheaply.

The *incomplete information* characteristic inherent in searches for content (digital and nondigital) is a substantial causal factor for participation in illegal file sharing. *Incomplete information* refers to a state in which the searcher does not have complete/perfect information about

1. Type of content sought
2. Price of content and affordability
3. Available alternatives
4. Location of content
5. Search costs

Illegal file sharing offers perhaps the best means of dealing with incomplete information because it provides the lowest search costs, selection costs, and choice-revision costs. These illegal virtual organizations do not have to *register* or provide credit card information in order to download files. Thus, the activity includes some anonymity that is a substantial motivating factor. The increasing incidence of *phishing*, tracking of consumers, CRM systems, and security breaches (particularly with the Windows browser) has made more people wary of disclosing personal information on the Internet and has also made them sensitive about privacy. Much of the illegal file sharing is done without people knowing each other or their email addresses, and the inherent anonymity provides a false sense of protection from identification and prosecution. The *community* that is often mentioned in the context of illegal file sharing is not a real community with meaningful social interactions but is only an *economically purposeful* community assembled for one reason. There are no *social contracts*, specific themes, or major rules of social interaction as in chat rooms. The existence of this *purposeful* community is an indication/result of further commercialization of most elements of daily life in developed countries, continued growth of individuality and encouragement of individual opinions, and increase in individuals' intentional separation of social and economic relationships.

All these factors make the structure of digital content very conducive to IOF. The information structure effect is manifested by (1) comparison of the number of online file sharing groups (legal and illegal) versus the number of offline file sharing groups; (2) the percentage of members of online file sharing networks (legal and illegal) who keep more than 50% of their content in digital formats; and (3) a comparison of the relative appeal of search results in various online file sharing networks.

2.4.4 Hypothesis-3: The Free-Products/Free-Search Effect

The advent of the Internet has resulted in numerous types of free promotions and price discounts for products and services. Prices offered on the web are often much lower than prices offered in physical *stores*. This has created a mentality among Internet technicians, web programmers, and web users that the Internet is a bastion and realm of free products and services and deeply discounted prices. Most online search services (Google, Yahoo, etc.) are free. IOF is essentially a form of Internet search. This mentality continues to be reinforced by marketing programs and promotions and partly accounts for the propensity of groups to develop P2P file sharing systems that in turn spawn illegal virtual organizations. Thus, traditional *free* Internet searches create subconscious emotions that cause developers of P2P file sharing systems to deem illegal file sharing to be comparable to normal/legal *free* Internet searches and hence either acceptable/justifiable or *forgivable* or *not deviant*. The process of IOF involves making a decision, sampling or downloading content, and revising the decision over time. This process may also create a habit and/or an addiction, depending on the individual's socioeconomic circumstances.

The free-products/free-search effect is manifested in (1) the percentage of participants in illegal file sharing networks that accept free products online or participate in online surveys in exchange for free products within two to three different time frames; (2) the weekly changes in the percentage of illegal file sharing network members that are willing to pay discounted prices for digital content and for physical content; (3) a comparison of the numbers of general free online searches and IOF searches conducted by an average consumer within a specific period of time; (4) a comparison of the changes in the volume of files transferred in IOF networks with the changes in the volume of free products/services distributed online within a specific period of time; and (5) a comparison of the changes in the number of free online searches with the changes in the volume of files transferred in illegal online networks within a specific period.

2.4.5 Hypothesis-4: The Failed Markets Effect

IOF can be construed as a group reaction to perceived ineffectiveness of and/or failure of traditional Internet markets (and even physical markets)—such as exchanges, eBay, auctions, barter markets, online stores, physical stores, and online catalogues. Ratchford et al. (2003) and Bolton et al. (2004) made tangential but useful comments. In traditional Internet markets, searches may not be efficient; customers may not be able to find items they seek; searches may take too long; desired items may be deemed too expensive when found in such markets; and there may be excessive competition for certain items that may temporarily drive up the prices. In traditional Internet markets, the required thresholds of trust are relatively significant.

The geographical dispersion of the Internet reduces psychological/mental barriers to participation in IOF because (1) perpetrators equate the substantial geographical dispersion of such networks to efficiency and larger volume of available digital content and (2) makers/developers of P2P systems perpetrators in different jurisdictions or countries are more likely to believe that they will not be prosecuted since foreign laws will not apply to them.

The *failed markets effect* is evident in (1) the changes in the locations of members of IOF networks; (2) the changes in volume of cross-border IOF; (3) the distribution of online file sharing networks by age of members, type of digital content, most active time periods (time of day, day of week), and concentration of members in a region; and (4) the changes in the number of monthly users of illegal P2P networks compared to changes in the monthly users of exchanges, eBay, auctions, barter markets, online stores, online catalogues, etc.

2.4.6 Hypothesis-5: The Payment Systems and Payment Divergence Effects

Information producers, ISP, and government regulators do not actively enforce IP laws in the Internet because of actual weaknesses in payment systems. The existing online payment systems in most legal file sharing and legal content download system always involve both individual pain and group pain (loss of money/wealth). Hence, people and groups opt to participate in illegal file sharing systems, which do not involve pain (most file sharing systems are free; computer costs are deemed nonexistent because the computer is used for many other purposes; bandwidth costs are paid monthly or quarterly; and time has less perceived costs).

Groups participate in IOF, and groups develop P2P file sharing systems because of substantial divergences between online payment systems and download systems. Many online payment systems are not fully integrated with content download systems. In such instances, the process of payment and the process of downloading are done through different websites and systems; and the process of downloading and the process of delivery (enjoyment by purchaser) are done through distinctly separate systems. There are no standardized online payment systems and each owner/distributor of content typically has their own file systems and payment system—and many do not use systems like Paypal. This *payment systems divergence* creates substantial incentives for consumers not to pay for digital content and also creates a state of inertia that results in lower willingness-to-pay for digital content.

2.4.7 Hypothesis-6: The Risk–Reward Moneyless-Trading Bias

Groups participate in IOF because the risk/reward ratio is very favorable. Only a relatively small percentage of IOF perpetrators are cautioned, prosecuted, or fined. In the United States, the penalties for illegal file sharing are relatively low and ineffective. On the other hand, perpetrators pay a fixed fee for Internet access and effectively convert their computers into servers with access to substantial digital content. Thus, the risk–reward profile for illegal file sharing is attractive to perpetrator groups and encourages participation. Groups and individuals with a high risk–reward bias are more likely to participate in illegal file sharing network and to download more files from such networks and to refer their friends to such file sharing networks. Note that there is a difference between individual risk–reward profile and group risk–reward profile.

Its conjectured here that the allure of *moneyless* trading in the United States and in many developed countries has increased during the last 5 years for several reasons: (1) the collapse of the emerging-growth-company sector (NASDAQ) stock market in 2000–2002, (2) the shift of assets from traditional bank accounts to securities accounts, (3) the broadening of the distribution of ages of people that participate in stock markets, and (4) the rapid increase in the popularity and volume of investments in securities. These factors have created a *trading mentality* that is now affecting other parts of daily life in the United States and most developed countries.

This *trading mentality* and *moneyless-trading bias* are evident in (1) increases in the volume of activity (trading, webpage listings, ads, email exchanges, etc.) in baseball cards, collectibles, and in auction-website activities; (2) the percentage of retailing websites that offer free products and product promotions; (3) the percentage of time spent on securities market transactions versus IOF networks; (4) the percentage of time spent on online auctions and price comparison websites versus IOF networks; and (5) the growth of websites that offer games in which either moneyless trading occurs or fake digital money is used. Illegal file sharing represents a form of moneyless trading that is substantially less risky than securities markets. Hence, people are more likely to prefer a legal online file sharing system than a download system and to prefer online purchase to physical purchase.

The group risk–reward bias is evident in (1) the percentage of IOF perpetrators who are arrested or prosecuted or punished compared to other forms of copyright infringement, (2) the percentage and effectiveness of punishment that targets groups only, and (3) the number of ISPs that penalize groups of illegal file sharing perpetrators (in addition to individuals).

2.4.8 Hypothesis-7: The Normality and Authority-Deficit Effect

IOF is often positioned and marketed as *normal* activity, whereas it is illegal. There are many academic science journals that have been publishing articles about sharing, reduction of free riding, and improvement of P2P file sharing systems without any consideration for the inherent misconduct or legal ramifications. Hence, some perpetrator groups internalize the misguided themes of legality of illegal file sharing networks. This normality effect seems to persist despite publicized prosecutions of illegal file sharing networks and associated perpetrators. The internalization process is reinforced by (1) relatively low Internet access costs, (2) the favorable risk–reward profile of IOF, (3) lack of enforcement by ISPs, (4) significant similarities between regular free Internet searches and participation in illegal file sharing networks, (5) the relative unsophistication of existing DRMSs, (6) ineffective penalties for IOF, (7) lax government enforcement of copyright laws, and (8) the absence of visible police presence in the Internet and absence of electronic tags on information goods (as in physical space), which increases consumers' propensity to engage in IOF—these web surfers view the Internet as a distinct world that is much less policed and, hence, much less punitive and more tolerant of criminal misconduct; and this type of thought process increases the propensity to participate in illegal file sharing networks.

2.4.9 Hypothesis-8: The Social Experimentation Effect

Illegal file sharing is a form of social experimentation in an increasingly diverse and information-deluged world, where people constantly seek to test relationships, limits, possibilities and consequences, and actions and relationships.

Groups are more likely to participate in IOF because the increase in popularity and availability of computer games has substantially changed modern culture and the mindset of people, making them much more prone to participate in online group activities and unregulated activities. In the United States, the computer games sector produces more annual sales revenues than the movie industry. Furthermore, the cost of participation in online digital games (at commercial locations) is relatively low, and this low-participation-cost effect reinforces consumers' propensity not to pay for digital content.

The social experimentation effect (SEE) is also related to anonymity. Developers of illegal file sharing software like the anonymity inherent in P2P networks (the activity includes some anonymity that is a substantial motivating factor). The increasing incidence of *phishing*, tracking of consumers, CRM systems, and security breaches (particularly with the Windows browser) has made more people wary of disclosing personal information on the Internet and has also made them sensitive about privacy. Much of the illegal file sharing is done without people knowing each other or their email addresses, and the inherent anonymity provides a false sense of protection from identification and prosecution. The *community* that is often mentioned in the context of illegal file sharing is not a real community with meaningful social interactions but is only an *economically purposeful* community assembled for one reason. There are no *social contracts*, specific themes, or major rules of social interaction as in chat rooms. The existence of this *purposeful* community is an indication/result of further commercialization of most elements of daily life in developed countries, continued growth of individuality and encouragement of individual opinions, and increase in individuals' intentional separation of social and economic relationships.

This SEE can account for the following:

1. The formation of groups that develop P2P software systems.
2. The inertia of legislators to enact efficient laws and penalties that will reduce or eliminate illegal file sharing. The pace and quality of statutes has not kept up with the evolution of P2P systems.
3. The inertia of government investigators and prosecutors to take timely action to prevent illegal file sharing.
4. The continuing evolution of P2P systems into more advanced versions that are more difficult to police.
5. The opposition of net neutrality statutes by ISPs. The reluctance of ISPs to help in regulating illegal file sharing or to implement network monitors that will reduce illegal file sharing.

SEE is conjectured to increase with (1) the popularity of the phenomenon, (2) the magnitude of intangibility of the subject asset or subject matter, (3) the geographical scope of the phenomenon, and (4) time—but only when many jurisdictions are affected. SEE is conjectured to decrease with (1) time—but only when relatively few jurisdictions are affected; (2) the magnitude of tangibility of the subject asset—the more tangible the asset, the lower the SEE; and (3) the amount of money that perpetrators spend in the illegal process.

2.4.10 Hypothesis-9: The Unstructured Growth Effect

Illegal P2P file sharing networks often grow in very unstructured patterns over time and cross physical regions; and it is fair to say that the physical configuration of a P2P file sharing network is never constant and is dynamic. The growth and speed of evolution of P2P software systems is also unstructured—investigators often discover new variants of P2P software by word of mouth. Such growth often cuts across jurisdictional, language, income, cultural, and technological barriers—which makes it more difficult to enforce IP laws and prosecute infringers. The unpredictability that is inherent in such unstructured growth makes it very difficult to plan for adequate regulation and policing of IOF. The anticipation of unstructured growth causes or can cause self-defeating behavior, group-think, group paralysis, and failed feedback systems in institutions associated with illegal file sharing.

Legislators are often exposed to entertainment and media industry lobbyists who seek new regulations for Internet and copyright matters. Within this context, perceptions are critical because it is very difficult or near impossible to gauge the true growth rate of P2P systems (physically and technologically). The unstructured growth effect raises the issue of commitment by trade associations and government prosecutors to effective enforcement of copyright statutes—commitment is conjectured to decline as the perceived rate of unstructured growth increases.

The unstructured growth effect can account for the following:

1. Allocation of inadequate government resources to combat copyright infringement, given the relatively high contribution of copyrights/trademarks to modern economies
2. Reluctance of legislators to enact new statutes (which may become outdated by the time that the bills are processed through the legislature)
3. The magnitude of interjurisdictional coordination in the enforcement and prosecution of perpetrators
4. The reluctance of ISPs to police their networks
5. The campaigns against net neutrality
6. The continuing change in the pricing of consumer network-access fees—to consumption-based pricing rather than flat-fee pricing
7. The ineffectiveness of penalties and the difficulties that judges and legislators have in determining the appropriate and sufficient type and magnitude of penalties for illegal file sharing
8. The low deterrence effect of existing antipiracy statutes

2.4.11 Hypothesis-10: The Phantom Adversary Problem

The *Phantom Adversary Problem* (PAE) refers to a state in which government investigators, private investigators, and prosecutors are relatively much more reluctant to prosecute or investigate misconduct because the adversary or perpetrators are not *visible* or physically perceptible. *Visibility* in this context means the extent to which the perpetrators are physically available and apprehensible or can be easily contacted by mail or phone. In this context, the geographical dispersion of the Internet makes most perpetrator *Phantom Adversaries*. The PAE raises the issue of the actual and perceived efficiency of interjurisdictional coordination in rule-making and enforcement—which has not been optimal or efficient in regulating illegal file sharing. The PAE can account for the following:

1. The reluctance of prosecutors to enforce copyright laws and to prosecute many perpetrators
2. The low level of cross-jurisdictional coordination in legislative processes pertaining to IOF
3. The lack of use of special taxes on ISPs and software firms to compensate information producers for illegal file sharing
4. The relatively slow reaction times of investigators when responding to complaints/reports of illegal file sharing

2.4.12 Hypothesis-11: The Liability Allocation Problem

The liability allocation effect is a state wherein the courts and prosecutors have substantial difficulty in allocating liability to perpetrators for any of the following reasons:

1. The complexity of the misconduct makes it difficult to allocate liability accurately.
2. The technological elements of processes or equipment used in the misconduct make it difficult to allocate liability accurately.
3. The applicable statutes are dormant and/or lag trends of misconduct, and thus, such statutes are not effective—that is, a state wherein statutes do not keep up with advances in P2P and other file sharing technologies, and/or the existing legislative processes are too cumbersome to react to both technological changes, and changes in human–computer interactions and data storage. When these conditions exist, then statutes become effectively dormant and cannot be effective against misconduct such as IOF.
4. The estimated costs of investigation and/or prosecution are substantial or are not justified by the expected deterrence effects of prosecution.
5. The allocation of liability can have collateral damage effects and may have adverse effects on overall social welfare.

Hence, the growth and increasing popularity of IOF can be attributed to the *liability allocation effect*.

2.5 Illegal Online File Sharing as Production Systems

Illegal online file sharing affects the economics, profitability, and business models of companies in many industries such as entertainment, education, travel, investments/finance, and any business where knowledge has value. Legal or illegal file sharing is essentially a production system that uses hardware, software, bandwidth, information (digital content), participant's time, software developers' time, and human capital as its inputs. Production in this instance consists of production of information, making digital content available to others, and successful online searches of digital content. In the United States, the Napster case illustrates some of the policy, technological, and economic issues inherent in systems for downloading content.[5]

2.5.1 Existing Literature on Legal File Sharing or IOF as a Production System

The existing relevant direct literature on online legal/illegal file sharing and associated production functions is very limited, although the literature on ordinary production functions is broad but not in-depth.

Baier et al. (2002), Brockett et al. (2005), Gandolfo (2008), Lindenberger (2003), and Atsushi (2002) analyzed services industry production functions. Gandolfo (2008), Lee and Keen (2004), McCombie and Dixon (1991), Shaikh (2005), Felipe et al. (2008), and other articles[6] critiqued traditional theories of production functions.

Merlone (2002), Khalil and Wang (2002), Roberts et al. (2005), and Nami et al. (2007) analyzed virtual organizations. Pickard et al. (1999), Wagner and Weitzel (2007), and Gurbaxani et al. (2000) analyzed production functions in software development.

Miklashevich (2003), Santin (2008), Fioretti (2007), Growiec (2008), and other articles[7] analyzed issues in the mathematical representations of social systems and production functions. Miller (2001), Lindenberger (2003), Wagner and Weitzel (2007), and Wall (1998) analyzed firms' production functions and cost functions. Mosca and Viscolani (2004) analyzed new product development within the context of production systems and marketing. Hinduja (2006) reviewed aspects of criminology. Pavlov and Saeed (2004), Netanel (2003), and Von Lohmann (2004) analyzed the file sharing phenomenon. Mosca and Viscolani (2004) analyzed optimization models for new product launches. Miller (2001) and Cooper (January 2006) studied elements of production functions. Beckenback (2000) modeled resource systems and markets.

The existing literature does not address the following issues:

1. Definition of production functions for IOF
2. Specification of appropriate amounts of monitoring, prosecution, and enforcement to deter illegal file sharing
3. Objectives of public and private efforts to deter IOF—substantial deterrence, complete deterrence, etc.
4. Optimal amount and type of punitive damages
5. The very minimal existing literature on online file sharing as production systems does not analyze the following factors:
   a. The conditions under which the information producer should increase, reduce, or cease efforts to eliminate IOF
   b. The information producer's objective function
   c. The optimal amount of effort that the information producer should allocate toward eliminating IOF
   d. The effects of knowledge and opportunity costs on the information producer's efforts to eliminate illegal file sharing
   e. The type and quality of coordination of information producer's efforts to curb illegal file sharing in physical space and online
   f. Effects of economic psychology factors and group dynamics on (i) propensity to share files illegally, (ii) deterrence effect of punitive damages and law enforcement activities, and (iii) consumer utility gained from IOF.
   g. Information producer's constraints and limitations imposed by corporate governance standards, public opinion considerations, and negative encouragement (by industry players who believe that illegal file sharing is beneficial to information producers)

2.5.2 The Production Model

Legal or illegal file sharing is essentially a production system that uses hardware, software, bandwidth, information (digital content), participant's time, software developers' time, and human capital as its inputs. This production system that is inherent in IOF has the following characteristics:

- It depends on cooperation rather than rights to property.
- It is completely self-sustaining.
- The product is not a public good.

- Each unit of product consists of the following: (1) utility from search, (2) utility from community, (3) utility from consumption of digital content, and (4) utility from absence of prosecution.
- Each unit of production creates highly varying amounts of utility for each participant in the file sharing network.

The following are the assumptions for the IOF production function models. T_v is the monetary value of total *valued time* spent by all participants in the file sharing network in time t. $T_v \in (-\infty, +\infty)$. B is the total cost of bandwidth used by all participants in the network in time t. $B \in (1, +\infty)$. B is assumed to increase with network congestion. H is the total cost of hardware (amortized over time t) and electricity used in time t, by participant i. $H \in (1, +\infty)$. D is the monetary value of total disutility of all participants, from unsuccessful searches in the network in time t. $D \in (-\infty, +\infty)$. S is the cost of developing file sharing software, amortized over time t. $S \in (-\infty, +\infty)$. ρ is the probability of prosecution for illegal file sharing. L is the actual loss incurred by participant i, if participant i is prosecuted and fined, where $i \in n$, and n is the number of participants in the file sharing network in time t. This includes time lost, penalties, and attorney costs. $L \in (-\infty, +\infty)$. N is the total number of searches for content in the network by participant i during time t. $N \in (0, +\infty)$. ϕ is the average marginal propensity to substitute digital content—to replace one unit of content from illegal file sharing with one unit of legal content. $\phi \in (-\infty, \infty)$. For example, where ϕ is equal to three, the web user is likely to substitute one unit of illegal content from illegal file sharing with three units of legal content. Where ϕ is equal to minus three (–3), the web user is likely to substitute one unit of illegal content from illegal file sharing with three units of content from illegal file sharing.

V is the monetary value of one unit of legal digital content. $V \in (0, +\infty)$.

Such a production system, P, can have one of the following alternative production functions:

$$P_1 = {}_0\!\int_0^t {}_0\!\int^V [(\Sigma_{i=t}T_v) + B + (\Sigma_{i=t}H) + (\Sigma_{i=t}U) + S + \{\Sigma_{i=n}(\rho * L)\} - \{(\Sigma_{i=n}N) * \phi * V\} + D]\partial t \partial V$$

$$P_2 = {}_0\!\int_0^t {}_0\!\int^V {}_0\!\int^\rho [(\Sigma_{i=t}T_v) + B + (\Sigma_{i=t}H) + (\Sigma_{i=t}U) + S + \{\Sigma_{i=n}(\rho * L)\} - \{(\Sigma_{i=n}N) * \phi * V\} + D]\partial t \partial V$$

$$P_3 = {}_0\!\int_0^t {}_0\!\int^V {}_0\!\int^\rho \left[(\Sigma_{i=t}T_v) + B + (\Sigma_{i=t}H) + (\Sigma_{i=t}U) + S + \left\{ (\Sigma_{i=n}(\rho * L)) * \left(\frac{\partial L}{\partial \rho} \right) \right\} \right.$$

$$\left. -\{(\Sigma_{i=n}N) * \phi * V\} - \left\{ D * \left(\frac{\partial \phi^2}{\partial N \partial V} \right) \right\} \right] \partial t \partial V \partial \rho$$

The foregoing models are somewhat self-explanatory. The differences among the foregoing production models can be attributed to types of networks, network topology, types of digital content being shared, etc.

2.6 Conclusion

IOF and content control remain the major problems with economic, psychological, technological, and policy ramifications. The rapid and continuing increases in the use of broadband Internet has exacerbated IOF. Given the nature of IOF, more effective regulations are required.

The illegal file sharing phenomenon is substantial evidence that the Diamond–Mortensen–Pissarides search models and the Koopman search models are grossly inaccurate or can be applied in only very few circumstances and with substantial limiting assumptions. The theories introduced in this chapter also limit the applicability of the Diamond–Mortensen–Pissarides search models and the Koopman search models. The advent of the Internet, substantial increases in the number of online/physical social networks, changes in the labor force, increasing mobility of households, and other factors have fundamentally changed the nature of search.

The production functions introduced herein can help in both (1) reducing IOF by identifying appropriate controls, profit mechanisms, opportunity costs, types of capital employed and appropriate regulations, and where best to focus enforcement and prosecution efforts and (2) improving legal online file sharing networks by identifying and optimizing key elements of online file sharing.

Notes

1 See Coyle et al. (2009); Jacobs et al. (2012); Steinmetz and Tunnell (2013); Wang and McClung (2012); Podoshen (2008); Cho et al. (2015); Cox and Collins (2014); and Aaltonen and Salmi (2013) analyzed elements of human behavior in the context of illegal file sharing. Bajari and Hortacsu (2004); Iwamura and Takefuji (2000); Janssen and Jager (2000); Beckenback (2000); Zimmerman et al. (2000); Balasko and Shell (1980); and Miklashevich (2003).
2 See Diamond (1971, 1982a,b,c, 1984, 1987a,b, 1993); Diamond et al. (1964); Diamond and Maskin (1981); and Diamond and Yellin (1987).
3 Hinduja (2006), Hughes et al. (2006), Gopal et al. (2002), and Jenny et al. (2006). Jenny et al. (2006) states in part:

>   …Accordingly, our hypotheses were the following:
>   I. Individual compliance with a rule is influenced by:
>   a) sanctioning costs;
>   b) general norm orientation;
>   c) social norms;
>   d) distributive justice;
>   e) procedural justice;
>   f) interactional justice (interpersonal and informational justice);
>   g) compatibility;
>   h) adequacy;
>   II. For an extended explanation, we assume that:
>   i) the individual's perception of sanctioning costs is based on the perceived possibility of non-compliant behavior being detected and the severity of the expected sanctions;
>   j) perceived compatibility depends on household characteristics (such as daily routines);
>   k) perceived adequacy of rules depends on the perceived state of the resource…

4 See Tsiros and Mittal (2000); Harrison et al. (February 2005); Bromiley et al. (1989); MacKinley (1997); McWilliams and Siegel (1999); Reagan (1998); Hosmer et al. (1991); and Tu et al. (2005).
5 See Schwab and Zampelli (1987); Richmond et al. (2007); Lence and Miller (1998); Hanoch and Rothschild (1972); Baier et al. (2002); and Neill (2003).
6 See Merlone (2002); Wall (1998); Battese and Coelli (1988, 1995); Ulieru (2002); Baker (1998).

Chapter 3

Illegal Online File Sharing and Information Producers' Strategies*

In the United States, Europe, and Asia, illegal online file sharing has resulted in billions of dollars of losses for many companies and many lawsuits by trade groups, government agencies, and entertainment companies. Illegal file sharing affects the economics, profitability, and business models of companies in many industries such as entertainment, education, travel, news, sports, investments/finance, and any business where information has value. The issue involves various policy, legal, technological, and economic problems that have not yet been resolved. This chapter introduces optimal strategies for owners and legitimate distributors of digital content—in terms of the optimal conditions for and the amount of effort to be allocated to reduction of illegal online file sharing.

3.1 Existing Literature

The literature on the information producers' business strategies is extensive and has been analyzed from strategy, law and economics, operations research, management science, technology, and computer science perspectives in the articles studied by Eliasson and Wihlborg (2003), Vaccaro and Cohn (2004), Hinduja (2006), and other articles.[1]

Halbheer et al. (2014), Gong et al. (2015), Grewal et al. (2010), Jeong et al. (2012), Krämer et al. (2013), and the authors of other articles[2] analyzed various elements of digital strategy.

Fazli et al. (2014), Bei et al. (2011), Melnik et al. (2013), Cao and Yang (2014), Georgiou et al. (2014), Kempe et al. (2013), and Kramer et al. (2015) studied *contagion in networks*.

---

* An earlier version of this chapter was published in 2009 as an article cited as: Nwogugu, M. (2009). Illegal online file sharing and information producers' strategies. *International Journal of Mathematics, Game Theory & Algebra*, 17(5/6), 329–342.

Anshelevich and Caskurlu (2011) and Ma et al. (2014) studied network structure and network formation.

Danaher and Smith (2014), Adermon and Liang (2014), Warr and Goode (2011), Wulandari (2014), Appleyard (2015), and the authors of other articles[3] studied *industrial organization* issues that pertain to IOF.

Benkler (2002) completely failed to show how intellectual property (IP) laws (mostly copyright laws) affect the business strategies used by producers and distributors of digital content. Benkler (2002) did not anticipate or analyze the implications of the (2004–2006) rulings by the U.S. Supreme Court and Australian Federal Courts on copyright infringement cases, all of which render the analysis by Benkler (2002) appellate meaningless. The *open-source* form of information production affects only a very small percentage of information producers. Similarly, the *appropriation* form of information production, which is described by Benkler (2002), also affects a relatively small percentage of information producers. Hence, the primary forms of digital information production are the *internally generated* model and the illegal file sharing and legal file sharing models. Von Lohmann (2004) made some useful comments.

Most of the literature on illegal file sharing and the content owners'/distributors' strategies does not analyze the following factors:

- The conditions under which the information producer should increase, reduce, or cease efforts to eliminate illegal online file sharing
- The optimal amount of effort that the content owner/distributor should allocate toward eliminating illegal online file sharing
- The effects of knowledge and opportunity costs on the content owner's/distributor's efforts to eliminate or reduce illegal online file sharing
- The type and quality of coordination of information producer's/distributor's efforts to curb illegal file sharing in physical space and online
- Effects of economic psychology factors and group dynamics on (1) propensity to share files illegally, (2) deterrence effect of punitive damages and law enforcement activities, and (3) consumer utility gained from illegal online file sharing (see Chapter 2 herein and earlier)
- The information producer's/distributor's constraints and limitations imposed by corporate governance standards, public opinion considerations, and negative encouragement (by industry participants who believe that illegal file sharing is beneficial to information producers)

3.1.1 An Analysis of Yoon (2002)

Yoon (2002) introduced several wrong contentions and contradictions about optimal copyright protection, some of which are as follows. First, contrary to Yoon (2002), increasing copyright protection does not decrease *social welfare* (SW) by limiting the unauthorized use of the works by consumers. The effect of copyright protection is a function of the utility/disutility the consumer gains from consumption of the works (i.e., the music may be demotivating or irritating), the associated opportunity costs (the works may be outdated, and using them will preclude search of more recent and useful information), and the associated use costs (the time spent searching for and consuming an illegal copy may be worth more than the time/cost of obtaining a legal copy). Yoon (2002) does not (1) distinguish between the proportion of total enforcement efforts that is attributable to the information producer and to government agencies and (2) distinguish between the proportion of total enforcement efforts by the information producer that is feasible compared to what is feasible for the government agencies.

Second, Yoon (2002) did not define an optimal level of copyright protection. *Underutilization* as defined and used by Yoon (2002) must be analyzed in the context of the incentives to create—the issue of incentives is almost completely omitted in the study by Yoon (2002). To be meaningful and effective, copyright protection must provide adequate psychological incentives (comfort, reassurance, trust in the system, recognition, etc.), physical incentives (money/value for products, safety, recognition, etc.), and monetary/wealth incentives (money, wealth, social capital, reputational capital, and brand equity) for people and companies to produce and market digital content; otherwise, creativity in the economy will decline.

Third, contrary to Yoon (2002), the relationship between the optimal level of copyright protection and the information producer's marginal cost is not as stated. The primary reason is that both elements are major components of two distinct phases in the information producer's supply chain, and both are typically implemented by very different entities—the production (CDs, tapes, etc.) is typically done by a third-party company (typically distinct from the distributor and the creator), while most copyright enforcement is done by government agencies, sometimes at the request of industry participants.

Fourth, contrary to Yoon (2002: 330), the information producer will still incur some costs even if it decides not to produce any digital content. This overhead cost is a substantial component of producers' costs. It includes administrative expenses, marketing expenses, and contractual payments to retain content creators.

Fifth, consumers can and do consume digital products in various ways. Yoon (2002) mentioned only two options—purchasing the product from the producer or borrowing it from someone and copying it. Yoon (2002: 331) omitted other alternatives such as moneyless exchanges of digital products, online file sharing (legal or illegal), sampling of digital content at stores and online, and consumption of very similar products.

Sixth, contrary to Yoon (2002: 331), the consumer's cost of reproducing digital content is typically relatively very low, so as to be almost negligible in the consumer's decision-making processes. Furthermore, the consumer's cost of reproduction does not always increase with the level of copyright protection because both phenomena are separated by technology, time, distance, observation, and rules. Regardless of the level of copyright protection, a consumer can still use a laptop to copy digital content despite the differences in distance (consumer's location vs. the creator's and the enforcer's location), time, technology (enforcer/government/creator often cannot observe or stop or technologically intervene in the illegal copying process), and rules (the rules of criminal procedure and evidence govern the collection and admissibility of evidence in prosecution of misconduct). The primary effects of most current copyright laws are ex post deterrence, a fear of consequences, and anticipation of the pain of post-misconduct penalties. Hence, the appropriate characterization of the relationships is more likely to be $-\infty < \partial z/\partial y < 1$.

Seventh, contrary to Yoon (2002), the rate of substitutability between the copy and the original digital content can be negative or positive depending on the type of content (e-books vs. videos vs. music), the use value, the quality of the pirated copy, etc. Furthermore, technology has advanced to the stage where digital copies are the same or almost of the same quality as the original digital content. Hence, contrary to Yoon (2002: 331), the consumer can derive greater utility from consuming the copy rather than from consuming the original digital content, particularly where: (1) the use value of information in the original and that in the copy are the same (i.e., digital academic books); (2) the search costs for obtaining the original digital content and the attendant use costs exceed those incurred for the copy; (3) ancillary services such as technical support are not relevant; (4) the consumer is skilled in technology and can do the same quality of work as the distributor/producer's customer service staff; and (5) the consumer derives utility from the act of illegal file sharing. Furthermore, *Propsition-2 in Yoon (2002: 334) is wrong* because, in many cases, the consumer's reproduction costs are much lower than the sale price of the digital content. Consumers have access to friends/family members who own equipment that can be used in reproducing digital content. Yoon (2002) erroneously concluded that no consumer has an incentive to reproduce the digital content since the price of the original content can be set low enough—this contention is wrong because Yoon's characterization of sets is wrong and assumes linear relationships among w, v, z, time, and ȧ. Furthermore, SW is not adequately defined in the study by Yoon (2002), and contrary to assumptions therein, SW does not have a linear relationship with w, z, or v. Hence, Proposition-6 in Yoon (2002: 340) is wrong.

Eighth, contrary to Yoon (2002), the production–consumption problem is a five-stage game:

1. The producer identifies talent and/or does market research.
2. The producer contracts for creation of content or creates content.
3. The producer develops a distribution system and channels.
4. The producer reproduces the digital content in files, CDs, tapes, etc.—often by third-party contractors.
5. The producer markets the product, and consumers choose and purchase the product.

Contrary to Yoon (2002), the game never ends with zero payoffs to all parties. The consumers gain by sampling the music or buying it. The contractor that reproduces the content makes profit. The information producer/distributor that does not sell any copy of the digital content can gain social capital, reputational capital, and a distribution network in the process. Yoon (2002) completely omits the critical relationships among the distribution channel, mode of consumption, and quantity consumed.

Ninth, contrary to Yoon (2002), the *no-protection* state has no basis in economic thought, facts, or logic. The majority of the existing literature on the economics of IP states that copyright protection is the very essence of viability of IP and the foundation of incentives to create. Most of the suggested departures from copyright protection in the literature, apply only to, and or are feasible only for artists/performances who have substantial audiences and name recognition. Contrary to Yoon (2002: 335), *full protection is never a possible state* because given the current state of technology and available resources (cash, computing power, staff, etc.) around the world, regulators and the information producer/distributor cannot observe all piracy/misconduct or obtain all resources required for enforcement and full protection. Furthermore, *full protection* may not be a viable or desirable option because it interferes with cultural and social patterns of sharing/reciprocity/gifts and personal beliefs (about fairness, equity, etc.). The resulting enforcement under *full protection* is very likely to create negative goodwill and boycott of products. Full copyright protection is not yet technologically feasible. Hence, *Proposition-5 in Yoon (2002: 338) is wrong* because the mathematical conditions for distinguishing between *full-protection* and *no-protection* regimes erroneously assume the following: (1) global continuous real-time observability by regulators and the information producer and minimal observation/monitoring costs; (2) minimal transaction costs and enforcement costs; (3) SW equates only to profits of information producers/distributors; (4) there is not any substitutability between digital content and other forms of property or entertainment; (5) there is a constant relationship/ratio between the producer's/distributor's marginal costs on one hand, and the producer's/distributor's development cost (D), profits, etc. on the other hand; (6) the information producer's monopoly is not a function of the nature of distribution channels, perceived product quality, and pricing, and depends solely on the level of copyright protection; (7) the proportions of enforcement costs that are attributable to the producer/distributor and the government remain constant over time; (8) consumers' switching costs are not relevant; (9) the decisions about levels of copyright protection do not depend on the deterrence effect and magnitude of possible sanctions; (10) rational consumers, no reciprocity, and no fairness-judgment effects; and (11) there are similar (or the same) utility scales for digital products and physical products and for various types of digital content.

Tenth, contrary to Yoon (2002: 339), while copyright protection provides significant incentives to innovate/produce, (1) the information producer's/distributor's decision to produce may not vary with the level of available copyright protection—depending on the audience, nature of distribution contract, revenue model (e.g., group licensing, public licenses), type of digital content, etc.; (2) it is not typically a requirement that profit (π) should cover development costs (D)—for example, this may be the case where sales of ancillary products and advertising can provide additional revenues; and (3) Yoon (2002) argues that the *no-protection* regime is a viable alternative and then makes a contradiction by stating that profit (π) is an increasing function of the level of copyright protection (z).

Eleventh, Yoon (2002) failed to analyze contagion in networks (social network, Internet networks). See articles about contagion that are cited herein and in earlier text.

Twelfth, Yoon (2002) failed to analyze digital-content strategies of information producers. See articles about digital-content strategy that are cited herein and in earlier text. Yoon (2002) also failed to analyze contagion in networks.

3.2 Business Strategies

In this context, information producers/distributors include legal P2P file sharing systems, legal download websites (where users can legally download digital content), record labels, and any company/individual/institution that produces any form of digital content that can be copyrighted. Although this chapter focuses on reduction of illegal file sharing, within the context of information production, *business strategies* is a term that refers to business models, innovation, and competition in the following dimensions: (1) modes of production, (2) modes of storage, (3) types of distribution and distribution channels, (4) types of transmission, (5) risk management, (6) pricing of digital content, (7) corporate/business structure, (8) DRM systems, (9) types of investment, and (10) monitoring and enforcement strategies.

Some of the main impacts of IP laws on business strategies of information producers are analyzed as follows. See Kim (2007).

3.2.1 Incentives to Produce Information

Varian (2005)[4] analyzed some conditions for illegal file sharing of content, and Boldrin and Levine (2002, 2005, 2012) made some useful comments. The content owner's/distributor's business strategies will change depending on the following variables:

IC is the amount and type of incentives that are provided by copyright laws.
T is the cost of achieving such incentives provided by copyright laws, which is a function of monitoring costs, enforcements costs, and cost of copyrighting content.

E is the information producer's effort (creative and business efforts).

R is resources devoted to developing content and will be much less in a *low-incentive regime* (denoted by LIC) than in a *high-incentive regime* (denoted by HIC). R is a function of human capital (h), cash (m), cost of capital (r), time (t), overhead (o), etc.

The 2004–2006 rulings by the U.S. Supreme Court (i.e., *MGM vs. Grokster*) and the Australian Supreme Court heralded the beginning of *high-incentive regimes.*

The information producer's multi-objective function is:

$$\text{Max}\Big[\big\{(I_t + D) - (IC - T - E - R)\big\}\Big]$$

$$\text{Min}\Big[\text{Max}(OC_t;0)\,\big|\,\big((\partial T_{HIC}/\partial T_{LIC}) \approx 1\big)\Big]$$

Hence, it will be most beneficial for information producers/distributors to continue production of I *iff*

$$\Big[\big\{(I_t + D) - (IC - T - E - R)\big\}\Big] > \Big[\text{Max}(OC_t,0)\,\big|\,\big((\partial T_{HIC}/\partial T_{LIC}) \approx 1\big)\Big]$$

where

OC_t is the opportunity cost of (E + R) in time t

T_{HIC} is the cost of achieving such incentives in a high-incentive regime

T_{LIC} is the cost of achieving such incentives in a low-incentive regime

D is the disutility experienced by actual and potential infringers due to perceived effectiveness and deterrence effects of copyright laws and associated punishment

3.2.2 The Cost of Acquiring Necessary Inputs for the Production Process

This becomes relevant only if any production input required for production of product I is acquired by payment, borrowing (loan, etc.), or barter from third parties. This applies only to IP that may be used in production, and hence the primary impacts are (1) cost of appropriation and (2) cost of probable future enforcement/prosecution and any related penalties. This issue arises in only the minority of circumstances. Benkler (2002) focuses almost exclusively on this issue but does not address it fully. The issue is more of a capital budgeting decision.

3.2.3 Optimal Conditions for Prosecution for Infringement

The probability of prosecution for infringement (ρ) is a function of various variables such as the following:

Ω is the prosecutor's resources. $0 < \Omega < \infty$. ψ is a function of municipal budget, staff costs, and case loads, and deterrence effect sought.

κ is the prosecutor's knowledge. $0 < \kappa < 1$.

Φ is the court environment. $0 < \Phi < 1$. τ is positive (Φ^+) if the court tends to convict infringers or find them liable, and negative (Φ^-) if the court is less likely to convict or rule against infringers.

χ is the threshold of infringement, which is the monetary value of infringement required for prosecution.

U_d is the expected deterrence effect of investigation and prosecution, which is a disutility that partly depends on the number of units of content that were not infringed because of information effects of investigation and/or prosecution.

U_p is the psychological utility provided to information producers by knowing that investigation and prosecution are possible and likely (U_p).

Λ_d is the perceived reactions by defendants/infringers to prosecution/enforcement, which is a function of the size of infringers, the number of infringers prosecuted, the resources available to infringers and prosecutors, and the court environment. i_d is the total cost of continued litigation and associated continued infringement by others, where infringers do not plead guilty.

Hence,

$$\rho = f\ (\Omega;\ \kappa;\ \Phi;\ \chi;\ \Lambda_d;\ i_d;\ U_p)$$

$$U_p \rightarrow 0, \quad \text{if } \partial\rho/\partial\chi = 0$$

Prosecution for infringement will be beneficial *iff* the following conditions exist:

1. $\partial U_p/\partial U_d > 1 > \partial\Lambda_d/\partial U_d$
2. $\partial\rho/\partial U_d > 1$
3. $\partial\rho/\partial\Lambda_d > 1$
4. $\partial\Phi/\partial k > 1$
5. $(\partial\Phi/\partial\chi \neq 0) \cap (\partial\rho/\partial\chi > 1)$

The makers of infrastructure include makers of Internet-based file sharing software, Internet access providers, and Internet backbones. The liability standards for infrastructure makers that are embodied in IP laws affect the information producer's business strategies to the extent that (1) such standards increase/reduce the variable costs of a given distribution channel—monitoring costs, maintenance costs, fees paid to the channel, and/or costs to achieve protection provided by IP laws (Eliasson and Wihlborg, 2003); (2) the standards provide a psychological comfort, incentives to produce and positive utility that vary directly with the severity and requirements of such standards; and (3) such standards increase/reduce the fixed costs of a given distribution channel—network construction costs, administrative costs, and maintenance costs.

3.2.4 *Method of Distribution of Content*

Copyright laws and the resulting probability of infringement affect producers' choices of distribution systems. Protection provided differs drastically depending on distributions methods. CDs and cassettes offer a different level of protection than digital files. Independent distributors, retail chain stores, specialized websites, online retailers, legal Internet-based file sharing networks, and legal content download websites all offer varying amounts of actual and perceived protection from infringement. These distribution channels all have various and different variable costs of distribution to the information producer, which in turn depends on copyright laws.

Assume that v is the content owner's variable cost of distribution. d is the fixed fees and per-unit fees charged by distributor. $-\infty < d < +\infty$. f is the incremental costs to deliver the unit of content to the distributor in the format that the distributor can work with. T is the per-unit costs of achieving protection—T is the per-unit cost of monitoring, investigation, and enforcement multiplied by the probability of infringement. a is the per-unit cost of marketing required if the distribution channel is used. $-\infty < a < +\infty$. I is the value of one unit of digital content (information product):

$$v = f + d + T + a$$

Hence, the information producer will select the distribution channel that has the following objective function:

Max [I – v]

s. t.

f > 0

T > 0

3.3 Conditions under which Content Owners or Distributors Will Change Their Efforts to Stop Illegal Online File Sharing

The content owner/distributor will be willing to make efforts to stop illegal online file sharing and will be economically better off by making such efforts, if and only if the following conditions exist:

1. $\text{Max}[0, (\xi + \beta)] < [U_{\text{illegal}} - \lambda_{\text{illegal}} - \tau_{\text{illegal}} + U_{\text{search}} - (\acute{\Gamma} * \rho_L) - \varepsilon]$
2. $\text{Max}[0,(\theta + \varepsilon)] < \gamma$
3. $\text{Max}[0,\{\sigma + U_{\text{legal}} - \psi_{\text{legal}}\}] < [U_{\text{illegal}} + U_{\text{search}} - \lambda_{\text{illegal}} - \psi_{\text{illegal}} - \omega - U_{\text{conf.}} - (\rho_L * \acute{\Gamma})]$
4. $\alpha \in \xi$; and $\mu, \beta \in \theta$
5. $[U_{\text{legal}} - \sigma - \psi_{\text{legal}} - \tau_{\text{legal}}] > \text{Max}[\{U_{\text{illegal}} - \tau_{\text{illegal}} - \psi_{\text{illegal}} + \omega\},0]$
6. $\partial\theta/\partial U_{\text{illegal}} < 1$
7. $\partial\theta/\partial\acute{\Gamma} < 1$
8. $\partial\theta/\partial\acute{\Gamma}_{\text{real}} < 1$
9. $\omega \approx 0$
10. $\lambda_{\text{illegal}} < \lambda_{\text{legal}}$ *and* $\omega \cong 0$ *and* $\psi_{\text{illegal}} < \psi_{\text{legal}}$
11. $(U_{\text{illegal}} - \psi_{\text{illegal}} - U_{\text{conf.}} - \lambda_{\text{illegal}} - [\acute{\Gamma} * \rho_L]) > \text{Max}[0,(U_{\text{legal}} - \sigma + \tau_{\text{legal}} + U_{\text{search}} - \tau_{\text{illegal}})]$
12. $\text{Max}[0,(\tau_{\text{illegal}})] < (\tau_{\text{legal}} + \sigma)$

13. $\text{Max}\left[0,\left\{\int_0^t (\tau_{\text{illegal}} + \psi_{\text{illegal}})\partial t\right\}\right] < \int_0^t \left[\tau_{\text{legal}} + \psi_{\text{legal}} + \sigma - (\acute{\Gamma} * \rho_L) + \lambda_{\text{illegal}}\right] S\partial t$

14. $\dfrac{\partial\acute{\Gamma}}{\partial\Pi_{\text{illegal}}} > 1;\ \dfrac{\partial\acute{\Gamma}^2}{\partial\Pi_{\text{illegal}}^2} > 0;$

15. $\dfrac{\partial\Pi_{\text{illegal}}}{\partial\rho_L} > 1;\ \dfrac{\partial^2\Pi_{\text{illegal}}}{\partial\rho_L^2} > 0;$

16. $\lambda_{\text{legal}} > (\lambda_{\text{illegal}} * (1-\rho_L));\ \dfrac{\partial(\lambda_{\text{illegal}} * (1-\rho_L))}{\partial\lambda_{\text{legal}}} < 0;$ and $\left\{\dfrac{\partial^2(\lambda_{\text{illegal}} * (1-\rho_L))}{\partial\lambda_{\text{legal}}^2}\right\} > 0$

17. $\dfrac{\partial \omega}{\partial \psi_{illegal}} > 0; \; \dfrac{\partial^2 \omega}{\partial \psi_{illegal}^2} > 0$

18. $\gamma > (\theta + \mu + \beta); \; \dfrac{\partial \gamma}{\partial (\theta + \mu + \beta)} > 1; \; \dfrac{\partial^2 \gamma}{\partial (\theta + \mu + \beta)^2} > 0$

where

θ is marginal cost of enforcement per unit of digital content

ξ is the actual cost of enforcement per unit of digital content

μ is the marginal costs of monitoring per unit of digital content

α is the actual cost of monitoring per unit of digital content

β is the marginal costs of identification of participants per unit of digital content

ε is the value of evidence/proof; $\varepsilon = \varepsilon_f + \varepsilon_{afv}$

ε_f is the value of fines

ε_{afv} is the present value of value of absence of future violations

γ is the profit from sale of one unit of digital content

π is the time spent by participant

$\tau_{illegal}$ is the monetary value of average time spent searching for one unit of digital content in illegal file sharing networks

τ_{legal} is the monetary value of time average spent searching for one unit of digital content in legal markets/sources

σ is the cost of legally purchasing one unit of digital content

U_{legal} is the utility gained from legally buying one unit of digital content

$U_{illegal}$ is the utility gained from illegally downloading one unit of digital content from the network and being able to share the file

U_{search} is the utility gained from searching in the file sharing network

$\psi_{illegal}$ is the marginal search costs per unit of digital content for illegal online file sharing, other than time, including bandwidth and proportional costs of hardware

ψ_{legal} is the marginal search costs per unit of digital content for legal purchases, other than time, including bandwidth, transportation/shipping, and proportional costs of hardware

ω is the marginal costs of substitution, that is, the cost of switching from one digital content to another similar content

U_{conf} is the disutility experienced by the participant by incorrectly configuring file sharing software and hence making the wrong files available to others

$\lambda_{illegal}$ is the monetary value of access rights in illegal file sharing networks—the right to participate in illegal file sharing network on the Internet and/or the right to access other participant's hard drives to download files (this includes the costs of access—such ISP fees charged to consumers and amortized hardware costs—and utility gained from participation in the network)

λ_{legal} is the monetary value of access rights in legal file sharing networks—the right to participate in legal file sharing network on the Internet (this includes the costs of access—such ISP fees charged to consumers and amortized hardware costs—and utility gained from participation in the network)

$\acute{\Gamma}$ is the perceived loss to participant from fine/penalty upon prosecution of the participant for illegal file sharing

ρ_L is the probability that the participant will be prosecuted for illegal file sharing

Γ'_{real} is the actual loss to the participant from fine/penalty upon prosecution of the participant for illegal file sharing

$\Pi_{illegal}$ is the cost of access rights in illegal file sharing networks (this includes ISP fees and hardware costs)

Π_{legal} is the cost of access rights in legal file sharing networks (this includes ISP fees and hardware costs)

The proofs for the foregoing conditions are relatively straightforward. The aforementioned conditions imply the following to deter illegal online file sharing:

- Penalties (for IOF) should be more dynamic in order to increase deterrence effects.
- The pricing of digital content and access rights should be more dynamic as opposed to using fixed amounts.

3.4 Conclusion

Illegal online/offline file sharing and content-control problems can be solved by (1) gaining a better understanding of the socioeconomic and behavioral issues inherent in P2P systems and distribution systems; (2) development of business models that minimize economic losses; (3) effective allocation of resources for monitoring, enforcement of IP laws, and digital rights management; (4) development of appropriate technology that considers legal and economic factors; and (5) enactment and implementation of IP laws that have significant deterrence effects, reduce monitoring and enforcement costs, and provide summary proceedings for prosecution.

Notes

1 See Xiao and Feng (2005); Yoon (2002); Cevik and Ozertan (2008); Netanel (2003); Lebowitz (2006); Zentner (2006); Bhattacharjee et al. (2006a,b); Gopal et al. (2002, 2006); Gopal and Bhattacharjee (2003); Gale and Rosenthal (1994); U.S. Federal Trade Commission (June 2005); Perritt (2007a,b); Banerjee (2003); Bae and Choi (2006); Peitz and Waelbroeck (2006); Kwan et al. (2008); Qiu (2006); Hui et al. (2008); Hanks (2004); Douglas et al. (2007); Choi and Perez (2007); Quiring et al. (2008); Gillespie (2006); and Jaisingh (2007).
2 See Lang et al. (2009); Cook and Wang (2004); Aron et al. (2006); Liu (2009); Lang et al. (2009); and Cook and Wang (2004).
3 Piolatto and Schuett (2012); Kim and Lee (2015); Bai and Waldfogel (2012); Zentner (2005); Mansell and Steinmueller (2013); and Jeong et al. (2012).
4 Varian (2005) stated in part:

> …The price to the group will then be p = p = k(v − t) so that the monetary price each person has to pay is (v − t). Plugging this group price back into expression (1), we see that the sharing outcome will occur when v > kt/(k − 1). Hence, large group sizes, large value for the work, and low transactions costs will lead to sharing. Note that this solution is socially inefficient. In equilibrium the consumers get zero surplus whether they share or not, but the monopolist gets lower profit under sharing due to the inefficient sharing technology…. The maximum price that just discourages sharing is p_n = tk/(k − 1). In the sharing equilibrium, the monopolist makes v − t per consumer. In the limit-pricing equilibrium the monopolist makes [tk/(k − 1)] per consumer. A little algebra shows that the limit-price equilibrium is

more profitable than the sharing equilibrium when $[((2k - 1)/(k - 1))^* t] \approx 2t > v$. In the limit-pricing equilibrium the surplus is shared between the monopolist and the consumer. Again, this is due to the fact that the possibility of sharing operates like a competitor for the monopolist, constraining the price that it can charge.... In the above analysis we assumed that all individuals had the same value for the work. When individuals have heterogeneous valuations for the work, the decision about whether to acquire a work that can subsequently be shared becomes a non-trivial public good problem. If k consumers share the item among themselves, what is the group demand function? There are (at least) two answers offered in the literature. One suggestion, put forth by Armstrong (1999), Bakos et al. (1999), and Bergstrom and Bergstrom (2004) is that the willingness to pay by the group is the sum of the willingness to pay of the individuals. That is, the group has some way to *solve* the public goods problem and elicit contributions from the members that cover the cost of the item being purchased whenever the sum of the valuations is greater than that cost.... *Video store model:* Suppose that consumers get utility from viewing a video and that the inverse demand function for viewing is given by p(x). If the marginal cost of the video is c, then the monopolist will choose output x* to maximize profit, [p(x)x − c x]. Suppose now that groups of size k form so that if x items are produced, there will be y = kx items viewed. The willingness to pay of the marginal individual is p(kx), so the willingness to pay of the marginal group is {k*p(kx)}. The monopolist now wants to chose x to maximize kp(kx)x − cx. If c = 0, then y* = kx*. That is, the monopolist just produces 1/kth as much when sharing is possible, and the marginal user ends up paying the same amount as he or she did before. When c > 0, the monopolist produces less when sharing is allowed, and makes more profit, due to the savings on production costs. Think of a situation where the users band together to form a private library and purchase some very expensive reference book. The publisher is better off printing a few of them and selling them to libraries at a high price than printing more and selling to every individual. In this case, sharing is a more efficient industry for selling downstream, so the monopolist wants to encourage downstream sharing. However, note that we have assumed that there is no cost to sharing. In reality, it is often inconvenient to share due to various forms of congestion. We could modify the above model by adding in a transactions cost of sharing, as was examined earlier. This task is pursued in Besen (1986) and Varian (2000), among others...

where

    k = the number of individuals in the group.

    v = value of content to the group.

    t = transaction costs of sharing the content.

    P = price of the content.

Varian (2005) also stated in part:

…Here is a brief list of business models that might work in a world without effective copyright.

Make original cheaper than copy:
This is basically the limit pricing model described earlier. If there is a transaction cost for a copy—a direct cost of copying, an inconvenience cost, or the copy is inferior to the original in some way—then the seller can set the price low enough that it is not attractive to copy.

Make copy more expensive than original:
The "cost of copying" is partially under the control of the seller, who could use a "digital rights management system," some anticopying technology, or threats of legal action which would increase the cost of copying and, therefore, increase the price that it could charge for its product.

Sell physical complements:
When you buy a physical CD you get liner notes, photos, and so on. Perhaps you could get a poster, a membership in a fan club, a lottery ticket, a free T-shirt, as well. These items might not be available to someone who simply downloaded an illicit copy of a song.

Sell information complements:
One can give away the product (e.g., Red Hat Linux) and sell support contracts. One can give away a cheap, low-powered version of some software and sell a high-powered version.

Subscriptions:
In this case, consumers purchases the information as a bundle over time, with the motivation presumably being convenience and perhaps timeliness of the information delivery. Even if all back issues are (eventually) posted online, the value of timely availability of current issues is sufficient to support production costs.

Sell personalized version:
One can sell a highly personalized version of a product so that copies made available to others would not be valuable. Imagine, for example, a personalized newspaper with only the items that you would wish to read. Those with different tastes may not find such a newspaper attractive. Selling works with digital fingerprints (encoding the identity of the purchaser) is an extreme form of this.
(*Playboy* has allegedly put digital fingerprints in online images.)

Advertise yourself:
A downloaded song can be an advertisement for a personal appearance. Similarly, an online textbook (particularly if it is inconvenient to use online) can be an advertisement for a physical copy. There are many examples of materials that are freely published on the Internet that are also available in various physical forms for a fee, such as US Government publications (e.g., *The 9/11 Commission Report*, or the National Academy of Sciences reports.

Advertise other things:
Broadcast TV and radio give away content in order to sell advertisements. Similarly, most magazines and newspapers use the per copy price to cover printing and distribution, while editorial costs are covered by advertising. Advertising is particularly valuable when it is closely tied to information about prospective buyers, so personalization can be quite important. In an extreme form, the advertisement can be completely integrated into the content via product placement.

Monitoring:
ASCAP monitors the playing of music in public places, collects a flat fee, which it then divvies up among its members. The shares are determined by a statistical algorithm. The Copyright Clearance Center uses a similar system for photocopying—a flat fee based on an initial period of statistical monitoring.

Site licenses:
An organization can pay for all of its members to have preferred access to some particular kinds of content. University site licenses to JSTOR content, Elsevier content, or Microsoft software are examples. This is particularly relevant when there are strong network effects from adopting a common standard, such as in the Microsoft example.

Media tax:
This is a tax on some physical good that is complementary to the information product (i.e., audio tape, video tape, CDs, TVs, hard drives, etc.). The proceeds from this tax are used to compensate producers of content. For example, the Audio Home Recording Act of 1992 imposes a media tax of 3 percent of the tape price. (http://www.brouhaha. com/~eric/bad_laws/dat_tax.html)

Ransom:
Allow potential readers to bid for content. If the sum of the bids is sufficiently high, the information content is provided. Various mechanisms for provision of public goods could be used, such as the celebrated Vickrey-Clarke-Groves mechanism. This could be used in conjunction with the subscription model. For example, Stephen King offered installments of his book *The Plant* on his web site. At one point he indicated he would continue positing installments if the number of payments received divided by the number of downloads from his site exceeded 75.6 percent. His experiment did not succeed, perhaps due to the poorly chosen incentive scheme. [http://www.writingonyourpalm.net/column001023. htm].

Pure public provision:
Artists and other creators of intellectual property are paid by the state, financed out of general revenues. This is not so different from public universities where research and publication is considered integral to the job.

Prizes, awards, and commissions:
Wealthy individuals, businesses or countries could commission works. The patronage system achieved some notable results in Europe for several centuries. The National Science Foundation or the National Endowment for the Humanities are examples of modern day state agencies that fund creative works using prize-like systems.

All of these business models have their problems, of course, and none is likely to yield any sort of social optimum. On the other hand, it should be kept in mind that copyright is a second-best solution to intellectual property provision as well...

Chapter 4

Complexity and Optimal Sanctions for Illegal Online File Sharing under Unconstrained Transferable Utility and Varying Compliance*

Illegal file sharing is an increasingly important determinant of profitability and distribution choices of companies in many industries. Illegal file sharing is often complicated by Internet congestion and lax enforcement. Thus, customer experience and firm-profitability can be vastly improved by piracy-minimizing and profit-maximizing sanctions that also reduce enforcement costs and monitoring costs. Such optimal sanctions are defined not only in terms of customers' opportunity costs (waiting time, search costs, value of customer's time, etc.) but also in terms of willingness-to-comply with intellectual property (IP) laws, expected post-purchase customer nonmonetary utility, customer's wealth and relative wealth, and customer's marginal propensity-to-substitute digital products. These optimal sanctions can minimize the firm's monitoring/enforcement costs and delivery costs and can also result in lower perceived prices for *high-priority* customers and uniform quality of service for all customers, all of which are socially more optimal outcomes when different customers place different values on compliance with IP laws. This article

* This chapter contains excerpts from an article written by Michael Nwogugu and cited as: Nwogugu (2015). Real options, enforcement of goodwill/intangibles rules and associated behavioral issues. *Journal of Money Laundering Control*, 18(3): 330–351.

(1) introduces models of information-producing firms that have unknown demand and that sell digital products to customers who have heterogeneous waiting costs and (2) introduces models of optimal sanctions (that incorporate evidence issues) that minimize losses from illegal file sharing, minimize monitoring/enforcement costs, and simultaneously maximize priority revenue for the information producer under different assumptions regarding customer behavior/utility and unknown demand.

BitTorrent is among the most widely used file sharing programs in the Internet. According to bandwidth management vendors in the United States, peer-to-peer applications represent a substantial percentage of all Internet traffic (but less than video traffic).

Some of the specific risks involved in illegal file sharing are as follows:

1. Criminal prosecution and fines.
2. Perpetrators face civil litigation, which could result in fines, injunctions, and damages awards.
3. The perpetrator's hard drive may be corrupted by viruses and adware embedded in shared files.
4. The perpetrator's employer can be subjected to fines and penalties for illegal file sharing activities on its computers.
5. The perpetrator–employee may be fired by his/her employer for illegal online file sharing.
6. The perpetrator may be blacklisted and denied service by ISPs for illegal file sharing.
7. The perpetrator may be suspended from college and from university housing.

4.1 Existing Literature on Perceptions of Risk in Illegal Online File Sharing

There is no direct literature on perceptions of risk in illegal online file sharing (IOF). There have been some industry surveys. Sang et al. (2015), Cox et al. (2010), Argan et al. (2013), Grüsser et al. (2007), Jambon and Smetana (2012), Borja et al. (2015), Coyle et al. (2009), Jacobs et al. (2012), Steinmetz and Tunnell (2013), and the authors of other articles[1] analyzed elements of human behavior in the context of illegal file sharing.

Ågotnes and Wooldridge (2010), Sterman (2008), and Ågotnes et al. (2010) studied compliance and optimal social laws. Bilò et al. (2013), Christodoulou et al. (2012), Anshelevich and Caskurlu (2011), Gabarró et al. (2011), Hegde et al. (2015), Emek and Feldman (2012), and Fiat and Saia (2007) studied network games and network-formation theories. Clark (2007) analyzed legal liability for illegal online downloads. Van Otterloo et al. (2006) analyzed *knowledge condition games*. Grant et al. (2014) analyzed the transformation of games by information sharing. Bachrach et al. (2013) analyzed *transformation games*, which are a form of coalitional games. Wooldridge et al. (2013) studied incentives in *Boolean games*.

4.1.1 Illegal File Sharing Networks as Chaotic Systems

Illegal P2P file sharing is a team effort, and some of the dynamical systems' *business team* principles in Losada and Heaphy (2004), Arthur (1999), and Sterman (1989) are relevant. Tussey (2005) analyzed the music distribution system within the context of chaos and complexity and concluded that music distribution systems exhibit the characteristics of complex systems and that several proposed models for regulating the music system fail to allow the system reasonable time to adapt without further legislative intervention. Ruhl and Ruhl (1997) explained various types of attractors. Kuhlman and Mortveit (2014) and Melnik et al. (2013) analyzed chaos and contagion in networks.

The typical P2P file sharing networks are complex adaptive systems, which are open, dynamic, nonlinear systems, and are characterized by self-organization or emergence. Emergence refers to unexpected system-wide behavioral patterns that arise from the predictable local interactions of the system's elements (nodes/participants, the physical network, digital content, bandwidth, regulation, monitoring, threat of prosecution, etc.), facilitating adaptation to changes in the surrounding environment. Within P2P networks, these adaptations include anonymity (very difficult to identify individual members of the network), BitTorrent streaming, and the dynamic form of the network that changes not only as members join or leave the network but also as members add or delete the amount of digital content in their computers' hard-drives.

In illegal file sharing networks, the *attractors* include the following: (1) social community; (2) economic gain (or absence of perceived economic loss); (3) the magnitude and quality/effectiveness of punishment delivered by government agencies; (4) the divergence between the perceived risk and the actual risk of participating in illegal file sharing networks; and (5) the changes in consumer tastes for digital content.

Gill (1996), Radzicki and Tauheed (2009), Lopucki (1997), and Post and Eisen (2000) discussed chaos and complex systems within the context of legal/regulatory systems and institutional economics. Coleman et al. (2007) analyzed chaos and dynamical systems in psychology research. Kuhlman and Mortveit (2014) and Melnik et al. (2013) studied chaos and contagion in networks. Kiel and Elliott (1997), Beesley (2010), Williams and Arrigo (2002), and Young (1997) analyzed the applications of chaos theory to crime and organized crime. Coleman et al. (2007) and Pavlov (2005) analyzed the elements of institutional conflict inherent in illegal file sharing. Huang et al. (2007) surveyed factors that influence people's perception of information security. Hennig-Thurau et al. (2007) found that movie purchases (both theater tickets and DVDs) are adversely affected by illegal file sharing.

Coleman et al. (2007) and Pavlov (2005) analyzed the elements of institutional conflict inherent in illegal file sharing. Huang et al. (2007) surveyed factors that influence people's perception of information security. Knoblich and Sebanz (2008) discussed four different mechanisms that enable social interactions, where these mechanisms differ in terms of how organisms are able to process and distinguish other organisms' intentions. These mechanisms include (1) entrainment and simultaneous affordance in *intentionally blind* individuals; (2) the interface between perception and action, which allows observers to simulate intentional action in others; (3) shared perceptions, partly based on the ability to distinguish other person's intentions; and (4) joint formation of intentions with simultaneous differentiation of intentions. Becker and Clement (2006)[2] analyzed the reasons why people illegally share files and concluded that pursing only a legal strategy will not work, and they suggested various strategies. Many of these strategies have already been tried in the United States and foreign countries and have not been successful in reducing IOF, and these strategies are not geared toward increasing the perception of illegal file sharing as a high-risk activity.

4.1.2 The Bhattacharjee et al. (2006) Study

Bhattacharjee et al. (2006) is notable because it is one of the first articles that attempted to address the issue of lawsuits and perpetrators' reactions to lawsuits for IOF.

The omissions and problems in Bhattacharjee et al. (2006) are as follows. The results of the tests are specific to the time period, type of content, type of audience, etc. The distinction between illegal *downloading* and illegal *sharing* of digital content is unnecessary because both are illegal. The results are not applicable to fourth-generation file sharing networks, for example, those that use streaming and encryption. While the two hypotheses that were tested are somewhat intuitive (lawsuits can reasonably be expected to reduce the occurrence of IOF), the studies are inconclusive because they do not indicate the type and magnitude of change in behavior of file sharers. The study omitted several critical hypotheses, some of which are introduced in this chapter. The study omitted testing for the effect of allocation of liability on risk perceptions. Given that the U.S. Supreme Court's ruling also allocates liability to ISPs and P2P software companies, the study should have tested for the effects of lawsuits on ISPs and software companies that make and distribute P2P software.

4.1.3 Damages and Sanctions for Illegal Online File Sharing

The optimal sanction for copyright infringement must incorporate not only costs of achieving desired levels of protection but also the deterrence effects of penalties and processes. The literature on punitive damages and sanctions is substantial but somewhat tangential to IOF and includes the following: Barr et al. (2003), Kleinman (1993), Miklashevich (2003), and Friehe (2008). Adermon and Liang (2014), Jeong and Khouja (2013), Kim and Lee (2015), Eivazi (2012), Synodinou (2015), Tang (2010), Banerjee (2003, 2006), Gunn (2015), and Ong (2015) studied issues that pertain to sanctions/punishment for IOF. Only Arai (2011) has attempted to directly address criminal and civil sanctions for IOF, but as explained herein and below, most of the analysis and models in Arai (2011) are wrong.

Bilò et al. (2013), Christodoulou et al. (2012), Anshelevich and Caskurlu (2011), Gabarró et al. (2011), Hegde et al. (2015), Emek and Feldman (2012), and Fiat and Saia (2007) studied network games and network-formation theories. Clark (2007) analyzed legal liability for illegal online downloads.

However, the significant gaps and omissions in the existing literature are as follows:

1. The analysis of the nonmonetary values and costs of prosecution
2. The objective function(s) for maximizing social welfare
3. The analysis of the deterrence effect as distinct from disutility experienced by infringers due to prosecution
4. How the proposed sanctions address and curtail the availability and use of the *currency* (time, cash, other property, Internet access rights, etc.) used in the illegal activities
5. Perpetrator's perceptions/judgments of the economic system and fairness of prices and the resulting impact on propensity to perform illegal acts
6. The conditions under which perpetrators will continue illegal activities
7. The content owner's/information producer's innate inertia, and its willingness to take action to enforce its rights effectively through monitoring and civil/criminal complaints
8. Sanctions as a direct or indirect function of perpetrator's risk aversion
9. Sanctions as a direct or indirect function of the infringer's marginal costs of substitution (substituting digital content for physical content, or substituting legal content for illegal content and vice versa)
10. The perceptions of risk of perpetrators in illegal file sharing networks
11. How perpetrators' behaviors differ from what is expected under existing theories
12. The conditions under which IOF will continue
13. The effects of incentives in IOF networks on perceptions of risk
14. Effects of penalties on perceptions of risk in IOF networks
15. Effect of allocation of liability on perceptions of risk

4.1.4 Enforcement Games

Leshem and Tabbach (2012) studied the role of commitment when enforcement can remedy harm from noncompliance. In their game, an enforcement authority (enforcer) and an offender may act as a Stackelberg leader, and the enforcer must choose whether to commit to an enforcement strategy or let the offender make the first move (thereby calibrating the level of enforcement to the actual level of noncompliance). Leshem and Tabbach (2012) concluded that the value of commitment to the enforcer depends on each player's responsiveness to a change in the other player's strategy choice and that commitment to an enforcement strategy is not always a good strategy for the enforcer. Helbing and Johansson (2010a,b), Helbing et al. (2010a,b), Perc et al. (2013), and Yeung et al. (2010) also studied *enforcement game*s.

Ohtsubo et al. (2010) examined whether violations of honesty norms would induce costly third-party punishments in two experiments, wherein participants in the third-party role observed a protocol of the trust game, in which the trustee solicited the trustor to transfer his/her endowment by stating that the trustee would return x units from the total resource. In both experiments, participants were willing to incur some cost to punish honesty-norm violators, even when the participants themselves were not harmed by the norm violation. They concluded that third-party punishment for norm violators can be an evolvable enforcer of social norms.

Although the credible announcement of thoroughly auditing insurance claim reports is a powerful deterrent, Lang and Wambach (2013) attempted to show that uncertainty about fraud detection can be an effective strategy to deter ambiguity-averse agents from reporting false insurance claims. They found that if, in addition, insurers' auditing costs are heterogeneous, it could be optimal not to commit to a fraud-detection strategy, because such commitment eliminates the ambiguity about auditing. Thus, strategic ambiguity can be an equilibrium outcome in the market, and competition does not force firms to provide the relevant information. They noted that their findings are applicable to other audit situations such as tax enforcement.

Mogy and Pruitt (1974) conducted a gaming experiment (prisoner's dilemma game) with 50 male undergraduates to determine the effects of a confederate's threats and subjects' perception of the credibility of those threats on subjects' compliance. Perception and credibility were measured by questionnaires after each threat trial. In the experiment, it was hypothesized that (a) threat credibility (and the probability of compliance) is inversely related to the threatener's cost of enforcement; (b) threats whose enforcement would hurt the recipient more than the threatener are more credible (hurt-more threats); (c) a threatener who enforces his threats is viewed as more hostile the greater the cost of his enforcement; and (d) a threatener who enforces non-hurt-more threats is seen as more hostile than the one who enforces hurt-more threats. Mogy and Pruitt (1974) stated that their results supported hypotheses (a) and (c) and partially support (b) and (d).

Miller and Watson (2013) proposed a new approach to equilibrium selection in repeated games with transfers, under the assumption that in each period, the players bargain over how to play. Miller and Watson (2013) developed predictions from three axioms wherein two axioms allow the players to meaningfully discuss whether to deviate from their plan and the third includes a *theory of disagreement*—that play under disagreement should not vary with the manner in which bargaining broke down. Miller and Watson concluded that equilibria that satisfy these axioms exist for all discount factors and all equilibria generate the same welfare; and optimal play under agreement generally requires suboptimal play under disagreement. They also found that whether patient players attain efficiency depends on both the stage game and the bargaining protocol and that their theory is applicable to games with imperfect public monitoring and heterogeneous discount factors.

Fehr et al. (2002) empirically showed that contrary to the *self-interest assumption* in the literature, *strong reciprocity* exists wherein many people have a tendency to voluntarily cooperate if treated fairly and to punish non-cooperators. They also found that people are willing to punish those who behaved unfairly toward a third person or who defected in a prisoner's dilemma game with a third person, and thus strong reciprocity is a powerful device for the enforcement of social norms. Fehr et al. (2002) noted that strong reciprocity cannot be rationalized as an adaptive trait by the leading evolutionary theories of human cooperation (in other words, kin selection, reciprocal altruism, indirect reciprocity, and costly signaling theory), but multilevel selection theories of cultural evolution are consistent with strong reciprocity.

Scholz (1991) noted that the control of policy outcomes is complicated by trade-offs between controllable versus effective implementation strategies. Scholz (1991) used a nested game framework and analyses of state-level Occupational Safety and Health Administration (OSHA, the United States) enforcement to explain why a cooperative strategy can increase enforcement effectiveness in the narrow administrative game and why principal-agent control problems and collective action problems associated with the strategy lead policy beneficiaries to oppose the effective strategy in the broader political games. Scholz (1991) found evidence that cooperation enhances the impact of enforcement in reducing workplace injury rates but that policy beneficiaries oppose and sabotage cooperation. Scholz (1991) also noted the usefulness of simultaneously analyzing the interactions between administrative effectiveness and interest group politics in implementation situations.

4.1.5 Empirical Enforcement Studies

The large-scale enforcement experiment in Fellner et al. (2013) consisted of varying the text of mailings sent to potential evaders of TV license fees. They found that the mailings caused a substantial increase in compliance and that a threat treatment that makes a high detection risk salient had a significant deterrent effect. They concluded that neither appealing to morals nor disseminating information about others' behavior enhances compliance on aggregate, but the information condition has a weak positive effect in municipalities where evasion is deemed to be common.

Using data from the Los Angeles Police Department (LAPD) and based on sparse observations of a combination of social interactions and geographic locations of the individual gang members, Van Gennip et al. (2013) identified social communities among gang members in the Hollenbeck policing district in Los Angeles. They constructed a similarity graph for the gang members and used spectral clustering to identify clusters in the graph, corresponding to communities in Hollenbeck, and compare these with the LAPD's knowledge of the individuals' gang membership. Using data from the LAPD, Short et al. (2010) found that there are two types of crime hotspots, which are *supercritical hotspots* (small spikes in crime that grow) and *subcritical hotspots* (hotspots where a large spike in crime pulls offenders into a central location). They also attempted to explain when law enforcement officials can expect crime to be suppressed by intensified police actions and when crime is or may be displaced to other neighborhoods.

Using microdata on compliance with TV license fees that allows classification between households that were subject to enforcement and those that were not, Rincke and Traxler (2011) identified spillovers from law enforcement. They found a significant response of households to increased enforcement in their vicinity, and on average, three detections made one additional household comply with the law. They also found that as compliance rose significantly among those who had no exposure to field inspections, there was a sizable externality in enforcement.

Jackson and Roe (2009) found that (1) private enforcement of investor protection via disclosure rules goes hand in hand with financial market development (but private disclosure rules do not); (2) there is a strong correlation between public enforcement and financial development (which should be considered in policy decisions); and (3) public enforcement is overall as important as disclosure in explaining financial market outcomes around the world and more important than private liability rules.

Antunes et al. (2008) found that differences across countries in intermediation costs and enforcement of laws generate differences in occupational choice, firm size, credit, output, and income inequality (experiments were performed for Latin American, European, transition and high-growth Asian countries, with empirical estimates of each country's financial frictions and U.S. values for all other parameters).

4.1.6 Political Theories of Enforcement

Bednar (2006), Tsebelis (1993), Urpelainen (2011), and De Mesquita and Stephenson (2006) analyzed crime, punishment, governance, and compliance within the context of institutions, but they focused on the *results* of risk perception rather than the causes and modifiers of risk perception.

4.1.7 The Selection of Disputes for Litigation

Heyes et al. (2004), Hylton (2002, 2008), Nwogugu (2008), Waldfogel (1998), Samuelson (1998), Chopard et al. (2010), Cornell (1990), Wang et al. (1994), and Marco (2005) analyzed the selection of disputes for litigation. Hylton and Lin (2009) surveyed the literature on *trial selection theory* and evidence and presented a model that includes the Priest–Klein theory and asymmetric information theories as special cases.

Demolombe (2011) analyzed how obligations on institutional agents are *propagated* to human and software agents, whose actions satisfy the obligations imposed on institutional agents, and concludes that the relationship between the different kinds of obligations and actions can be represented in terms of the concept of *count as* proposed by Searle, of role, and of causality. Balke et al. (2013) noted that scalability and complexity issues arise when modeling large-scale realistic systems and described how to achieve verification of a formal specification combined with the testing of large-scale systems with numerous different actor configurations. The result is an institutional agent-based model methodology that allows for reasoning about policies, policy making, and their consequences on a more comprehensive level (combines institutional frameworks with agent-based simulations).

Burgemeestre et al. (2011) noted that corporate values motivate the selection of control measures (actions), which aim to fulfill control objectives, and tried to show how value-based argumentation theory can be applied to the compliance domain and how to formalize the audit dialogue in which companies justify their compliance decisions to regulators using value-based argumentation. Andrighetto and Conte (2012) presented an integrated, cognitive view of different mechanisms, reasons, and pathways to norm compliance and noted that theories of norm compliance can be grouped into the following four main typologies: the rational choice model of norm compliance, theories based on conditional preferences to conformity, theories of thoughtless conformity, and theories of norm internalization. They also introduced the normative architecture *EMIL-A*.

Chapman (2013) noted that, sometimes, the values confronted in legal decision-making appear to be incommensurable, which is unnecessarily undesirable to some legal theorists. Chapman (2013) hypothesized that if incommensurability creates a problem of public significance in the proportional satisfaction of values, when two values are commensurable, this public significance is provided by the mediating effects of the overarching third value that provides the common measure of the values; but without this common measure, the public significance of value satisfaction must be otherwise achieved. Chapman (2013) proposed *equal proportional value satisfaction* as the most appropriate proportionality maxim (i.e., wherein the proportional satisfaction of any one value has significance for each and every other value) and stated that the legal process that is most appropriate to equal proportionality is a process that implements defeasible legal rules.

Zhang and Walton (2010) studied the history of evidence theory in China and its gradual shift from a pluralistic evidence law to evidence-based scholarship and also compares fundamental distinctions on evidence and judicial proof in China and those in Anglo-American law. Bex and Walton (2012) developed a formal logical model of evidential reasoning with proof standards and burdens of proof, which facilitates evaluation of evidential reasoning by comparing statements of opposing litigants, and they conclude that the model has implications for modeling and using traditional proof standards such as preponderance of the evidence and beyond reasonable doubt. Miller (2012) noted that the function of the required level of statistical significance in the scientific method is not analogous to that played by the standard of proof in the legal process.

Barnett (2011) studied the risks and rewards involved in the litigation process and whether it is beneficial for a victim to file a lawsuit against the injurer. The analysis can be used to determine whether a victim should have legal representation and how much a victim should accept in an out-of-court settlement. Barnett (2011) noted that the *minimax theorem*, the *maximax principle*, and the *minimize the maximum regret principle* all follow the Von Neumann and Morgenstern linearity axiom, which states that numbers in the game matrix must be cardinal utilities and can be transformed by any positive linear function f(x) = ax + b; a > 0, without changing the information that they convey. Barnett (2011) described risk-averse strategies for a two-person zero-sum game, where the linearity axiom may not hold, and obtained an *arbitration value* in a litigation game, where the amount awarded to the victim is less than expectation and is shown to be *airer* when compared with the amount obtained using the Von Neumann and Morgenstern game theory framework.

Prakken (2008) developed a formal reconstruction of a Dutch civil legal case in Prakken's formal model of adjudication dialogues in order to test whether AI and law models of legal dialogues in general and Prakken's model in particular are suitable for modeling particular legal procedures and legal dispute.

Kacsuk (2011) used the approach of the European Patent Office (patent claims as a set of independent features that are examined separately in a more or less formal way) to develop a simple mathematical model that treats patent claim features as logical statements and patent claims as compound statements wherein the individual statements are connected by logical connectives. Kacsuk (2011) stated that the proposed mathematical model provides a uniform system for examining various legal questions that are dealt with separately under case law, and it facilitates the development of an expert system for resolving complex legal situations and for automating the evaluation of a large number of patent claim variants.

Kim (2014) analyzed the properties and relative efficiency of the inquisitorial system and the adversarial system of dispute resolution. Daughety and Reinganum (2000) modeled the adversarial provision of evidence as a game in which two parties engage in strategic sequential search and characterized a court's decision based on the evidence provided. Daughety and Reinganum (2000) noted that (1) even though evidence submissions are handled in an unbiased way, the equilibrium outcome may still exhibit bias that arises from differences in the cost of sampling or asymmetry in the sampling distribution; (2) in a multistage model, a prodefendant bias arises in the first stage from a divergence between the parties' stakes; and (3) the adversarial process generates additional costs that screen out some otherwise meritorious cases.

Farmera and Pecorino (2002) incorporated *self-serving bias* into the Bebchuk (*Rand Journal of Economics*, 15 (1984): 404) model in which court trials result from asymmetric information, and they characterized the equilibrium and noted that an increase in the *self-serving bias* of a defendant who receives an offer can sometimes reduce the incidence of trial, while an increase in the *self-serving bias* of either player increases the incidence of trial. They also observed that *self-serving bias* serves as a commitment mechanism not to accept offers that are too unfavorable, but players with such a bias typically end up in trial more often, and for the offering player, an increase in *self-serving bias* unambiguously lowers social welfare.

Klement and Neeman (2005) introduced a strategic model of liability and litigation under court errors wherein the model allows for endogenous choice of level of care and endogenous likelihood of filing and disputes. Klement and Neeman (2005) derived sufficient conditions for a unique universally divine mixed-strategy perfect Bayesian equilibrium under low court errors and also found that court errors in the size of the award, as well as damage caps and split awards, reduce the likelihood of trial but increase filing and reduce the deterrence effect of punitive damages.

Friedman and Wickelgren (2010) noted that allowing or promoting settlement of lawsuits does not necessarily enhance social welfare, and settlement can lower social welfare because it reduces the accuracy of legal outcomes, which in turn reduces the ability of the law to deter harmful activity without chilling legitimate activity that might be mistaken for harmful activity (i.e., the welfare loss from the chilling of legitimate activity can outweigh the gains from litigation cost savings, even if there are no restrictions on the damage rule).

Avraham and Liu (2012) analyzed the nonbreaching party's option to not sue for damages upon breach, when her/his expected payoff from suing is negative, given the contractual terms and her/his private information about her post-breach loss. They concluded that (1) courts should commit to awarding fixed damages, because awarding flexible damages based on ex post information will distort the incentives to breach; (2) the option of acquiescing to the breach expands the breach set under specific performance, which can be more efficient than other remedies; and (3) the efficiency advantage of ex ante expectation damages over ex post actual damages is further enhanced when we account for the possibility of renegotiation.

Using evolutionary game theory, Bar-Gill (2005) attempted to provide a theoretical explanation for the persistence of the *optimism bias* among litigants and their attorneys and noted that optimistic lawyers succeed in extracting more favorable settlements by credibly threatening to resort to costly litigation, and thus equilibrium should include a positive level of optimism. Bar-Gill (2005) concluded that the design of legal rules affects the equilibrium level of optimism, which in turn affects the relative efficiency of the different legal designs. Methodologically, by enabling a more systematic exploration of the perception-shaping role of the law, this chapter seeks to expand the conventional boundaries of behavioral law and economics. Baker and Mezzetti (2001) analyzed the strategic interaction between a defendant and a prosecutor during the plea bargaining process and developed a four-stage game where the defendant's guilt or innocence is private information but the amount of resources available to the prosecutor is common knowledge. Baker and Mezzetti (2001) noted that equilibrium is semi-separating; the plea offer is accepted by a proportion of the guilty defendants and is rejected by all of the innocent defendants and the remaining guilty defendants. Baker and Mezzetti (2001) found that an increase in the resources available to the prosecutor increases the proportion of guilty defendants who accept plea offers.

Chen and Wang (2007) theoretically compared the British and American fee-shifting rules in their influences on the behavior of the litigants and the outcomes of litigation—specifically in terms of equilibria under both American and British rules, equilibrium settlement amounts and rates, and expenditures incurred in trials, as well as the plaintiff's chances of winning and incentive to sue.

Daughety and Reinganum (2010) studied how plaintiffs' pre-litigation incentives differed between lawsuits associated with stand-alone tort cases (individual-based liability determination or IBLD) and lawsuits that involve mass torts (population-based liability determination or PBLD). Daughety and Reinganum (2010) observed that PBLD causes a *rational optimism effect* that affects plaintiffs and creates incentives for higher settlement demands and results in greater interim expected payoffs for plaintiffs and, thus, an increased propensity to file a lawsuit. As a result, defendants in PBLD cases face increased ex ante expected costs compared with the IBLD regime, and that increases the incentives to be more diligent.

Friedman and Wittman (2007) developed game-theoretic foundations for bargaining in the context of a trial, wherein the plaintiff and the defendant make simultaneous offers to settle, and they settle where feasible. Otherwise, both litigants incur additional litigation cost and the judgment is imposed at trial. They obtained and characterized an essentially unique Nash equilibrium and observed that an increase in trial cost (or a decrease in the range of possible outcomes) reduces the probability of a trial, and trials are possible even when the defendant's signal indicates a higher potential judgment than the plaintiff's signal. They also noted that when trial costs are low, middling cases (rather than extreme cases) are more likely to settle.

Using docket-level U.S. federal district court data, Boyd and Hoffman (2013) analyzed how motion practice (particularly nondiscovery motions) can affect the timing/occurrence of settlement and the parties' knowledge about their cases. Boyd and Hoffman (2013) found that the filing of a motion significantly speeds case settlement, that granted motions are more immediately critical to settlement timing than motions denied, and that plaintiff victories have a stronger effect than defendant victories.

4.1.8 Psychological Theories of Enforcement

Henrich and Boyd (2001) proposed a cultural evolutionary model in which norms for cooperation and punishment are acquired through (1) payoff-biased transmission, a tendency to copy the most successful individual, and (2) conformist transmission, a tendency to copy the most frequent behavior in the population. Henrich and Boyd (2001) noted that if a finite number of punishment stages are permitted, then an arbitrarily small amount of conformist transmission will stabilize cooperative behavior by stabilizing punishment at some nth stage; and once cooperation is stabilized in one group, it may spread through a multigroup population via cultural group selection. Henrich and Boyd (2001) concluded that once cooperation is prevalent, prosocial genes favoring cooperation and punishment may invade in the wake of cultural group selection.

Piercey (2009), Tetlock (2002), De Dreu et al. (2006), and Bodenhuasen et al. (2003) analyzed and introduced psychological theories pertaining to enforcement of statutes and/or implementation of accounting regulations.

4.2 Risk

Illegal file sharing contravenes almost all known theories of risk aversion. In existing risk and decision-making literature, studies have indicated that people are more risk-averse in the domain of profits and are more risk-seeking when experiencing losses. Most participants in illegal file sharing networks know that ISPs can easily identify them and that free online file sharing is illegal. In illegal file sharing, the longer an individual participates successfully in the network, the higher the probability that the ISPs will identify and report the individual, but then it also becomes more likely that the probability that the individual will continue to participate in the network will increase substantially.

The notions of *gain* and *loss* are very likely to be somewhat different in online file sharing *markets* because of the nature of the *property* being traded, perceptions of time, and the dynamics of human–computer interaction. In illegal file sharing, gain is conjectured to be measured in terms of (1) finding specific digital content, (2) the ability to sample specific digital content, (3) successfully downloading digital content, (4) the range of choices available to the participant, (5) relatively minimal time spent successfully searching for digital content, and (6) emotional attachment to downloaded digital content. In illegal file sharing, losses are conjectured to be measured in terms of (1) time wasted unsuccessfully searching for content, (2) inability to find specific digital content, (3) to a much lesser extent, warnings by ISPs and content owners about file sharing, (4) making the individual's hard drive accessible to other members of the P2P file sharing network, (5) uploading digital content, and (6) emotional dislike for downloaded digital content.

In illegal file sharing, risk is conjectured to be measured in terms of (1) being reported to regulators by ISPs; (2) prosecution by content owners, trade groups, and/or government regulators; (3) erroneously providing access to various parts of the individual's hard drive; (4) downloading computer viruses and spyware; and (5) spending substantial amounts of time and not finding content sought.

Human perceptions of risk in illegal file sharing are also conjectured to be linked to the dynamic mental rebalancing between human *anticipation* and a *retrospection gap* as described in the study by Van Boven and Ashworth (2007). *Retrospection gap* refers to a mental chasm, wherein an illegal file sharing perpetrator's brief mental reviews of prior illegal file sharing activity and prior copyright infringements do not reveal any harm or warnings or other economic or psychological *losses*. *Anticipation* refers to (1) consumer expectations of positive economic/psychological utility from illegal file sharing, (2) expected cost savings, (3) anticipation of no or low prosecution, (4) confidence in the anonymity of P2P file sharing system, and (5) anticipation of interaction.

IOF contravenes all theories of risk aversion:

■ *Reference dependence*—in illegal file sharing, the following is likely to be no reference points for individuals, and perpetrators just search, to sample and download content. The exponentially greater amount of choice in file sharing networks (compared to ordinary stores) results in continuous changes in consumer tastes, such that there are no reference points. Because of the ease of search, minimal transaction costs, and broad choice, individuals are very likely to switch to brands/themes other than their original objectives (and are more likely to switch to brands/themes in online file sharing markets than in physical stores).

■ *Loss aversion*—contrary to the existing theory, in illegal file sharing networks, losses most probably do not loom larger than corresponding gains because money is not used as currency, and time is the main *currency*; gains create more incentives for continued participation in the network, and there is a perceived low probability of prosecution and perceived high enforcement costs among participants.

- *Diminishing sensitivity*—contrary to the existing theory, in illegal file sharing, the marginal value of gains probably does not decrease as more gains are achieved, but rather it is very likely to increase as more successful downloads are completed, because utility-creating expectations will rise, the online file sharing system will be validated, and the absence of fees (for downloading digital content) increases the marginal value of perceived gains. Similarly, the marginal value of losses is very likely to increase as more time is spent unsuccessfully searching for digital content, because as the individual spends more time searching unsuccessfully, he/she will begin to mentally account for lost time and his/her expectations will decline rapidly.

- *Endowment effect*—This does not apply because increased levels and magnitude of choices in file sharing networks create a situation in which utility loss from giving up a valued good (e.g., access to files on the person's hard drive) is less than utility gain associated with receiving a good (i.e., access to other participant's files). This situation accounts for the *free rider problem* in file sharing networks and provides incentives for people to participate in illegal file sharing.

- *Status quo bias*—This does not apply in online file sharing networks, primarily because the bare essence of file sharing networks is to change the participant's economic and psychological state.

4.3 The Currency and Conditions for Voluntary Participation in Illegal Online File Sharing

In new generation online file sharing, the *currency* is a mix of (1) time spent, (2) access rights, (3) utility values traded, and (4) expectations (including the ability to gather evidence of infringement and admissibility of evidence). Time is the most measurable of these indications of value and utility. The psychology of spending time is very different from the psychology of spending money to purchase/obtain a specific good. Delgado (2003), Lea and Webley (2006), Saini and Ashwani (2008), Perritt (2007a,b), and the authors of other articles[3] analyzed elements of intertemporal decision-making.

Okada and Hoch (2004) found that when individuals pay in time rather than money, they seem to have greater willingness to pay for riskier alternatives. Okada and Hoch (2004) stated that "...ex-post, people tend to more easily adapt to losses and negative outcomes by changing the value of the temporal inputs. Ex-ante, people are more willing to spend more time for higher risk, higher return alternatives, but if spending money, the opposite becomes the case...." This may be because time has a lower *exchange value* than money (it is easier to buy/sell items with money than with an individual's time), and it is easier to mentally and physically adjust the amounts of time contributed to a loss-producing activity than to adjust amounts of money spent in loss-producing activities. This divergence in behavior that is solely attributable to the differences between two *currencies* (money versus time) may partly explain why many people continue to participate in IOF (and remain members of illegal file sharing networks), even when experiencing *losses*. Zauberman and Lynch (2005) found that time expenditures are discounted more than money expenditures because of a difference in how perceived surplus changes from the present to the future and because change in perceived surplus is greater for time than for money. Saini and Ashwani (2008) found that consumer decision-making differs when consumers evaluate expenditures based on time spent instead of money and that consumers considering expenditure of time are more likely to rely on heuristics than on the analysis of the information presented. In the Saini and Ashwani (2008) study, participants were asked to evaluate the mentioned results of an Internet search on a used-car website, which had provided 80 cars that met their criteria but that viewing each accident record would take either US $1 or 5 minutes of time. Before indicating the specific number of records they would view, participants were asked whether they would view *up to 2* or *up to 40* records. The use of *up to 2* or *up to 40* records as *anchor values* seemed to have had a significant impact for participants thinking in terms of time expenditure. The number of records consumers in the *money-condition* chose to view was statistically the same, irrespective of whether the anchor value was high or low. On the contrary, when the anchor value was low in the *time-condition*, consumers chose to view an average of 9.1 accident reports versus 23.7 when the anchor value was high. However, when participants under both time and money conditions were asked to account for their expenditures, they no longer differed in their use of heuristics. The Saini and Ashwani (2008) study provides substantial evidence that the time expenditure inherent in IOF causes perpetrators not to fully evaluate the risks (including criminal penalties) inherent in IOF. Soman (2001) found that the consideration of past investments (sunk costs) was weaker when consumers are required to pay with time. However, none of these empirical studies tested for differences in cognition/perception of study participants, the conditions under which IOF will continue, or the effects of incentives in IOF networks on perceptions of risk, or the effects of evidence and the ability to gather evidence in IOF networks on perceptions of risk, or the effects of penalties on perceptions of risk in IOF networks.

In the case of illegal file sharing, consumers' time is a large component of value because (1) other *elements of currency* are not easily measurable and cannot be converted to cash and (2) the value of other *elements of currency* is not as perceptible as time. Thus, in illegal file sharing, the perpetrator's valuation of the sum of two components of the *currency* (time and access rights) should typically be less than any amount spent to buy the content legitimately.

In the following models, the following assumptions hold. IOF is partially observable, because after downloading, perpetrators may share the files in physical space, and the P2P network is not controlled or fully monitored by either regulators or the information producer. *Net neutrality* prevails—ISPs are not required to enforce IP laws. Consumers have strictly *monotonic consumption functions* wherein consumption of illegally downloaded files increases in direct proportion as illegal file sharing activity, knowledge, and leisure time. There are *constantly increasing returns to enforcement costs* wherein every enforcement expenditure produces some deterrence effects (enforcement costs include the cost of gathering and assessing evidence).

The following are assumptions for the subsequent models. θ is the marginal cost of enforcement per unit of digital content. Ξ is the actual cost of enforcement per unit of digital content. μ is the marginal costs of monitoring per unit of digital content. α is the actual cost of monitoring per unit of digital content. β is the marginal costs of identification of participants per unit of digital content. ε is the value of evidence/proof; $\varepsilon = \varepsilon_f + \varepsilon_{afv}$, where ε_f = value of fines. ε_{afv} is the present value of the absence of future violations. γ is the profit from sale of one unit of digital content. π is the time spent by the participant. $\tau_{illegal}$ is the monetary value of average time spent searching for one unit of digital content in illegal file sharing networks. τ_{legal} is the monetary value of average time spent searching for one unit of digital content in legal markets/sources. σ is the cost of legally purchasing one unit of digital content. U_{legal} is the utility gained from legally buying one unit of digital content. $U_{illegal}$ is the utility gained from illegally downloading one unit of digital content from the network and being able to share the file. U_{search} is the utility gained from searching in the file sharing network. $\psi_{illegal}$ is the marginal search costs per unit of digital content for IOF, other than time, including bandwidth and proportional costs of hardware. ψ_{legal} is the marginal search costs per unit of digital content for legal purchases, other than time, including bandwidth, transportation/shipping, and proportional costs of hardware. ω is the marginal costs of substitution, that is, the cost of switching from one digital content to another similar content. $U_{conf.}$ is the disutility experienced by the participant by incorrectly configuring file sharing software and hence making the wrong files available to others. $\lambda_{illegal}$ is the monetary value of access rights in illegal file sharing networks—the right to participate in illegal file sharing network on the Internet and/or the right to access other participant's hard drives in order to download files. This includes the costs of access (such ISP fees charged to consumers and amortized hardware costs) and utility gained from participation in the network. λ_{legal} is the monetary value of access rights in legal file sharing networks—the right to participate in legal file sharing network on the Internet. This includes the costs of access (such ISP fees charged to consumers and amortized hardware costs) and utility gained from participation in the network. $\acute{\Gamma}$ is the perceived loss to the participant from fine/penalty upon prosecution of the participant for illegal file sharing. ρ_L is the probability that the participant will be prosecuted for illegal file sharing. $\acute{\Gamma}_{real}$ is the actual loss to the participant from fine/penalty upon prosecution of the participant for illegal file sharing. $\Pi_{illegal}$ is the cost of access rights in illegal file sharing networks. This includes ISP fees and hardware costs. Π_{legal} is the cost of access rights in legal file sharing networks. This includes ISP fees and hardware costs.

Then for illegal file sharing to continue voluntarily, the following conditions must exist:

$$\{\tau_{illegal} + \lambda_{illegal} + \psi_{illegal} + U_{illegal} - (\acute{\Gamma} * \rho_L) - U_{conf.} + U_{search}\} \geq [\tau_{legal} + \sigma + \psi_{legal} + U_{legal}] \quad (4.1)$$

$$U_{illegal} \geq 0; \frac{\partial U_{illegal}}{\partial \pi \geq 0} \quad (4.2)$$

$$U_{legal} \geq 0; \frac{\partial U_{legal}}{\partial \pi \geq 0} \quad (4.3)$$

$$U_{search} \geq 0 \quad (4.4)$$

$$\frac{\partial U_{search}}{\partial \pi \geq 0} \quad (4.5)$$

This condition (4.5) applies only if a certain minimum number of files are downloaded during time π.

$$\psi_{illegal} \geq 0; \psi_{legal} \geq 0; \psi_{legal} \geq \psi_{illegal} \quad (4.6)$$

$$U_{illegal} + U_{search} \geq U_{legal} \quad (4.7)$$

$$0 \geq \omega \leq +\infty \quad (4.8)$$

$$\acute{\Gamma}_{real} \geq \acute{\Gamma} \quad (4.9)$$

$$\frac{\partial U_{illegal}}{\partial \pi \geq 0} \quad (4.10)$$

This condition (4.10) applies only if a certain minimum number of files are successfully downloaded during time π.

The implications of these models are that:

1. In order to reduce infringement, ISPs should share some liability for IOF and should be required to report illegal or suspicious activity in their networks.
2. The past and current schemes of punitive measures (for illegal file sharing) in most countries have not worked. Thus, there is a need to increase the perception of illegal file sharing as highly unacceptable misconduct. This can be achieved in several ways:
   a. Punitive sanctions should be criminal and should focus on taxing the total wealth of perpetrators rather than jail sentences.
   b. ISP should be required to permanently bar illegal file sharing perpetrators from Internet access, without any court proceedings. ISPs should participate in a government-sponsored consortium wherein ISPs will report (1) persons suspected of IOF, (2) persons permanently barred from Internet access for illegal file sharing, and (3) persons barred from Internet access for specific periods for illegal file sharing. This will enable other ISPs to easily identify potential offenders. Thus, persons that seek Internet access must provide multiple valid proof of identification. Legal file sharing network will have to be registered with this consortium.
   c. ISPs should be required to display warnings in the screens of illegal file sharing perpetrators once the ISP identifies suspicious activities.
   d. As the P2P file sharing network grows and becomes successful (more uploads), people will be more likely to join.
   e. More effort should be allocated to shutting down not only illegal file sharing websites but also websites that provide links/access to illegal file sharing systems and websites.

The impact of time constraints on choice and propensity-to-purchase is discussed in Weenig et al. (2005), Mogilner and Aaker (2009), and Okada and Hoch (2004). Within the file sharing context

1. Time limits search, $\partial \pi / \partial \sigma > 1$ (this condition always exists).
2. Time creates an opportunity cost that is often greater that the legal market price of the digital content.

However, the designation of time as the *currency* must be weighed within the context of *valued time* (the proportion of time is or can be compensated) and *leisure time* (the proportion of time that is leisure, for which there cannot be any compensation). In this chapter, most references to time are to *valued time*.

4.4 Criteria for Choosing between Criminal and Civil Prosecution

Generally, content-owners and government prosecutors have a choice of civil litigation and/or criminal litigation (the content owner can file a criminal complaint that triggers criminal prosecution, and the government can file a civil lawsuit). As mentioned herein and earlier, in many jurisdictions, each of the content owner and the government can simultaneously pursue both criminal and civil claims for copyright infringement.

To date, both civil lawsuits and criminal prosecutions have been used by content owners and trade groups to fight infringement of digital content. There has not been any definitive empirical study of the effectiveness of either criminal prosecution compared to civil lawsuits.[4] Miles (2004) and Bakker (2005) addressed some of these issues.

Some of the main differences between criminal and civil lawsuits are in (1) social capital and the stigma of criminal conviction, (2) enforcement costs (litigation costs, public relations costs, etc.), (3) civil procedure versus criminal procedure, (4) rules of evidence, (5) sentencing guidelines (criminal proceedings) versus judicial discretion or jury discretion (in civil lawsuits), (6) affordability and negotiations for the payment of penalties, and (7) deterrence effect.

4.4.1 A Critique of Arai (2011)

Arai (2011) attempted to analyze the *choice* between criminal and civil prosecution for IOF. As explained herein and earlier, most of the analysis and models in Arai (2011) are wrong (see Nwogugu (2013), which addressed similar issues). The obvious weaknesses and errors in the Arai (2011) analysis are as follows:

1. The major assumption in Arai (2011) that civil and criminal cases are distinguished by whether or not the perpetrator pays *transfers* (sanctions/fines) to copyright holders (or to the government) is wrong. First, when an IOF perpetrator is sentenced to a long prison term (e.g., 5–10 years), the content owner can indirectly gain an important economic *transfer* in the form of reduced loss of revenues from lower volumes of copyright infringement activity. Second, when an IOF perpetrator is fined a large amount of money that is a substantial percentage of his/her wealth, the content owner can indirectly gain an important economic *transfer* in the form of reduced loss of revenues from a substantial reduction of the perpetrator's ability to infringe copyrights. Third, to the extent that all or a portion of fines (imposed on perpetrators by a court) are used by the government for monitoring and enforcement of copyright laws, the content owner gains another important economic *transfer* in the form of increased government monitoring/enforcement and the reduction of its own monitoring/enforcement requirements. Fourth, in some jurisdictions, in criminal prosecutions for IOF, the perpetrators can be ordered to pay statutory and common law restitutions and punitive damages to the content owners.
2. For an individual copyright infringement, the content owner and the government can choose to simultaneously execute both civil and criminal prosecution. In criminal prosecutions initiated by the government in most jurisdictions, the content owner is usually a major prosecution witness and participant. The content owner can also initiate criminal prosecutions by filing a criminal complaint at the government prosecutor's offices or in court. Thus, the Arai (2011) social welfare analysis that is erroneously based on distinctions between criminal and civil prosecution is entirely wrong.
3. The optimality of criminal sanctions versus civil sanctions cannot really be accurately modeled based on a narrow set of parameters as in Arai (2011) and depends on the circumstances of each case. What is clear is that the current criminal penalty statutes in the United States do not provide sufficient deterrence effect to reduce IOF and often bear no relationship to the perpetrators' total monetary/nonmonetary wealth and illegal profits.
4. Arai (2011) makes a wrong assumption that the consumer's valuations of the digital goods are uniformly distributed across an interval. Furthermore, and as explained in Chapter 2, in many instances, IOF is often not motivated by the consumer's valuation of the digital content but rather by other factors such as psychological states, nonmonetary impulses, and external influences.
5. Contrary to Arai (2011), if a consumer does not use any product, his/her utility is not necessarily zero and may be positive or negative depending on his/her utility/disutility gained

from membership in a P2P file sharing system, his/her views about other people's comments about the products, and his/her ability to sample the products.

6. The analysis in Arai (2011) fails to distinguish between the *probability-of-detection* and the *probability-of-enforcement*, and the (historical) plaintiff's *probability-of-winning* such cases.

7. Arai (2011) completely omits the government's and the content owners' prosecution costs.

8. Contrary to Arai (2011), for most digital content, (1) the content producer's production costs are not fixed but rather have variable components, and the full costs are also determined by the nature of the distribution channels; (2) the content owner's production costs change drastically as time progresses with the bulk of the costs incurred at the initial production stages while the per-unit marginal production cost declines drastically after the first batch is produced.

9. Contrary to Arai (2011), the government's goal of maximizing a social surplus function (the consumer and producer surplus) by setting the penalty for copyright infringement at the *optimal level* (1) is not an appropriate goal because of the large numbers and geographic dispersion of perpetrators; (2) is not an appropriate goal because the demand for and supply of the enforcement of IP laws is often distorted by technological constraints, enforcement costs, limitations of monitoring, jurisdictional restrictions, etc.; and (3) is never achievable in the way described in Arai (2011).

10. The conclusions by Arai (2011) that social surplus is a decreasing function of the penalty because the number of participating consumers decreases as the penalty increases and that the producer's profit is an increasing function of the penalty are both wrong. This is because the size of the penalty is not always directly proportional to its deterrence effect particularly where the perpetrator believes that the *probability-of-detection* and the *probability-of-enforcement/litigation* are low, the enforcement costs are prohibitive, and/or the possible probability-adjusted penalties are far outweighed by his/her nonmonetary/monetary profits from infringement.

11. The Arai (2011) analysis of *social surplus* omits the concept of *substitutability* wherein a consumer can substitute with and gain utility from similar or even dissimilar products. When the penalty is low and the production cost is high, the content producer may decide not to create digital goods at all and instead, make the same or greater profits by legally distributing/reselling legal digital goods that are produced by others; and in such circumstances, the social surplus will not be zero.

12. The Arai (2011) conclusions/propositions that, under some circumstances, the government should set the civil penalty equal to zero and that the government should set the civil penalty to a level that makes the producer's profit zero, are wrong and misguided.

4.5 Factors to Be Considered When Developing Optimal Sanctions

In developing optimal sanctions, for IOF, legislators/regulators must strike a balance among several factors. The unique features of and criteria for illegal file sharing liability are as follows:

1. Both the infringer and the content owner/distributor suffer losses when infringement occurs—the infringer's losses could be from (a) viruses/adware embedded in the shared digital content, (b) time spent, (c) psychological discomfort from probability of prosecution, and (d) cost of bandwidth and hardware.

2. Fourth-generation file sharing systems use *streaming* technologies and anonymity features, which makes it difficult to determine the exact source of digital content.
3. New P2P file sharing systems are completely decentralized, which makes it more difficult to establish the liability of companies that produce P2P software, and infringers.
4. Most P2P infringers are price-sensitive and have limited wealth.
5. Sampling of digital content provides an alternative to IOF.
6. The existing liability framework acts as a *floor* and insurance for perpetrators and P2P software companies—the fines and penalties do not vary with wealth of intensity of infringement, or duration of infringement; and the probability of prosecution remains low.
7. Content owners and distributors incur significant monitoring and enforcement costs, and their marginal cost of enforcement can be relatively very high.
8. There is the requisite *knowledge* element for culpability because the P2P software company, the ISP, and the P2P member know exactly what P2P network does.
9. Incentives to produce valuable information.
10. The psychological comfort provided by IP rights.
11. Impact of proposed sanctions on creativity and advancement of technology.
12. Deterrence effect (negative or positive) of information from investigations and prosecutions.
13. The impact of proposed sanctions on transaction costs, monitoring costs, and public-perception costs.
14. Reputation effects, particularly in criminal prosecutions.
15. Transfers of *social capital*.
16. Wealth of perpetrators—monetary fines must be sufficiently significant to discourage future infringement.
17. Wealth of companies that build and distribute P2P software.
18. The key employees of companies that build and distribute P2P software.

The literature on the theories of and allocation of liability for torts is extensive and includes Jain and Kundu (2006), Rouillon (2008), and Bhole and Wagner (2008). There has been some debate about property rules versus liability rules—some of which were discussed in Lemley and Weiser (2007).

The following are the omissions and gaps in the literature. Unfortunately, most of the literature does not pertain to and is not applicable to information goods, or impulse goods (except a few articles such as Thoman (1994)). Most of the literature is not applicable in situations where leisure time is substituted for money (such as illegal file sharing). The existing literature does not account for the significant information asymmetry inherent in IOF—among the P2P software companies, infringers, content owners, and government prosecutors. The literature does not consider the effects of the cost structure of producers/distributors of digital content (high fixed costs and sunk costs and relatively low marginal costs). The models and theories assume (1) some measure of familiarity and unstructured contacts among joint tortfeasors, (2) some uniformity in diffusion of information among joint tortfeasors. In reality, in most P2P systems, there is significant anonymity and only very structured communications among joint tortfeasors. The models and theories do not incorporate the highly structured nature of P2P systems—once the individual downloads the P2P software and his/her computer becomes a node, the searches, protocols, and transfer of data are highly automated. In their pure forms, the traditional models of strict liability and vicarious liability are limited and insufficient to address third-generation and fourth-generation IOF. Vicarious liability theories and models often assume a major dichotomy between the P2P software company (i.e., company that produces P2P software) and its agents. Most of the theories in the existing literature were developed for situations where (1) there is only one occurrence of the tort, (2) there is only one tortfeasor and only one victim or there are joint tortfeasors and only one victim, and (3) there may be differences in knowledge between any two joint tortfeasors. On the contrary, in IOF, (1) there are many joint tortfeasors and many victims, (2) the tort occurs many times, and (3) with the exception of the P2P software company, all other joint tortfeasors are essentially *nodes* and have the same *knowledge* that is distinct from the files being shared.

The traditional basis of liability for illegal file sharing has included negligence, strict liability, and vicarious liability. Bonadio (2008), Peguera (2008), Sugden (2008), and Vincents (2007, 2008) analyzed European law aspects of these issues. Leong and Saw (2007) studied copyright infringement. The U.S. Supreme Court and many terminal courts in other countries have established the liability of ISPs for IOF, and some courts have imposed affirmative duties on ISPs to prevent and stop IOF. However, the liability of infringers and companies that produce P2P software can still be established based on

1. Negligence—companies that make P2P software face absolute negligence or contributory negligence: (a) strict liability—where both the P2P software company and each P2P member that functions as a node are liable, and (b) vicarious liability—where each P2P member is deemed as both agent of the P2P software company and agent of other P2P members.
2. Collusion—between the P2P software company and network members; and collusion among network members.
3. Common law fraud.
4. Common law conversion.
5. Statutory criminal misconduct or civil misconduct—with vicarious liability, personal liability, or strict liability.

4.6 Liability and Sanctions Models

The following are the assumptions for the models. U_{dp} is the disutility experienced by infringers from prosecution. This is a function of loss of income, fees/costs, loss of social capital, mental processes, biological functions, aspirations, perception, reputation, actual/perceived wealth, temporal dislocations, etc. This is a negative dollar amount. $U_{dp} \in (-\infty,0)$. U_{di} is the disutility experienced by infringers from investigation. This is a function of loss of income, fees/costs, loss of social capital, possible adverse action by the ISP, mental states/processes, biological functions, aspirations, perception, reputation, temporal dislocations, etc. $U_{di} \in (-\infty,0)$. U_{dc} is the disutility experienced by the P2P software company from public prosecution and/or private lawsuits. This is a function of loss of income, fees/costs, actual/perceived wealth, loss of social capital, mental states/processes, biological functions, aspirations, perception, reputation, temporal dislocations, etc. $U_{dc} \in (-\infty,0)$. χ_i is the cost of investigation incurred by the society. It includes business interruption costs; staff costs; and cost of lost customers for ISPs, universities, and other entities involved. χ_p is the cost of prosecution for the government and the content owners/distributors. This includes attorney's fees, discovery costs, etc. Ω is the liability assigned to the P2P company and all individuals involved in illegal file sharing (infringers, employees, and managers of the P2P software company, such as Grokster) as a percentage of economic losses caused by IOF during t. $\Omega \in (0,1)$; $\Omega = (\Omega_e + \Omega_u + \Omega_c)$. Ω_e is the proportion of total liability that is allocated to employees of the file sharing company. $\Omega_e \in (0,1)$. Ω_u is the proportion of liability assigned to individuals (nonemployees of P2P companies) that use the online file sharing network. $\Omega_u \in (0,1)$. Ω_c is the proportion of liability that is allocated to the P2P software company. $\Omega_c \in (0,1)$. Ω_f is the proportion of total liability that the individual(s) (employees of the file sharing company) expects will be assigned to him and/or other individuals (before investigation and prosecution or lawsuit). $\Omega_{ef} \in (0,1)$. F_e is the portion of total fines/penalties (at the time of sentencing) that is allocated to employees of the file sharing company. $F_e \in (0, \infty)$. F_u is the proportion at sentencing of total penalties/fines that is assigned to individuals (nonemployees of P2P companies) who use the online file sharing network. $F_u \in (0, \infty)$. F_c is the proportion of total fines/penalties that is allocated to the P2P software company at sentencing. $F_c \in (0, \infty)$. F_f is the proportion of total liability that the individual(s) (employees of the file sharing company) expects will be assigned to him and/or other individuals (before investigation and prosecution or lawsuit). $F_{ef} \in (0, \infty)$. ω_e is the total wealth of the liable employees of the P2P software company. Wealth includes social capital, reputation, opportunity costs, and loss of opportunity set. $\omega_e \in (-\infty, +\infty)$. ω_c is the total wealth of the P2P software company. Wealth includes social capital, reputation, opportunity costs, and loss of opportunity set. $\omega_c \in (-\infty, +\infty)$. ω_u is the total wealth of individuals (nonemployees of P2P companies) who are found liable for using the online file sharing network. Wealth includes social capital, reputation, opportunity costs, and loss of opportunity set. $\omega_u \in (-\infty, +\infty)$. ρ_i is the probability of identification/detection and investigation. ρ_r is the probability of recurrence of infringement after investigation and/or prosecution. ρ_p is the probability of prosecution. U_r is the utility equal to monetary benefit gained by infringers in a P2P network by recurrence of infringement after investigation and/or prosecution. $-\infty < U_r < +\infty$, because some people will start/try illegal file sharing simply because it is illegal. U_i is the utility equal to monetary benefit to a group of content owners/distributors from investigation = the monetary value of units of content that would have otherwise been infringed, but for investigation. U_p is the utility equal to monetary benefit to a group of content owners from prosecution. This includes the monetary value of units of content that would have otherwise been infringed, but for investigation. $-\infty < U_p < +\infty$, because some people will start/try illegal file sharing simply because it is illegal. **T**, **M**, **U**, **A** are *states* that represent the various *currencies/elements* used in IOF: T is the time; M is money, U is utility, and A is access rights to online file sharing networks. These *currencies* and associated penalties will have different values that vary depending on jurisdiction, type of digital content, types of content delivery system, mental states, biological functions, aspirations, perception, temporal dislocations, family structure, concentration of P2P network members, and the type of audience. For example, consider two P2P illegal file sharing networks (Network A, Network B) where members of Network A are mostly working professionals, each of whom can afford to purchase entire libraries of digital music but instead chooses to participate in illegal file sharing, and members of Network B are mostly college students, many of whom cannot afford to purchase most of the illegally downloaded content. Clearly, the leisure time and utilities of members of Network A are more valuable that their access rights or the cash value of the downloaded digital content. In the case of members of Network B, the cash value of the downloaded content is probably greater than the monetary value of their leisure times or their access rights. This implies that sanctions should vary depending on the *currency* that has the highest value to the perpetrator. Hence, P_m, P_t, P_a, P_u represent penalties/sanctions under various *states* representing various *currencies* used in IOF. P_{ci} and $\mathbf{P}_{cr}$ are the monetary values of civil and criminal penalties, respectively, if the perpetrators in IOF are convicted or found liable—including fines, lost wages, court costs, and attorney's fees. P_{ci}, $P_{cr} = (F_e + F_u + F_c)$. n is the number of individuals in the file sharing network. t is the duration of operations of the P2P software company.

The objective functions for maximizing social welfare from punishment are as follows:

$$\text{Max } \{(U_i * \rho_i) + (U_p * \rho_p) + \left|U_{dp}\right| + \left|U_{di}\right| - [(\chi_i + \chi_p) * \rho_i * \rho_p]\} | \text{Max}(P_m, P_c, P_a, P_u) \quad (4.11)$$

$$\text{Min}\{[(\chi_i + \chi_p) * \rho_i * \rho_p]\} | \text{Max}(P_m, P_c, P_a, P_u) \quad (4.12)$$

s.t.:

$P_m, P_c, P_a, P_u > 0$
$U_i, U_p > 0$
$\chi_i, \chi_p > 0$
$\Omega_e, \Omega_u > \Omega_c$

4.6.1 Conditions for Optimal Sanctions in Civil Prosecution

In a civil proceeding, the optimal sanction (with total value γ) for IOF must satisfy *all* the following conditions:

$$[\{(U_i * \rho_i) + (U_p * \rho_p) - [(\chi_i + \chi_p) * \rho_i * \rho_p]\} | \text{Max}(P_m, P_c, P_a, P_u)] > 0 \quad (4.13)$$

$$\text{Max}[0, \{((\chi_i + \chi_p) * \rho_i * \rho_p) + U_{dc} + U_{dp} + U_{di}\}] < P_{ci} \quad (4.14)$$

$$\left\{\partial\rho_r / \partial\left(\rho_p | \rho_i\right)\right\} < 0 \quad (4.15)$$

Thus, (4.15) implies that evidentiary standards for liability must be amended, to facilitate early intervention by investigators.

$$[\{P_{ci} - (U_r * \rho_r)\} | \text{Max}(P_m, P_c, P_a, P_u)] > 0 \quad (4.16)$$

$$\frac{\partial\Omega_e}{\partial\Omega_u} > \text{Max}\left[1, \left(\frac{\partial P_{ci}}{\partial\rho_p}\right), \left\{\frac{\partial(U_{di} + U_{dp})}{\partial(\chi_i + \chi_p)}\right\}, \left\{\frac{\partial U_{di}}{\partial U_{dp}}\right\}\right] \quad (4.17)$$

$$\Omega_e \in (0,1); \Omega_e > 0 \quad (4.18)$$

$$\{(\chi_i + \chi_p) * \rho_i * \rho_p\} < (F_u + F_c) \quad (4.19)$$

$$\frac{\partial F_c}{\partial\left\{\left[(\chi_i + \chi_p) * \rho_i * \rho_p\right]\right\}} > 1 \quad (4.20)$$

$$\Omega_e, \Omega_u > \Omega_c \quad (4.21)$$

$$\frac{\partial^2 P_{ci}}{\partial n \partial t} > \text{Max}\left[1, \frac{\partial\Omega_e}{\partial n}, \frac{\partial P_{ci}}{\partial\left(\chi_i + \chi_p\right)}\right] \quad (4.22)$$

$$\frac{\partial U_{dp}}{\partial P_{ci}} > \text{Max}\left[0, \frac{\partial U_{dp}}{\partial\left(\chi_i + \chi_p\right)}\right] \quad (4.23)$$

$$\frac{\partial P_{ci}}{\partial\left(\chi_i + \chi_p\right)} > \text{Max}\left[1, \frac{\partial P_p}{\partial P_i}, \frac{\partial U_{dp}}{\partial n}\right] \tag{4.24}$$

$$\left[\frac{\partial U_{dc}}{\partial n} + \frac{\partial U_{dp}}{\partial n}\right] > \left[\frac{\partial^2 U_p}{\partial n \partial t} + \frac{\partial^2 U_i}{\partial n \partial t}\right] \tag{4.25}$$

$$\frac{\partial F_e}{\partial F_u} > \text{Max}\left[1, \left(\frac{\partial P_{ci}}{\partial \rho_p}\right), \left\{\frac{\partial\left(U_{di} + U_{dp}\right)}{\partial\left(\chi_i + \chi_p\right)}\right\}, \left\{\frac{\partial U_{di}}{\partial U_{dp}}\right\}\right] \tag{4.26}$$

$$\frac{\partial F_e}{\partial F_u} \leq \frac{\partial \Omega_e}{\partial \Omega_u} \tag{4.27}$$

$$\frac{\partial F_c}{\partial F_u} \leq \frac{\partial \Omega_c}{\partial \Omega_u} \tag{4.28}$$

$$\frac{\partial F_u}{\partial \Omega_u} \leq \frac{\partial F_c}{\partial \Omega_c} \tag{4.29}$$

$$\frac{\partial F_e}{\partial \Omega_e} \leq \frac{\partial F_c}{\partial \Omega_c} \tag{4.30}$$

$$\left(\frac{F_c}{\omega_c}\right) > \left(\frac{F_e}{\omega_e}\right), \left(\frac{F_u}{\omega_u}\right) \tag{4.31}$$

$$\frac{\partial\left(U_i + U_p\right)}{\partial \text{Max}\left\{\left(\omega_c - F_c\right), \left(\omega_e - F_e\right)\right\}} < 0 \tag{4.32}$$

$$\frac{\partial U_r}{\partial\left(\omega_u - F_u\right)} > 0 \tag{4.33}$$

$$\frac{\partial U_{dc}}{\partial\left(\chi_i + \chi_p\right)} \geq 1 \tag{4.34}$$

$$\frac{\partial^2 U_{dc}}{\partial\left(\chi_i + \chi_p\right)^2} \geq 0 \tag{4.35}$$

$$\frac{\partial\left(U_{dp} + U_{di}\right)}{\partial\left(\chi_i + \chi_p\right)} \geq 1 \tag{4.36}$$

$$\frac{\partial^2\left(U_{dp} + U_{di}\right)}{\partial\left(\chi_i + \chi_p\right)^2} \geq 0 \tag{4.37}$$

The foregoing analysis implies that the legal processes (discovery, subpoenas, etc.) must also be modified so that (1) transaction costs and prosecution costs are reduced and (2) investigation alone causes substantial disutility and is sufficient ground for informal and civil sanctions by other parties such as ISPs, telephone companies, and small claims courts.

The aforementioned models assume that (1) *sanctions* include the acts of investigation and prosecution—this partly accounts for social capital and reputation effects—and (2) a significant portion of liability that is attributable to the company that produces P2P software is allocated to its employees. The problems of corporate liability for criminal misconduct and torts have been noted in the literature. Corporate civil and criminal liability remains necessary in order to discourage funding of illegal activities and in order to encourage good governance—where the members of the board of directors and/or officers can be held responsible for corporate misconduct.

4.6.2 Conditions for Optimal Sanctions in Criminal Prosecution

In a criminal proceeding/prosecution, the optimal sanction (with total value γ) for IOF must satisfy all the following conditions:

$$[\{(U_i * \rho_i) + (U_p * \rho_p) - [(\chi_i + \chi_p) * \rho_i * \rho_p]\} \mid Max(P_m, P_c, P_a, P_u)] > 0 \tag{4.38}$$

$$Max[0, \{((\chi_i + \chi_p) * \rho_i * \rho_p) + U_{dp} + U_{dc} + U_{di}\}] < P_{cr} \tag{4.39}$$

$$\frac{\partial \rho_r}{\partial (\rho_p \mid \rho_i)} < 0 \tag{4.40}$$

This condition (4.40) implies that evidentiary standards for liability must be amended, to facilitate early intervention by investigators.

$$[\{P_{cr} - (U_r * \rho_r)\} \mid Max(P_m, P_c, P_a, P_u)] > 0 \tag{4.41}$$

$$\frac{\partial \Omega_e}{\partial \Omega_u} > Max\left[1, \left(\frac{\partial P_{cr}}{\partial \rho_p}\right), \left\{\frac{\partial (U_{di} + U_{dp})}{\partial (\chi_i + \chi_p)}\right\}, \left\{\frac{\partial U_{di}}{\partial U_{dp}}\right\}\right] \tag{4.42}$$

$$\Omega_e \in (0,1); \ \Omega_e > 0 \tag{4.43}$$

$$\{(\chi_i + \chi_p) * \rho_i * \rho_p\} < F_u \tag{4.44}$$

$$\frac{\partial P_{cr}}{\partial \{(\chi_i + \chi_p) * \rho_i * \rho_p\}} > 0; \ \text{and} \ \frac{\partial F_c}{\partial \{(\chi_i + \chi_p) * \rho_i * \rho_p\}} > 1 \tag{4.45}$$

$$(F_e + F_c) > \{(\chi_i + \chi_p) * \rho_i * \rho_p\} \tag{4.46}$$

$$\Omega_e, \Omega_u > \Omega_c \tag{4.47}$$

$$\frac{\partial^2 P_{cr}}{\partial n \partial t} > Max\left[1, \frac{\partial \Omega_e}{\partial n}, \frac{\partial P_{cr}}{\partial (\chi_i + \chi_p)}\right] \tag{4.48}$$

$$\frac{\partial U_{dp}}{\partial P_{cr}} > Max\left[0, \frac{\partial U_{dp}}{\partial (\chi_i + \chi_p)}\right] \tag{4.49}$$

$$\frac{\partial P_{cr}}{\partial(\chi_i + \chi_p)} > Max\left[1, \frac{\partial P_p}{\partial P_i}, \frac{\partial U_{dp}}{\partial n}\right] \tag{4.50}$$

$$\left[\frac{\partial U_{dc}}{\partial n} + \frac{\partial U_{dp}}{\partial n}\right] > \left[\frac{\partial^2 U_p}{\partial n \partial t} + \frac{\partial^2 U_i}{\partial n \partial t}\right] \tag{4.51}$$

$$\frac{\partial^3 P_{cr}}{\partial \omega_e \partial \omega_c \partial \omega_u} > 0 \tag{4.52}$$

$$\left\{\left(\frac{\partial F_e}{\partial \Omega_e}\right)*\left(\frac{\partial \omega_e}{\partial F_e}\right)\right\} = \left\{\left(\frac{\partial F_u}{\partial \Omega_u}\right)*\left(\frac{\partial \omega_u}{\partial F_u}\right)\right\} = \left\{\left(\frac{\partial F_c}{\partial \Omega_c}\right)*\left(\frac{\partial \omega_c}{\partial F_c}\right)\right\} < 0 \tag{4.53}$$

$$\left(\frac{\partial F_c}{\partial \Omega_c}\right) > Max\left[0; \left(\frac{\partial F_e}{\partial \Omega_e}\right), \left(\frac{\partial F_u}{\partial \Omega_u}\right)\right] \tag{4.54}$$

$$\left(\frac{\partial^2 \omega_e}{\partial F_e^2}\right), \left(\frac{\partial^2 \omega_u}{\partial F_u^2}\right), \left(\frac{\partial^2 \omega_c}{\partial F_c^2}\right) < -1 \tag{4.55}$$

$$\left[\left(\frac{\partial \omega_c}{\partial F_c}\right) + \left(\frac{\partial \omega_e}{\partial F_e}\right) + \left(\frac{\partial \omega_u}{\partial F_u}\right)\right] > Max\left[0, \frac{\partial(\omega_c + \omega_e + \omega_u)}{\partial P_{cr}}\right] \tag{4.56}$$

$$Min\left[\left(\frac{\partial \omega_c}{\partial F_c}\right), \left(\frac{\partial \omega_e}{\partial F_e}\right), \left(\frac{\partial \omega_u}{\partial F_u}\right)\right] > \frac{\partial(\omega_c + \omega_e + \omega_u)}{\partial P_{cr}} \tag{4.57}$$

$$\left[\left\{\left(\frac{\partial \omega_e}{\partial F_e}\right)*U_r\right\} + \left\{\left(\frac{\partial \omega_u}{\partial F_u}\right)*U_{dp}\right\} + \left\{\left(\frac{\partial \omega_c}{\partial F_c}\right)*U_{dc}\right\}\right] > (U_p + U_i) \tag{4.58}$$

Here (in condition 4.58), $(\partial \omega_e/\partial F_e)$, $(\partial \omega_u/\partial F_u)$, and $(\partial \omega_c/\partial F_c)$ function as proxies for and equivalents to *probabilities of occurrence* and *probabilities of effectiveness* of the associated utilities/disutilities.

$$\frac{F_e}{\omega_e} > \frac{F_u}{\omega_u} > \frac{F_c}{\omega_c} \tag{4.59}$$

$$[U_r + U_{dp} + U_{dc}] < (U_p + U_i) \tag{4.60}$$

$$\frac{\partial(U_{dp} + U_{dc})}{\partial P_{cr}\partial(\chi_i + \chi_p)} < Min\left[0, \frac{\partial(U_p + U_i)}{\partial(\chi_i + \chi_p)}\right] \tag{4.61}$$

The aforementioned conditions and the proofs are relatively straightforward and are applicable to all types of digital content.

The foregoing analysis implies that the legal processes (discovery, subpoenas, etc.) must also be modified so that (1) transaction costs and prosecution costs are reduced and (2) only investigation (by government agencies) causes substantial disutility and is sufficient ground for informal and civil sanctions by other parties such as ISPs, telephone companies, and small claims courts.

The aforementioned models assume that a significant portion of liability that is attributable to the company that produces P2P software is allocated to its employees.

4.7 Conclusion

Illegal online file sharing (IOF) and online content control remain major problems with economic, technological, and policy ramifications. These problems can be solved by (1) incorporating economic psychology factors in both the design of online systems and legal processes, (2) development and implementation of appropriate sanctions for the various parties involved in IOF, (3) development of appropriate business models that minimize economic losses. In IOF, the perpetrators' perceptions of risk vary with various factors such as knowledge, cognition, peer pressure, and the enforcement/prosecution activities of content producers and distributors. Unfortunately, most existing user interfaces and the file sharing software systems are not designed to affect risk perceptions of users, and file sharing software systems actually reduce the risk perceptions of users by *normalizing* illegal file sharing, significantly simplifying and enhancing the illegal file sharing process, substantially reducing the economic and psychological search costs that may have served as deterrent to illegal file sharing, and reducing the perceived threat of apprehension. It is now clear that for copyright statutes to function effectively, the perceived risks inherent in illegal file sharing must be exponentially increased. ISPs can help in achieving this objective.

Notes

1 See Wang and McClung (2012); Podoshen (2008); Golle et al. (2001); Clark and Tsiaparas (2002); Cho et al. (2015); Cox and Collins (2014); and Aaltonen and Salmi (2013).
2 Becker and Clement (2006). This article stated in part:

> …The current strategy to increase the costs of participating in P2P networks by systematically suing users who illegally supply copyright protected material may help to reduce the willingness to share. Our results indicate a negative influence of costs on sharing behavior. However, there is a segment of heavy sharers that internalizes the costs and keeps providing a substantial number of files. The fewer the users who provide files to the network, the more these heavy sharers feel important and get an image of being a rebel—an argument often stated by users to engage in file sharing or open source projects. The results of our study also show negative effects when the music industry only follows a legal strategy. The underlying motives of the users intensify the open source development of anarchic p2p networks like Mute that encrypt the communication between the peers in such a way that the RIAA or MPAA will hardly be able to identify the user. Because Mute is an open source project, the development will attract users who want to feel secure from legal actions by the music industry…. Therefore, we suggest expanding the current strategy of the music industry by using several other elements. First, if the users just perceive very little reciprocity for their offer, they will reduce their supply. The same can be said for a user who believes that his offering is no longer important. Thus, any strategy that influences this perception will reduce the supply because the majority of the users do not wish to satisfy the demand of free riders. Second, the easier a user can access legal files in legal services such as iTunes or Napster 2.0, the less attractive are the illegal alternatives because participating in these networks not only implies legal risk but also a high uncertainty of the quality of the file, spyware, and so on. Therefore, we suggest that the music industry should license their content to other parties extensively. Third, some of the p2p networks have already installed barriers against free riders (i.e., some OpenNap servers) or use incentive mechanisms to reduce the free riding within the network. For instance, KaZaA is providing higher download priorities to heavy sharers. However, the software KaZaA Lite (which does not originate from the founders of KaZaa) allows the usage of the KaZaA network without download restrictions—a paradise for free

riders and an interesting issue to communicate to reduce the perceived reciprocity. Instead of flooding the networks with corrupted files, the RIAA or MPAA should enter the networks as free riders…

http://www.warsystems.hu/wp-content/uploads_bodo/becker-Dynamics%20of%20Illegal%20 Participation%20in%20file-sharing%20networks.pdf.

3 See Liu (2001); Kernochan (1989); Leclerc et al. (1995); Soman (2001); and Zauberman and Lynch (2005).

4 See *Viacom International Inc., v. YouTube, Inc.*, Complaint for Declaratory and Injunctive Relief and Damages, March 13, 2007 (filed in the U.S. District Court for the Southern District of New York; 2007).
See *Arista Records LLC. v. Lime Wire*, Civil Action No. 06 CV. 5939 (GEL) (filed S. D. N. Y. 2006).
See *In re: Aimster Copyright Litigation* 334 F. 3d 643 (7th Circuit 2003).

Chapter 5

Economics of Digital Content: New Digital Content-Control and Anti-P2P Systems/Methods*

This chapter introduces new content-control and anti-P2P-file sharing systems that are designed to reduce/eliminate illegal file sharing and improve control of digital content. Golle et al. (2001) studied incentives for sharing in peer-to-peer (P2P) systems. The earlier chapters in this book provide an analysis of some economic, legal, and psychological issues inherent in digital rights management (DRM) systems for digital content.

5.1 Constraints

In analyzing illegal downloads of content, there are several constraints on the efficiency of systems:

- Cost and availability of bandwidth
- ISPs' willingness to cooperate in enforcement activities
- Costs of security
- Network congestion costs
- Pricing difficulties (determining the exact number of players and the number of times each digital content file is played)

---

* An earlier version of this chapter was published as an article cited as follows: Nwogugu, M. (2008). Economics of digital content: New digital content-control and anti-P2P systems/methods. *Computer and Telecommunications Law Review*, 14(6), 150–159.

- Cost of hardware for playing content (introducing specialized hardware will only increase the final cost of downloading digital content and also increase complexity)
- The control of content and the form of content that will be transferred (different companies have different file formats)
- The physical structure/configuration of the network
- Cost of enforcing intellectual property rights (lawsuits, investigations, staff, etc.)

5.2 Existing Literature and Existing P2P and File Sharing Systems

Mertzios et al. (2013), Beekhuyzen et al. (2015), Avinadav et al. (2014), Blum et al. (2010), Feige and Vondrak (2010), and Gavalda-Miralles et al. (2014) and other articles[1] analyzed various content-protection and infrastructure methods and issues. Fetscherin and Knolmayer (2004) analyzed business models for content delivery.

Some courts have imposed criminal and civil sanctions on peer-to-peer (P2P) file sharing software companies. Online file sharing systems have evolved from a centralized model (Napster, etc.) to second-generation hybrid decentralized systems (Direct Connect Servers, eDonkey, etc.) and third-generation and fourth-generation wholly decentralized systems (Kazaa, BitTorrent, Videora, etc.) primarily because of lawsuits and criminal prosecution. More recently, legal/authorized file sharing systems have been implemented and are commercially available. Meisel (2008) described some of their business models. To date, there are very few commercially viable anti-P2P systems (Audible Magic and SafeMedia developed anti-P2P systems based on pattern recognition and dynamic profiling). Many internet service providers (ISPs) now have systems that block downloading of certain digital content and also block access to known illegal file sharing networks. SafeMedia (www.safemedia.com) developed portable and scalable P2PActive Denial Systems to detect, intercept, capture, and deny all illegal sharing of copyrighted digital files from P2P networks, encrypted or nonencrypted, without any measurable latency on the network (http://www.articlesbase.com/press-releases-articles/technology-that-stops-illegal-copyright-file-sharing-366243.html). Audible Magic's *CopySense* Network appliance does not disable P2P systems or restrict available bandwidth but rather blocked the exchange of copyrighted material while allowing transmission of legitimate files.

The main elements of the four generations of P2P systems are described as follows:

1. First-generation P2P systems:
   a. First-generation P2P is comprised of a centralized server and list. Hence, the company supplying is at fault for any illegal material.
   b. Centralized server system controlled all traffic among users. Central servers stored lists of shared files of network members.
   c. Central servers were updated regularly. Users would query central severs for location of desired media files.
   d. Examples are Napster, eDonkey2000, Soulseek, and DirectConnect.
2. Second-generation P2P systems:
   a. There is no centralized server—all file sharing is done by P2P connections.
   b. Nodes were not designed to be *equal*—some nodes have priority, some nodes were designated as indexing nodes, and some were designed to be high-capacity or low-capacity nodes.
   c. These systems contain distributed hash tables, which facilitate rapid scaling of the network—certain nodes are designated to index some hashes. However, users cannot

search for content through keywords but must use the exact description of the exact file that is sought.

d. Examples are LimeWire, *Gnutella, Kazaa, eMule, Kademlia,* FastTrack, and Ares Galaxy.

3. Third-generation P2P systems:

a. Anonymity—traffic is routed through other network members' clients, which function as network nodes. For example, A sends a file to B and then B gives the file to C. A and C do not become acquainted and thus are protected under most copyright laws. In many instances, these systems use virtual IP addresses, which obfuscate A's, B's, and C's location in the network and also hide the key elements of culpability—the justification for these systems is that virtual IP addresses make it very difficult to determine whether C requested for the file, and whether A sent the file or if A just forwarded the file. However, liability can be established based on theories of aiding-and-abetting, vicarious liability, and collusion.

b. Encryption of media files—which makes it very hard for network managers to identify illegal activity.

c. User-created list of acceptable people to share files with—similar to an instant messaging buddy list.

d. These systems are relatively slower due to encryption of media files and the smaller number of network members.

e. Examples of such systems include Tor (http://www.torproject.org/), *ANts P2P, RShare, Freenet, GNUnet,* Entropy, I2P (I2Phex, iMule, Azureus), and Waste.

4. Fourth-generation P2P systems:

a. Data are sent in the form of streams over P2P networks (instead of being sent as files).

b. There is no server involved in the system. Files are not transferred between users but the information is shared over streams in P2P networks.

c. The data are not stored on consumer's computer but rather are confined to an Internet connection and a host page.

d. Examples include YouTube, Peercast, Miro, Cybersky, and DemoTV.

Illegal file sharing in any form (1) compounds pricing of content, because the owner does not know the exact number of users/players and the number of times each user downloads the digital content, and (2) violates most intellectual property laws and provisions inherent in digital content.

5.3 Systems Requirements and Legal Standards for *Legal* File Sharing Networks

The demise of Napster and lawsuits against Internet companies, websites, and individuals have created a need for certain general criteria or standards for downloading and file sharing, which are deemed legal—this issue of criteria has not been completely resolved, even though the U.S. Supreme Court has ruled on some of the issues in *MGM v. Grokster*, 125 SCT 2764 (2005).[2] Adkinson (March 2004), Bakker (2005), Choi (2006), Depoorter and Parisi (2002), and Samuelson (2005) discussed associated legal and economic issues. *MGM v. Grokster* imposes an affirmative duty on makers/distributors who attempt to build devices that cannot be used for illegal file sharing. In June 2007, Belgium's Court of First Instance held that an ISP named Scarlet Extended SA was responsible for blocking illegal file sharing on its network—the ruling was based on the European

Union's Information Society Directive and, thus, will probably set a precedent in Europe. See comments in Perritt (2007a,b)(*supra*).

It is relevant to establish specific criteria for allocation of liabilities so that programmers, developers, and business professionals can improve their product development processes. Von Lohmann (2003)(*supra*) stated in part:

> ...In order to prevail on a contributory infringement theory, a copyright owner must prove:
> 1. *Direct Infringement*: There has been a direct infringement by someone.
> 2. *Knowledge*: The accused contributory infringer knew of the underlying direct infringement. This element can be satisfied by showing either that the contributory infringer *actually* knew about the infringing activity, or that he reasonably *should have known* given all the facts and circumstances. At a minimum, however, the contributory infringer must have some specific information about infringing activity—the mere fact that the system is capable of being used for infringement, by itself, is not enough.
> 3. *Material Contribution*: The accused contributory infringer induced, caused, or materially contributed to the underlying direct infringement. Merely providing the site and facilities" that make the direct infringement possible can be enough... in order to prevail on a vicarious infringement theory, a copyright owner must prove each of the following:
> **a.** *Direct Infringement*: There has been a direct infringement by someone.
> **b.** *Right and Ability to Control*: The accused vicarious infringer had the right and ability to control or supervise the underlying direct infringement. This element does not set a high hurdle. For example, the Napster court found that the ability to terminate user accounts or block user access to the system was enough to constitute *control*.
> **c.** *Direct Financial Benefit*: The accused vicarious infringer derived a *direct financial benefit* from the underlying direct infringement. In applying this rule, however, the courts have not insisted that the benefit be especially *direct* or *financial*—almost any benefit seems to be enough. For example, the Napster court found that "financial benefit exists where the availability of infringing material acts as a draw for customers" and the growing user base, in turn, makes the company more attractive to investor....

See comments in Lemley and Reese (2004), which stated in part:

> ...In addition, some recent suits appear to be based on a new theory that might be called 'tertiary' liability that seeks to reach those who help the helpers. Cases in this vein include lawsuits filed against those who help others crack encryption (for example by providing links to software that can be used to crack encryption), the copyright lawsuit against backbone providers for providing the wires on which copyrighted material flows, the claims filed against the venture capital firm of Hummer Winblad for its role in funding Napster, and (with an unusual twist) the malpractice suit against the law firm of Cooley Godward for advising mp3.com that it could assert defenses to copyright infringement. The anti-circumvention provisions of the Digital Millennium Copyright Act (DMCA) provide by statute for one particular type of tertiary liability (for providing tools that circumvent encryption protecting a copyrighted work and that can help another get access to a copyrighted work in order to infringe that copyright), and there have even been suggestions that there should be a claim for contributory violation of the DMCA's anti-circumvention provisions, which should perhaps be termed quaternary liability for copyright infringement...

Under existing U.S. case law and U.S. federal statutes,[3] and *Metro-Goldwyn-Mayer vs. Grokster Ltd.*, 125 S.CT. 2764 (2005) (henceforth, *MGM v. Grokster*), and under *Universal Music Australia Pty Ltd and Others v. Sharman License Holdings Ltd and Others 220 A.L.R 1* (2005) (Australia), in order for any P2P platform to be deemed *legal*, it should conform to the following criteria:

- The platform must not store content/files.
- The platform must be decentralized.
- The platform must not instruct users on what to do.
- The platform/system must not show users where to locate files.
- The platform must not advertise its ability to provide free copies of protected works.
- The platform must not aid users in uploading/downloading copyrighted digital content (files).
- The maker of the platform/device must not promote the device for illegal uses. *Promotion* in this context refers to marketing, advertising, tutorials, advice, online customer service, etc., which could directly or indirectly cause users to use the device for illegal purposes.
- The maker of the device must not foster infringement in any way.
- The device must contain filters or other mechanisms that will identify, reduce, or eliminate infringement.
- The device must not provide access to network-members' files that are not intended to be shared—the device must request for specifically designated file-folders (in network-members' hard drives) that will be used in file sharing operations. The device must not access other parts of the network-member's hard drives.
- The device/system should not be bundled with or transmit privacy-invasive software such as spyware, viruses, or adware.
- The platform must not store content/files.
- The platform must be decentralized.
- The platform must not instruct users on what to do. The maker of the device must not foster, promote, or encourage infringement in any way.
- The platform/system should encrypt files to ensure control.
- The platform must not permit files to be copied by any internal mechanism.
- The platform should ensure that only specific and controllable types of files can be transmitted using the system.

Meisel (2008), Choi (2006), Landes and Lichtman (2003), and Samuelson (2005) discussed the *MGM v. Grokster* case and related issues.

5.4 Solutions to the File Sharing and Content-Control Problems

This section presents several new solutions for the content-control problem. The technical issues in P2P systems and content control have been analyzed in several articles. The existing literature omits the following:

- Efficient solutions to the P2P and content-control problems
- Legal requirements and their impact on design of technology

- Economic psychology issues and their impact on design of technology
- Solutions at the browser level (most solutions have been developed at the server and router/gateway levels, and these have not been effective because P2P traffic is sometimes disguised as other traffic or consists of encrypted files or streams)
- Solutions that minimize the use of bandwidth

Building browser-based systems raises security, user psychology, and human–computer interaction issues, some of which are addressed in Ye et al. (2005).

5.4.1 New P2P Control Systems

This section describes several new systems (P2PMonitor™ system) that prevent illegal file sharing in P2P systems and reduce P2P traffic problems.[4] The economic rationale for these proposed solutions are as follows:

- They minimize the use of bandwidth—illegal communications are detected before they commence.
- They minimize detection costs.
- They prioritize traffic.
- They are effective against fourth-generation P2P systems that are based on streaming technologies.

5.4.1.1 P2PMonitor-A™

This system is based on a browser-add-in. Once the consumer requests for a website/URL (which presumably may contain *torrent files* or links to files available for sharing), the browser-add-in will automatically extract and store the IP address of the server and URL of the website requested and then compare such information to a database of similar data of known P2P websites and P2P servers and to several criteria such as the type/structure of URL/IP address, source of transmission (originating layer; port) of packets arriving from other computers or the company's servers to the browser, number of IP addresses (i.e., dynamic IP addresses, virtual IP addresses), activities of a server and frequency of uploads/downloads, contents of website, type and frequency of activity/data extracted from the requested website/server, file type, file size, packet size, grouping of packets, completeness of packets, average transmission bit rate and volume, etc. The browser-add-in will automatically corrupt any torrent files and determine whether the computer is part of a P2P network, and if so, it will terminate the transmission. These prespecified criteria will be coded into the browser-add-in. If the URL/IP address and the data analysis confirm that the requested website is a P2P website and/or that the requested data are from an illegal P2P network or that the file was prepped for sharing, then the browser-add-in will not process the consumer's request for the website or from another server or a computer in the P2P network. All tests/extractions will be done within the browser-add-in.

The browser-add-in will test for whether the computer/PC/server is part of a P2P network by (1) noting the layer from which the computer/server/PC's data are being sent; (2) noting whether the packets sent in any transmission constitute a complete file; (3) noting the type of protocols used in the transmission; (4) noting what percentage of the file is transmitted within a specific unit of time t—before transmission is initiated, the browser-add-in will request for and get data on the file size/type/location/features/protocol; and (5) noting the nature of a transmission between the computer/PC's hard drive and another PC's browser. If the results of any of these tests are negative, then the browser-add-in will terminate the transmission. All tests/extractions will be done only within the browser-add-in.

The browser-add-in will have an embedded personal firewall that will cover and override/protect the underlying browser. The firewall will be programmed to reject traffic with the following prespecified characteristics: (1) bandwidth intensity/use, (2) whether its traffic from P2P connections (the firewall will be able to determine the source/type/layer/port of the packet-traffic as it arrives from the server[s]), (3) packet characteristics, etc. Similar firewalls can also be embedded at the network level.

5.4.1.2 P2PMonitor-B™

This system is based on a browser-add-in. The browser-add-in will analyze incoming traffic and if it identifies any bandwidth-intensive traffic, the browser-add-in will immediately terminate receipt of the packets—thus, there will be predetermined thresholds for bandwidth use per millisecond and for total bandwidth used for a specified percentage of each transaction. Alternatively, if any bandwidth-intensive traffic begins to be sent, the browser-add-in will immediately determine the source-URL and source-server, determine whether it is a server used in P2P activities (such as *tracker servers* and centralized servers used in Napster-like systems and *designated servers* used in Kazaa-type systems) or a website associated with P2P activities (where files or links to files are posted), and if necessary, then terminate receipt of the packets.

The browser-add-in will have an embedded personal firewall that will cover and override/protect the underlying browser. The firewall will be programmed to reject traffic with the following prespecified characteristics: (1) bandwidth intensity/use, (2) whether its traffic from P2P connections (the firewall will be able to determine the source/type of the packet-traffic as it arrives from the server), packet characteristics, etc. Similar firewalls can also be embedded at the network level.

5.4.1.3 P2PMonitor-C™

The browser-add-in in the consumer's device will analyze incoming web traffic, and if it identifies any group of similar packets being sent by two or more different computers/servers/devices, the browser-add-in will immediately terminate receipt of the packets. The browser-add-in will control membership in any network (by controlling performance of various layers and traffic through such layers)—and membership in known illegal P2P networks will not be physically possible. The browser-add-in will be designed to identify the characteristics of a packet—whether it is a music/video/audio/data file, the total size of the file, etc. Thus, the browser-add-in will ensure that the following conditions must exist: (a) for each file, all packets must be received from one source; (b) for each file, a certain minimum volume of packets must be received within a second/millisecond (depending on the connection speed being used); otherwise, the transmission of the packets will be terminated; and (c) within any network that the user/consumer belongs to, there cannot be any simultaneous transfer of data from more than two other network members to the user/consumer within a prespecified time frame (e.g., 30 min).

In addition, the browser-add-in will immediately (1) obtain the source-URL and determine whether it is a website associated with P2P activities (where files or links to files are posted) and (2) obtain the IP address of the source-server and determine whether it is a server that is used in illegal P2P activities (such as *tracker servers* and centralized servers used in Napster-like systems). Thereafter, if necessary, it will then terminate receipt of the packets. The browser-add-in will have an embedded personal firewall that will cover and override/protect the underlying browser. The firewall will be programmed to reject traffic with the following prespecified characteristics: (1) bandwidth intensity/use, (2) whether its traffic from P2P connections (the firewall will be able to determine the source/type of the packet-traffic as it arrives from the server), packet characteristics, etc. Similar firewalls can also be embedded at the network level.

5.4.2 New Content-Control Systems

These proposed systems assume that other *traditional* techniques such as watermarking and fingerprinting are also used (Table 5.1).[5] The ContentControl™ systems described in this section provide solutions for online file sharing and content control. The economic rationales for these systems are as follows:

- They minimize the use of bandwidth and minimize network congestion.
- They reduce infringement and, hence, reduce enforcement and monitoring costs.
- They are neutral to different types of media files.
- They reduce security costs.
- They reduce the computing capacity required by the content distributor and the consumer.

Table 5.1 Some Effects of Restrictive Policies

Restrictive Policy	Potential Alienation or Subscriber Concern	Alternative Smart Policies
Block (or significantly limit) access to certain P2P applications	May aggravate subscribers using the blocked P2P applications, potentially causing bad publicity.	• Deprioritize P2P during congestion periods. • Throttle upstream (file upload) traffic and do not limit downstream (file downloads). • Limit P2P access during certain periods of the day/week (e.g., business hours). • Limit P2P traffic traversing expensive peering points or transits. • Provide unrestricted subscription plans for an additional charge.
Subscriber byte caps (e.g., up to 1 GB daily, followed by an additional surcharge or block of access)	May cause concern that application unaware byte caps do not provide the desired application isolation for the subscriber, as excessive P2P use might penalize other critical applications (e.g., VPN, email). This is especially true for cases in which one broadband connection is used by a number of different users.	• Provide a P2P quota, which once depleted will throttle P2P traffic but will not affect other application uses. • Provide optional P2P bandwidth-on-demand for an additional charge to allow subscriber access to more bandwidth even if quota has been depleted.

Source: P-Cube (2003).

5.4.2.1 *ContentControl-1*™

This is a mechanism to process and control digital content. The main component is browser-add-in software that will contain an online payment system and a content download system. In essence, the content owner/rights holder will store content as encrypted files in its servers or as secure URLs. Upon online payment by the consumer, the online payment system automatically sends instructions to the download mechanism in the browser-add-in about the number of downloads that have been paid for and the browser-add-in then processes requests to the company's servers the same number of times. Once the consumer pays to access the content, the consumer's browser-add-in will send a request to the content owner's servers to encrypt (and fingerprint/watermark) the requested content, and the browser-add-in will then initiate send–receive protocols pertaining to the encrypted data residing in the content owners'/distributor's servers/URLs at another location, such that the servers *process* the content and the sound/video/data are sent over the Internet as encrypted packets (streams or files) to the browser-add-in. The download mechanism in the browser-add-in is linked to the online payment system on a website (or alternatively, the online payment system is built into the browser-add-in). Upon online payment by the consumer, the online payment system automatically sends instructions to the browser-add-in stating the number of downloads that have been paid for, and the browser-add-in then downloads the content as encrypted file-in-a-file series or streams and processes the file/streams. In the case of encrypted files, the *main* encrypted file contains a series of encrypted files A_1, A_2, A_3,... A_n, where A is the same encrypted content, A_1 contains files A_2 ... A_n, and encrypted file A_i contains encrypted files A_{i+1}... A_n. N is the number of times the file A can be downloaded after online payment. After file A_1 is processed, A_1 self-destructs and only file A_2 remains and becomes the *main* encrypted file. (Alternatively, the browser-add-in will download a series of encrypted files/streams A_1, A_2, A_3,... A_n, where A is the same encrypted content and N is the number of times that the consumer has paid to download content A. Files that are not being played are cached in the browser-add-in.) Each file is processed while encrypted (there is no decryption), and after *processing*, the file automatically partially self-destructs and leaves only the secondary file that was embedded. Processing the media file or stream while encrypted eliminates the possibility of copying the file or stream because the encryption is specific to the consumer's IP address(es), consumer's profile, the ISP, and to each browser-add-in. Each file is encrypted such that there can be fast-forwards, pauses, and rewinds.

All content-manipulation functions (fast-forward, pause, play, etc.) will be requested by the consumer's browser-add-in as queries to the content distributor's servers/URLs. The browser-add-in then immediately converts the packets into recognizable sound/data/images as they arrive at the browser. These encrypted packets will self-destruct immediately after being received and processed by the browser-add-in such that they cannot be copied due to the encryption and the self-destruction. *The encrypted file is never stored in the user's hard drive and is never cached in the browser-add-in.* The encryption of the file is browser specific and is also specific to an IP address—a PC, mobile phone, or handheld device. That is, the encryption is keyed to (1) IP address, (2) browser address (each browser will have a specific address/ID), (3) consumer name and personal info (obtained through payment system), (4) consumer location, (5) type of device, and (6) ISP used by the consumer.

A search algorithm can also be included in the browser—the download mechanism, a search algorithm, and an online payment system are all embedded in the browser-add-in. The search algorithm searches for and retrieves specific content on servers of prespecified companies.

5.4.2.2 ContentControl-2™

This system is primarily for persons who want to build digital libraries/collections. The system is structured such that the digital content will always reside with and be controlled by the consumer but with some control by the content owner/distributor. This system downloads encrypted content (music, video, etc.) in the form of a file or stream only when the consumer has paid the download fee. The main component is a browser-add-in. The download mechanism, a search algorithm, and an online payment system are all embedded in the browser-add-in. The search algorithm searches for and retrieves specific content from the content owner's servers. The browser-add-in downloads the encrypted stream or media file onto the consumer's hard drive—this process will involve partitioning the consumer's hard drive (and perhaps creating a *virtual drive* that will be erased once the content has been processed). The downloaded/stored media file/stream is designed to become useless code unless activated. The encryption is coded such that:

1. The media file or stream is specific to the device (handheld, PC, laptop, etc.) and the browser and the IP address.
2. The media file can be processed only by the consumer's browser-add-in (a media player is embedded in the browser-add-in).
3. The encryption and watermarking of the file/stream is specific to a browser/IP address—the encryption is keyed to (a) the consumer's IP address(es), (b) the consumer's browser address (each browser will have a specific address/ID), (c) consumer name and personal info (obtained through payment system), (d) consumer location, (e) the type of device, and (f) ISP used by the consumer.

Once the browser-add-in is instructed to process the media file/stream, it sends several messages to the content owner's servers as follows: (1) a *request for confirmation*, (2) the IP address and location of the file, and (3) the *state* of the file. If the file has been copied, moved, or changed in any way, the content owner's servers will not send any confirmation code and the file will automatically disintegrate and erase itself. Otherwise, the content owner's servers will confirm and send a confirmation code to the browser-add-in. Thus, the media file is independently

1. *State* aware—the encryption processes analyze the future storage processes (partitioning of the hard drive), file size, exact arrangement of bits in file/stream, etc., and any changes in any of these characteristics will result in automatic self-erasure of the file.
2. *Location* aware—the encryption (and the underlying file/stream) includes matching codes for the IP address(es).
3. *Activity* aware—the encryption (and the underlying file/stream) records how many times the file/stream has been accessed.
4. *Attempts* aware—the encryption specifically notes any attempts to copy or move or access the file.

The browser-add-in will use the confirmation code to activate and access the stored media file. While the file/stream is being accessed, every 30 seconds, the content owner's servers will send similar confirmation codes and will continue to do so until the *session* expires. The length of each session will depend on the content (which ranges from 1 min to 3 h). Functions such as rewinds and fast-forwards are done using the browser-add-in. The embedded media player in the browser-add-in (1) automatically blocks out any other media player in the device once the browser-add-in receives the confirmation code, (2) does not have any *save* or *record* functions, and (3) is not linked to the hard drive and cannot play any other files in the consumer's hard drive. The download mechanism in the browser-add-in is linked to the online payment system in the browser-add-in. Upon online payment by the consumer, the browser-add-in notes the number of downloads that are being paid for, and the browser then downloads the encrypted files or file-in-a-file series and processes the files.

5.4.2.3 ContentControl-3™

In all the aforementioned alternatives, the digital content (sound/images/data) will be programmed so that it cannot be copied by any built-in mechanism in the consumer's device (computer, mobile phone, handheld, etc.). The next problem is to prevent the content (sound/images) from being copied by external devices. In the case of images, the pixels used will be sufficient only for viewing the screen of the device with the naked eye but will not be adequate for printing the screen or for photographing the image. In the case of sound, external copying can be eliminated by embedding high-pitched sounds in the file or stream (that contains the content) during the process of encrypting the media files. The human ear cannot hear these high-pitched sounds when the content is processed/played. However, when the waves of these high-pitched sounds come into contact with any external recording devices, (a) the friction produced, (b) the resulting distortion of the surrounding sound, and (c) the reflection of the waves will all make it impossible to successfully record the sound.

5.4.2.4 ContentControl-4™

Digital content is typically transported by different types of Internet protocols, and this creates problems of control. The main issue then is to design a protocol that links the online payment system to the media file/stream and the file/stream transfer process while eliminating illegal online file sharing. The file/stream encryption is keyed to the following: the consumer's IP address(es), the consumer's browser address (each browser will have a specific address/ID), consumer name and personal info (obtained through payment system), consumer location, the type of device, and the ISP used by the consumer.

The protocol is described as follows:

1. The exchange and file transfer process is initiated by the content owner/distributor, only after online payment by the consumer. Online payment is the catalyst for the entire file transfer process and determines whether there will be *loop* processes in the protocol. Without a particular payment system and online payment, the consumer cannot initiate or participate in the protocol.
2. Every 5–20 seconds, the consumer's computer/device will send confirmations of payment (a code number is assigned to the device's browser after online payment—the payment code), consumer's IP address (the IP code), port identifier (the port ID code), and

consumer's location (location code—based on ISP and phone number). If the confirmation is not received, the file transfer (from the owner's servers) will be automatically terminated.

3. The media file is encrypted such that it can be accessed and processed only by the consumer's browser-add-in. The encryption carries the payment code, the IP code, the port ID code, and the location code.

4. The media file is encrypted such that wherever it is located, it sends intermittent messages to the content distributor's servers (similar to a search agent).

5. The content distributor's servers will be able to set the user's device browser-add-in/ media player to one of the three states—*blocked*, *enabled*, and *pending*—only for purposes of a specific file transfer session; but for other purposes, the browser-add-in/media player will work as normal. In the *blocked* state, no transactions are possible. In the *pending* state, verifications and payments are possible. In the *enabled* state, actual transfer of bits occurs.

6. The protocol effectively modifies the behavior of at least one router and switches by instructions in packet headers: (a) instructing the router to compare the code assigned to the file's packets to a code supplied by the content owner's servers—if there is no match, the router terminates the transmission and does not allocate any bandwidth, and (b) instructing the router to check for file completeness, and if more than 10% of the file is missing, the router will terminate the file/stream transfer.

7. The protocol causes messages to be sent between the consumer's browser and the content owner's servers.

5.5 Conclusion

Most existing anti-file sharing systems and content-control systems remain deficient and, sometimes, do not comply with case law and statutes. The existing legal framework in most jurisdictions is not completely adequate to regulate the new and evolving models/systems of online file sharing. Illegal file sharing and content-control problems can be solved by (1) relating economic issues and legal requirements to technological solutions and capabilities and (2) developing appropriate business models that create value and minimize economic losses for content distributors.

Notes

1 See Steinmetz and Wehrle (eds) (September 2005); Kolpakov and Raffinot (2008); Lin and Wu (2008); Swangmuang and Krishnamurthy (2008); Shao (2007); Wu and Pang (2008); Chen and Horng (2007); and Stutzbach et al. (2008).

2 See *Feist Publications, Inc. vs. Rural Telephone Service Co.*, 499 U.S. 340, 111 S. Ct. 1282 (1991; USA court case).
See *American Geophysical Union v. Texaco, Inc.*, 60 F.3d913 (2d Cir. 1995; USA).
See *Princeton University Press v. Michigan Document Services*, Inc. (6th Cir. 1996; USA).
See U.S. Patent 7187678—Authentication for use of high speed network resources. Available at http://www.patentstorm.us/patents/7187678.html.

3 See *Viacom International Inc., v. YouTube, Inc.*, Complaint for Declaratory and Injunctive Relief and Damages, March 13, 2007 (filed S.D.N.Y. 2007).

See *Arista Records LLC. v. Lime Wire*, Civil Action No. 06 CV. 5939 (GEL) (filed S. D. N. Y. 2006).

See *In re: Aimster Copyright Litigation* 334 F. 3d 643 (7th Circuit 2003).

4 See *Technology That Stops Illegal "copyright" File Sharing*. http://www.articlesbase.com/press-releases-articles/technology-that-stops-illegal-copyright-file-sharing-366243.html.

5 See U.S. Patent 6917975—Method for role and resource policy management. Available at http://www.patentstorm.us/patents/6917975/description.html.

See USPTO Patent Application 20050273714—Systems and methods for an embedded collaboration client. http://www.freshpatents.com/Systems-and-methods-for-an-embedded-collaboration-client-dt20051208ptan20050273714.php?type=description.

Chapter 6

The Free Rider Problem, Inequality in Networks, and a Critique of Tit-for-Tat Mechanisms

This chapter introduces new solutions to the free rider problems in networks. The chapter explains why FairTorrent (a peer-to-peer [P2P] model) and similar tit-for-tat (TFT) P2P systems are not efficient and how, contrary to the literature, free riding may be beneficial. The information producer modeled herein is not a traditional profit-maximizing entity but rather is piracy averse, has limited control over the P2P network or client–server network, sells short-lived products, and is most interested in long-term profits. The *free riders* (network members) are generally self-interested, *loss-averse*, and price-sensitive persons who derive mostly nonmonetary utility from consumption of digital content. Free riding can be knowing or involuntary. The P2P and client–server networks discussed herein are anonymous legal networks, and thus the effects of actual or potential coordination and/or altruism among customers are somewhat limited.

6.1 The Existing Literature on the Free Rider Problem and Incentives in Networks

Free-riding also occurs in other nontraditional forms such as uploading of useless content and/ or malicious content and misreporting of bandwidth capacity by peers. The literature on free riding in various types of networks (social networks, Internet networks, electricity distribution networks, etc.) is extensive. Huo (2011), Tseng and Chen (2011), and Feldman et al. (2006) analyzed the free riding problem in P2P networks. Bloch and Quérou (2013), Candogan et al. (2012), Galeotti et al. (2010), and Adlakha et al. (2015) analyzed games and networks. Ramaswamy et al. (2012) and Feldman et al. (2006) analyzed and surveyed incentive systems in P2P networks within the context of game theory (i.e., repeated games). The solutions to free riding that were presented in Chen et al. (2012), Feldman et al. (2006), Huo (2011), Hua et al. (2012), and Tseng and Chen (2011) are not feasible because weaknesses in TFT mechanisms; the principles in Coleman et al. (2007), Pavlov (2005), and Diederich and Busemeyer (1999) which analyzed various elements of conflict within the context of decision-making, and the principles in Gradwohl and Reingold (2010) which provided some useful critiques of theories of large games.

Hamida et al. (2008), Anshelevich and Caskurlu (2011), Azar et al. (2005), Giotis and Guruswami (2006), Bei et al. (2011), Feige and Vondrak (2010), and Blum et al. (2010) analyzed network formation games and node interactions in networks. Fiat and Saia (2007) and Nisgav and Patt-Shamir (2011) analyzed patterns in networks.

6.1.1 Free Riding Can Be Beneficial and Can Increase Social Welfare in Some Very Rare Circumstances

The general consensus in the existing literature is that free riding is bad for, and reduces social welfare in, every type of network. On the contrary, in P2P Internet networks and some social networks, free riding may be beneficial and improve social welfare if any of the following conditions exists:

1. The cost savings achieved by having other network members download whole or partial units of digital content (or other social goods) from the free rider are greater than the value of partial or whole units of content (or other social goods) downloaded by the free rider. This implies that the free rider's location (and resources) must be of great value and, in the case of P2P networks, that the free rider node is constantly functioning and accessible; and the *centrality* of the node within the P2P system is high/significant. That is, the node serves as a *quasi client–server node within the P2P network* and thus saves bandwidth costs and search time. Bei et al. (2011) discussed the *centrality* of network nodes.
2. The content-distributor's cost-adjusted revenues that are lost by free riding are lower than the revenues gained by having other network members download content (or other social goods) from the free rider.
3. The free rider increases the actual and perceived choice in the network (at least during the times that the network has its high traffic/activity) and thus enhances the brand equity of the network. Choice here refers to availability of digital content (or social goods).
4. The free rider substantially reduces the network-monitoring and enforcement costs and facilitates enforcement of IP laws, and such cost savings are greater than the revenues lost from the free rider's downloading.

Free riders that exhibit such characteristics are henceforth referred to as *valuable free riders*.

6.1.2 A Critique of FairTorrent, Tit-for-Tat Mechanisms, and Sherman et al. (2012)

The supposedly new P2P algorithm that was introduced by Sherman et al. (2012) and is named *FairTorrent* is not efficient and is a development/extension of existing systems. The *normalized generosity measure* in Feldman et al. (2006) and Feldman et al. (2004) was the precursor to *FairTorrent*.

Ballester and Seigneur (2015) surveyed/reviewed several "trust" mechanisms in networks. The problems inherent in *FairTorrent* are as follows:

1. FairTorrent is really designed for illegal P2P networks. Note that the whole debate about the fairness of allocations in P2P systems has been about illegal P2P networks. In legal P2P file sharing systems, the distributor can charge free riders higher prices (and possibly redistribute a portion of such prices to other peers), can reduce downloading by known free riders, or can provide incentives to reduce free riding.

2. FairTorrent results in the creation and use of *suboptimal peers*, which reduces overall social welfare in the network. The *suitability* of a peer is defined in terms of speed, bandwidth capacity, disclosure of resources, etc. Within the TFT and FairTorrent frameworks, the concept of *suboptimal peers* is hereby defined as (1) *suitable* peers that are physically farther away from the subject peer and for which more bandwidth is required for any uploads/downloads; (2) peers that do not have sufficient resources/capacity (e.g., bandwidth); (3) peers for which reciprocal downloads are improbable or unlikely (because such peers have preferences and/or habits that differ from those of the subject peer); (4) peers that are not active within the P2P system and are not functioning when most searches by other peers occur (i.e., the peer is switched off); (5) any peer that does not truthfully disclose its resources and bandwidth capacity (i.e., download/upload speeds); (6) any peer that values bandwidth on a scale that differs from the typical valuation of other peers and/or any peer that has low value for bandwidth; or (7) any peer/member that values leisure time on a scale that differs from the typical valuation of other peers/members and/or any peer that has low value for leisure time.

3. Contrary to Sherman et al. (2012), and given their definitions and notations, FairTorrent requires predictions of peers' rates (i.e., upload/download rates in the Internet, social communication in social networks). *FairTorrent* still requires node-discovery that may be of the same or greater magnitude as in other TFT mechanisms (depending on the physical/social dispersion of the network, the percentage of nodes that are functioning at the time of search, etc.).

4. The definitions/notions of fairness and stability within the TFT and FairTorrent frameworks (a peer receives bandwidth equal to what it contributes) are wrong and very misplaced because of the following reasons. One of the greatest advantages of a P2P file sharing system is that it can take advantage of the differences in resources available to, and differences among preferences of, each peer. Different peers place different monetary and nonmonetary values on bandwidth, other search costs, and on time spent searching for content in the file sharing system. Different peers have different raw-access prices and get different bandwidth allocations from their internet service providers (ISPs)—that is, different peers pay different access prices to their ISPs who provide different bandwidths. In most instances, each peer's processing capacity and bandwidth is not available at all times—FairTorrent may work only if all peers are constantly active or are active in the network at the same time and have similar bandwidth allocations from their ISPs. There is a distinction between the individual human who does the search in the P2P system and what happens at the node level where P2P systems use proximity, rates, and incentives to attempt to ensure fairness. In file sharing networks, there can be economic value for waiting time—that is, some nodes may prefer and/or accept time-deferred downloads either for nothing or in exchange for incentives or in exchange for grant of future priority in downloading. In most instances, the network structure is dynamic over most time intervals. As a result, there is never any *market equilibrium* with respect to bandwidth

allocations in such networks. Finally and as mentioned earlier, free riders can be beneficial to networks under some rare circumstances.

5. The effectiveness of FairTorrent and all TFT mechanisms depends on the skewness of the distribution of nodes based on the following measures: (1) their download volumes, (2) their *net upload/download* volumes (i.e., aggregate upload volume minus download volume), (3) their physical location, and (4) the duration of time that each node/computer is functioning. If the P2P network is significantly physically dispersed (a substantial percentage of nodes/members are geographically spread out) or if a high percentage of members/nodes use different ISPs, FairTorrent or any TFT mechanism is less likely to work because of the greater distances between matched *suitable* peers (which incurs greater bandwidth), bottlenecks in transmission, greater interconnection fees, etc. Moreover, high-capacity users (HCUs) are very likely to contribute more than they receive, because such HCUs are very likely not to find any *suitable* node with whom they have a deficit. In the context of TFT mechanisms, *distance* means not only physical distance between nodes/members but also *transmission distance* (which includes actual distance along transmission lines) and *ISP distance* (which includes distance in the context of the specific ISPs that support each node/member, and thus considers routers). Note that within TFT mechanisms and FairTorrent, making up a deficit can have two possible meanings: (1) the debtor node has the content that is sought by the creditor node and will use its bandwidth to upload such content when requested or (2) the debtor node does not have the content that is sought by the creditor node but will use its bandwidth to help upload part of the content obtained from other peers. The criticisms of TFT introduced herein remain valid under both definitions.

6. FairTorrent and all TFT mechanisms are based on the erroneous and implicit assumption that the series of downloads and uploads within a file sharing system occur over one long continuous period of time. On the contrary, for each peer and for all possible groups of peers in a system, the downloads/uploads occur in a relatively short period (minutes or hours) and are not continuous and there are gaps when there is no activity and/or when some nodes are switched off.

6.1.3 Conditions under which FairTorrent and All Tit-for-Tat Mechanisms May Work

FairTorrent and all TFT mechanisms may work if *all* the following conditions exist simultaneously during each search-and-transmission session *t*:

1. The greater of the average or median of the distances between each pair of connected nodes is below a certain threshold distance (λ_1); and the greater of the average or median of the distances between each pair of unconnected nodes is below a certain threshold distance (λ_2); and the greater of the average or median of the distances between each pair of unconnected node and connected node is below a certain threshold distance (λ_3).

2. The cost of bandwidth ($\mathcal{b}_1$) required to transmit content over λ_1 remains relatively constant and is the same around all parts of the network at all times, and the cost of bandwidth ($\mathcal{b}_3$) required to transmit content over the distance λ_3 remains relatively constant and is the same around all parts of the network at all times.

3. $\mathcal{b}_1 < \mathcal{b}_3$ in either all parts of the network or at least in q% of the network—where q% is the minimum percentage of the geographic spread of nodes in the network that is required to maintain the cost-advantage and constant-cost of transmitting bandwidth over λ_1.

4. $\lambda_1 < \lambda_3 < \lambda_2$ in either all parts of the network or at least in q% of the network.
5. The rate of change of λ_1 with respect to λ_2 is either constant or is less than 1—that is, $d(\lambda_1)/d(\lambda_2) < 1$.
6. $d(\mathcal{C}_1)/d(\lambda_1) < \text{Max}[d(\mathcal{C}_3)/d(\lambda_3), 1]$.
7. The probability of establishing a link/connection between an unconnected node and a connected node (p3) is less than the probability of establishing an active upload/download link/connection between any two connected nodes (p1)—these probabilities also include the truthfulness of each node and the cost of verification of each node's disclosures.
8. The aggregate net upload/download volume is balanced (near-zero)—that is, if the individual net upload/download volumes for more than a majority of *active* nodes is negative (i.e., more downloads than uploads for each such node), then a majority of such nodes will owe deficits that may never be fulfilled and then FairTorrent (or any TFT mechanism) will be ineffective. Similarly, if the net upload/download volumes for more than a simple majority of nodes is positive (i.e., more uploads than downloads for each such node), then a majority of nodes will have (be owed) deficits, which if not fulfilled in the short run or long run will render FairTorrent (or any TFT mechanism) ineffective.
9. If for the majority of search-and-transmission sessions in any time interval (t), more than a majority of *active* nodes are primarily downloading, then such majority of notes will owe deficits to a minority. If those deficits are never fulfilled, then FairTorrent (or any TFT mechanism) will be ineffective.
10. All nodes have the same/similar bandwidth capacity and have the same relative per-unit nonmonetary valuation and monetary valuation of bandwidth (which is almost never the case because members typically have different ISP service plans than provide different amounts of bandwidth, e.g., a node that has excessive bandwidth capacity will have a relatively lower valuation of bandwidth than another node that has lower volumes of bandwidth).

6.2 Inequality in Networks

Within the context of networks and TFT mechanisms, the concepts of inequality and fairness are related because they both deal with allocations to/from nodes, deviations, and coalition formation.

6.2.1 A Critique of Kets et al. (2011) and Lorenz Dominance

The existence and feasibility of the new classes of games introduced in this chapter implies that the theories and conclusions in Kets et al. (2011) are wrong. Kets et al. (2011) found the following. First, if players can jointly deviate only if they form a clique in the network, then the degree of inequality that can be sustained depends on the cardinality of the maximum independent set. Second, for bipartite networks, the size of the maximum independent set fully characterizes the degree of inequality that can be sustained. Third, this result extends partially to general networks and to the case in which a group of players can deviate jointly if they are all sufficiently close to each other in the network. Fourth, there is a link between extremal inequality on a network and a natural measure of the sparseness of a network (the size of its maximum independent set)—and this connection is especially strong in the case of bipartite networks, which have unique extremal distributions and can be completely ordered. Fifth, bipartite networks with larger maximum independent sets can sustain greater levels of extremal inequality. Sixth, for general networks with arbitrary clique sizes, for any two networks, extremal inequality cannot be greater in the one with the smaller maximum independent set. However, the Kets et al. (2011) findings and conclusions are error because of the following reasons.

Kets et al. (2011) did not distinguish among intentional/knowing deviations and unintentional deviations and involuntary deviations and also did not distinguish among intentional/knowing coalitions and unintentional coalitions and involuntary coalitions. In many P2P networks, the deviations and the formation of new coalitions (for uploads or downloads) are automatically determined by the software program and are thus involuntary.

In many instances, joint deviation or compact-sequential deviation in a network implies the existence of a coalition.

The Kets et al. (2011) notions and definitions of *inequality* are wrong for the following reasons. First, the Kets et al. (2011) *inequality* does not address psychological benefits/disutility, altruism, temporal discounting in valuation, information asymmetry and differences in knowledge of coalition/clique members. Second, the Kets et al. (2011) concept of *inequality* is inaccurate unless the coalition members reveal their true preferences and valuations (of the benefits gained or to be gained from both joint deviation and coalition formation) to other coalition members. Third, a typical coalition member requires a certain minimum amount of benefit/allocation or incentive (the *minimum benefit*) within a specific time frame in order to agree to intentionally deviate and/or to form a coalition. This *minimum benefit* may also be sufficient for the member to condone specific levels of inequality up to some limits without deviating. Thus, contrary to the existing literature, inequality can be relative (inequality is perceived and measured primarily with respect to other members' allocations) and dynamic (i.e., even with allocations of fixed amounts to the network member, perceived inequality changes as the members' valuations, preferences, altruism, greed, and regret change) rather than absolute. Fourth, an inequality is more likely to exist only if all coalition or clique members have the same or similar discount rates and valuation criteria. Fifth, members that benefit from inequality in a distribution are assumed to have the same votes or influence as members that suffer from inequality in the distribution. Sixth, disclosed or undisclosed side payments between members can be used to modify actual or perceived inequality in each distribution (the existence or possibility of side payments can drastically alter the rate of deviations and coalition formation).

If achievement of the *minimum benefit* is dependent on *both* the formation of the coalition/clique and the joint deviation from actual/perceived equilibrium, then the larger the *independent set*, the lower the probability of achieving the *minimum benefit*—and the independent set is irrelevant if sparseness of the network is not directly proportional to physical proximity of the nodes; and if achievement of this minimum benefit is dependent on only joint deviation but not coalition formation, then the larger the independent set, the lower the probability of their being individual or joint knowledge of existence of an inequality, and the less relevant the inequality becomes.

The sparseness of a network cannot be measured by the size of its maximum *independent set*—because the independent set completely ignores physical proximity, and connectedness differs from physical proximity; physical proximity differs from the actual length of the connection in both wireless and physical networks (due to physical obstructions, weakness of signals, etc.); and the connections between any two nodes may be temporary or even instantaneous.

Within the context of inequality in allocations within cliques/coalitions, *Lorenz Dominance* and *extremal distributions* are completely irrelevant for the following reasons. There can be only one *best* allocation/*distribution* for each clique or coalition. Without the use of the median or the average, the ascending/descending ordering of allocations within each distribution is irrelevant to the issue of inequality in networks—because what matters is the absolute differences among the allocations (maximum and minimum) in each distribution. *Lorenz Dominance* does not address the issue of whether the pairs of distributions are statistically related—that is, whether the occurrence of x is wholly or partly dependent on y and vice versa, or whether choosing x will result in future imposition of y, or choice between y and another distribution. *Lorenz Dominance* implicitly and erroneously assumes that nodes/members in each distribution have equal and complete knowledge about each other's allocations—in reality, members of cliques/coalitions often do not have the opportunity to compare alternative allocations or allocations of other members and often do not know the final allocations until both coalition formation and joint deviation occur. The sequence of occurrence of deviation, joint deviation, and coalition formation affects the validity of allocations in *Lorenz Dominance* and the usefulness of the concept of extremal distributions. *Lorenz Dominance* does not address the possibility or existence of side payments—which can alter the probabilities of deviation and coalition formation. *Lorenz Dominance* may become applicable only if pairs of alternative allocations (distributions) remain constant throughout coalition formation and joint deviation and if the distributions are revealed to clique members (or coalition members) during these distinct stages. *Lorenz Dominance* is applicable only if clique/coalition members value information about the pairs of distributions in the same way and in the same amounts and use such information to make decisions. *Lorenz Dominance* deals with the total sums of benefits allocated in each distribution, and not to the magnitude of the absolute or relative inequality within each *distribution*, where basic inequality is defined within the context of differences in allocations within a given distribution—thus, the *Lorenz Dominance* and *extremal distributions* can significantly distort inequality within a distribution, and for any two distributions that have the same sum total, the magnitude of the inequality within each distribution can vary drastically.

The cardinality of pairs of distributions is also irrelevant because of the following reasons. The relationship between any two distributions and the existence of one as a function of the other may not affect the choice patterns of members/nodes. Second, in the context of inequality, the number of nodes/members in each distribution may not be relevant if such members/nodes have heterogeneous preferences and criteria.

The constraint that players/members *cannot divide more than they produce* (Equation 3.2 in Kets et al. (2011)) is unrealistic because one of the key features of a P2P network is that the system takes advantages of resources and capabilities of all nodes, such that players both individually and as a group can gain more than they *produce*. Equation 3.1 (in Kets et al., 2011) does not consider the differences in valuations of allocations by members; or altruism, regret, members' need for deferral of losses/gains; and the differences between individual utility and group utility—that is, a member may be willing to accept a lower allocation in one distribution (x) compared to another distribution (y), in order to facilitate coalition formation or joint deviation, where x > y, etc. Moreover, Equations 3.1 and 3.2 in Kets et al. (2011) erroneously assume that coalition formation or joint deviation occurs simultaneously and that the sequence of their occurrence does not matter.

Lorenz Dominance measures only inequality between two distinct distributions and in only two dimensions but does not measure the nature of inequality within a distribution, and in the context of human/nonhuman biases and or human emotions.

6.3 Some Nontechnical Pricing-Only Solutions to the Free Rider Problem

Given the foregoing issues about free riding, some nontechnical pricing-only solutions to the free rider problem are described as follows.

6.3.1 Solutions for Pay-per-Download Pricing Systems in P2P Networks

The following recommendations should be read in the context of the aforementioned conjecture that free riding can be beneficial in some circumstances. In legal P2P networks that use pay-per-download pricing, the sponsor/distributor can completely eliminate or reduce free riding by using the following pricing methods:

1. Charge free riders higher prices (a *bandwidth premium*) for each download—*personalize* prices based on the system-wide costs of free riding to the system during time *t*.
2. Identify and exclude (full or partial exclusion) members/nodes who are known as free riders.
3. Pay cash and noncash incentives to members who upload more than average volumes of digital content and whose content get downloaded more than the average.
4. Cap the number of downloads per period for known/classified free riders.
5. Charge free riders higher prices (a *bandwidth premium*) for each download that occurs after a set threshold number of downloads in each billing period.
6. Implement bundled-pricing wherein prices are based on blocks of downloaded content and the per-unit prices increase as download volume increases—that is, a block of 5 units costs $10, and blocks of 10, 20, and 50 units cost $13, $54, and $140, respectively.
7. Increase the per-unit prices for the most popular (top 20th percentile) units of content.
8. Charge the free rider a bandwidth premium when it downloads content that is not a member of a *Designated–A pair*. *Designated–A pairs* are any two different units of content that are not popular (are not sought or downloaded by at least a specific percentage of nodes) and/or require low bandwidth (and are usually downloaded around the same time or may be complementary).
9. Charge the free rider a bandwidth premium only when its net upload/download volume is negative (when its downloads exceed its uploads with respect to the same units of content during a specified time period).
10. Implement a prioritization scheme wherein after the free rider exceeds a threshold number of downloads per period, known free rider download requests are treated as second-priority or third-priority traffic and are deferred to periods of low traffic and are fulfilled in whole or part by only nodes that have excess bandwidth capacity and/or low valuation for bandwidth.
11. Implement a prioritization scheme wherein non-free rider nodes are given incentives (e.g., reduced prices) to defer their downloads to low-traffic periods, and such requests will be fulfilled first by free rider nodes and then by nodes that have low valuation for bandwidth (i.e., high bandwidth capacity).
12. Identify *valuable free riders* and allow them to continue participating in the network (based on their nonmonetary contributions, *centrality*, and other considerations) and create conditions that foster favorable conditions for more valuable free riders.
13. Provide incentives for free riders to help improve the efficiency of networks.

6.3.2 Solutions for Flat-Fee Subscription Pricing in P2P Networks

In legal P2P networks that use flat-fee subscription pricing, the sponsor/distributor can completely eliminate or reduce free riding by the following pricing methods, which implemented in the context of the aforementioned conjecture that free riding can be beneficial in some circumstances:

1. Set access prices in order to reduce the negative effects of free riders (i.e., the distributor/sponsor can charge known or suspected free riders more money for monthly/weekly subscriptions).
2. In addition to the periodic subscription fee, charge members an additional fee on a pay-per-download basis wherein the prices will reflect free riding activities (i.e., free riders will pay higher prices for each download above a periodic maximum, and such incremental fess will be in the form of *bandwidth premiums*).
3. Identify and exclude members/nodes who are known free riders.
4. Limit the number of downloads per node/member per subscription period.
5. Pay cash and/or noncash incentives to members who upload more than average volumes of digital content and whose content get downloaded more than the average.
6. Increase the periodic subscription fees in towns/cities where free riding activity is high.
7. Designate the free rider node as a major *source node* so that a greater-than-average number of files will be downloaded or *sent* from the free rider's node, which will cost the node some bandwidth.
8. Implement a prioritization scheme wherein after the free rider exceeds a threshold number of downloads per period, known free rider download requests are treated as second-priority or third-priority traffic and are deferred to periods of low traffic and are fulfilled in whole or part by only nodes that have excess bandwidth capacity and/or low valuation for bandwidth.
9. Implement a prioritization scheme wherein non-free rider nodes are given incentives (e.g., reduced prices, bonuses, free content) to defer their downloads to low-traffic periods, and such requests will be fulfilled first by free rider nodes and then by nodes that have comparatively low valuation for bandwidth (i.e., high bandwidth capacity). Note that various authors have developed reputation-based systems.

6.4 Conclusion

The *free rider problem* and *inequality* in networks are central elements of the content distributor's challenge of minimizing illegal file sharing and maximizing both profits and brand equity. Thus, customer experience in legal P2P networks and firm profitability can be vastly improved by either eliminating free riders, fostering *valuable free riders*, or providing incentives for free riders to help improve the efficiency of networks. TFT mechanisms and *Lorenz Dominance* are grossly inefficient. The principles derived in this chapter are also applicable to other types of networks such as social networks and electricity distribution networks.

Chapter 7

Pricing Digital Content: The Marginal Cost and Open-Access Controversies*

The marginal cost and open-access controversies have had substantial effects on the debate about the pricing of digital content. Unfortunately, all existing studies of pricing of digital content have not explored the full ramifications of marginal costs and open access. Contrary to some *open-access* theories in the literature, copyright law is necessary—for incentives, for trade (transfer, pledging, sale, documentation) in intellectual property (IP) rights, and to preserve social order (to reduce crime, breaches of contracts, and torts). This chapter introduces new elements of marginal cost analysis in the pricing of digital content, illustrates how the present mispricing of digital content contributes to illegal online file sharing (IOF), and illustrates how the various elements of marginal cost analysis can be used to allocate resources for enforcement of IP rights.

7.1 Existing Literature

The literature on net neutrality and the marginal costs of digital content is significant and burgeoned during 2002–2010[1] and includes the following: Bhargava and Choudhary (2008), Jin and Kato (2007), and other articles.[2] Krämer et al. (2013), Bauer and Obar (2014), and Cerf et al. (2014) discussed net neutrality. The omissions in the existing literature include the following:

1. An accurate analysis of the economics and cost structure of digital content.
2. Accurate valuation of digital content within the context of marginal costs and the existing legal framework for IP rights.

---

* An earlier version of this chapter was published by the author as an article cited as: Nwogugu, M. (2008), "Pricing digital content: The marginal cost and open access controversies," *Computer & Telecommunications Law Review* (2008; Issue #6).

3. Changes in marginal costs as volume, time, spatial coverage as distribution costs change, and the many elements of the content owner/distributor's marginal costs.
4. The elements of the consumer's marginal costs of legally or illegally purchasing digital content, or participating in legal or IOF.
5. The economic effects of copyright laws and net neutrality on maintenance of social order (reduction of crime, torts, and breaches of contract).

However, the marginal cost controversy and the open-access debate are better understood and developed within the context of network games and contagion. Bilò et al. (2010) and Gabarró et al. (2011) developed various types of network games. Cao and Yang (2014), Fazli et al. (2014), Melnik et al. (2013), and Kempe et al. (2013) analyzed influence and contagion in networks. Georgiou et al. (2014), Hegde et al. (2015), and Fiat and Saia (2007) analyzed exchanges, censorship, and interactions in networks.

7.2 Net Neutrality

Network neutrality (net neutrality) has remained a contentious issue that many governments (including the U.S. Congress, the U.S. FCC, and the U.S. Justice Department) have been analyzing. Although large Internet service providers (ISPs) like Comcast and Verizon had argued against such a reclassification, on or around February 26, 2015, the U.S. Federal Communications Commission approved new network neutrality rules under which broadband services will be treated like traditional phone services under Title II (which will also restrict the FCC from imposing rate regulation, tariffs, or limits on bundling). On net neutrality, see Yoo (Fall 2005), Spangler (March 4, 2015),[3] and Johnson (Variety) (February 26, 2015).[4]

Many different proposed laws on network neutrality have been introduced in the U.S. Congress and various countries during 2005–2015.[5] Cheng et al. (2011), Choi and Kim (2010), Hogendorn (2007), Economides and Tag (2012), Economides (2008), Economides and Hermalin (2012), and Musacchio et al. (2009) analyzed Internet access pricing within the context of net neutrality and the reasons for and against net neutrality. Ewing (2003) also discussed net neutrality. However, there seem to be common fallacies and errors among these articles, some of which are as follows:

1. Most of the theories and models completely omitted any analysis of bandwidth markets without which such studies are meaningless. There is now an active market in bandwidth which affects routing algorithms and peering agreements.
2. Most of the analysis omits the relative costs of building traditional physical networks versus the cost of mobile networks.
3. Most of the theories and analysis in these articles omit the feasibility of defection by ISPs solely due to customer tastes.
4. Within the context of two-sided markets (i.e., Economides 2008; Hagiu 2009; Musacchio et al. 2009; Weyl 2010; Economides and Tag 2012; and Economides and Hermalin 2012), most of the theories in these articles are wrong.

On alternative approaches to network access pricing, see Gupta and Zhang (2008), Andersen (2005), Cao et al. (2002), Gupta et al. (2006), Kodialam and Venkateswaran (2003), and Chen and Savage (2011).

7.2.1 The Yoon (2002) Study

The critique of Yoon (2002) (also stated in Chapter 3) is repeated here. Yoon (2002) is important because it tried to analyze the optimal level of copyright protection; and also attempted to use game theory to model the information producer's alternatives. However, Yoon (2002) introduced several wrong contentions and contradictions, some of which are described as follows.

Yoon (2002) did not define an optimal level of copyright protection. Contrary to Yoon (2002), increasing copyright protection does not decrease social welfare by limiting the unauthorized use of the works by consumers. The effect of copyright protection is a function of the utility/disutility the consumer gains from consumption of the works (i.e., the music may be demotivating or irritating), the associated opportunity costs (the works may be outdated, and using them will probably preclude the search for more recent and more valuable information), and the associated use costs (the time spent searching for and consuming the illegal copy may be worth more than the time/cost of obtaining a legal copy).

As defined and used in Yoon (2002), *underutilization* should be analyzed in the context of the incentives to create—the issue of incentives is almost completely omitted. To be meaningful and effective, copyright protection must provide adequate psychological incentives (comfort, reassurance, trust in the legal system, recognition, etc.), physical incentives (money/value for products, safety, recognition, etc.), and monetary/wealth incentives (money, wealth, social capital, reputational capital, and brand equity) for people and companies to produce and market digital content, and otherwise, creativity in the economy will probably decline.

Contrary to Yoon (2002), the *no-protection* state has no basis in economic thought, facts, or logic. Most of the existing literature on the economics of IP state that copyright protection is the very essence of viability of IP and the foundation of incentives to create. In the existing literature, most of the suggested departures from copyright protection apply only to and/or are feasible only for artists/performances that have substantial audiences and name recognition.

The actual relationship between the optimal level of copyright protection and the information producer's marginal cost is different from what was described in Yoon (2002), because both elements are major components of two distinct phases in the information producer's supply chain; and both are typically implemented by very different entities—the production of content (CDs, tapes, DVDs, MP3s, etc.) is typically done by a third-party company (typically distinct from the distributor and the creator), while almost all copyright enforcement is done by government agencies, sometimes at the request of industry participants.

In contrast to theories/models in Yoon (2002: 330), the information producer will still incur some costs even if it decides not to produce any digital content. Such costs are a substantial component of the information producer's costs and include administrative expenses, marketing expenses, and contractual payments to retain content creators.

While consumers can consume digital products in various ways, Yoon (2002) mentions only two options—purchasing the product from the information producer or borrowing it from someone and copying it. Yoon (2002: 331) omits other alternatives such as moneyless exchanges of digital products, online file sharing (legal or illegal), sampling of digital content at physical stores and online, and consumption of very similar products.

Contrary to Yoon (2002: 331), the consumer's cost of reproducing digital content is typically relatively very low, so as to be almost negligible in consumer decision-making. Furthermore, the consumer's cost of reproduction does not always increase with the level of copyright protection because both phenomena are separated by technology, time, distance, observation, and rules. Regardless of the level of copyright protection, a consumer can still use a laptop to copy digital content—but the differences in distance (consumer's location vs. the creator's and the enforcer's location), time, technology (enforcer/government/creator often cannot observe or stop or technologically intervene in the illegal copying process), and rules (the rules of criminal procedure and evidence govern the collection and admissibility of evidence in prosecution of misconduct). The primary effects of most existing copyright laws are ex-post deterrence, a fear of consequences of infringement, and anticipation of the pain of post-conduct penalties. Hence, the appropriate characterization of the relationships is more likely to be $-\infty < \partial z/\partial y < 1$. Furthermore, Proposition-2 in Yoon (2002: 334) is wrong because in most cases, the consumer's reproduction costs are much lower than the sale price. Consumers have access to friends/family members who own equipment that can be used in reproducing digital content. Yoon (2002) erroneously concludes that consumers do not have any incentives to reproduce content because the price of the original content can be set low enough—this contention is wrong because the Yoon (2002) characterization of sets is wrong and erroneously assumes linear relationships among w, v, z, time, and ά.

Yoon (2002) does not define social welfare (SW) adequately, and contrary to assumptions in Yoon (2002), social welfare (SW) does not have a linear relationship with w, z, or v. Hence, Proposition-6 (Yoon [2002: 340]) is wrong.

The rate of substitution between the copy and the original digital content can be negative or positive depending on the type of content (videos, news, books vs. music), the use value, etc. Hence, contrary to Yoon (2002: 331), the consumer can derive greater utility from consuming the copy rather than from consuming the original, particularly where (1) the use value of information in the original content and the copy are the same (i.e., digital academic books), (2) the search costs for obtaining the original and the attendant use costs exceed those of the copy, (3) ancillary services such as technical support are not relevant, and (4) the consumer is skilled in technology and can do the same quality of work as the distributor/producer's customer service staff.

Contrary to Yoon (2002), the production–consumption problem is a five-stage game:

1. The producer identifies talent and/or does market research.
2. The producer contracts for creation of content or creates content.
3. The producer develops a distribution system and channels.
4. The producer reproduces the digital content in files, CDs, tapes, etc.—often by third-party contractors.
5. The producer markets the product, and consumers choose and purchase product.

The game never ends with zero payoffs to all parties—this is in contrast to the Yoon (2002) theories/models. The consumers gain by sampling the content and/or buying it. The contractor or content owner that reproduces and/or distributes the content typically earns profits and/or gains brand equity. The producer that does not sell one copy of the content can gain social capital, reputational capital, and a distribution network in the process. Yoon (2002) completely omits the critical relationships among distribution channels, the mode of consumption, and the quantity consumed.

Yoon (2002) does not (1) distinguish between the proportion of total enforcement efforts that is attributable to the information producer and that which is attributable to government agencies and (2) distinguish between the proportion of total enforcement efforts by the information producer that is feasible compared to what is feasible for the government agencies. Contrary to Yoon (2002: 335), full protection is never a possible option because regulators and the information producer/distributor cannot observe all piracy/misconduct (at any given time-frame), or obtain all resources required for full protection. Furthermore, full protection may not be a viable or desirable option because it interferes with cultural and social patterns of sharing/reciprocity/gifts and personal beliefs (about fairness, equity, etc.)—the resulting enforcement under full protection is very likely to create negative goodwill and boycott of products. Full copyright protection is not yet technologically feasible. Hence, Proposition-5 in Yoon (2002: 338) is wrong because the stated mathematical conditions for distinguishing between *full-protection* and *no-protection* regimes erroneously assume the following: (1) global real-time observability by regulators and the information producer and minimal observation/monitoring costs; (2) minimal transaction costs and enforcement costs; (3) social welfare that equates only to profits of information producers; (4) no substitutability between digital content and other forms of property/entertainment; (5) constant relationship/ratio between the producer's marginal costs on one hand and the producer's development cost (D), profits, etc., on the other hand; (6) that the information producer's monopoly is not a function of distribution channels, perceived product quality and pricing, and depends solely on the level of copyright protection; (7) that the proportions of enforcement costs that are attributable to the producer and the government remains constant over time; (8) that consumer switching costs are not relevant; (9) the decisions about levels of copyright protection do not depend on the deterrence effect and magnitude of possible sanctions; (10) consumers are rational; there is no reciprocity; and there are no fairness-judgment effects; and (11) similar utility scales for digital products and physical products, and for various types of digital content.

In contrast to the theories/models in Yoon (2002: 339), while copyright protection provides significant incentives to innovate/produce, (1) the producer's decision to produce content may not vary with the level of available copyright protection and (2) Yoon (2002) argues that the *no-protection* state is a viable alternative and then makes a contradiction by stating that profit (π) is an increasing function of the level of copyright protection (z).

Yoon (2002) completely omitted any analysis of contagion in networks. Fazli et al. (2014), Bei et al. (2011), Melnik et al. (2013), Cao and Yang (2014), Georgiou et al. (2014), Kempe et al. (2013), and Kramer et al. (2015) studied contagion in networks.

Yoon (2002) completely omitted any study of the relationship between optimal copyright protect and the firm's digital-content strategy. Halbheer et al. (2014), Gong et al. (2015), Grewal et al. (2010), Jeong et al. (2012), Kramer et al. (2013), and other articles[6] analyzed various elements of digital strategy.

7.3 Some Economic Effects of Illegal File Sharing

Borkotokey and Sarangi (2011) critiqued the Myerson value, the Position value (for communication games only), and Jackson's flexible network values and stated that these rules do not consider simultaneous multilateral interactions and do not consider the notion of simultaneous multilateral interaction in a network.

Danaher et al. (2010), Clement et al. (2012), Ouellet (2007), Sinha et al. (2010), and Brynjolfsson et al. (2011) reviewed the effects of consumer responses to IOF.

Several authors have documented four specific economic effects (consumer welfare, substitution, loss, and sampling) of consumer participation in IOF,[7] which are described as follows:

1. The *consumer welfare effect*—the downloaded content represents consumption of content for which the consumer is willing to pay a price that is less than the market price but is greater than the marginal cost of distribution.
2. The *substitution effect*—downloaded content substitutes for purchases that the consumer otherwise would have been willing to make at market price.

3. The *sampling effect*—downloading content may eventually lead to the consumer paying for the content at market prices as a result of experiencing the content. Downloading content may increase the artist's/creator's name recognition and brand equity and, hence, lead to future sales. The sampling effect was mentioned in Gopal et al. (2006) and Liebowitz (2005).
4. The *wealth effect*—the downloaded content is consumption of content for which the consumer is never willing to pay the market price or the marginal cost of production because the consumer cannot afford the content.

These four effects will be totally valid *iff all* the following conditions exist:

1. All consumers have the same price sensitivity to digital content.
2. All consumers value the unit of digital content at the same price.
3. All consumers have the same utility for any one specific unit of digital content; and factors such as attachment, affinity for certain types of entertainment/content, differences in perceived value, etc. do not matter.
4. The magnitude of supply of digital content has minimal effect on price sensitivity of consumers.
5. All sampling results in subsequent purchases of digital content.

7.3.1 A New Definition of the Sampling Effect

As described in the literature, the *sampling effect* is not entirely accurate and refers only to the increase in sales revenues and sales volume that is attributable to sampling. A more complete definition of the *sampling effect* consists of the following:

1. The *loss in sales revenues* (not sales volume, because sampling is often combined with discounts, promotions, and free giveaways) that is solely attributable to allowing consumers to sample digital content. Sampling loss occurs when consumer curiosity is satisfied by sampling, and the consumer does not purchase digital content, that he/she would have otherwise purchased.
2. The *gain in sales revenues* (not sales volume, because sampling is often combined with discounts, promotions, and free giveaways) that is solely attributable to allowing consumers to sample digital content. Sampling gain occurs when consumer curiosity is increased by sampling of digital content, and the consumer purchases the unit of digital content because of the sampling.
3. The lack of change in *sales revenues* (not sales volume, because sampling is often combined with discounts, promotions, and free giveaways) that is solely attributable to allowing consumers to sample digital content. A *sampling-neutral* consumer is not affected (is indifferent) after sampling digital content.

Chapter 2 of this book introduces other different economic psychology effects that cause or are results of consumer participation in IOF networks including perceived unfairness of prices—wherein the consumer is never willing to pay any price for downloaded content because the consumer believes that the content is overpriced (relative to the marginal cost of production). However, all these economic effects have not been fully incorporated into the pricing of digital content.

7.4 The Marginal Cost Controversy

Within the context of reduction of IOF and the production, pricing, and distribution of digital content, the marginal cost controversy is very relevant because unlike many industries, (1) the marginal cost of producing a unit of digital content is relatively very low compared to the average cost of production; (2) the marginal cost of distributing/selling a unit of digital content is also relatively very low compared to the average cost of distribution/selling; (3) most digital content are leisure goods and also *impulse goods*; (4) consumers are more price sensitive to digital content compared to other products; (5) digital content is an *experience* good whose value is not fully known until the consumer fully experiences the product—and pricing the product above average cost creates the risk of reduced future propensity to buy digital content; (6) consumers know that the costs of reproducing digital content are relatively low and hence their propensity to participate in IOF is a function of their perceptions of the distributor's marginal costs versus its average cost per unit; (7) the relationship between average cost and marginal cost of producing and distributing digital content is unusual; and (8) marginal cost analysis aligns content pricing with the distributor's strategies and opportunity set.

This rare cost structure has significant implications for product pricing, IOF (online and offline), copyright regulation, and the choice of distribution channels. Most of the economic psychology effects that cause or result in IOF, which were introduced in Chapter 2 in this book, are affected by the (consumer's and distributor's) marginal costs that are inherent in the production and distribution of digital content.

Furthermore, marginal cost analysis is a critical element of the efforts to reduce IOF because (1) marginal cost analysis can help determine where and when to allocate resources for enforcement, monitoring efforts, and digital rights management systems (DRMSs); (2) consumers' propensity to participate in IOF is a function of their perceptions of the distributor's marginal costs versus its average cost per unit; and (3) marginal cost analysis can help determine the best distribution channels given specific IP laws and enforcement costs and monitoring costs.

Within the context of digital content, the marginal cost controversy has been addressed primarily and almost exclusively from the perspective of the marginal cost of producing one unit of digital content—as illustrated in the articles cited earlier (existing literature) and Karp (1996), Khouja et al. (2007), King and Lampe (2003), Khouja and Smith (2007), and Boldrin and Levine (2005). Hence, most analysis about costs of and pricing of digital content have been insufficient and inaccurate. There are several aspects of marginal costs within the realm of pricing of digital content, which are explained as follows.

This section summarily introduces new elements of marginal cost analysis (in the pricing of digital content), which can be used for the allocation of resources for the enforcement of IP rights by both government agencies and companies in industry (either individually or by combination of efforts) and for the pricing of digital content in order to reduce IOF. The new elements are as follows: (1) the marginal cost of digital product substitution (MCDPS); (2) the marginal cost of cross product substitution (MCCPS); (3) the marginal cost of enforcement of IP laws (MCEIP); (4) the marginal cost of Internet consumer search (MCICS); (5) the marginal cost of physical consumer search (MCPCS); (6) the marginal costs of time substitution (MCTS); (7) the marginal cost of illegal diffusion (MCID); and (8) the marginal cost of channel choice (MCCC). In many countries, the nature and success of enforcement of laws, and the selection of disputes and offences for prosecution/litigation, and the actual/perceived credibility of enforcement threats often depend on the perceived affordability of enforcement costs.

7.4.1 Marginal Cost of Producing One Unit of Digital Content

In the realm of digital content, the average cost of production (AC_p) will always exceed the marginal cost of production (MC_p), primarily because (1) AC_p and MC_p decline as the unit volume (V) increases ($\partial MC_p/\partial V < 0$; $\partial AC_p/\partial V < 0$) and (2) because $\partial MC_p/\partial V$ is almost always greater than $\partial AC_p/\partial V$, (3) MC_p is a subset of AC_p and the cost of reproducing one more unit of digital content is relatively very low primarily due to technology. The marginal cost is the direct cost of producing one unit of digital content. MC_p is highly dependent on skill/knowledge, access to marketing channels, manufacturing/production systems, regulatory costs (attorneys, filing fees, etc.), type of media used, and associated bandwidth costs.

7.4.2 The Rights Holder's/Distributor's Marginal Cost of Distributing/Selling One Unit

In the realm of digital content, the average cost of distribution (AC_d) will usually exceed the marginal cost of distribution (MC_d), primarily because (1) AC_d and MC_d generally decline as the unit volume (V) increases ($\partial MC_d/\partial V < 0$; $\partial AC_d/\partial V < 0$), but will tend to increase as time progresses and as spatial coverage increases ($\partial^2 MC_d/\partial V \partial t > 0$ and $\partial^2 AC_d/\partial V \partial t > 0$); ($\partial^2 MC_d/\partial V \partial S > 0$ and $\partial^2 AC_d/\partial V \partial S > 0$, where S is the spatial coverage of distributor's marketing efforts) and (2) because $\partial MC_d/\partial V$ is almost always greater than $\partial AC_d/\partial V$, (3) MC_d is a subset of AC_d. The marginal cost is the direct cost of producing and selling one unit of digital content. Marginal cost is highly dependent on reputation, network effects, access to marketing channels, manufacturing/production systems, storage costs and database costs, regulatory costs—attorneys, filing fees, etc., distribution channel, and type of medial file used and associated bandwidth costs.

Most articles in the literature do not distinguish between the MC_p and the MC_d, which can behave differently as unit volume, time, and spatial coverage change, depending on the distribution channel (Internet vs. physical stores; P2P vs. client–server systems), media (DVDs vs. CDs vs. flash drives vs. various types of media files), type of content (news, educational material, music, movies, entertainment, etc.), and bandwidth requirements. In the context of digital content, pure marginal cost pricing may not be feasible because the total pre-reproduction cost of producing digital content is typically substantial (time, financing costs, intangibles, and money) and pure marginal cost pricing will not result in adequate cost recovery over any time horizon or spatial coverage. Also, for most types of digital content, the consumer's marginal utility from consuming one unit of digital content (MU) declines over time (t), such that $\partial MU/\partial t < 1$ and $\partial^2 MU/\partial t^2 < 0$. Hence, to maintain the same sales volume over time, the content owner/distributor must spend more money on advertising and promotions.

7.4.3 The Consumer's Marginal Cost of Digital Product Substitution (MCDPS)

The consumer's MCDPS refers to the consumer's costs of substituting one unit of digital content with another unit of digital content. MCDPS is a function of bandwidth costs, access to databases and file sharing networks, time, etc., and applies in both legal and IOF networks. The consumer's marginal cost of products substitution is a significant determinant of his/her propensity to seek participation in file sharing and to copy files. In the present regime, the cost of bandwidth, broadband availability, the cost of processing power, and consumer's time are the major elements of the marginal cost of substitution. The consumers' *propensity to substitute* one specific unit of digital content for another and his/her marginal cost of substitution have a substantial impact on profitability of content owners and network effects. The consumers' *propensity to substitute* affects the content owner's marginal cost because *propensity to substitute* determines whether the content owner will incur bandwidth costs, content replication costs, storage costs, and encryption costs when the consumer does substitute.

7.4.4 The Consumer's Marginal Cost of Cross Product Substitution (MCCPS)

The consumer's MCCPS refers to the consumer's costs of substituting one unit of *digital* content with another unit of *physical* content. The MCCPS is a significant determinant of the consumer's propensity to participate in file sharing and infringe on IP rights. In the present regime, the cost of bandwidth, broadband availability, the cost of computer processing power, access to databases and file sharing networks, transportation costs, price of CDs, value of time, etc., are the major elements of the marginal cost of substitution. The MCCPS has a substantial impact on profitability of content owners and network effects. The MCCPS affects the content owner's marginal cost because *propensity to substitute* determines the content owners choice of channel and also determines whether the content owner will incur bandwidth costs, certain content replication costs, storage costs, and encryption costs when the consumer does substitute. MCCPS also determines the content owner's profit margins and future channel selection strategies (margins vary dramatically across various distribution channels). Kannan et al. (2009: 7) found that there were some customers who would switch from the print form to the PDF form even if it were priced at 110% of the print price—this article states in part:

> …These were customers who had much higher preference for the PDF form as compared to the print form and were willing to pay higher prices than prevailing print prices for obtaining the PDF form. That is why we see in Table 1 that even with PDF form at 100% and 110% of the print price, the online publisher would have still come out ahead in terms of overall revenue. The optimal pricing policy was, obviously, to price PDF forms at 75% of the print book prices. Going from 75% to 50% made the cannibalization impact much higher than the market expansion effect and as a result the impact swings from positive net of approximately one million dollars to a negative net of one million dollars….

7.4.5 The Content Owner's/Rights Holder's Marginal Cost of Enforcement of IP Laws (MCEIP)

The content owner's/rights holder's MCEIP includes attorney's fees, monitoring costs (liaising with ISPs and networks), court costs, etc. Ramello and Silva (2007) discussed some of these costs. Various industry groups and companies have pursued court claims against individuals. It is not clear whether content owners include enforcement costs in their prices of digital content. Under the present IP regime in most jurisdictions, it is very expensive to pursue claims against IP rights infringers because (1) claims have to be filed against individuals and not groups—group liability and mass-litigation processes should be built into statutes and evidentiary standards in order to facilitate enforcement and prosecution, (2) the ISPs may not cooperate in investigations unless there are court orders and subpoenas, (3) IOF is not punished with severe penalties that have sufficient deterrence effects, (4) the proportion of perpetrators that is prosecuted is very low, (5) the court procedures are time consuming, (6) the statutes do not provide for summary low-cost court proceedings for adjudication of infringement cases, (7) the evidentiary standards for proof of infringement remain relatively high in most common law jurisdictions, and (8) recent and continuing technological advancements have made it more difficult to track the source and/or destination of illegally shared files. Thus, given these high MCEIP in most jurisdictions, which is known to and understood by perpetrators, illegal sharing and/or copying of digital content is likely to continue. The MCEIP affects the content owner's marginal cost because (1) it influences the content owner's choice of distribution channel (e.g., the Internet vs. independent stores vs. chain stores); (2) it affects the costs of encryption, monitoring, and systems development; and (3) it affects perceived profitability of various types of digital content and, hence, affects capital budgeting, resource allocation, and decisions pertaining to creative ventures.

7.4.6 The Consumer's Marginal Cost of Internet Consumer Search (MCICS)

The consumer's MCICS is the consumer's marginal cost of searching for a unit of digital content. It consists of mostly the consumer's leisure time (which can have a lower value than the consumer's work time) and the associated opportunity costs (price of bandwidth is typically fixed and minimal).

7.4.7 The Consumer's Marginal Cost of Physical Consumer Search (MCPCS)

The consumer's MCPCS is the consumer's marginal cost of searching for a unit of physical content in the physical domain. It consists of the consumer's leisure time (which can have a lower value than the consumer's work time) and the associated opportunity costs, transportation costs, hardware costs, and software costs (price of bandwidth is typically fixed and minimal).

7.4.8 The Consumer's Marginal Costs of Time Substitution (MCTS)

The consumer's MCTS refers to the value (in monetary amounts) of the time that the consumer spends to search for and download one unit of digital content within the IOF networks. Many consumers that participate in IOF networks do not have adequate funds for purchases or may not want to pay cash for digital content, but have significant leisure time. At the present time, the average costs (per unit of digital content) of computer hardware and bandwidth are relatively low and declining; IOF network members are essentially trading in *currency* that consist of mostly *leisure time*. MCTS affects the rights holder's average costs and marginal costs of production and distribution because (1) MCTS is a major determinant of the consumer's perceived value of content and propensity to purchase digital content, (2) MCTS affects right holder's/distributor's costs—encryption/DRM, systems development costs, etc., (3) MCTS affects content owner's distribution channel decisions, and (4) MCTS determines the consumer's willingness to substitute original physical content for pirated digital copies. MCTS indicates the degree to which scarcity of digital content in P2P networks and illegal downloading websites affects the consumer's propensity to participate in IOF—such scarcity can be achieved by encryption, reducing the download speed for digital content, cooperation by ISPs that will not agree to carry certain watermarked digital content. Hence, digital content should be priced to reduce the consumer's propensity to substitute search time for spending cash to purchase digital content.

7.4.9 The Marginal Cost of Illegal Diffusion (MCID)

MCID is the loss incurred by the content owner/distributor when one consumer illegally downloads one unit of digital content and shares such unit with persons who are not members of the IOF network. MCID affects the rights holder's average costs and marginal costs of production and distribution because (1) MCID is an indicator of network externalities, and the consumer's perceived value of content, and propensity to purchase digital content; (2) MCID affects right holder's/distributor's costs—encryption/DRM, systems development costs, etc.; and (3) MCID affects the content owner's/distributor's channel decisions. MCID can help in (1) determining how liability and punitive sanctions should be apportioned among ISPs, members of P2P networks, and persons who share files but are not members of P2P networks, (2) determining how much an owner/distributor should spend on enforcing IP rights in the physical domain, and (3) determining the effects of size of the P2P on *leakage*.

7.4.10 The Marginal Cost of Channel Choice (MCCC)

MCCC is the per-unit loss (reduced margin) that the content owner incurs, if any, by selling one unit of content through an independent record store or chain stores (CDs, DVD, Flash drives) rather than through the Internet. The MCCC affects the rights holder's or distributor's average costs and marginal cost because (1) it affects right holder's distribution costs (encryption, reproduction costs, marketing costs, etc.) and the prices it charges for products; (2) it affects the rights holder's/distributor's profit margins; (3) it affects content owner's distribution channel decisions and allocation of resources to marketing efforts; (4) MCCC helps in developing pricing strategies for digital content that is sold in both the Internet and physical domains; and (5) MCCC is an indicator of consumer preferences for various channels for different forms of content. Hence, digital content should be priced to reduce the propensity to substitute search time for spending cash to purchase digital content.

7.4.11 Sunk Costs and Valuation of Digital Content

Contrary to assertions in some articles, under no circumstances can piracy increase the value of digital content—see the analysis in Chapters 9 and 10 on valuation of digital content. The value of digital content directly depends on the utility of people/groups that access it. Because consumers derive substantial utility from digital content, differences among content owners/distributors cannot be explained entirely by differences in sunk costs (marketing, distribution networks, overhead costs, advertising, financing costs, etc.), costs of preparing the prototype, etc.

7.5 The Open-Access Controversy

There is an inherent trade-off between open access to digital content on the web, and the regime (and associated incentives) provided by IP laws. The trade-off between the benefits of open access on the Internet and the incentive effects of IP laws depends on the following factors:

- The strategy a firm employs to obtain IP rights—the costs of obtaining IP rights and the terms of such rights will substantially affect benefits of open access versus regulation.
- The type, amount, and efficiency of protection provided by laws, and the associated costs of monitoring and enforcement, will affect the benefits of open access compared to regulation.
- Competitors' actions will affect consumer's perceptions of products and their reactions to prices. If competitors choose a different strategy, the content owner may lose substantial market share and revenues.
- Consumer's economic utilities.
- Available technology.
- To encourage creativity and resourcefulness, content owners must be rewarded in some manner. Thus, pure open-access schemes are inefficient. Open-access initiatives must incorporate some form of private *taxation* (similar to the system for radio broadcasts) to provide incentives for commerce.

While IP laws provide substantial incentives for private individual/group initiative, the key issue is moderating pricing of products to increase accessibility. The incentive effects of IP laws are not limited to the realm of intangible property but affect associated tangible property, lifestyles, family dynamics, regional economies (i.e., Microsoft in Seattle, WA; EDS in Texas, United States; Disney in Florida and California, United States; etc.), firm structure, nature of competition, investment, etc.

Deterrence of crime cannot justify open access to digital content. The objective of IP laws should be to provide profits for creators and to provide an orderly regime for the advancement of innovation. These objectives cannot be achieved under an open-access regime.

7.5.1 Benkler (2002), Ku (2002), and Benkler (2004)

Benkler (2002) completely fails to show how IP laws (mostly copyright laws) affect the business strategies used by producers and distributors of digital content. Benkler (2002) did not anticipate or analyze the implications of the (2004–2006) rulings by the U.S. Supreme Court (as explained in Nwogugu 2006) and Australian Federal Courts on copyright infringement cases, all of which render the analysis in Benkler (2002) meaningless.

Ku (2002) is notable because it supports a previously proposed regime of IP law that essentially eliminates all incentives and reward systems for innovation and enterprise. Contrary to Ku (2002) and Benkler (2004), information in digital content is not a public good. Since there is differentiation in the nature of different units of digital content, in private effort and creativity, and hence inherent value, digital content cannot be considered a public good.

Ku's (2002) main rationales were that (1) the economics of digital technology undercuts prior assumptions about the efficacy of a private property regime for information, a public good; (2) copyright is primarily an argument for protecting content distributors in a world in which middlemen are obsolete, and copyright is no longer needed to encourage distribution because consumers themselves build and fund the distribution channels for digital content; (3) exclusive rights to reproduce and distribute copies provide little, if any, incentive for creation; and (4) that digital technology makes it possible to compensate artists without control. All of Ku's (2002) contentions and theories are invalid.

The existing property rights regimes are suited to digital content but may need modification to improve enforcement and reduce transaction costs, and as described, the key issue is accurate pricing of digital content in order to facilitate access. Contrary to Ku (2002), copyright is not an argument to protect middlemen but a mechanism that ensures reward of content creators, recognition of creative activity, and incentives for innovation, all of which are critical for continued economic activity. Contrary to Ku (2002), copyright is needed to *encourage distribution* even though many of the content creators and rights holders (e.g., large entertainment companies, individual artist's websites) can afford to and do distribute digital content themselves without middlemen (see Bockstedt et al. 2005). The exclusive rights to reproduce and distribute copies are the essence of the incentive system and reward system that are inherent in IP laws—without these legally enforceable rights, the entire value system in property and digital content would dissipate. Copyright is necessary for transfer, sale, and collateralization of digital content. The advent of digital technology does not preclude or eliminate the need for enforceable IP rights—content creators will always demand economic compensation for their products, and furthermore, given the economic valuation of digital content explained in this chapter, content control remains necessary.

Ku (2002) fails to distinguish between the cost of distributing content and (1) value in digital content arising from differentiation, personal effort, and creativity; (2) incentive effects of IP laws—the incentive to engage in economically profitable activities, where such profits are protected by IP laws; (3) value in digital content arising solely by existence of IP laws without regard to the quality of the digital content; and (4) economic utility gained by consumers from consuming digital content and physical content.

7.5.2 Does Piracy/Infringement Substantially Help Content Owners and/or Distributors?

Several studies (such as Von Lohmann [2004], Danay [2005], Barnett [2006], Ghosh [2006], Khong [2006], Campbell and Picciotto [2006], and Yuan [2007]) have suggested that copyright and IP laws are inefficient and/or that piracy/infringement actually helps content owners and/or distributors. However, those articles and theories (and especially Boldrin and Levine [2002, 2005, 2012] and Oberholzer-Gee and Strumpf [2007]) are inaccurate for the following reasons.

1. They are based on the *sampling effect*, which, as described herein, can have positive and negative effects. It is most probable that for any given unit of digital content, *sampling losses* will exceed *sampling gains* because most consumers that sample are price sensitive.
2. Several studies have clearly documented the benefits of copyright and trademark laws and the negative effects of infringement/piracy—those include Picard (2004), Greenhalgh and Rogers (2007), Subirana (2000), Horan et al. (Office of Industries—U.S. International Trade Commission) (October 2005), Gopal et al. (2006), Choi and Perez (2007), DeCastro et al. (2008), and Ouma (2006).
3. Zenter (2006), Michel (2005), Hennig-Thurau et al. (2007), Liebowitz (2007, 2008), and Liebowitz (2005) specifically contradict the results/conclusions of Oberholzer-Gee and Strumpf (2007), Danay (Autumn 2005), Zhang (2003), Netanel (2003), Von Lohmann (2004), and Jaisingh (2007). Like most empirical studies in the literature, the Michel (2005) study is subject to methodological limitations. Gopal et al. (2006) also specifically

contradict the results of Oberholzer-Gee and Strumpf (2007), Danay (Autumn 2005), Zhang (2003), Netanel (2003), Jaisingh (2007), and Von Lohmann (2004) and render these results moot but with the additional findings that (1) sampling and the cost of sampling can affect IOF and sales volume; (2) IOF reduces the *superstar phenomenon* in entertainment, which is a significant element of value of digital content; and (3) the assumed probability distribution of the values of digital content will have a significant effect on sampling, sales volume, and piracy.

4. The proposals and theories introduced in Netanel (2003) (noncommercial use levy) and Von Lohmann (2004) and similar studies are irrational because (1) the proposals are not based on accurate values of digital content (cash value, utility value, and use value); (2) the proposals assume that every consumer values any one unit of digital content in the same way and at the same amount; (3) the proposed compensation to be paid to content owners/distributors may not have a relationship to the values of the digital content; (4) the proposals do not contain any efficient or fair mechanism for allocating fees to content owners/distributors; (5) the proposals do not set forth a viable distinction between *commercial* and *noncommercial* use in the online file sharing context—IOF in P2P networks is a form of sale; (6) the proposals can greatly reduce the incentive to create content—by capping fees paid to content owners/distributors; (7) contrary to Netanel (2003) some enforcement efforts have been successful in reducing IOF; and (8) at best, the noncommercial use levy should be an adjunct to but not a replacement mechanism for traditional sales of digital content and enforcement of IP rights.

5. The main argument in Conner and Rumelt (1991) is that in the presence of network externalities, the value a user derives from digital content depends on the size of the audience (users) and, hence, the utility of the software increases with piracy (i.e., the utility of consumption of digital content increases with the total number of individuals using it including those using pirated copies). This proposition is not always true and does not justify acceptance of IOF because (1) increasing the *group experience* and/or ordinary utility of users should not be done at the expense of content owners/distributors, (2) piracy reduces the incentive to create, (3) the proposition may be relevant only within the context of complementary goods, (4) Conner and Rumelt's (1991) results are not generalizable to other forms of digital content (movies, news, educational materials, and some types of music), and (5) with network effects, a smaller user base does not always result in lower value of digital content, where the sale of complementary goods and/or ancillary services can provide revenues.

6. In the realm of IOF, consumer tastes, technologies, and enforcement patterns change—and hence the results of Oberholzer-Gee and Strumpf (2007) (and many similar empirical studies) cannot be generalized and are highly specific to the time period during which data were collected, the type of digital content (music vs. movies vs. educational material vs. news), the type of transfer (files vs. streaming), the time intervals between observations, the number of observations, and the country/region from which the data were collected.

7. The Zhang (2003) concept of *social welfare* is inaccurate and misplaced. That losses incurred by content owners/distributors flow to the public do not constitute an increase in social welfare—such a situation will drastically reduce the incentives to innovate and reduce the volume of products.

8. Hennig-Thurau et al. (2007)[8] also stated that the results in Oberholzer-Gee and Strumpf (2007) were wrong.

Deterrence of crime is not a sufficient justification for open access to digital content. The key issue is that the present regime of criminal sanctions for IP infringement in most jurisdictions is not effective. The nature of crime involved in IP infringement is similar to white-collar crime in that it is not life threatening and does not involve any threat of bodily harm, and is mostly economic crime. The key issue is that the negative effects of IP infringement on innovation and enterprise and associated losses far outweighs any societal damages harm that may be caused by the imposition of criminal sanctions for IP infringement (indeed it is unlike that such criminal sanctions will cause any such harm).

The objective of IP laws should be to provide profits for creators and rights holders, to provide recognition for creative effort, to provide adequate incentives for further innovation, and to provide an orderly regime for the transfer, collateralization, exchange, and use of IP rights. These objectives cannot be achieved under an open-access regime—as supported by theories and models in Asvanund et al. (2004)[9] and Sag (2006).[10]

7.6 Conclusion

Marginal cost analysis can help in the enforcement of IP laws and in developing appropriate pricing strategies for digital content within the context of IOF. The open-access controversy is moot, given the many benefits and incentive effects of IP laws, the content owner's/distributor's fixed costs, advances in DRM technology, and different utilities for different individuals and groups.

Notes

1 See network neutrality debate: (a) The *Internet Freedom Preservation Act of 2007* (S.215) was introduced by Sen. Byron Dorgan (D-N.D.) on January 9, 2007 (United States); (b) *H.R.5252* (*109th Congress)—Communications Opportunities Promotion and Enhancement* (COPE) bill (United States); (c) S.2686, the *Communications, Consumers' Choice, and Broadband Deployment Act of 2006* (U.S. Senate); (d) H.R.5273 (109th Congress)—*Network Neutrality Act of 2006* (U.S. Congress); (e) *S.2360* (*109th Congress)—Internet Non-Discrimination Act of 2006* (United States).
See Digital pricing model patent—U.S. Patent 7383207—http://www.freepatentsonline.com/7383207.html.
See Domon (2006).
See Madrigal and LaFrance (April 25, 2014).
See Newman (January 21, 2014)
See Mari (March 26, 2014)
See "As debate over net telephony rages, Govt to re-examine services offered by Skype, Google." *The Hindu Business Line.* 11 February 2013. http://www.thehindubusinessline.com/industry-and-economy/info-tech/as-debate-over-net-telephony-rages-govt-to-reexamine-services-offered-by-skype-google/article4404537.ece.
See "Not just Airtel Zero: Facebook to WhatsApp, everyone has violated Net Neutrality in India." *Indian Express.* 18 April 2015. http://indianexpress.com/article/technology/social/net-neutrality-debate-its-not-just-limited-to-airtel-zero/
See Singh (April 8, 2015).
See Gandhi (April 8, 2015).
See "The Netherlands Passes Net Neutrality Legislation." Electronic Frontier Foundation. May 21, 2012. https://www.eff.org/deeplinks/2012/05/netherlands-passes-net-neutrality-legislation.

See *Letter expressing strong opposition to proposals to classify broadband as a 'Title II' service*, to U.S. congressional leaders and members of the FCC, from representatives of a wide range of technology companies, December 10, 2014. http://www.tiaonline.org/sites/default/files/pages/Internet_ecosystem_letter_FINAL_12.10.14.pdf.

See Staff (February 26, 2015). "FCC Adopts Strong, Sustainable Rules To Protect The Open Internet" (PDF). Federal Communications Commission. http://transition.fcc.gov/Daily_Releases/Daily_Business/2015/db0226/DOC-332260A1.pdf.

See Ruiz and Lohr (February 26, 2015).

2 See Bakos and Brynjolfsson (1999); Duffy (2004); Delgado (2003); Schmidt (2006); Domon (2006); Belleflamme and Picard (2007); Yoon (2002), Singleton (December 2007); Latcovich and Smith (2001); Michel (2005); Hitt and Chen (2005); Wu et al. (2008); and Bhargava and Choudhary (2008).

3 See Spangler (March 4, 2015).

4 See Johnson (Variety) (February 26, 2015) stated in part:

> …The FCC approved robust rules of the road for the Internet on Thursday, a move that supporters believe will prevent conglomerates from consolidating control over the flow of online content, but that critics characterize as a huge regulatory overreach. The FCC's approach is one favored by many public interest groups, Hollywood content creators and a large number of Web companies including Netflix and Twitter: It is reclassifying Internet service as a Title-II telecommunications service, a regulatory designation akin to that of a utility. The move is intended to give the FCC solid authority to impose rules over Internet service. The new rules prohibit ISPs from blocking or throttling content, as well as from collecting payments from content providers for speedier access to their subscribers. The latter has been commonly referred to as the notion that ISPs would eventually create Internet "fast lanes.…

5 See https://en.wikipedia.org/wiki/Net_neutrality—for summaries of net neutrality statutes that were enacted in various countries.

See U.S. Government Printing Office (2006-05-15). Communications Opportunity, Promotion and Enhancement Act of 2006 (H.R. 5252).

6 See Lang et al. (2009); Aron et al. (2006); Cook and Wang (2004).

7 See US Federal Trade Commission (Staff Report) (2005). *Peer-to-Peer FileSharing Technology: Consumer Protection and Competition Issues*. http://www.ftc.gov/reports/p2p05/050623p2prpt.pdf.

8 Hennig-Thurau et al. (2007) stated in part:

> …Oberholzer-Gee and Strumpf (2007) present empirical results that show no negative impact of file sharing on traditional music distribution channels. Over the course of four months, they monitor 1.75 million file downloads on filesharing networks and then match the downloads to U.S. album sales data. Their empirical analysis shows that music file sharing has no significant impact on album sales. Again, however, the generalizability of their findings is somewhat limited because the authors use the 'number of German school kids on vacation' as an instrumental variable for file sharing activity to bypass endogeneity problems caused by the simultaneity of downloading and purchasing activity in their aggregate level data… To summarize, movie industry representatives argue that file sharing serves as a substitute for commercial movie consumption, but no peer-reviewed research has studied this relationship for movies, and the results from music filesharing research are inconclusive and limited by methodological constraints. Moreover, no existing study has surveyed actual consumer decision making on an individual level, and no study has used longitudinal data…

9 Asvanund, Clay, Krishnan, and Smith (2004) stated in part:

> …The services provided over P2P networks have some of the characteristics of public goods… Further, in the absence of free-riding, song replication should scale with network size, creating a situation where the consumption of network resources is non-rivalrous…

There are, however, several notable differences between the content offered in P2P networks and typical public and club goods. First, in public and club goods environments the endowment typically is discrete and fixed (e.g., radio broadcast, swimming pool). In contrast, the endowment of P2P goods is based on the number and character of content shared by users within the community, and thus is relatively continuous and variable. Second, in a typical public or club goods settings, non-contribution is the 'default' choice, whereas typical P2P client programs are designed to contribute (share files) as the default. Turning off contribution requires the P2P user to take action. Strahelivitz (2002) suggests that making contribution the default action of P2P clients substantially decreases free-riding. Third, in typical public and club goods environments, contribution is in the form of monetary outlay and is separate from consumption....

10 Sag (2006) stated in part:

...Both legal and illegal music acquisition result in three types of benefits to individuals: (1) the *functional value* of individual music files (F), (2) the *normative value* of the method of acquisition (N), and (3) the *law-abidingness value* of the method of acquisition (L)... Anecdotal reports suggest that free riding has diminished the attractiveness of peer-to-peer distribution, but exactly how much remains unclear... consumers will continue to buy the industry's products if $(BL - CL) > (BU - CU)$, constrained by $(BL - CL) > 0$. Expanding this inequality to take into account the variables that comprise these costs and benefits results in

$(FL + NL + LL) - (ML + TL + VL + SL) > (FU + NU + LU) - (MU + TU + VU + SU)$.

This can be simplified if we assume that VL (the expected cost of viruses), SL (the expected cost of sanctions) and MU (expected monetary cost) are each equal to zero for the reasons given above. This results in

$(FL + NL + LL) - (ML + TL) > (FU + NU + LU) - (TU + VU + SU)$.

The recording industry's optimal strategy is not to make the left-hand side of this equation dominate for every single potential music consumer. That is an unrealistic objective given the likely variation of individual valuations of functional attributes, money, time and effort, the risk of viruses and legal sanctions...

Chapter 8

New Models of Dominance of Allocations (in Network Games) That Solve Some of the Problems Inherent in Lorenz Dominance, Higher-Order Stochastic Dominance Models and Higher-Order Prospect Theory

Digital piracy is often complicated by anonymous online *coalitions* (that thwart enforcement efforts) and offline/online coordination by digital pirates. Such coordination is often complex and can be intended or unintended and both observable and unobservable. Thus, customer experience and firm profitability can be vastly improved by developing new models of stochastic dominance (SD) in P2P networks. Such SD models incorporate a *prioritization scheme* where the *priority* is defined not only in terms of customers' opportunity costs (waiting time, search costs, etc.) but also in terms of willingness-to-comply with IP laws, prepurchase, and post-purchase regret, customer's relative wealth, and customer's marginal propensity-to-substitute digital products. The new SD models can minimize the firm's production/delivery costs and can also result in lower perceived prices for *high-priority* customers and uniform QoS for all customers, all of which are socially more optimal outcomes when different customers place different values on compliance with IP laws.

This chapter critiques SD models and introduces new models of SD of allocations (in network games) that solve some of the problems inherent in *Lorenz dominance* and other forms of SD. The chapter also critiques cumulative prospect theory and prospect theory (PT) (and by extension higher-order PT).

8.1 Existing Literature

Stochastic dominance (SD) has been analyzed extensively in the literature and in various contexts including decision-making, inequality, choice, and networks. Generally, the same classes of SD models have been applied across various fields. Within the context of social networks, Internet networks, and electricity distribution networks, SD is relevant in the following ways:

1. The allocations (of anything) among nodes in a network
2. The voluntary or involuntary *deviation* of one or more nodes, and the formation of some types of coalitions among nodes
3. The choice of an individual between purchasing legal digital content and joining an illegal file sharing network
4. The choice of an individual between leaving an illegal network and purchasing legal digital content
5. The choices made by network nodes with regard to routing and distribution

Guo (2012) surveyed the general SD literature and summarized the various tests for SD. Guo (2012) compared the SD rules with variance, semivariance, value at risk, the expected shortfall, and the coherent risk measure and found that expected shortfall is consistent with both the SD rules and the coherent risk measure. Guo (2012) also compared the SD linear programs with other portfolio selection models and found that the SD efficient set is inconsistent with the mean-variance efficient set, but the SD efficient set contains the mean-semivariance, the global minimum variance, the global minimum semivariance, and the minimum shortfall efficient sets. Note that Nwogugu (2013) proved that semivariance, variance, and correlation are irrelevant in risk analysis. Guo (2012) also noted that (1) SD rules are consistent with the expected utilities that characterize general investors' preference without any restricted assumptions on return distributions, (2) SD is useful when researchers have limited information about the shapes of investors' utilities, (3) SD takes higher moments into account beyond the first two moments and incorporates more information about empirical cumulative distribution functions (CDFs), and (4) SD serves as a supplement to other portfolio selection models when they fail. Guo (2012) introduced optimal SD rules via the CDF approach (the mathematical approach to define, prove, and develop SD tests), the Neumann–Morgenstern utility approach (more often used in finance to link investors' risk preference with their decision-making), and the quantile approach (or p-approach) (to prove and develop SD tests because the domains of quantiles are constrained in [0,1] and provide a bridge between the SD rules and value-at-risk).

Biswas (2012) analyzed SD and risk aversion. Lamberson (2009) surveyed the SD literature as it pertains to networks. Mellers et al. (1992), Birnbaum (2005b,c), Diederich and Busemeyer (1999), and Post and Kopa (2013) found various violations of *SD*. Birnbaum (2005b) compared five models that predicted violations of first-order SD in risky decision-making. Stein and Pfaffenberger (1987) analyzed problems inherent in SD models. Castellano and Cerqueti (2012) and Gradwohl and Reingold (2010) provided some useful critiques of theories of large-games. Coleman et al. (2007), Pavlov (2005), and Diederich and Busemeyer (1999) analyzed various elements of conflict within the context of decision-making.

Fong et al. (2008) and Eeckhoudt et al. (2009) analyzed *SD* and risk. Baucells and Heukamp (2006) studied *SD* and *cumulative prospect theory* (CPT). Gollier and Muermann (2010) studied choice and beliefs.

Nisgav and Patt-Shamir (2011) analyzed patterns in networks. Blavatskyy (2008) developed stochastic utility theorem. Ogryczak and Ruszczynski (1999) recommended the use of *standard semideviation* (square root of the semivariance) because it makes the mean-risk model consistent with the second degree SD, provided that the trade-off coefficient is bounded by a certain constant. However, the critique of variance and semivariance in Nwogugu (2013) is also applicable to *standard semideviation*. Wu and Nie (2011), Boujelben et al. (2009), and Blavatskyy (2012) analyzed various elements of SD. Loomes et al. (2002) and Birnbaum (2005a) tested models of decision-making. Blavatskyy (2006) analyzed possible violations of the *betweenness* principle.

Troquard et al. (2011), Ågotnes et al. (2009), and Wolter and Wooldridge (2011) studied logic and the aggregation of preferences and judgments in games.

8.1.1 Weaknesses Inherent in Current SD Models and Lorenz Dominance

The existing literature contains many studies of similar *first-order stochastic dominance* (**FSD**) models, *second-order stochastic dominance* (**SSD**) models, *third-order stochastic dominance* (**TSD**) models, and *higher-order stochastic dominance* (**HSD**) models. Davidson (2008) noted that *Lorenz dominance* is just an SSD. Heathcote et al. (2010) studied distribution-free tests of SD for small samples. The main weaknesses and problems inherent in FSD/SSD/TSD/HSD models, in *Lorenz dominance*, and in tests for SD are as follows:

1. Most FSD/SSD/TSD/HSD models and SD tests are based on specific known statistical distributions—and the models do not work when the data/allocations do not fit any distributions.
2. The *orders* of FSD/SSD/TSD/HSD models and *Lorenz dominance* are often defined in terms of *levels* of calculus and statistical measures, rather than in terms of *levels* of human behavior and biases (which are more relevant to and more directly connected to choice/decisions). Human behaviors are often *derivative* in nature, wherein one bias/behavior arises partly or solely from or is ancillary to another behavior/bias. Similarly, human groups are often *derivative* in nature. Bernard (1926a) distinguished *primary groups* from *derivative groups* and gave specific examples of derivative groups in their order of *derivativeness*. Bernard (1926b) distinguished between *primary* and *derivative* attitudes and ideals. Bernard (1936) analyzed conflicts between *primary group attitudes* and *derivative group ideals*. *Hullian Theory* in psychology also distinguishes between *direct* and *derivative* human (individual and group) behaviors. Noussair et al. (2013) explained how *prudence* and *temperance* have been applied to bargaining, rent-seeking, auctions, and savings. While Ebert (2013) noted that prudence or Intemperance do not necessarily arise from risk-loving behavior; Crainich et al. (2013) analyzed third-order and fourth-order risk attitudes and concluded that risk lovers can be both *intemperate* and *prudent*. Nwogugu (2005a,b)[1] specifically noted that agents and decision-makers can be *risk loving* or *risk seeking* if risks and losses can be sold and/or deferred and/or transferred, or if losses have inherent utility (e.g., such as the tax

benefits derived from losses), all of which violate principles of prospect theory (PT) and CPT. The biases and preferences discussed or introduced in Nwogugu (2006) and in Chapters 4, 5 and 15 in Nwogugu (2012) and in Chapter 2 of this book are *higher-order* biases and risk preferences. Bergemann and Morris (2005) discussed higher-order beliefs within the context of mechanism design. Thus, the analysis in Deck and Schlesinger (2014) and Noussair et al. (2013) is not entirely new. Deck and Schlesinger (2014) noted that a significant minority of the global population do not exhibit both risk aversion (a second-order risk preference) and other higher-order risk preferences such as *prudence* (third-order risk preference) and *temperance* (fourth-order risk preference). Deck and Schlesinger (2014) attempted to study fifth-order and sixth-order *attitudes* and risk preferences in a laboratory setting and to show (1) how both risk-averse and risk-loving behaviors can be developed from a basic lottery preference for either combining *good* outcomes with *bad* ones, *or* combining *good with good* or mixing *bad with bad*, respectively; and (2) that this dichotomy is fairly robust at explaining higher-order risk attitudes in the laboratory.

3. Most importantly, *Lorenz dominance* and most FSD/SSD/TSD/HSD models are not directly/ indirectly derived from or related to any of the following four classes of behavioral factors:
    a. *Human feelings*—Such as jealousy, anger, motivation, apathy, empathy, confusion, inertia, relative poverty, happiness, regret, etc.
    b. *Human behaviors*—Such as greed, altruism, regret, risk aversion, risk seeking, shirking, etc.
    c. *Behavioral outcomes*—Such as cooperative/noncooperative behaviors, deviation, formation of coalitions, cognitive deficits.
    d. *Knowledge*—That is, common knowledge, information asymmetry, learning patterns, information-processing capabilities, cognitive deficits, etc.
    e. Individual-to-group, group-to-group, and group-to-individual contagions and behavior transitions.
    f. *primary* vs. *derivative* human behaviors and biases (both for groups and individuals)
4. Most FSD/SSD/TSD/HSD models and tests cannot handle transformations of the allocations/distributions.
5. Most FSD/SSD/TSD/HSD models and tests erroneously assume that each pair of distributions (or each node in each distribution) has the same valuation scale/measure and the same timescale (or time valuation).
6. The SSD/TSD/HSD models that are based on derivatives and derivative functions are wrong because (1) as explained in Chapter 14 in Nwogugu (2012), the fundamental theorems of calculus are wrong, (2) the derivative functions alter/transform the allocations and/or the relationships among the allocations in each distributions and between pairs of distributions, and (3) the derivatives often do not account for time and assume that there are equal valuation scales/measures among different pairs of distributions/choices; the higher-order derivatives do not account for many human biases and behaviors.

8.2 Some New Types of SD in Network Games

8.2.1 Properties of Efficient SD Models

Given the foregoing weaknesses and limitations inherent in *Lorenz dominance* and in SD models in general, this section introduces new types of SD that can be used to measure inequality in networks (and in public choice matters). See Aaberge and Mogstad (February 2010)—which cites

Aaberge (2009), Weymark (1981), and Muliere and Scarsini (1989). The main and necessary characteristics of these new types of dominance are as follows:

1. *Distribution invariance*—The dominance is invariant to the type of distribution within each allocation.
2. *Transformation invariance*—The dominance is invariant to all types of transformations of the allocations within each distribution.
3. *Knowledge sensitive*—The dominance can account for differences in knowledge among members of each distribution.
4. *Utility discriminant*—Some of these types of dominance can distinguish between group utility and individual utility—that is, the members' predecision knowledge of the sum total allocations of two choices x and y (and/or allocations to each individual member) may not affect the decisions of the individual members about choosing between x and y. Hence, x may be chosen over y, where a majority of members get lower allocations in x than in y. These characteristics can account for differences among network members' perceptions of time, cross-sectional choice, inequality, regret, etc.
5. *Attribute elicitation*—Some of these types of dominance can elicit preferences and attributes of members across various dimensions (time, cross-sectional choice, inequality, regret, etc.).
6. *Discounting*—These types of dominance can account for differences in discounting among members.
7. *Sequence neutral*—The sequence of occurrence of individual deviation, joint deviation, and coalition formation does not affect the validity of these types of dominance and also does not affect the nature of each distribution.
8. These types of dominance account for differences between *primary* and various *derivative* behaviors of both individuals and groups.

8.2.2 New SD Models

This section introduces new classes of SD models that can be categorized as HSD models because they incorporate second-order, third-order, and higher-order human behaviors such as irrationality, regret, intertemporal choice, WTAL Nwogugu (2006), and other biases (e.g., some in Chapters 4 and 5 in Nwogugu, 2012).

Definition 8.1 Type-1 Dominance

For any two nonrelated/independent distributions (x and y), and for nodes/individuals in each such distribution (where the nodes are named 1,2,3,4,.........ith node ε m; such that an allocation to node #1 in x is x_1, and an allocation to node #1 in y is y_1; and each allocation to a node may be negative or positive), x is said to be *Type-1 dominant* over y *iff* the following conditions exist:

a) $\sum_{i=n} |x_i - x_a| < \sum_{i=n} |y_i - y_a|$

b) $\sum_{i=n} x_i \geq \sum_{i=n} y_i$

The following condition is referred to as a *Type-1A Dominance* of x over y:

a) $\sum_{i=n} |x_i - \ddot{x}| > \sum_{i=n} |y_i - \ddot{y}|$

b) $\sum_{i=n} x_i \geq \sum_{i=n} y_i$

The following condition is referred to as a *Type-1B Dominance* of x over y:

a) $\sum_{i=n} |x_i - x_m| > \sum_{i=n} |y_i - y_m|$

b) $\sum_{i=n} x_i \geq \sum_{i=n} y_i$

The following condition is referred to as a *Type-1C Dominance* of x over y:

a) $\sum_{i=n} |x_i - x_m| < \sum_{i=n} |y_i - y_m|$

b) $|x_1 - x_a| > |y_1 - y_a|; |x_2 - x_a| > |y_2 - y_a| \ldots |x_n - x_a| > |y_n - y_a|$

The following condition is referred to as a *Type-1D Dominance* of x over y:

a) $\sum_{i=n} |x_i - x_a| > \sum_{i=n} |y_i - y_a|$

b) $|x_1 - x_a| > |y_1 - y_a|; |x_2 - x_a| > |y_2 - y_a| \ldots |x_n - x_a| > |y_n - y_a|$

c) $x_1 \geq y_1, x_2 \geq y_2, \ldots x_n \geq y_n$; (ie. $x \geq y$) for a majority or super-majority of members

where

$\ddot{x}$ is the maximum allocation to any node/member in distribution x

$\ddot{y}$ is the maximum allocation to any node/member in distribution y

x_m is the median of the allocations in distribution x

y_m is the median of the allocations in distribution y

x_a is the average of the allocations in distribution x

y_a is the average of the allocations in distribution y

This class of *Dominance* is applicable in any or all of the following circumstances:

i) The members/nodes are sensitive about the absolute magnitude of allocations.

ii) The ordering of the allocations in each distribution is irrelevant to the decision or to stability.

iii) A majority or super majority of members must choose nondeviation in order to maintain stability.

iv) The members are very concerned about inequality within any distribution and are as equally concerned about their relative allocations between the two distributions (x and y).

v) For all or members, regret, greed, and altruism are bigger decision factors than inequality.

vi) Each member knows the sum-total allocation for each distribution and also knows about allocations to other members.

vii) The occurrence of x and y are mutually exclusive (i.e., if x is chosen, y will never be allocated or the members will not have to choose between y and other allocations and vice versa).

Definition 8.2: Type-2 Dominance

For any two nonrelated/independent distributions (x and y) and for nodes/individuals in each such distribution (where the nodes are named 1,2,3,4,…ith node ε n, such that an allocation to node #1 in x is x_1, and an allocation to node #1 in y is y_1, and each allocation to a node may be negative or positive), x is said to be Type-2 dominant over y *if* the following conditions exist:

1. $\sum_{i=n} (x_i - x_s) < \sum_{i=n} (y_i - y_s)$

2. $\sum_{i=n} x_i \geq \sum_{i=n} y_i$

The following condition is referred to as a *reverse Type-2A dominance* of x over y:

1. $\sum_{i=n}(x_m - x_i) > \sum_{i=n}(y_m - y_i)$
2. $\sum_{i=n}x_i \geq \sum_{i=n}y_i$

The following condition is referred to as a *reverse Type-2B dominance* of x over y:

1. $\sum_{i=n}(x_m - x_i) < \sum_{i=n}(y_m - y_i)$
2. $\sum_{i=n}x_i \geq \sum_{i=n}y_i$

where
$\quad$ x_s is the smallest of the allocations in distribution x
$\quad$ y_s is the smallest of the allocations in distribution y

This type of dominance is applicable in the following circumstances:

1. The members/nodes are not sensitive about the absolute magnitude of allocations.
2. The ordering of the allocations in each distribution is relevant to the decision or to stability.
3. A majority or supermajority of members must choose nondeviation in order to maintain stability.
4. The members are very concerned about inequality within any distribution and are less concerned about their relative allocations between the two distributions.
5. For all or members, regret, greed, and altruism are as important or less important than inequality as decision factors.
6. Each member not only knows the sum total allocation for each distribution but also knows about allocations to other members.
7. The occurrence of x and y are independent but mutually exclusive (i.e., if x is chosen, y will never be allocated or the members will not have to choose between y and other allocations, and vice versa).

Definition 8.3: Type-3 Dominance

For any two nonrelated/independent distributions (x and y), and for nodes/individuals in each such distribution (where the nodes are named 1,2,3,4,…*i*th node ε n, such that an allocation to node #1 in x is x_1, and an allocation to node #1 in y is y_1, and each allocation to a node may be negative or positive), x is said to be Type-3 dominant over y *if* the following conditions exist:

1. $\sum_{i=n}(x_i - x_m) < \sum_{i=n}(y_i - y_m)$
2. $\sum_{i=n}x_i \geq \sum_{i=n}y_i$

The following condition is referred to as a *Type-3A dominance* of x over y:

1. $\sum_{i=n}(x_m - x_i) < \sum_{i=n}(y_m - y_i)$
2. $\sum_{i=n}x_i \geq \sum_{i=n}y_i$

where
$\quad$ x_m is the median of the allocations in distribution x
$\quad$ y_m is the median of the allocations in distribution y

This type of dominance is applicable in the following circumstances:

1. The allocations in one or both distributions are skewed above the median—with nodes in upper two quartiles getting numerically larger positive allocations (Type-3).
2. The allocations in one or both distributions are skewed below the median—with nodes in lower two quartiles getting numerically larger negative allocations (Type-3A).
3. Low inequality is the objective.
4. All nodes have information about all allocations in a distribution.
5. Greed, regret, and altruism are or can be decision factors for members of each distribution (Type-3A).
6. The members/nodes are not sensitive about the absolute magnitude of their allocations.
7. The ordering of the allocations in each distribution is relevant to the decision or to stability.
8. A majority or supermajority of members must choose nondeviation in order to maintain stability.
9. The members are very concerned about inequality within any distribution and are less concerned about their relative allocations between the two distributions.
10. For all or members, regret, greed, and altruism are as important or less important than inequality as decision factors.
11. Each member not only knows the sum total allocation for each distribution but also knows about allocations to other members.
12. The occurrence of x and y are independent but mutually exclusive (i.e., if x is chosen, y will never be allocated or the members will not have to choose between y and other allocations, and vice versa).

Definition 8.4: Type-4 Dominance

For any two nonrelated/independent distributions (x and y), and for nodes/individuals in each such distribution (where the nodes are named 1,2,3,4,…ith node ε m, such that an allocation to node #1 in x is x_1, and an allocation to node #1 in y is y_1, and each allocation to a node may be negative or positive), x is said to be Type-4 dominant over y *if* the following conditions exist:

1. $\sum_{i=n}(\ddot{x} - x_i) < \sum_{i=n}(\ddot{y} - y_i)$
2. $\sum_{i=n}x_i > \sum_{i=n}y_i$

The following condition is referred to as a *Type-4A dominance* of x over y:

1. $\sum_{i=n}(x_i - \ddot{x}) > \sum_{i=n}(y_i - \ddot{y})$
2. $\sum_{i=n}x_i \geq \sum_{i=n}y_i$

The following condition is referred to as a *Type-4B dominance* of x over y:

1. $(\ddot{x} - x_m) < (\ddot{y} - y_m)$
2. $\sum_{i=n}x_i > \sum_{i=n}y_i$

The following condition is referred to as a *Type-4C dominance* of x over y:

1. $(\ddot{x} - x_a) > (\ddot{y} - \tilde{y})$
2. $x_1 \geq y_1, x_2 \geq y_2,…x_n \geq y_n$; (i.e., $x \gtreqqless y$) for a majority or supermajority of members

The following condition is referred to as a *Type-4D dominance* of x over y:

1. $\sum\limits_{i=n}(x_i - \ddot{x}) > \sum\limits_{i=n}(y_i - \ddot{y})$
2. $x_1 \geq y_1, x_2 \geq y_2, \ldots x_n \geq y_n$; (i.e., $x \geq y$) for a majority or supermajority of members

where
    $\ddot{x}$ is the maximum allocation to any node/member in distribution x
    $\ddot{y}$ is the maximum allocation to any node/member in distribution y

Definition 8.5: Type-5 Dominance

For any two nonrelated/independent distributions (x and y), and for nodes/individuals in each such distribution (where the nodes are named 1,2,3,4,...*i*th node ε m, such that an allocation to node #1 in x is x_1, and an allocation to node #1 in y is y_1, and each allocation to a node may be negative or positive), x is said to be Type-5 dominant over y *if* the following conditions exist:

1. $(\ddot{x} - x_m) < (\ddot{y} - y_m)$
2. $\sum\limits_{i=n}x_i \geq \sum\limits_{i=n}y_i$

The following condition is referred to as a *Type-5A dominance* of x over y:

1. $\sum\limits_{i=n}(x_m - \ddot{x}) < \sum\limits_{i=n}(y_m - \ddot{y})$
2. $\sum\limits_{i=n}x_i \geq \sum\limits_{i=n}y_i$

The following condition is referred to as a *Type-5B dominance* of x over y:

1. $\sum\limits_{i=n}(x_m - \ddot{x}) < \sum\limits_{i=n}(y_m - \ddot{y})$
2. $\sum\limits_{i=n}x_i > \sum\limits_{i=n}y_i$
3. $\left|x_1 - x_a\right| > \left|y_1 - y_a\right|; \left|x_2 - x_a\right| > \left|y_2 - y_a\right| \ldots \left|x_n - x_a\right| > \left|y_n - y_a\right|;$

The following condition is referred to as a *Type-5C dominance* of x over y:

1. $(\ddot{x} - x_m) < (\ddot{y} - y_m)$
2. $x_1 \geq y_1, x_2 \geq y_2, \ldots x_n \geq y_n$; (i.e., $x \geq y$)
3. $\left|x_1 - x_a\right| \geq \left|y_1 - y_a\right|; \left|x_2 - x_a\right| \geq \left|y_2 - y_a\right| \ldots \left|x_n - x_a\right| \geq \left|y_n - y_a\right|;$ for a majority of members

where
    $\ddot{x}$ is the maximum allocation to any node/member in distribution x
    $\ddot{y}$ is the maximum allocation to any node/member in distribution y
    x_a is the average of the allocations in distribution x
    y_a is the average of the allocations in distribution y
    x_m is the median of the allocations in distribution x
    y_m is the median of the allocations in distribution y

This type of dominance is suitable in the following circumstances:

1. Many of the allocations in each distribution are clustered around the median of the distribution.
2. Greed, wealth comparison, and regret are factors.
3. Low inequality is the objective.

Definition 8.6: Type-6 Dominance

For any two nonrelated/independent distributions (x and y), and for nodes/individuals in each such distribution (where the nodes are named 1,2,3,4,...ith node ε m, such that an allocation to node #1 in x is x_1, and an allocation to node #1 in y is y_1, and each allocation to a node may be negative or positive), x is said to be Type-6 dominant over y *if* the following conditions exist:

1. $x_1 \geq y_1, x_2 \geq y_2, \ldots x_n \geq y_n$; (i.e., $x \geqq y$)
2. $\left| x_1 - x_a \right| \geq \left| y_1 - y_a \right|$; $\left| x_2 - x_a \right| \geq \left| y_2 - y_a \right|$ $\ldots$ $\left| x_n - x_a \right| \geq \left| y_n - y_a \right|$; for a majority of members
3. $\left| x_1 - y_a \right| \geq \left| y_1 - x_a \right|$; $\left| x_2 - y_a \right| \geq \left| y_2 - x_a \right|$ $\ldots$ $\left| y_n - x_a \right| \geq \left| x_n - y_a \right|$; for a majority of members

The following condition is referred to as a *Type-6A dominance.*

1. $\sum\limits_{i=n} (x_m - \ddot{x}) < \sum\limits_{i=n} (y_m - \ddot{y})$
2. $\left| x_1 - x_a \right| \geq \left| y_1 - y_a \right|$; $\left| x_2 - x_a \right| \geq \left| y_2 - y_a \right|$ $\ldots$ $\left| x_n - x_a \right| \geq \left| y_n - y_a \right|$; for a majority of members
3. $\left| x_1 - y_m \right| \geq \left| y_1 - x_m \right|$; $\left| x_2 - y_m \right| \geq \left| y_2 - x_m \right|$ $\ldots$ $\left| y_n - x_m \right| \geq \left| x_n - y_m \right|$; for a majority of members

The following condition is referred to as a *Type-6B dominance*:

1. $\sum\limits_{i=n} (x_m - \ddot{x}) < \sum\limits_{i=n} (y_m - \ddot{y})$
2. $\sum\limits_{i=n} x_i > \sum\limits_{i=n} y_i$
3. $\left| x_1 - x_a \right| > \left| y_1 - y_a \right|$; $\left| x_2 - x_a \right| > \left| y_2 - y_a \right|$ $\ldots$ $\left| x_n - x_a \right| > \left| y_n - y_a \right|$;

The following condition is referred to as a *Type-6C dominance*:

1. $(\ddot{x} - x_m) < (\ddot{y} - y_m)$
2. $x_1 \geq y_1, x_2 \geq y_2, \ldots x_n \geq y_n$; (i.e., $x \geqq y$)
3. $\left| x_1 - x_a \right| \geq \left| y_1 - y_a \right|$; $\left| x_2 - x_a \right| \geq \left| y_2 - y_a \right|$ $\ldots$ $\left| x_n - x_a \right| \geq \left| y_n - y_a \right|$; for a majority of members

where
  $\ddot{x}$ is the maximum allocation to any node/member in distribution x
  $\ddot{y}$ is the maximum allocation to any node/member in distribution y
  x_a is the average of the allocations in distribution x
  y_a is the average of the allocations in distribution y
  x_m is the median of the allocations in distribution x
  y_m is the median of the allocations in distribution y

This type of dominance is suitable in the following circumstances:

1. Many of the allocations in each distribution are clustered around the median of the distribution.
2. Greed, wealth comparison, and regret are factors.
3. Low inequality is the objective.

8.3 Cumulative Prospect Theory (CPT), Prospect Theory (PT), Third-Generation Prospect Theory (PT³), and Networks

Baucells and Heukamp (2006) analyzed SD and CPT. Several authors have tried to apply PT and CPT to network analysis—such as Li et al. (2012, 2015), Jou and Chen (2013), Wu and Yang (2013), Xia et al. (2012), Zhang and He (2014), and Li and Mandayam (2014) and other articles.[2]

Nwogugu (2005a,b,c, 2006a) explained why PT/CPT (and implicitly, *third-generation prospect theory* [PT³]) are wrong. Nwogugu (2006b) introduced new models of *regret* and also introduced *willingness to accept losses*. Furthermore, the existence of P2P networks is perhaps one of the largest empirical evidence that CPT, PT, and PT³ are wrong and are not applicable to any network. This is because the functions/preferences implied by CPT/PT/PT³ are not the same as the functions/preferences of P2P nodes/users and P2P networks in general as illustrated in the existing literature (i.e., as illustrated in the many network games described in mathematics, economics, operations research, and computer science literatures). Furthermore, CPT/PT/PT³ preferences and functions cannot exist in most P2P networks and many social networks. See comments in Nwogugu (2005a,b,c, 2006a). Some of the CPT/PT/PT³ preferences include *reference dependence*, the *reflection effect*, *certainty effect*, the *endowment effect*, and the *isolation effect*.

8.4 Conclusion

Lorenz dominance and FSD/SSD/TSD/HSD models are problematic. Nwogugu (2013) illustrated weaknesses inherent in the mean-variance framework—many of which can be extended to other statistical distributions. Many of the weaknesses in FSD/SSD/TSD/HSD models can be reduced by incorporating measures of human behavior, irrationality, availability of resources, substitutability, time, *intertemporal choice*, and other factors. CPT/PT/PT³ are not generally applicable (or are applicable only in a minute set of circumstances) in the analysis of social networks and P2P Internet networks.

Notes

1 Nwogugu (2005a,b) stated in part:

> …Contrary to PT/CPT, risk is not always expressed in terms of monetary losses. There are many situations in which risk can be expressed in terms of excessive gains, increased regulation, increased compliance requirements, changes in consumer attitudes, changes in tax consequences, loss of time/effort, etc. PT/CPT and EUT do not consider that the decision

maker can control and reduce risk and losses through insurance, contracts, and the use of derivative securities. The decision maker can sell or transfer risk and losses, and the decision maker can defer the impact of risk over time by the use of specific corporate/organizational structures, derivative securities, contracts, enforcement of government regulations, etc. There may be other factors—e.g., public policy, etc.—that affect decision making. The decision maker's preferences may remain constant when expected values and probabilities and decision weights change if the decision maker can transfer/sell/modify/defer risk and losses and if there are public policy and regulatory issues that affect decisions and outcomes....

2 See De et al. (2011), Gao et al. (2010), Wang et al. (2010), Zhao and Zhang (2007), and Hjorth and Fosgerau (2012).

Chapter 9

Consumer Surplus, Producer Surplus, Equilibrium Prices, and the Enterprise Value of Digital Content

9.1 Introduction

It is not clear whether Nash Equilibrium, Bayesian Nash Equilibrium, or similar equilibria are suitable for analysis of prices of digital content because of the following reasons:

1. Consumers' switching costs are or can be very low; there are several alternatives to traditional digital content (CDs, real-live education, home study, other forms of entertainment, etc.), and the illegal file sharer can easily and *profitably* deviate from any perceived Nash Equilibrium and at low costs (*profit* refers to both monetary and nonmonetary gains such as cost savings, excitement, reduced search costs, and group activities).
2. Given that time is a major search cost, the transaction costs and opportunity costs inherent in maintaining any Nash Equilibrium, Bayesian Nash Equilibrium, or similar equilibria can be prohibitive.
3. The amount and duration of information asymmetry inherent in the price discovery process and in maintaining any Nash Equilibrium, Bayesian Nash Equilibrium, or similar equilibria can be prohibitive and precludes any such equilibria.
4. The operations of information producers often differ substantially and they have or can have different cost structures and very different production costs, and consumers' tastes/preferences and the temporal manifestations of such preferences differ substantially, all of which affect the probability of existence of equilibria.
5. Nash Equilibria does not implicitly or explicitly consider regulations (unlike *competitive regulatory equilibria*); but regulation affects or can affect consumers' preferences and information producers' pricing and distribution channels.

6. Nash Equilibrium does not consider the absolute/relative values of, and changes in, social welfare; and thus, Nash Equilibria may not necessarily result in optimal outcomes in terms of maximization of social welfare.

In many existing models of pricing of digital content in the literature, *equilibrium* is rarely defined or is rarely defined accurately even though it is one of the main elements of both conceptual and analytic solutions. Govindan and Wilson (2006) analyzed the conditions sufficient for *equilibrium*. Kohlberg and Mertens (1986) stated the required properties of a good normal form solution concept and the three types of stability (KM stability, full stability, and hyperstability) that satisfy some, but not all, of those properties. Goodman and Porter (1988) addressed *competitive regulatory equilibrium* in general. Although Virag (2011) addresses concepts of *competitive nonregulatory equilibrium*, most of the theorems in Virag (2011) are wrong and equations 2,5,4,8,9, and 13 in Virag (2011) are also wrong because (1) sellers have brand equity and buyers have individual preferences that evolve (symmetry of buyers' preferences across sellers is rare/uncommon and an unreasonable assumption); (2) zero-utility equilibrium is rare but possible and the article does not state conditions under which it occurs; (3) a seller's market power is not always inversely proportional to the market size, even in a market that is not an oligopoly/duopoly/monopoly (because of pricing, service/delivery terms, promotions/discounts, complimentary goods, regulation, product quality, lack of substitutes, etc.); (4) the anonymity of buyers varies or can vary across sellers; and (5) in the equations in which *limits* are mentioned, the formulas do not behave as stated when the variables tend to positive or negative infinity. These concepts/definitions of *equilibrium* differ from and can be more efficient than *Nash Equilibrium* in many dimensions and circumstances.

Within the context of equilibrium in the pricing of digital content, *social welfare* and thus *equilibrium* can be defined in various ways including but not limited to any of the following: (1) pricing changes are timely and accurate (they match and are related to information producers' costs), and illegal file sharing is substantially reduced or eliminated, and (2) harmful freeriding and collusion among illegal file sharers are minimized, and perpetrators face penalties for inaccuracy and or collusion, and enforcement and investigation costs are minimized.

Traditional contract theory is not suitable for analysis of pricing of digital content and the process of enforcement of intellectual property (IP) law because the associated compliance burdens are one-sided (most obligations and regulations apply to consumers); and consumers are often irrational. Thus, incentive systems and/or pricing systems that are heavily dependent on the volume of trades/transactions or on consumers are likely to be inappropriate. The enforcers' (both government agencies and private parties) and ISPs' parties' ability to contract is statutorily limited; and in most IOF systems, perpetrators' ability to contract is physically and psychologically limited. Licensing and regulation of ISPs and the *entrenchment* of ISPs impose or can impose artificial price floors for digital content. The entrenchment is often caused by the cost of ownership of physical network infrastructure, cost of licensing/permits, and the actual and perceived costs of network agreements among internet service providers (ISPs).

9.2 Existing Literature

Aoki and Yoshikawa (2009) critiqued traditional *equilibrium* within the context of search theory. Risse (2000) critiqued Nash Equilibrium within the context of one-time interactions. Daskalakis (2008) noted that the credibility of the Nash Equilibrium depends on whether such equilibria are efficiently computable and that computing Nash Equilibria is an intractable problem. Aumann and Dreze (2008) critiqued Nash Equilibrium. Bernheim (1984) and Pearce (1984) introduced the concept of *rationalizability* and critiqued Nash Equilibrium.

9.3 Within the Context of Illegal Online File Sharing: There Is No Consumer Surplus or Producer Surplus or Equilibrium Price

In the context of illegal online file sharing and P2P networks, the concepts of consumer surplus, equilibrium, and *equilibrium price* are either not practical or rarely useful because of the following reasons:

1. In most instances, the per-unit marginal cost of a unit of digital content is always much less than the per-unit average cost; the per-unit total cost of a unit of digital content is always greater than the per-unit average cost and marginal cost.
2. The actual per-unit content delivery cost differs dramatically for each consumer in the P2P network, depending on their geographical location and the type of content; hence, the true price for each unit differs depending on the consumer.
3. The demand for the digital content varies dramatically and constantly fluctuates such that there is no steady measurable demand curve—both for each consumer as an individual and for the entire P2P system as a whole. Demand in the P2P system is a function of not only the consumer's tastes but also of (1) the reputation of the P2P network, (2) the perceived fairness of the P2P network, (3) the *willingness to comply* of each network member, (4) the availability of similar products in the P2P system, (5) the extent to which each network member can see the holdings of other members' networks, (6) the amount and availability of cash and noncash incentives in the P2P system, (7) the amount of cash that the consumer is obliged to pay to get digital content (after subtracting any incentives), and (8) the combined effects of peer pressure and network effects.
4. The supply for the unit of digital content varies dramatically and constantly fluctuates such that there is no steady or measurable supply curve—both for each consumer as an individual and for the entire P2P system as a whole. Supply in the P2P system is a function of not only each network members' tastes but also of (1) the reputation of the P2P network, (2) the perceived fairness of the P2P network, (3) willingness to comply of each network member, (4) the availability of similar products in the P2P system, (5) the extent to which each network member can see the holdings of other members' networks, (6) the amount and availability of cash and noncash incentives in the P2P system, (7) the amount of cash that the consumer is obliged to pay to get digital content in the P2P system (after subtracting any incentives), (8) the combined effects of peer pressure and network effects, and (9) whether or not each network member can upload content for sharing in the P2P system.
5. There is never *equilibrium* because one network member or a group of network members can improve their positions either by purchasing the digital content from a legal file sharing network or by purchasing the unit from a discount store or by offline sharing.
6. The unit of digital content is often sold at a substantial discount to both the retail and wholesale prices of a physical product.
7. There are significant differences between the *stated price* and the *net effective price* of the unit of digital content in a legal P2P network or client–server network. The *net effective prices*

vary substantially depending on (1) the amount of incentive payments paid to the member, (2) the cost of bandwidth incurred, (3) the density of the network, and (4) the owner/distributor's cost of monitoring and enforcement. Note that these additional costs are not considered as *operating expenses* or *cost of services* because they are integral to the revenue process (similar to some discounts and trade credit terms).

8. The rate of change of both the demand and supply curves precludes any stable *equilibrium price*.

Similarly, in the context of illegal file sharing and P2P networks and client–server networks, the concept of *producer surplus* either does not exist or is rarely useful because of the following reasons:

1. In most instances, the per-unit marginal cost of a unit of digital content is always far below the per-unit average cost; the per-unit total cost of a unit of digital content is always greater than the per-unit average cost and marginal cost.

2. The actual per-unit content delivery cost differs dramatically for each consumer in the P2P network, depending on their geographical location and the type of content; hence, the true price for each unit differs depending on the consumer.

3. Demand for the digital content varies dramatically and constantly fluctuates such that there is no steady measurable demand curve—both for each consumer as an individual and for the entire P2P system as a whole. Demand in the P2P system is a function of not only the consumer's tastes but also of (a) the reputation of the P2P network, (b) the perceived fairness of the P2P network, (c) willingness to comply of each network member, (d) the availability of similar products in the P2P system, (e) the extent to which each network member can see the holdings of other members' networks, (f) the amount and availability of cash and noncash incentives in the P2P system, (g) the amount of cash that the consumer is obliged to pay to get digital content (after subtracting any incentives), and (h) the combined effects of peer pressure and network effects.

4. The supply for the unit of digital content varies dramatically and constantly fluctuates such that there is no steady or measurable supply curve—both for each consumer as an individual and for the entire P2P system as a whole. Supply in the P2P system is a function of not only each network members' tastes but also of (a) the reputation of the P2P network, (b) the perceived fairness of the P2P network. (c) willingness to comply of each network member, (d) the availability of similar products in the P2P system, (e) the extent to which each network member can see the holdings of other members' networks, (f) the amount and availability of cash and noncash incentives in the P2P system, (the amount of cash that the consumer is obliged to pay to get digital content in the P2P system after subtracting any incentives), (g) the combined effects of peer pressure and network effects, and (h) whether or not each network member can upload content for sharing in the P2P system.

5. In most instances, the supply does not reflect the owner/distributor's cost of enforcement and monitoring, losses attributable to piracy, or the marginal cost of the unit of digital content.

6. The unit of digital content is often sold at a substantial discount to both the retail and wholesale prices of a physical product.

7. There is never equilibrium because one network member or a group of network members can improve their positions either by purchasing the digital content from an illegal file sharing network or by purchasing the unit from a discount store or by offline sharing.

8. The rate of change of both the demand and supply curves precludes any steady equilibrium price.

9.4 Enterprise Value of Digital Content

9.4.1 The True Enterprise Value of Digital Content Is Dynamic

Enterprise value of digital content refers to the value of one unit of digital content (e.g., a movie CD, or a music file, or a vinyl record, or a digital book). A *unit* of such digital content is the individual unit that is sold to each consumer. Contrary to the existing literature on valuation of digital content, the enterprise value of digital content is not fixed and does not decline as many people copy/access the mentioned digital content (Klein et al. 2002, Krishnan et al. 2003). The reasons are as follows.

Each person who has access to a specific unit of digital content derives some positive or negative utility, which has monetary value that can change exponentially and is dynamic. This dynamic value is a function of consumer tastes, economic/social profile, wealth, leisure time, affinity for certain subjects, type of digital content, disposable income, etc. Similarly, each person who knows about but does not have access to a unit of digital content is conjectured to derive some positive or negative utility from such knowledge and *relative scarcity*, which has monetary value that can change exponentially.

The perceived value of downloaded digital content is affected by the magnitude of network congestion, which is dynamic, and the size of the available illegal P2P networks and ability to locate the digital content within such illegal networks. Hence, even as the number of legal downloads increases, if the digital content is not available on illegal P2P networks, the digital content's perceived value may increase.

9.4.2 The Enterprise Value of One Unit of Digital Content

In most existing content distribution systems, digital content is substantially mispriced, because a consumer pays a price P for almost perpetual access to content, regardless of how many times he or she accesses the content and the number of people who access the content. To price the digital content accurately, there should be some assumptions about the number of times any person/group accesses the content, the number of persons in the *audience/group* each time there is access, the timing of each access, the value (negative or positive utility) derived by each person each time he or she accesses the digital content, an appropriate discount rate, perpetuity factors, and the probability that each user will share the file with another user.

The content pricing models introduced in this chapter distinguish between the *enterprise value* of one unit of digital content to the content owner/rights holder, and the per-unit price of one unit of digital content that is distributed by the content owner or the distributor.

Assume that one unit of digital content is distributed only by downloading the product from a website or legal P2P system where the consumer pays for the item. If there are α consumers who have access (via links or direct connections) to the website during n periods, and each consumer has utility/satisfaction U_i (for the ith consumer), then the true *enterprise value* of the digital content to the owner is as follows. r is the periodic interest rate. t is the number of time periods during which the system will function. S is the geographical coverage of the network. C_i is the cost of creating the digital content—this includes costs such as initial production costs, manufacturing/replication costs, testing costs, and overhead costs; marketing studies; etc. Π_r is the marginal cost of reproducing a unit of digital content. This includes overhead, production costs, and replication costs. Π_d is the marginal cost of distributing a unit of digital content and includes overhead, system, bandwidth, distribution, and marketing costs. This amount includes Internet congestion costs incurred by the distributor (including any fee paid for priority access during peak usage periods). Π_m is the distributor's/owner's marginal cost of creating and distributing one unit of digital content and includes production, manufacturing/replication, distribution, and marketing costs. $\Pi_m = \Pi_d + \Pi_r$. Π_{ms} is the consumer's marginal costs of searching for one unit of digital content.

Π_{mps} is the consumer's marginal cost of product substitution for one unit of digital content. This includes the effects of price discounts, promotions, coupons, and free products, etc. Π_p is the distributor's/content owner's marginal cost of enforcement of IP rights. Π_{ts} is the consumer's *marginal cost of time substitution* (which is a function of background, education, temporal coordination, hobbies/leisure, income, social networks, cognition, mental processes, aspirations, biological conditions, affinity for online search, actual/perceived wealth, etc.). U_i is the utility for each individual who accesses the digital content. U_i has monetary value. U_i is a function of several variables, including age, background, education, hobbies, social life, location of access to the content, mental processes, aspirations, biological conditions, affinity for online search, cognition, altruism, greed, etc. U_i accounts for differences in age, location, type of device (wireless versus desktop versus laptop, types of content, scarcity values, etc.). $\infty < U_i < \infty$. Golle et al. (2001) also described a utility function. U_g is the utility for each group of persons that accesses the digital content at any time. U_g has monetary value. U_g is a function of several variables, including age of group members, location of group, group cohesion, background, education, hobbies, social life, social networks, cognition, mental processes, aspirations, biological conditions, affinity for online search, altruism, greed, location of access to the content, etc. $\infty < U_g < \infty$. U_g partly accounts for group interactions, some file sharing activities, etc.

For content in general, the *enterprise value* of such content is as follows:

$$V_1 = \left(\sum_{i=\alpha} U_i * e^{tr} \right) + \left(U_g * e^{tr} \right) - C_i - \sum_{i=\alpha} \left(\Pi_m * e^{-tr} \right) - \sum_{i=\alpha} \left(\Pi_p * e^{-tr} \right) - \sum_{i=\alpha} \left(\Pi_r * e^{-tr} \right) \quad (9.1)$$

$$V_2 = \left[\left(\sum_{i=\alpha} \left(U_i / (1+r)^t \right) \right) + \left\{ \left(U_g * e^{-tr} \right) \right\} - C_i - \sum_{i=\alpha} \left\{ \left(\Pi_m * e^{-tr} \right) \right\} - \sum_{i=\alpha} \left\{ \left(\Pi_p * e^{-tr} \right) \right\} \right.$$

$$\left. - \sum_{i=\alpha} \left(\Pi r * e^{-tr} \right) * \text{Max} \left\{ 1, \left(\partial^2 \Pi_d / \partial \Pi_{mps} \right) \right\} \right] \quad (9.2)$$

For digital content, the *enterprise values* V are as follows:

$$V_3 = \left[\left(\sum_{i=\alpha} U_i * e^{tr} \right) + \left(U_g * e^{tr} \right) - C_i - \sum_{i=\alpha} \left(\Pi_m * e^{-tr} \right) - \sum_{i=\alpha} \left(\Pi_{ms} * e^{-tr} \right) \right.$$

$$\left. - \sum_{i=\alpha} \left(\Pi_p * e^{-tr} \right) + \sum_{i=\alpha} \left(\Pi_{mps} * e^{-tr} \right) - \sum_{i=\alpha} \left(\Pi_r * e^{-tr} \right) \right] \quad (9.3)$$

$$V_4 = \left[\left(\sum_{i=\alpha} U_i * e^{-tr} \right) - C_i - \sum_{i=\alpha} \left(\Pi_m * e^{-tr} \right) - \sum_{i=\alpha} \left(\Pi_{ms} * e^{-tr} \right) - \sum_{i=\alpha} \left(\Pi_p * e^{-tr} \right) \right.$$

$$+ \sum_{i=\alpha} \left(\Pi_{mps} * e^{-tr} \right) - \sum_{i=\alpha} \left(\Pi_r * e^{-tr} \right) \right] * \text{Max} \left[1, \left[\left(\text{Max} \left\{ 0, \left(\frac{\partial^2 \Pi_d}{\partial \Pi_{mps}} \right) \right\} \right) \right. \right.$$

$$\left. \left. + \text{Max} \left\{ 0, \left(\frac{\partial^2 \alpha}{\partial \lambda \partial \Pi_d} \right) \right\} + \text{Max} \left\{ 0, \left(\frac{\partial \Pi_d}{\partial \Pi_r} \right) \right\} \right] \right] \quad (9.4)$$

$$V_5 = \text{Min}\left[\left\{\sum_{i=\alpha}\left(\Pi_{ms} + \Pi_{ts}\right)\right\}; \left\{\left(\sum_{i=\alpha}U_i * e^{-tr}\right) + \left(U_g * e^{-tr}\right) - C_i - \sum_{i=\alpha}\left(\Pi_m * e^{-tr}\right)\right.\right.$$

$$\left.\left. - \sum_{i=\alpha}\left(\Pi_p * e^{-tr}\right) - \sum_{i=\alpha}\left(\Pi_r * e^{-tr}\right) - \left(\sum_{i=\alpha}\left(\Pi_{mps} * e^{-tr}\right)\right)\right\}\right] \qquad (9.5)$$

In the foregoing formulas, the summations of Π_m, Π_p, and U_i represent the addition of these costs or utilities for all customers that purchase the digital content. There are different formulas for the *enterprise value* of digital content because there are different types of digital content (news, educational materials, music, videos, etc.) and different types of content formats (MP3, streaming, etc.), various broadband speeds are available in different countries/cities, and different network models are used (P2P versus client–server). Moreover, most digital content is *experience goods*, for which the consumers and distributors do not know the value until the consumer experiences the product; hence, U_i and U_g are estimated in part by historical analysis.

9.5 Conclusion

The value of a specific unit of digital content can either increase or decrease as many people access it; and the direction of change of value is a function of the popularity of the content, consumer tastes, consumer wealth, consumer utility/disutility created, distribution channels, magnitude of communication among groups that have and do not have access to the digital content, consumers' disposable incomes, consumer affinity for specific types of content, etc. Furthermore, there is a distinction between (1) the economic value of digital content and (2) the loss of economic value to the digital content owner. Content owners lose economic value when one unit of content is copied and accessed by people who have not paid for it. This is very different from the economic value of content that depends on individual and group utilities/wealth/tastes/preferences and can *increase or decrease* as the audience increases.

Chapter 10

Human Decisions, Optimal Search, and Stopping, the Pricing of Differentiated Digital Goods in Legal P2P and Client–Server Networks under Unconstrained Transferable Utility and Unknown Demand, and Three New Network-Allocation Mechanisms

10.1 Introduction

Although the number of *legal* online file sharing networks has increased, digital piracy has become more pervasive and affects several industries such as news/information, entertainment, education, and sports. One of the content distributor's challenges is to find the price that minimizes IOF. Digital piracy is often complicated by Internet congestion, informal online *coalitions* that thwart enforcement efforts, lax enforcement, and offline/online coordination by digital pirates. Such coordination is often complex and is intended or unintended and both observable and unobservable. Thus, customer experience and firm profitability can be vastly improved by piracy-minimizing and profit-maximizing pricing of digital goods. Such pricing schemes incorporate elements of a *prioritization scheme* where the *priority* is defined in terms of not only customers' opportunity costs (waiting time, search costs, etc.) but also willingness to comply with intellectual property (IP) laws, prepurchase and postpurchase regret, customer's relative wealth, and customer's marginal propensity-to-substitute digital products. These pricing schemes can minimize the firm's production/delivery costs and can also result in lower perceived prices for *high-priority* customers and uniform Quality of Service (QoS) for all customers, all of which are socially more optimal outcomes when different customers place different values on digital content, time, and compliance with IP laws. The interactions among the members of peer-to-peer (P2P) networks are forms of network games.

This chapter (1) introduces three new classes of dynamic anonymous random network matching games (Transferrable Utility [TU] noncooperative repeated games in client–server networks and TU cooperative repeated games in P2P networks for which it is possible to calculate the payoffs of individual members/nodes), (2) introduces three new network-allocation mechanisms for sharing the benefits of P2P and client–server networks wherein the mechanism is embedded in the pricing formula that can optimize both consumer welfare and producer/distributor welfare, (3) develops pricing models that can minimize the firm's piracy losses and simultaneously maximize revenue for the information producer under different assumptions regarding customer behavior and utility, (4) develops models of information-producing firms and content-distribution firms that sell differentiated digital products to customers who have heterogeneous online/offline search costs, and (5) develops conditions for *optimal search* and a *stopping point* in the file sharing network (without using stochastic calculus which has been shown to be deficient).

The information producer modeled herein is not a traditional profit maximizing entity, but rather is piracy-averse, has limited control over the P2P network or client–server network, sells short-lived products, and is most interested in long-term profits. Customers (network members) are generally self-interested, *loss-averse*, and price-sensitive persons who derive mostly nonmonetary utility from consumption of digital content. The P2P and client–server networks discussed herein are anonymous legal networks, and thus the effects of actual or potential coordination and/or altruism among customers are somewhat limited. Within this framework, the marginal cost and marginal price of a unit of digital product become relevant, contrary to the analysis in the existing literature.

10.2 Existing Literature

The literature mentioned herein should be considered in the context of the critique of Nash equilibrium in Chapter 9 in this book. Cao and Yang (2013) introduced a new simple game known as the *complementary weighted multiple majority game* (the *C-WMMG game*). Nikoletseas et al. (2015) introduced a new *swap-based network creation game*, in which selfish costs depend on the immediate neighborhood of each node (and the profit of a node is defined as the sum of the degrees of its neighbors). Hegde et al. (2015) introduced *flow games*. Qiaolun et al. (2008) developed three closed-loop supply chain–based models of pricing, which are *model CMRC* (the manufacturer for collecting), *model CRMRC* (the retailer for collecting), and *model CTMRC* (the third party for collecting). Antos et al. (2013) developed classifications of *finite partial monitoring games*. Bei et al. (2011) introduced the *bounded budget betweenness centrality game* (the ℓ-*B3C game*), which is a strategic network formation game wherein nodes build connections subject to a budget constraint in order to maximize their *betweenness* in the network (the *betweenness centrality* of a node indicates the amount of information passing through the node when all pairs are conducting shortest-path exchanges). Grüner et al. (2013) introduced a game-theoretic model for the study of dynamic communication networks that are subject to failure of nodes and where the restoration needs resources, and the two-player game is played between a *destructor* (who can delete nodes) and a *constructor* (who can restore or create nodes under certain conditions). Bilò et al. (2013) analyzed six *social-context games* in which the underlying games were linear congestion games and Shapley cost-sharing games, and the aggregation functions were min, max, and sum, and for each game, they characterized the class of social context graph topologies guaranteeing the existence of pure Nash equilibria and provided optimal or asymptotically optimal bounds on the price of anarchy of 22 out of the 24 cases obtained by considering four social cost functions, namely, max and sum of the players' immediate and perceived costs. Bilò et al. (2006) developed network cost-sharing games. AhmadiPourAnari et al. (2013) developed pricing games. Kawase and Makino (2013) introduced the concepts of *potential-optimal price of anarchy* (POPoA) and *potential-optimal price of stability* (POPoS), where "POPoA" is the ratio between the worst cost of Nash equilibrium with optimal potential and the minimum social cost and "POPoS" is the ratio between the best cost of Nash equilibrium with optimal potential and the minimum social cost. Kawase and Makino (2013) noted that (1) the POPoA and POPoS for undirected broadcast games with n players are $O(\sqrt{\log n})$; (2) the POPoA and POPoS for undirected broadcast games with $|V|$ vertices are O(log $|V|$); (3) there exists an undirected broadcast game with n players such that POPoA, POPoS $= \Omega(\sqrt{\log \log n})$; and (4) there exists an undirected broadcast game with $|V|$ vertices such that PPPoA, POPoS $= \Omega(\log|V|)$. Anshelevich and Caskurlu (2011) analyzed *group network formation games* (where agents can attempt to satisfy different connectivity requirements by purchasing links in the network) and found that the *price-of-stability* is one when all nodes in the network are owned by players and that doubling the number of players creates an equilibrium as good as the optimum centralized solution, and there exists a two-approximate Nash equilibrium that is as good as the centralized optimum solution.

Van Otterloo et al. (2006) analyzed *knowledge condition games*. Grant et al. (2014) studied the transformation of games by information-sharing. Bachrach et al. (2013) reviewed *transformation games*, which are a form of coalitional games. Wooldridge et al. (2013) studied incentives in *Boolean games*.

Ågotnes et al. (2009), Rahwan et al. (2012), Dunne et al. (2007, 2010), Wooldridge (2012), and Phelps and Wooldridge (2013) studied logic and *coalitional games*.

Brynjolfsson et al. (2011) studied the effects of search costs on product sales. Wei and Zhao (2011), Wang and Tung (2011), Pal and Hui (2013), AhmadiPourAnari et al. (2013), and Chen and Chang (2013) analyzed the pricing of goods within the context of supply chains. Avinadav et al. (2014), Li (2010), Kogan et al. (2013), Liu et al. (2011), and Yu et al. (2011) studied pricing strategies for digital goods within the context of reducing piracy. Basu et al. (2015) and Pal and Hui (2013) researched the pricing of cloud services. Gans (2012) studied the pricing of mobile applications. Kumar et al. (2011) analyzed a mechanism for pricing and resource allocation in peer-to-peer networks. Jena and Sarmah (2014), Li et al. (2009), and Xiong et al. (2014) studied the pricing of remanufactured goods. Bilò et al. (2006, 2010), Fotakis et al. (2009), and Balcan and Blumm (2007) reviewed algorithms and costs in the context of network games. Nisgav and Patt-Shamir (2011) and Fiat and Saia (2007) analyzed censorship and patterns in networks. Iamnitchi et al. (2011), Liu et al. (2015), Matsuda et al. (2010), Albert and Barabási (2002), Watts and Strogatz (1998), Tauhiduzzaman and Wang (2015), Stutzbach et al. (2008), Chen et al. (2012), and Mertzios et al. (2013) commented on the structure and evolution of networks. However, the theories in this chapter contradict most theories in the foregoing articles.

Gavalda-Miralles et al. (2014) studied 10,000 anonymous BitTorrent users (users of the BitTorrent plug-in named *Ono*) and found that most BitTorrent users are *content specialists* and users in countries with similar economies tend to download similar types of contents. Matsumoto (2003), Khouja et al. (2007), Danaher et al. (2010), and Sinha et al. (2010) analyzed pricing issues. Wingrove et al. (2010), Clement et al. (2012), and OECD (2008) studied behavioral patterns in IOF.

Asvanund et al. (2003) introduced some characterizations of the individual's utility from digital content and from participating in IOF networks with respect to the size of the network and network congestion. The Asvanund et al.'s (2003) characterizations are as follows:

1. $U(F(N), C(N)) = UF(F(N)) + UC(C(N))$
2. $\partial U/\partial f > 0$; $\partial U/\partial c < 0$; $\partial f/\partial N > 0$; $\partial c/\partial N > 0$; $\partial^2 U/\partial f^2 \leq 0$; $\partial^2 U/\partial c^2 \leq 0$
3. $\partial U/\partial N = [\partial U/\partial f \cdot \partial f/\partial N] + [\partial U/\partial c \cdot \partial c/\partial N]$
4. $\partial^2 U/\partial N^2 = [\partial^2 U/\partial f^2 * (\partial f/\partial N)^2] + [\partial U/\partial f \cdot \partial^2 f/\partial N^2] + [\partial^2 U/\partial c^2 \cdot (\partial c/\partial N)^2] + [\partial U/\partial c \cdot \partial^2 c/\partial N^2]$

where
    N is the number of network users
    U is the network member's utility from participation in the IOF network
    F is the utility from the availability and replication of a vector of content that the network member is interested in (f is an element of the content vector F)
    C is the disutility of a vector of congestion effects that network members face (c is an element (subset) of the congestion effects vector C)

Congestion measures include login time, query time, and download times.

However, those characterizations in Asvanund et al. (2003) will be valid, *iff* all the following conditions exist simultaneously:

1. $\partial c/\partial t = 0$
2. $\partial^2 U/\partial c \partial t < 0$
3. $\partial S/\partial N > 0$
4. $\partial^2 c/\partial N \partial S > 0$
5. $\partial^2 U/\partial N > 0$; and $\partial^2 U/\partial N \partial S > 0$
6. The network is a first-generation, second-generation, or perhaps third-generation network, but definitely not a fourth-generation or higher network.
7. The network is a consumer P2P file sharing network.
8. The rate of arrival of consumers to the network fits a known probability distribution.
9. The size of the network includes only consumers that are connected to the network—the consumer does not have to be actively searching for content on the network.
10. The network is assumed to be spatially distributed evenly across the country, such that there is no spatial concentration of network members—any spatial concentration may reduce the utility of both the network and the downloaded content.

where
    t is the session time
    S is the magnitude of the geographical dispersion of the network

Note that the results in Asvanund et al. (2003) are valid only for the time period from which the data were extracted (the nature and magnitude of enforcement and prosecution efforts have since increased and have been diversified since then).

Varian (2005)[1] introduced some models of content pricing that reduce illegal file sharing and also analyzed the conditions under which purchasing digital content will be preferable to illegal sharing.

The key issues in Varian (2005) are (1) the omission of the customers' ability and willingness to pay for the right to copy/share digital content and (2) the assumption that the distributor's/content owner's marginal cost can be zero.

Kannan et al. (2008) introduced models of pricing digital content based on LOGIT analysis. Kannan (2013) also discussed pricing issues. The Kannan et al. (2008) analysis can be valid *iff* all the following conditions exist simultaneously: (1) The data are normally distributed; (2) the rate of arrival of consumers to the website follows a Poisson distribution or is constant; (3) the website is the only place where customers can purchase the digital content (PDF) in the Internet; (4) customers who purchase the PDF forms do not share it with other customers (this may increase the cannibalization impact of the digital content on the print version); (5) the transaction costs involved in downloading the PDF file (allocated hardware costs, bandwidth, consumer's leisure time, storage devices, etc.) is relatively minimal and comparable to the transaction costs involved in purchasing a print copy (such as transportation costs, taxes, purchase price, consumer's leisure time); (6) the consumers propensity to substitute between the PDF and physical copies of the content remains constant over any time interval (the model does not fully capture the propensity to substitute between the PDF file and physical print, because of the assumptions underlying the LOGIT model—normality of data, treatment of outliers, rate of change of probability density at tails, etc.); and (7) the utility that the consumer gains from substituting the PDF and physical copies of the content remains constant over any time interval.

The analytical approach in Hachez (2003) is perhaps suitable for traditional application software, but not for digital content that is typically exchanged or frequently purchased over the Internet. Hachez (2003)[2] built on a prior model introduced by Devanbu and Stubblebine (2002). Hachez (2003) modified the Devanbu and Stubblebine (2002) model by adding a new variable—a new cost "C_{eu}" that reflects the burden imposed on the customer when he/she legally possesses the software (e.g., privacy loss, technical requirements, etc.) such that the objective is to achieve the following (using notations in Hachez (2003)):

$$\{n * (C_b + C_{eu})\} \gg [C_h + \{n * C_c\} + \{P_l(n) * C_l(n)\}]$$

s.t.

$$C_{rw} \ll C_s + \{P_l(n) * C_l(n)\}$$

$$C_{rw} \ll C_e + \{P_l(n) * C_l(n)\}$$

Sundararajan (2004)[3] introduced some content pricing models. The theories and comments in Sundararajan (2004) are wrong because making customers indifferent between legal use and piracy is not a sufficient incentive to curb/eliminate piracy losses. Sundararajan's (2004) model attempts to develop a continuous pricing schedule (rather than a single variable price, or a pair of prices for two quality-differentiated products), which accounts for the different values of pirated products to different customers. However, the problems and issues in Sundararajan (2004) are as follows:

1. The utility function $U(q, \theta) = (\theta + \omega)q - (0.5 * q^2)$ is not feasible because its elements (type, ω, etc.) are quantitatively very difficult to define. The term "q" also has limited usefulness because it does not account for illegal use of products. The second term in the equation $(0.5 * q^2)$ has no meaning. The term ω is not defined.

2. It is wrong to use the same variable (s) to measure the quality of the pirated good and also measure the level of piracy—the assumption that at a higher level of piracy, the quality of the pirated good is higher is inaccurate. It is also incorrect to assume that in all cases, the pirated good is always strictly inferior to the legal good (many infringers also have advanced technology for copying content), or that the seller can make a nonzero profit only when the legal good is superior to pirated goods. Sundararajan (2004) states the following in part:

   > … The 'level' of piracy referred to here is distinct from the piracy rate. The former measures the extent to which the legal good can be pirated (and therefore determines the quality of the pirated good, perhaps indirectly through its availability as well), while the latter is a measure of how many customers are actually using the pirated good….

3. Pirated goods are not entirely *free*. There are costs of reproduction, the psychological cost of apprehension/prosecution (in developed countries), etc.

4. It is wrong to assume that the monopolist or any content distributor knows the probability distribution of types in the customer population ($F(\theta)$).

5. The use of the hazard rate function erroneously assumes normality of data. In reality, the distribution of *types* is very likely to vary across different types of contents (music, videos, educational materials, news, sports, etc.), devices (laptop vs. cellphone vs. handheld device), location, age, and Internet access (dial-up, slow broadband, fast broadband). The *normalization* of the total number of customers to one is also error. The actual total number of customers in the market is a dynamic number that changes with time, mobility, wealth, disposable income, consumer tastes, proximity to Internet access points, group socialization, reactions to marketing efforts, etc.

6. The use of quantity–price pairs in the models is inappropriate because in most instances (and especially digital content) the consumer rarely purchases more than one unit of content (news, newspapers, books, music DVDs, etc.) at any time interval.

7. The models erroneously assume that given a pricing schedule $q(x)$, $\tau(x)$ for the legal good, customers of type θ will choose to buy the legal good if their surplus from doing so is at least as much as the value they would derive from the (free) pirated good. First, there is difference between the actual-consumer-surplus and the perceived-consumer-surplus (there are often divergences between perceived-consumer-surplus and actual-consumer-surplus). The actual-consumer surplus is capped/limited primarily by the consumer's wealth, tastes, and budget. The actual-consumer-surplus is entirely based on monetary/cash considerations. The perceived-consumer-surplus has monetary and nonmonetary (emotions, satisfaction, value, peace of mind, perceived savings) components. The consumer surplus is meaningful and is a basis for consumer choice only within certain domains of prices of digital content. Below a certain price threshold (P_l), any consumer surplus that results from choosing either a legal good or a pirated good is not a major decision factor for the consumer simply because the price is very low relative to other household expenses or operating expenses—in such instances, there is significant divergence between actual-consumer-surplus and

perceived-consumer-surplus. Above a certain price threshold (P_h), consumer surplus and price becomes more of a concern and a major decision factor because the price is high relative to other household expenses or operating expenses.

8. The analysis does not account for the costs of monitoring/enforcement of IP laws, the probability of apprehension/prosecution, and transaction costs.

9. Most of the lemmas and proofs in Sundararajan (2004) are based on the consumer being economically indifferent between the legal good and the pirated good—this approach is wrong because such *indifference* is not sufficient incentive for customers to avoid piracy. First, most consumers do not perceive or calculate consumer surplus when choosing between legal content and pirated content. The consumer surplus derived from purchasing the legal unit of content is almost never the same or larger than the consumer surplus from the pirated unit of content—as described earlier, the actual-consumer-surplus is bounded by the consumer's wealth and periodic budget. Furthermore, in most instances, there is typically no material difference in quality between the legal good and the pirated copy (infringers also have advanced technology for copying content). Consumers measure their consumer surplus in terms of not only actual cash expenditures (as in equilibrium prices), but also cash saved (as in zero prices in illegal P2P networks). Unlike consumer surplus for pirated content, the consumer surplus for legal content is *contingent* on paying the cash *equilibrium price*. Thus, consumer surplus for legal content is conjectured to have lower economic value than that for pirated content, for most types of digital content. Its conjectured here that the equilibrium prices for pirated content in illegal file sharing networks are either zero or very close to zero; and the demand/supply curves for pirated content are usually steeper than those for legal content (primarily due to enforcement, punitive damages, and the risk of apprehension), and so the consumer surplus for pirated content is usually greater than that for legal content for most types of digital content. The only condition under which the consumer surplus derived from purchasing the legal good can be the same or larger than the consumer surplus from the pirated good is if the consumer (and the merchant) faces a real and significant risk of apprehension, prosecution, and large fines (i.e., probability greater than 75%)—which flattens the supply curve or steepens the demand curve or shifts the supply curve downward and thus reduces classical consumer surplus.

10. The models do not account for sunk costs and associated economic and psychological effects (e.g., capital budgeting, managerial risk taking, choice of channels).

11. The content pricing models do not have any relationship to the content distributor's strategies and opportunity set.

12. The models erroneously assume that variable production costs and distribution costs are zero or near-zero. Studies of real, large-scale file sharing systems have shown that online distribution of digital content creates long waiting queues that prompt many consumers to abort their download service requests before data transmission has been completed or, in many cases, before downloading has even started.

Lang and Vragov's (2005) model is applicable because it recognizes that the distributor's variable distribution costs can be significant and it introduces pricing models for both P2P and client–server structures. The problems and errors in Lang and Vragov (2005) are as follows:

1. The models erroneously assume that in the client–server model, the customers are served (purchase products) in *generations*.

2. The models erroneously assume that values of digital content follow a uniform distribution in every generation.

3. The P2P pricing model is not meaningful (note that most content distributors use a client–server model for selling digital content). In many instances, all P2P network members know that the distributor is monitoring them on the P2P network—this factor alone indicates that the P2P pricing model is inaccurate because it eliminates the major advantage of illegal P2P network, which provides anonymity and low monitoring and hence low risk of fines. Furthermore, a rational profit maximizing distributor would not pay a *compensation fee* to a P2P network member for making files available for download in a P2P network, where the distributor can easily implement a client–server system and earn the full price for the unit of digital content—the additional bandwidth costs incurred for a download under the client–server model are relatively low compared to the price of the unit of digital content.

4. The models erroneously assume that in the P2P network the distributor's variable cost decreases with every *generation* (or *node-level* of distribution), and becomes negligibly small as the number of *generations* (*node-level*) goes to infinity. In reality, the distributor incurs several variable costs (network monitoring cost that consists of labor, bandwidth, and software costs; payment processing costs), which increase as the number of *generations/node-levels* increases. Furthermore, in third- and fourth-generation P2P systems, the distributor's servers may also distribute some parts of a unit of digital content to various *generations/node-levels*, depending on the location of the purchasing customer—this effectively increases the distributor's variable costs as the number of *generations/node-levels* increases.

5. The models erroneously assume that in the P2P network, the distributor's variable cost is significant only in the beginning of the distribution process (first purchase) when the distributor is most actively involved. In reality, the distributor's variable costs (in *secondary* sales/purchase) are a direct function of the (1) size of the digital content (in bytes); (2) the physical distances between the network members, and the distance between the distributor's servers and the members; and (3) the distributor's cost of monitoring the network that varies with the size of the network. Hence, for any given *secondary* download (from one network member to another network member), where the distributor's cost of monitoring the network (bandwidth, human labor, hardware, software) is greater than the cost of a direct *first-generation* download (from distributor's servers to the network member), then the P2P model is not efficient or feasible. In some instances, the client–server model is more efficient than the P2P model because in the former, the distributor often uses dispersed servers that cache the content at various known locations (chosen in order to achieve a known maximum distance to each network member), while in the P2P system the maximum distance between any two communicating members is unknown or very difficult to predict.

6. The content pricing models do not have any relationship to the content distributor's strategies and opportunity set.

7. The models do not account for sunk costs and associated economic and psychological effects (e.g., capital budgeting, managerial risk taking, choice of channels).

8. The models erroneously assume that the spatial coverage (number of nodes/members per square mile/kilometer) of the network is uniform and remains constant over time.

9. Monopolistic pricing is not applicable, because, in either the client–server or P2P models, the content owner–distributor does not have a true monopoly on the digital content: (1) for most digital content, the Internet is only one of several distribution channels and (2) the customer can always purchase illegal copies.

10. The P2P models that were developed involve copyright infringement, because under most terms of sale of content consumers are not permitted to trade or upload content.

11. The concept of pricing digital content based on the volume of content (in bytes) delivered is or can be ineffective and very inaccurate—because it does not consider the differences in intrinsic value and utility of digital content and does not distinguish between the business of content delivery and that of content production, which have different characteristics.

12. The formulas (Equations [2] and [3] in page 126 of Lang and Vragov [2005]) for the expected value of the number of clients who decide to download the file in generation (*node-level*) *g* are inaccurate and do not consider the following: (1) differences in utility values and content valuation erroneously assume that utility is the same across all consumers; (2) the changes in the total population over time (not all nodes are functioning at all times); (3) Internet congestion is also considered; and (4) in most client–server models, there are no *generations*, customers download content when they desire, and the pattern of downloads typically does not fit any specific distribution.

13. The equations for the total profit and the profit-maximizing price (Equations [5] and [6] in Lang and Vragov [2005:127]) are inaccurate because they do not account for the following factors: (1) breakeven volumes and (2) the fixed costs of production are calculated; (3) variable costs not only include bandwidth costs but also amortize contracting costs and network monitoring costs; and (4) in most client–server models, there are no *generations*, (*node-levels*) customers download content when they desire, and the pattern of downloads typically does not fit any specific distribution.

14. The equations for the total profit and the profit-maximizing price in decentralized P2P systems (Equations [12] and [13] in Lang and Vragov [2005:129]) are inaccurate because they do not account for the following issues: (1) breakeven volumes and (2) the fixed costs of production are calculated; (3) variable costs not only include bandwidth costs but also amortized contracting costs and network monitoring costs; (4) in most P2P systems, *generations* are not rigidly defined in terms of time and/or group identity and/or download/upload capacity (the number of nodes in each *generation* changes over time, and not all nodes in any *generation* function at exactly the same time); (5) there are significant differences in download/upload capacity among nodes in any given generation and between nodes in any two contiguous generations; and (6) the geographical dispersion of nodes in the network.

15. The pricing schemes described may be feasible only in flat-rate access-pricing regimes.

10.2.1 The Price of One Unit of Digital Content in a Legal Cooperative Nonmonitored Open P2P Distribution System

10.2.1.1 A New Form of Cooperative Network Game

This section introduces a new class of TU dynamic cooperative games (within legal P2P networks), which is henceforth referred to as the repeated TU anonymous matching cooperative nonmonitored open (RTAMNO) games. Anagnostakis and Greenwald (2006), Despotovic and Aberer (2005), Li and Shen (2012), Chen and Liu (2011), Zhang and Van Der Schaar (2012), Padhariya et al. (2013), Shen and Li (2015), Xiao and Yeh (2012), Tang et al. (2015), Xu and Van Der Schaar (2013), Yang et al. (2005), and Li et al. (May 2007) and other articles[4] analyzed games and networks. Let Q be the space of feasible types of players, and let F be the space of all feasible actions of nodes/players. Q and F are fixed subsets of some Euclidean spaces.

The following characterizes a class of Bayesian games $G(Q; F; N, d1; d3; p3; u_i)$ known as RTAMNO games.

1. There are N players $\{i = 1,\ldots, N\}$. Each *player, member,* or *node* is a combination of the node (which is partly controlled by the system software) and individual human user.
2. The type of each player/node i is drawn independently from a type space Q_i, where Q_i is a compact subset of Q. Players know only their own type space. Each player i chooses actions from his or her action space F_i, which is a compact subset of F. The type distributions are common knowledge.
3. Let p3 be a probability that an unconnected node will be verified and included in the active part of the network.
4. $u = (u_1, \ldots, u_n)$ is the vector of payoff functions.
5. Let d1, d2, and d3 be distances between various types of nodes as defined earlier.
6. Each node is required to publish its capacity and content to other nodes in the P2P system.
7. Each node connects to one or more nodes. Node A cannot store any files in Node B or any other node—it can only download files from other nodes. Storage is a commodity for which supply is not limited.
8. Legal file sharing is the distribution mode—illegal file sharing is not permitted in the P2P network, and, regardless of the structure of the P2P system, the distributor's servers are the primary source for *first purchases* (a *first purchase* is the initial download of the digital content by any node in the P2P system).
9. The distributor controls the network but does not actively monitor the network. The network sponsor/distributor controls the file-folder in the peers' hard drives where the downloaded content is stored, and such content cannot be copied from the file-folder or processed on another device. The content owner/distributor knows (or can reasonably estimate) the distribution of consumers' prior valuations of available similar digital content. There is partial monitoring of each game, because the network members are anonymous and cannot monitor each other. The network sponsor monitors all network members—the network is decentralized and each node is required to publish its capacity and content to other nodes in the P2P system.
10. Members of the network are not paid when they upload any files to their hard drive folders that are designated for participation in P2P systems, and generally members can upload any files (stored in a member's hard drive and made accessible to other nodes), but each member/ node can upload files into the system/network only if (1) the member has obtained verifiable permission from the owner of the content (and the uploading member agrees to bear all liability, if any, for infringement), or (2) the distributor has entered into an agreement with the content owner to either allow the distributor to circulate a copy of the content in the system or allow persons who legally purchase a legal copy of the content to circulate such unit of content in the system.
11. All payments that pertain to each member are made to, or by, the distributor. There are no *referrals fees* for nodes that do not have requested digital content—this is because queries are a commodity in P2P systems, and the bandwidth costs for a system of referrals may be greater than the bandwidth costs incurred when a member queries all network members.
12. Each peer/node has fixed upload and download capacity, but the upload capacity is more likely to be the resource bottleneck than the download capacity. The P2P system supports partial transfers such that each peer/node can download different parts of the same unit of content concurrently from multiple sources (the number of source nodes is capped, and all source nodes share the bonus for each secondary download).
13. Any coalitions that are formed among the network members are anonymous, involuntary (or voluntary if members can guess their presence based on their holdings), and

temporary and depend on the geographic location of the nodes/members and the permitted content that each node stores.

14. The cooperative game has many geographically dispersed heterogeneous players and is repeated each time a member searches for, uploads, or downloads content.

15. Bandwidth is a commodity with nonnegligible costs.

16. There is anonymous and simultaneous multiple matching in each game because members do not know the identity of other members; and in each game, each member may match simultaneously with one or more members, depending on the geographical location of the nearest nodes.

17. Each new member of the network can be admitted into the network by simply registering and agreeing to comply with the rules.

18. Unlike most cooperative games, it is possible to derive payoffs for both individual players and *coalitions* that are subsets of the total population of members (both intentional and unintentional coalitions as defined in this section). Any distribution of value (derived from existence of, membership of, and/or participation in the network) must be stable with respect to coalitional deviations.

19. The structure of the network determines the types and durations of intentional and unintentional coalitions that may be formed.

20. Each member can see the holdings of other members. Deviations and the formation of coalitions can be *intentional/knowing* (when members can guess or estimate each other's presence/membership based on their holdings of digital content) or *unintentional*. Not only groups of players that are mutually connected in the network can jointly and unintentionally deviate and form unintentional coalitions, but also both unconnected and mutually connected members can form coalitions if they guess/estimate each other's membership in the network. Thus, the set of unintentional and intentional coalitions is limited.

21. The distributor sets prices that can be either (1) a periodic subscription fee or (2) a pay-per-use fee. The prices charged to each participant may differ from those charged to others. The distributor may decide to cap the prices charged to each member.

22. The content owner/distributor sets the price based on consumer's expected valuations and utility, and on the volume of digital content sold to customers. The content creator takes on the dual roles of creator and distributor or contracts with a third-party distributor to distribute the content.

23. The consumer's *utility value* of the unit of digital content typically exceeds its monetary value, but the content owner/distributor cannot charge a price equal to the true utility value of the unit of digital content because in the realm of digital content the consumer's marginal propensity to substitute is relatively high (compared to other products), the consumer's marginal cost of substitution is relatively low, and the consumer's search costs are relatively low.

24. The consumer does not know the content owner's or the distributor's true production and distribution costs. The distributor's marketing costs have some effect on consumer choice and such effects vary across time, type of digital content, and consumer profiles.

25. The digital distributor is not a monopolist in the typical meaning of the word—because the same distributor typically uses other channels (record stores, retail stores, DVDs, CDs, mail order, etc.), and the consumer can choose to obtain illegal copies of the content from other sources. Due to pirating, for any given unit of digital content, at any time, there are many suppliers/sellers, intensive price-based competition, and low switching costs. Thus, customer experience and the average download time can be enhanced by

piracy-minimizing pricing. Such a pricing scheme incorporates elements of a prioritization scheme and will necessarily reduce the download speed and QoS experienced by lower-priority customers.

26. The information producer is not a traditional revenue maximizing entity, but rather is piracy-averse, has limited control over the P2P network, and is willing to incur lower profits in the short term in order to preserve capacity to generate long-term profits.

27. Customers are generally self-interested, *loss-averse*, and price-sensitive persons who derive mostly nonmonetary utility from consumption of digital content.

28. The P2P network is a legal network and thus the effects of coordination among customers are somewhat limited.

The game is a cooperative game because (1) regardless of whether the network is decentralized or centralized, members do not always compete for allocation of portions of the processing capacity of the distributor's servers (because all or portions of each unit of content can be simultaneously downloaded from various nodes); (2) the network members do not always compete for the distributor's finite bandwidth because all or portions of each unit of content can be simultaneously downloaded from various nodes (and for any two network members or for any coalition that is a subset of the population of all network members, the allocation of bandwidth [for proposes of downloading or uploading content] is never a zero-sum subgame); (3) network members directly and indirectly assist each other in their respective search and download efforts; and (4) network members do not necessarily compete based on the amount of content that they upload and make publicly available (partly because content can be partly or wholly downloaded from one or more members [in some of these networks and games, the more content that a member makes available, the more incentives he or she earns]).

The utility that each network member gains from each repeated game is *transferable* without the member incurring any losses because (a) the players have common currencies that they all value equally or may value equally during specific units of time—and the common currencies are as follows: (1) the value of the time spent by the member on searching for digital content is transferable to other members (i.e., by making content available in his or her hard drive) and may be deemed to be equal across some members; (2) the member's opportunity cost of searching for digital content in the network is transferable to other members (i.e., by making content available in his or her hard drive) and may be deemed to be equal across members; (3) each member's enjoyment of the actual unit of digital content (separate from the monetary cost/value of the unit) is transferable (i.e., by making content available in his or her hard drive) and may be deemed equal across some members; (4) the utility gained by each member by his or her ability to search the network for digital content and to see the holdings of other network members is transferable to other members (by making his or her hard drive available) and may be deemed to be equal across some members; and (5) the transfer of utility associated with a unit of content does not reduce the value/appeal/perception of the unit of content.

In RTAMNO P2P games, the core is empty because (1) the games are anonymous and the network members cannot voluntarily communicate with each other, and thus *voluntary coalitions* cannot be formed; (2) the matching is done automatically and anonymously by the P2P software; (3) for each member that sends a query, he or she can be matched with more than one member and simultaneously download content from multiple members; and (4) any *involuntary anonymous coalitions* that are formed cannot leave the P2P system—such coalitions are very temporary and are based on the P2P software systems' determination of the most efficient paths for downloading content.

In RTAMNO P2P games, there is never equilibrium because one network member or a group of network members can improve their position either by downloading the digital content from an illegal file sharing network or by purchasing the unit from a discount store or by offline sharing.

10.2.1.2 A New Network-Allocation Model for Cooperative-Open P2P Incentive Systems (Which Is More Efficient Than Shapley Value and Stackelberg Allocations)

This section summarizes the problems inherent in P2P incentive systems and especially for RTAMNO P2P games and introduces a new allocation mechanism that allocates the benefits of cooperative-open P2P networks among network members and thus reduces the prices of digital content.

Most proposed solutions to the cooperative-open P2P incentive problems focus on developing incentives to reward cooperative peers (by a system of fees and compensation), but there are several problems inherent in such systems. First, in such systems, the resulting system load is not balanced. Second, most of these models erroneously assume that the network is uniformly spatially dispersed. Third, the models erroneously assume that each peer/node has the same utility and value for each unit of digital content and also has the same utility for uploading and downloading digital content. Fourth, the models are designed for illegal P2P file sharing—the models assume that each node can upload and download files. Finally, the full potential of such systems is not fully used.

The price per unit of content distributed in a client–server model (P_c) differs from the price per unit in the P2P model (P_p) in the following ways. The distributor/owner's marginal cost of distributing content is likely to be lower in a P2P system. Π_{mps} is the consumer's marginal cost of product substitution for one unit of digital content (this includes the effects of price discounts, promotions, coupons, and free products), which is likely to be greater in a P2P system. Π_{ms} is the consumer's marginal costs of searching for one unit of digital content, which are likely to be slightly lower in a P2P system due to lower bandwidth costs. Π_{ts} is the consumer's *marginal cost of time-substitution*, which is likely to remain the same in client–server or P2P systems.

Each P2P network member gains certain benefits from the use of the P2P model, some of which are as follows:

β_n are cash benefits from reduced network congestion, if any, and from savings in bandwidth.

β_w are cash benefits from savings in bandwidth.

β_d are cash benefits of faster download times—lower search-time and lower congestion.

β_p are cash benefits of increased probability of completing a purchase. Only digital content that is provided by the distributor can be shared in the P2P system—but the distributor's website may not be functioning at certain times, and there could be packet losses and bottlenecks.

β_b are psychological benefits of being a member of an online community (a function of mental processes, aspirations, biological conditions, affinity for online search, altruism, greed, etc.).

β_c are total cash values of these benefits. $\beta_c = \beta_n + \beta_d + \beta_p + \beta_n + \beta_w$.

β_u are total nonmonetary utility values of these benefits. $\beta_u = \beta_n + \beta_d + \beta_p + \beta_b + \beta_w$.

β_f is the total *compensation fee* paid by the distributor to one or more P2P network *primary* members (each unit of content can be downloaded from one or more members), each time that a *secondary* member–purchaser downloads a unit of content from one or more *primary* member's hard drive.

The sum of the cash and utility values of these benefits are β_c and β_u, respectively. In typical P2P content pricing models, the distributor pays each member a *compensation fee* for transferring the content to other members. However, this *compensation fee* is erroneously calculated and modeled as if each member's computer is always on. Hence, the P2P benefits (β_c, β_u) are limited by (1) the number of consumer's computers that are functioning and connected to the network (η_c) (thus, $\partial\beta_c/\partial\eta_c > 0$); (2) the number of P2P network members that have already downloaded the content (η_d) (thus, $\partial\beta_c/\partial\eta_d > 0$); and (3) the geographical dispersion of the network members that have already downloaded the content (S) (hence, $\partial\beta_c/\partial S < 0$).

The P2P network member's possible reaction to any *incentives to share* in P2P networks is limited, given the structure of the network because sharing in P2P systems is not optional and the network member must participate in the network once he or she signs on—the only two variables are the following:

1. The network member can choose to leave his or her computer on and connected permanently—but even then, the member may not have downloaded *desirable* content that others seek; and the cost of leaving the computer on is usually relatively minimal.
2. The network member should download as much *desirable* digital content as possible but at market price. Hence, any incentive payment made to the network member has limited value, because the downloaded content may not be desired by other network members. Even if the distributor assigns *compensation fees* to specific content based on each unit-type's popularity and utility-value, then the *compensation fee* will either be reduced or will become less meaningful as many network members choose to download only the most popular types of digital contents.

In the P2P model, the distributor's marginal cost of distribution/selling is a function of (1) the number of consumer's computers that are functioning and connected to the network (η_c) (thus, $\partial\Pi_d/\partial\eta_c < 1$); (2) the number of P2P network members that have already downloaded the content (η_d) (thus, $\partial\Pi_d/\partial\eta_d < 0$); (3) the geographical dispersion of the nodes (network members) that have already downloaded the content (S) (and thus, in most instances, $\partial\Pi_d/\partial S < 0$); (4) administrative costs; (5) the size of the unit of digital content; (6) the distributor's per-unit cost of monitoring the P2P network (C_m) (this cost does not exist in the client–server model, and, generally, $\partial\Pi_d/\partial C_m \geq 0$).

In most instances, the member's cost of distributing the digital content (secondary purchases) typically consists of bandwidth costs, marketing costs (online and offline marketing), and amortized hardware costs. Note that each network member in each *generation* (first, second, third, etc.) is assumed to pay the same price for each unit of digital content regardless of the source (the distributor's servers or other members' servers). The distributor is the *primary source*. After the primary purchase, the purchasing member becomes a *secondary source*.

Definition 10.1: Incentive Stability

Incentive stability refers to a state wherein the existence of a set of conditions and/or incentives is required to provide sufficient inducement for an incentive-based coalition in time t and to remain active and valid (without any member deviation).

Theorem 10.1

For the defined legal cooperative nonmonitored open P2P system, there are minimum incentive-stability conditions for distributors for secondary purchases.

Proof: The content owner/distributor will pay a *compensation fee* β_f to secondary-source members of this legal-P2P network for each secondary purchase, *iff* all the following conditions exist:

$$\beta_f < \beta_u, \beta_c \tag{10.1}$$

$$(\Pi_d + C_m) \geq \beta_u, \beta_c, \text{ for } secondary\ purchases \tag{10.2}$$

$$[\text{Min}(\beta_c, \beta_u) - (C_p * \gamma)] \geq (\Pi_d + C_m) \tag{10.3}$$

$$\frac{\partial \beta_u}{\partial \beta_f} \geq 0, \quad \text{and} \quad \frac{\partial^2 \beta_u}{\partial \beta_f^2} > 0, \quad \text{and} \quad \frac{\partial^2 \beta_u}{\partial \beta_f \partial \beta_c} \geq 0; \tag{10.4}$$

$$0 < \frac{\partial^2 C_m}{\partial \eta \partial S} \leq 1 \tag{10.5}$$

$$\frac{\partial \rho_s}{\partial \eta} \geq 0, \quad \text{and} \quad \frac{\partial \rho_{sd}}{\partial C_p} < 1 \tag{10.6}$$

$$\frac{\partial^2 \rho_s}{\partial \gamma \partial \eta} \geq 0 \tag{10.7}$$

$$\frac{\partial^2 \rho_{sd}}{\partial \beta_c \partial \gamma} \geq 0, \text{ and } \frac{\partial \rho_{sd}}{\partial \gamma} \geq 0; \text{ this implies that network effects are a requirement} \tag{10.8}$$

$$\frac{\partial C_m}{\partial \gamma} \leq 1, \quad \text{and} \quad \frac{\partial^2 C_m}{\partial \gamma \partial \eta} \leq 1 \tag{10.9}$$

$$\frac{\partial^2 \Pi_d}{\partial \gamma \partial n} \leq 1, \quad \text{and} \quad \frac{\partial \Pi_d}{\partial P_{sd}} \geq 0, \quad \text{and} \quad \frac{\partial^2 \Pi_d}{\partial P_{sd}^2} \geq 0, \quad \text{and} \quad \frac{\partial \Pi_d}{\partial C_m} \leq 1 \tag{10.10}$$

$$\frac{\partial \Pi_d}{\partial \beta_c} \leq 1, \quad \text{and} \quad \frac{\partial^2 \Pi_d}{\partial \beta_c \partial n} \leq 1 \tag{10.11}$$

$$\frac{\partial C_m}{\partial \gamma} \leq 1, \quad \text{and} \quad \frac{\partial^2 C_m}{\partial \gamma \partial n} \leq 1 \tag{10.12}$$

$$\frac{\partial \beta_c}{\partial \gamma \partial n} \leq 1; \frac{\partial \beta_c}{\partial \Pi_d} \leq 1; \frac{\partial \beta_c}{\partial \Pi_d \partial \gamma} \leq 1 \tag{10.13}$$

where

C_p are member's average bandwidth costs and hardware costs for distributing one unit of content in a secondary purchase.

γ is the expected minimum number of secondary downloads/purchases per primary purchase.

ρ_{sd} is the probability of a secondary purchase/download.

η is the number of network members.

C_m is the owner's/distributor's per-unit cost of monitoring the network.

S is the vector for geographical dispersion of the P2P network members that have already downloaded the digital content (S → 1, as geographical dispersion increases).

C_v are the costs incurred by the member when the member's computer contracts a virus because of participation in the P2P network, for example, repairs and new hard drive.

ρ_v is the probability that the purchasing member will contract a virus in any sale *after the primary sale* and that the owner/distributor and/or the P2P software firm will be held partly liable for such viruses—probability given the occurrence of secondary sale and partial or full download of one unit of digital content.

ρ_f is the probability that the member will be detected in an illegal P2P network and fined.

C_f is the applicable fine for participating in IOF.

R_1 is the average ratio of *first purchases* (distributor to member) to *second purchases* (member to member) in the P2P system (If one unit of digital content is downloaded from more than one node/peer, the calculation assumes that the download is from one node/peer. For any given unit of digital content, there can be more than one *first purchase* depending on the relative location and proximity of the owner's/distributor's servers and the nearest node that has the desired content. R_1 is calculated from the historical performance of the same or comparable digital content.).

R_2 is the average ratio of *second purchases* to all other subsequent derivative purchases in the system (R_2 is determined by historical performance of the same or comparable digital content.).

For any given unit of digital content purchased by primary sale, and for a given probability of a secondary sale (ρ_{sd}), if the primary member knows about the incentives that will be provided in exchange for sharing digital content, then the primary member will want to realize at least γ secondary sales in order to mentally justify the cost of primary download. This justification process may not exist where incentives (for sharing) are not offered. ■

Theorem 10.2

For the defined legal cooperative-nonmonitored-open P2P system, there are minimum incentive-stability *conditions for* primary purchases *that are also akin to optimal search and stopping points.*

Proof: A network member may have sufficient incentives to purchase a unit of digital content in a *primary purchase* in this legal P2P system, *iff* all of the following conditions exist simultaneously:

$$Max(0,P_{p2}) * h \leq (\beta_f * \gamma), \text{ where } 0 < h < 1 \tag{10.14}$$

and h measures the network member's perception of price fairness. As h → 1, prices are deemed to be more fair.

$$\frac{\partial R_2}{\partial R_1} \geq 0; \frac{\partial R_1}{\partial \eta} \leq 0 \tag{10.15}$$

$$\{Max(0,P_{p2}) * h\} \leq \{\beta_c - ((\beta_f - C_m) * \gamma)\}; \text{ where } 0 < h < 1 \tag{10.16}$$

$$[\{Max(0,P_{p2}) * h\} *](1 - \rho_f)] \leq \{\beta_c - ((\beta_f - C_m) * \gamma) - (\Pi_{ms} + \Pi_{mps} + \Pi_{ts}) - (\rho_v * C_v)\} \tag{10.17}$$

$$Max(0,P_{p2}) \leq \{(\Pi_{ms} + \Pi_{mps} + \Pi_{ts}) - (P_v * C_v)\} \tag{10.18}$$

$$\frac{\partial U_i}{\partial \beta_u} \geq 0, \quad \text{and} \quad \frac{\partial^2 U_i}{\partial \beta_c \partial \beta_f} \geq 0 \tag{10.19}$$

$$\frac{\partial^2 U_i}{\partial \Pi_{ms} \partial \Pi_{mps}} \leq 0 \tag{10.20}$$

$$\frac{\partial U_i}{\partial U_g} \geq 0, \quad \text{and} \quad \frac{\partial^2 U_i}{\partial \gamma \partial \Pi_{ts}} \geq 0 \tag{10.21}$$

$$\frac{\partial \beta_c}{\partial P_{p2}} \geq 0, \quad \text{and} \quad \frac{\partial^2 \beta_c}{\partial \Pi_{ms} \partial \Pi_{mps}} \tag{10.22}$$

$$\frac{\partial \beta_u}{\partial \beta_f} \geq 0, \quad \text{and} \quad \frac{\partial^3 \beta_f}{\partial U_g \partial n \partial S} \geq 0 \tag{10.23}$$

$$\left[\left\{ \text{Max}\left(0, P_{p2}\right) + \left(C_m * \gamma\right) + \Pi_{ms} + \Pi_{mps} + \left(P_v * C_v\right) \right\} * \left(1 - \rho_f\right) \right]$$
$$\leq \left[\left(\beta_f * \gamma\right) + U_i + \left(\frac{U_g}{\eta}\right) + \beta_u \right] \tag{10.24}$$

$$\left[\left\{ \text{Max}\left(0, P_{p2}\right) + \left(C_m * \gamma\right) + \Pi_{ms} + \Pi_{mps} + \left(\rho_v * C_v\right) \right\} \right] \leq \left[\left(\beta_f * \gamma\right) + U_i + \left(\frac{U_g}{\eta}\right) + \beta_u \right] \tag{10.25}$$

$$\left[\left(\rho_v * C_v\right) + \left(\rho_f * C_f\right) \right] \leq \left[P_{p2} - \left(\left(\beta_f * C_m\right) * \gamma\right) - \beta_c + \left(\rho_v * C_v\right) \right] \tag{10.26}$$

assuming that Π_{ms}, Π_{mps}, and Π_{ts} are the same for both legal and illegal P2P networks.

where P_{p2} is the price of one unit of digital content in a secondary sale.

These conditions can be weighted and converted into a score (or an index) that can be calibrated to determine an *optimal stopping point*. Thus, the conditions mentioned earlier are analogous to conditions for *optimal search* and a *stopping point* in this P2P network—all of which are derived without the use of stochastic calculus. The weighted scores can indicate the areas of optimal search and a stopping point. ■

It may not be necessary to pay the secondary source any incentive benefits for tertiary purchases or any further sales for several reasons. First, after the secondary purchase, the secondary purchaser expands both the size of the network and the number of nodes that have the content; hence, the value of the service provided by the primary purchaser's node immediately declines substantially—the magnitude of the decrease in value is a function of the size of the network, and the location of the nodes that demand the content. Second, after the secondary purchase, the cost advantage of downloading from the primary purchaser (secondary source) declines substantially. Third, continuing to pay B_f to the primary purchaser for all subsequent derivative downloads after the secondary purchase provides substantial incentives or basis for (1) *network collusion* in which network members will *knowingly cooperate* (only if they can guess or estimate each other's presence/membership in the network—e.g., by their user-names, and/or by the type/names of files that they make publicly available in their hard drives) and download only very few files directly from the distributor but share the files among themselves, such that for any one unit of content the ratio of primary purchases to secondary purchases is very small (less than 1/100 or 0.001) and/or (2) *incentive failure* wherein network members will *unknowingly cooperate* and download only very few files directly from the distributor but share the files among themselves many times, such that for any one unit of content the ratio of primary purchases to secondary purchases (R_1) is very small (less than 1/100 or 0.001). Fourth, continuing to pay β_f to the primary purchaser for all subsequent derivative downloads after the secondary download provides a strong incentive for some members to withdraw downloaded content from the file-folder that is used for file sharing, because of fear of security breaches and also provides a strong incentive for network members to load extraneous materials (like spyware and adware) into the file-folder that is used for file sharing. Fifth, according to Golle et al. (2001), empirical evidence suggests that users strongly dislike micropayments: having to decide before each download if a file worth a few cents imposes mental decision costs. Finally, if pricing mechanisms used to calculate prices and *compensation fees* are not made completely transparent to the network members, then the P2P system is likely to have a high cost in terms of *user attention* and *complexity deficit* (wherein the member's lack of knowledge and perceptions of complexity of the system preclude or reduce the participation rate in and adoption rate of the system).

10.2.2 Price of One Unit of Digital Content in a Cooperative-Open P2P Incentive System

The price of one unit of legal content in a legal P2P file sharing system is modeled as follows. The price for a primary purchase (P_{p1}) (downloaded directly from the content distributor/owner) is the same as in a client–server model, which is defined herein and in the following, and differs from the price for a *secondary purchase* (P_{p2}), which is downloaded from another node (or group of nodes), and both are described in the following models. P_{p2} does not include β_u or β_f, which are paid net of the price.

$$P_{p1} = \text{Max}\left[\left\{\left(U_i\left(e^{-tr}\right) + \left(\frac{U_g * e^{-tr}}{\pi}\right) - \left(C_v * \rho_v\right)\right\}; \left\{X + Y_p - \left(\Pi_{ms}\right) + \text{Max}\left(0, \text{Min}\left(\Lambda_p, \Pi_p\right)\right)\right.\right.$$

$$\left.\left. - \text{Max}\left(0, \Pi_{mps}\right) - \left(C_v * \rho_v\right) + \beta_c + \lambda + L + C_m + S_1\right\}, 0\right] \tag{10.27}$$

$$P_{p2} = \text{Max}\left[\left\{\left(U_i * e^{-tr}\right) + \left(\frac{\left(U_g * e^{-tr}\right)}{\pi}\right) - \left(C_v * \rho_v\right)\right\}; \left\{X + Y_p i - \left(\Pi_{ms}\right)\right.\right.$$

$$+ \text{Max}\left(0, \text{Min}\left(\Lambda_p, \Pi_p\right)\right) - \text{Max}\left(0, \Pi_{mps}\right)$$

$$\left.\left. - \left(C_v * \rho_v\right) - \beta_c + \lambda + L + + C_m + S_1\right\}; 0\right] * \text{Max}\left[1, \left\{\left(\frac{\partial^2 \Pi_{mps}}{\left(\partial \Pi_{ts} \partial \Pi_{ms}\right)}\right)\right\}\right] \tag{10.28}$$

$$P_{p2} = \text{Max}\left\{0, \text{Min}\left[\left\{\Pi_{ms} - \text{Max}\left(0, \Pi_{mps}\right) + C_m - \left(C_v * \rho_v\right) + \Pi_{ts}\right\};\right.\right.$$

$$\left\{\left(U_i * e^{-tr}\right) + \left(\frac{\left(U_g * e^{-tr}\right)}{\pi}\right) - \left(C_v * P_v\right)\right\}; \left\{X + Y_p + \text{Max}\left(0, \text{Min}\left(\Lambda_p, \Pi_p\right)\right)\right.$$

$$\left.\left. - \text{Max}\left(0, \Pi_{mps}\right) - \left(C_v * \rho_v\right) + \lambda - \beta_c + L + C_m + S_l\right\}\right]\right\} \qquad (10.29)$$

$$P_{p2} = \text{Max}\left[\left\{X + Y_p - \Pi_{ms} + \text{Max}\left(0, \text{Min}\left(\Lambda_p, \Pi_p\right)\right)\right.\right.$$

$$\left. - \text{Max}\left(0, \Pi_{mps}\right) - \left(C_v * \rho_v\right) + \lambda - \beta_c + L + C_m + S_l\right\}, 0\right]$$

$$* \text{Max}\left[\left\{\left(\partial^2 S / \partial\Pi_{ts}\partial\Pi_{ms}\right) + \left(\partial L / \partial\Pi_{ts}\right) + \left(\partial S / \partial n\right)\right\}; 1\right] \qquad (10.30)$$

$$P_{p2} = \text{Max}\left[\left\{\left(U_i * e^{-nr}\right) + \left(\frac{\left(U_g * e^{-nr}\right)}{\pi}\right) - \left(C_v * \rho_v\right)\right\}; \left\{X + Y_p - \left(\Pi_{ms}\right)\right.\right.$$

$$\left. + \text{Max}\left(0, \text{Min}\left(\Lambda_p, \Pi_p\right)\right) - \text{Max}\left(0, \Pi_{mps}\right) - \left(C_v * \rho_v\right) + \lambda - \beta_c + L + C_m + S_l\right\}; 0\right]$$

$$* \text{Max}\left[1, \left\{\text{Max}\left(0, \left(\frac{\partial^2 \Pi_{mps}}{\partial\Pi_{ts}\partial\Pi_{ms}}\right)\right)\right\}\right] \qquad (10.31)$$

s.t.:

$$\beta_f < \beta_u, \beta_c \qquad (10.32)$$

$$\left(\Pi_d + C_m\right) > \beta_u, \beta_c, \text{ for } secondary\ purchases$$

$$\left[\text{Min}(\beta_c, \beta_u) - \left(C_p * \gamma\right)\right] \geq \left(\Pi_d + C_m\right) \qquad (10.33)$$

$$\frac{\partial\beta_u}{\partial\beta_f} \geq 0, \quad \text{and} \quad \frac{\partial^2\beta_u}{\partial\beta_f^2} \geq 0, \quad \text{and} \quad \frac{\partial^2\beta_u}{\partial\beta_f\partial\beta_c} \geq 0 \qquad (10.34)$$

$$0 < \frac{\partial^2 C_m}{\partial\eta\partial S} < 1 \qquad (10.35)$$

$$\frac{\partial\rho_s}{\partial\eta} \geq 0, \quad \text{and} \quad \frac{\partial\rho_{sd}}{\partial C_p} < 1 \qquad (10.36)$$

$$\frac{\partial^2\rho_s}{\partial\gamma\partial\eta} \geq 0 \qquad (10.37)$$

$$\frac{\partial^2\rho_{sd}}{\partial\beta_c\partial\gamma} \geq 0, \quad \text{and} \quad \frac{\partial\rho_{sd}}{\partial\gamma} \geq 0; \text{ this implies that } network\ effects \text{ are a requirement} \qquad (10.38)$$

$$\frac{\partial C_m}{\partial \gamma} < 1, \quad \text{and} \quad \frac{\partial^2 C_m}{\partial \gamma \partial \eta} \leq 1 \tag{10.39}$$

$$\frac{\partial^2 \Pi_d}{\partial \gamma \partial n} \leq 1 \quad \text{and} \quad \frac{\partial \Pi_d}{\partial P_{sd}} \geq 0, \quad \text{and} \quad \frac{\partial^2 \Pi_d}{\partial P_{sd}^2} \geq 0, \quad \text{and} \quad \frac{\partial \Pi_d}{\partial C_m} \leq 1 \tag{10.40}$$

$$\frac{\partial \Pi_d}{\partial \beta_c} \leq 1, \quad \text{and} \quad \frac{\partial^2 \Pi_d}{\partial \beta_c \partial n} \leq 1 \tag{10.41}$$

$$\frac{\partial C_m}{\partial \gamma} \leq 1, \quad \text{and} \quad \frac{\partial^2 C_m}{\partial \gamma \partial n} \leq 1 \tag{10.42}$$

$$\frac{\partial^2 \beta_c}{\partial \gamma \partial n} \leq 1; \frac{\partial \beta_c}{\partial \Pi_d} < 1; \frac{\partial^2 \beta_c}{\partial \Pi_d \partial \gamma} \leq 1 \tag{10.43}$$

$$\Pi_{ms}, \Lambda_p, \Pi_p, \Pi_{mps}, \Pi_{ts}, \Pi_{ms}, \Pi_{ts} > 0 \tag{10.44}$$

$$-\infty < U_i, U_g < +\infty \tag{10.45}$$

where

B_p is the *bandwidth premium* that is the amount charged to a free rider for above-average use of other peers' bandwidth. The distributor can then share portions of the bandwidth premium among the peers that download content to the free rider. The bandwidth premium can be imposed in various ways: (1) imposed as to only one free rider only when the free rider has exceeded a certain number of downloads per period (in a *net* version, only when the free rider exceeds a specific net download [excess of downloads over uploads]), (2) imposed as to only the members of the highest/upper quartile of actual/perceived free riders only when this group has exceeded a certain number of downloads per period (in a *net* version, only when this group of free riders exceed a specific number of *net downloads* [i.e., excess of downloads over uploads]), and (3) the bandwidth premium that is necessarily dynamic and is adjusted to reflect existing and recent download/upload patterns. Let:

B_d be the average amount of bandwidth used by a peer to download one unit of content directly from the distributor

B_{na} and B_{nt} be the average and total amounts, respectively, of bandwidth expended by each *downloading peer* when two or more peers simultaneously download one unit of content to the free rider

B_{nt} be the total amount of bandwidth expended by all *downloading peers*, each peer, when two or more peers simultaneously download one unit of content to the free rider

A be any incremental advertising or sponsorship or loyalty-program revenues that the distributor generates from the simultaneous multipeer download to the free rider

C be the cost of one unit of bandwidth

Thus,

$$B_p \text{ is } Max(B_{nt}; B_d) - A.$$

The foregoing pricing models for digital content can also be solved as optimization models and are self-explanatory. These conditions can be weighted and transformed into scores (or an index) that can be calibrated to determine an *optimal stopping point*. Thus, the conditions are akin to conditions for *optimal search* and an *optimal stopping point* (when such scores reach a certain magnitude).

Jiang (2012), Yuan and Tsao (2010), Xu et al. (2007), Ekstrom and Lu (2011), Guo et al. (2006), Chin et al. (2015), Zhang et al. (2012), Ting and Xiang (2015), and Ghosh and Rao (2012) and other articles[5] analyzed optimization. On fuzzy sets, see Lin et al. (2010).

There are various feasible pricing models because information-producer firms differ (sometimes substantially) in various dimensions—distribution channels, knowledge, emphasis on pricing, scope of anti-piracy efforts, industry, form of digital content and digital rights management (DRM), etc.

10.2.3 Price of One Unit of Digital Content in a Legal Monitored and Closed P2P Distribution System

10.2.3.1 A New Form of Cooperative Network Game

Most P2P systems that distribute digital content are illegal—but the P2P network defined herein is *legal*. The interactions among the network members and the sponsor of the network are a form of a transferable utility cooperative game. This section introduces a new class of TU dynamic cooperative game, which is henceforth referred to as the repeated TU monitored matching closed games (RTMMC games). Despotovic and Aberer (2005), Buchegger and Le Boudec (June 2004), Yang et al. (2005), Li and Shen (2012), Chen and Liu (2011), Zhang and Van Der Schaar (2012), Padhariya, et al. (2013), Shen and Li (2015), Xiao and Yeh (2012), Tang et al. (2015), Xu and Van Der Schaar (2013), and Li et al. (May 2007), and other articles[6] discussed networks and games.

The following are characteristics of the *RTMMC* network games.

1. The owner/distributor creates a list of digital content that can be legally shared in its P2P system—any content that is not on this list will not be distributed in the distributor's P2P system Let Q be the space of feasible types of players, and let F be the space of all feasible actions of nodes/players. Q and F are fixed subsets of some Euclidean spaces. The following characterizes a class of Bayesian games G(Q; F; N, d1; d3; p3; ui) known as RTAMNO games. There are N players {i = 1,…, N}. Each "player," "member," or "node" is a combination of the node (which is partly controlled by the system software) and individual human user. The type of each player/node i is drawn independently from a type space Q_i, where Q_i is a compact subset of Q. Players know only their own type space. Each player i chooses actions from his or her action space F_i, which is a compact subset of F. The type distributions are common knowledge. Let p3 be a probability that an unconnected node will be verified and included in the active part of the network. $u = (u_1, …, u_n)$ is the vector of payoff functions. Let d1, d2, and d3…dn be distances between various types of nodes as defined earlier. Each node is required to publish its capacity and content to other nodes in the P2P system. Each node connects to one or more nodes. Node A cannot store any files in Node B or any other node—it can only download files from other nodes. Storage is a commodity for which supply is not limited.
2. The distributor contracts with the owners of each listed digital content such that the content owner will permit consumers who have legally purchased the listed content from other sources to upload and share the content in the distributor's P2P system, and the distributor will pay a fee to the owner each time so that the listed content is downloaded by a network member, or, alternatively, the distributor will pay a one-time licensing fee to the content owner.
3. Each member of the network cannot upload any new digital content—the only content that can be distributed in the network are those that originate from the distributor's servers. The distributor can upload files into the system/network only if (1) a member has obtained verifiable permission from the owner of the content (and such a member agrees to bear all

liability, if any, for infringement), and the member transfers the file for free (or in exchange for incentives) to the distributor for inclusion/uploading in the network or (2) the distributor has entered into an agreement with the content owner to either allow the distributor to circulate a copy of the content in the system or allow persons who legally purchase a legal copy of the content to circulate such unit of content in the network.

4. Each member of the network serves as a distribution node in the network.

5. Data storage is a commodity for which supply is not limited (within the reasonable bounds of mounts of traffic in the Internet).

6. Node-A (in the network) cannot store any files in Node-B or any other node—it can only download files from other nodes.

7. Legal file sharing is allowed in the P2P network, and, regardless of the structure of the P2P system, the distributor's servers are the primary source for *first purchases* (a *first purchase* is the initial download of the digital content by any node in the P2P system).

8. All payments are made to, or by, the distributor/sponsor.

9. There are no *referrals fees* for nodes that do not have requested digital content—this is because queries are a commodity in P2P systems, and the bandwidth costs for a system of referrals may be greater than the bandwidth costs incurred when a member queries all network members.

10. Each peer/node has fixed upload and download capacity, but the upload capacity is more likely to be the resource bottleneck than the download capacity.

11. The P2P system supports partial transfers such that each peer/node can download different parts of the same unit of content concurrently from multiple sources (the number of source nodes is capped, and all source nodes share the bonus for each secondary download).

12. The network distributor/sponsor controls the file-folder in the peers' hard drives where the downloaded content is stored, and such content cannot be copied from the file-folder or processed on another device.

13. Any coalitions that are formed among the network members are anonymous, involuntary, temporary, and dependent on the geographic location of the nodes/members and the permitted content that each node stores.

14. There is asymmetric monitoring of each game, because the network members are anonymous and cannot monitor each other, but all network members are monitored by the network sponsor/distributor. Each node is required to publish its capacity and content to other nodes in the P2P system.

15. The cooperative game has many geographically dispersed heterogeneous players and is repeated each time a member searches for, uploads, or downloads content.

16. Bandwidth is a commodity with nonnegligible costs.

17. Each new member of the network can be admitted only by the network sponsor/distributor.

18. The content owner/distributor knows (or can reasonably estimate) the patterns/distribution of consumers' prior valuations of available similar digital content—from historical sales.

19. The content owner/distributor sets the price based on consumer's expected valuations and utility and based on the volume of digital content sold to customers.

20. The content creator takes on the dual roles of creator and distributor or contracts with a third-party distributor to distribute the content.

21. The consumer's *utility value* of the unit of digital content typically exceeds its monetary value, but the content owner/distributor cannot charge a price equal to the true utility value of the unit of digital content because its conjectured here that in the realm of digital content, the consumer's marginal propensity to substitute is relatively high (compared to other products), the consumer's marginal cost of substitution is relatively low, and the consumer's search costs are relatively low.

22. The consumer does not know the content owner's or the distributor's true production and distribution costs.

23. The distributor's marketing costs have some effect on consumer choice and such effects vary across time, type of digital content, and consumer profiles.

24. The digital distributor is not a monopolist in the typical meaning of the word—because the same distributor typically uses other channels (record stores, retail stores, DVDs, CDs, mail order, etc.), and the consumer can choose to obtain illegal copies of the content from other sources.

25. Due to pirating, for any given unit of digital content, at any time, there are many suppliers/ sellers, intensive price-based competition, and low switching costs.

26. It is possible to derive payoffs for both individual players and for *coalitions* (both intentional and unintentional coalitions as defined in this section).

27. The game is a cooperative game because (1) regardless of whether the network is decentralized or centralized, members do not compete for allocation of portions of the processing capacity of the distributor's servers, because except for *first downloads*, all or portions of each unit of content can be simultaneously downloaded from various nodes; (2) the network members do not compete for the distributor's finite bandwidth because all or portions of each unit of content be simultaneously downloaded from various nodes, and for any two network members or for any coalition that is a subset of all network members, allocation of bandwidth (for proposes of downloading or uploading content) is never a zero-sum subgame; (3) network members directly and indirectly assist each other in their respective search and download efforts; and (4) network members do not necessarily compete based on the amount of content that they upload and make publicly available, partly because content can be partly or wholly downloaded from one or more members (in some of these networks and games, the more content that a member makes available, the more incentives he or she earns).

28. The utility that each network member gains from each repeated game is *transferable* without the member incurring any losses because (a) the players have common currencies that can be valued equally or are valued equally by all players during specific units of time—the common currencies are (1) the value of the time spent by the member on searching for digital content, (2) the member's opportunity cost of searching for digital content in the network, (3) the member's enjoyment of the actual unit digital content (separate from the monetary cost/value of the unit), (4) the member's ability to search the network for digital content and to see the holdings of other network members, and (5) the transfer of utility associated with a unit of content, which does not reduce the value/appeal/perception of the unit of content.

29. Tny distribution of value (derived from existence of, membership of, and/or participation in the network) must be stable with respect to coalitional deviations.

30. The structure of the network determines the types and durations of intentional and unintentional coalitions that may be formed.

31. Each member can see the holdings of other members. Deviations and the formation of coalitions can be *intentional/knowing* (when members can guess or estimate each other's presence/membership based on their holdings of digital content) or *unintentional*. Not only groups of players that are mutually connected in the network can jointly and unintentionally deviate and form unintentional coalitions, but also both unconnected and mutually connected members can form coalitions if they guess/estimate each other's membership in the network. Thus, the set of unintentional and intentional coalitions is potentially unlimited.

32. The distributor sets prices that can be either a periodic subscription fee or a pay-per-use fee. The prices charged to each participant may differ from those charged to others. The distributor may decide to cap the prices charged to each member.

The distributor/sponsor's challenge is to find a price that minimizes illegal file sharing. In RTMMC games, the core is empty for the following reasons:

1. The network members cannot voluntarily communicate with each other, and thus *voluntary coalitions* cannot be formed.
2. While there is monitoring by the distributor, the matching is done automatically and anonymously by the P2P software.
3. For each member that sends a query, he or she can be matched with more than one member and simultaneously download content from multiple members.
4. Any *involuntary anonymous coalitions* that are formed cannot leave the P2P system—such coalitions are very temporary and are based on the P2P software systems' determination of the most efficient paths for downloading content.

In *RTMMC games*, there is never equilibrium because one network member or a group of network members can improve their position either by purchasing the digital content from an illegal file sharing network or by purchasing the unit from a discount store or by offline sharing.

10.2.3.2 A New Network-Allocation Model for Monitored-Closed P2P Systems

This section summarizes the problems inherent in monitored-closed P2P incentive systems and especially for RTMMC games and introduces a new allocation mechanism that allocates the benefits of the network among network members and thus reduces the prices of digital content.

Most proposed solutions to the monitored closed P2P incentive problems focus on developing incentives to reward cooperative peers (by a system of fees and compensation), but there are several problems such as the following. In such systems, the resulting system load is not balanced. Most of these models erroneously assume that the network is uniformly spatially dispersed. The models erroneously assume that each consumer/node has the same utility and value for each unit of digital content and that each consumer/node has the same utility for uploading and downloading digital content. The models are designed for illegal P2P file sharing—the models assume that each node can upload and download files. The full potential of such systems is not fully used.

The price per unit of content distributed in a client–server model (P_c) differs from the price per unit in the P2P model (P_p) in several ways, which are as follows. The distributor/owner's marginal cost of distributing content is likely to be lower in a P2P system. Π_{mps} is the consumer's marginal cost of product substitution for one unit of digital content (this includes the effects of price discounts, promotions, coupons, and free products), which is likely to be greater in a P2P system. Π_{ms} is the consumer's marginal costs of searching for one unit of digital content, which are likely to be slightly lower in a P2P system due to lower bandwidth costs. Π_{ts} is the consumer's *marginal cost of time-substitution*, which is likely to remain the same in client–server or P2P systems.

Each P2P network member gains certain benefits from the use of the P2P model, some of which are as follows:

β_n are cash benefits from reduced network congestion, if any, and from bandwidth savings (for each transmission of files).

β_d are cash benefits of faster download times—lower search-time and lower congestion.

β_p are cash benefits of increased probability of completing a purchase. Only digital content that is provided by the distributor can be shared in the P2P system—but the distributor's website may not be functioning at certain times, and in the client–server model there could be packet losses and bottlenecks.

β_b are psychological benefits of being a member of an online community.

β_c are total cash values of these benefits. $\beta_c = \beta_n + \beta_d + \beta_p$.

β_u are total utility values of these benefits. $\beta_u = \beta_n + \beta_d + \beta_p + \beta_b$.

β_f is the total *compensation fee* paid by the distributor to one or more P2P network *primary* members (each unit of content can be downloaded from one or more members), each time that a *secondary* member–purchaser downloads content from one or more *primary* member's hard drive.

The sum of the cash and utility values of these benefits are β_c and β_u, respectively. In typical P2P content pricing models, the distributor pays each member a *compensation fee* for transferring the content to other members. However, this *compensation fee* is erroneously calculated and modeled as if each member's computer is always on. Hence, the P2P benefits (β_c, β_u) are limited by (1) the number of consumer's computers that are functioning and connected to the network (η_c) (thus, $\partial\beta_c/\partial\eta_c > 0$), (2) the number of P2P network members that have already downloaded the content (η_d) (thus, $\partial\beta_c/\partial\eta_d > 0$), and (3) the geographical dispersion of the network members that have already downloaded the content (S) (hence, $\partial\beta_c/\partial S < 0$).

The P2P network member's possible reaction to any *incentives to share* in P2P networks is limited, given the structure of the network because sharing in P2P systems is not optional and the network member must participate in the network once he or she signs on—the only two variables are the following:

1. The network member can choose to leave his or her computer on and connected permanently—but even then, the member may not have downloaded *desirable* content that others seek, and the cost of leaving the computer on is minimal.
2. The network member should download as much *desirable* digital content as possible but at market price. Hence, any incentive payment made to the network member has limited value, because the downloaded content may not be desired by other network members. Even if the distributor assigns *compensation fees* to specific content based on each unit-type's popularity and utility-value, then the *compensation fee* will either be reduced or will become less meaningful as more network members choose to download only the most popular types of digital content.

In the P2P model, the distributor's marginal cost of distribution/selling is a function of (1) the number of consumer's computers that are functioning and connected to the network (η_c) (thus, $\partial\Pi_d/\partial\eta_c < 1$), (2) the number of P2P network members that have already downloaded the content (η_d) (thus, $\partial\Pi_d/\partial\eta_d < 0$), (3) the geographical dispersion of the nodes (network members) that have already downloaded the content (S) (and thus, in most instances $\partial\Pi_d/\partial S < 0$), (4) administrative costs, (5) the size of the unit of digital content, and (6) the distributor's per-unit cost of monitoring the P2P network (C_m) (this cost does not exist in the client–server model, and, generally, $\partial\Pi_d/\partial C_m > 0$).

In most instances, the member's cost of distributing the digital content (secondary purchases) typically consists of bandwidth costs, marketing costs (online and offline marketing), and amortized hardware costs. Note that each network member in each *generation* (first, second, third, etc.) is assumed to pay the same price for each unit of digital content regardless of the source (the distributor's servers or other members' servers). The distributor is the *primary source*. After the primary purchase, the purchasing member becomes a *secondary source*.

Theorem 10.3

For the defined legal monitored-closed P2P system, there are minimum incentive-stability conditions for distributors for secondary purchases.

Proof: The content owner/distributor will pay a *compensation fee* β_f to secondary-source members of this legal monitored-closed P2P network for each secondary purchase, *iff* all the following conditions exist simultaneously:

$$\beta_f < \beta_u, \beta_c \tag{10.46}$$

$$(\Pi_d + C_m) > \beta_u, \beta_c, \text{ for } secondary\ purchases \tag{10.47}$$

$$[\text{Min}(\beta_c, \beta_u) - (C_p * \gamma)] \geq (\Pi_d + C_m) \tag{10.48}$$

$$\frac{\partial \beta_u}{\partial \beta_f} \geq 0, \quad \text{and} \quad \frac{\partial^2 \beta_u}{\partial \beta_f^2} \geq 0; \quad \text{and} \quad \frac{\partial^2 \beta_u}{\partial \beta_f \partial \beta_c} \geq 0 \tag{10.49}$$

$$0 < \frac{\partial^2 C_m}{\partial \eta \partial S} < 1 \tag{10.50}$$

$$\frac{\partial \rho_s}{\partial \eta} > 0, \quad \text{and} \quad \frac{\partial \rho_{sd}}{\partial C_p} < 1 \tag{10.51}$$

$$\frac{\partial^2 \rho_s}{\partial \gamma \partial \eta} \geq 0 \tag{10.52}$$

$$\frac{\partial^2 \rho_{sd}}{\partial \beta_c \partial \gamma} \geq 0, \quad \text{and} \quad \frac{\partial \rho_{sd}}{\partial \gamma} > 0; \text{ this implies that network effects are a requirement} \tag{10.53}$$

$$\frac{\partial C_m}{\partial \gamma} < 1, \quad \text{and} \quad \frac{\partial^2 C_m}{\partial \gamma \partial \eta} < 1 \tag{10.54}$$

$$\frac{\partial^2 \Pi_d}{\partial \gamma \partial n} \leq 1, \quad \text{and} \quad \frac{\partial \Pi_d}{\partial P_{sd}} > 0, \quad \text{and} \quad \frac{\partial^2 \Pi_d}{\partial P_{sd}^2} \geq 0, \quad \text{and} \quad \frac{\partial \Pi_d}{\partial C_m} < 1 \tag{10.55}$$

$$\frac{\partial \Pi_d}{\partial \beta_c} < 1, \quad \text{and} \quad \frac{\partial^2 \Pi_d}{\partial \beta_c \partial n} \leq 1 \tag{10.56}$$

$$\frac{\partial C_m}{\partial \gamma} < 1, \quad \text{and} \quad \frac{\partial^2 C_m}{\partial \gamma \partial n} < 1 \tag{10.57}$$

$$\frac{\partial^2 \beta_c}{\partial \gamma \partial n} \leq 1; \frac{\partial \beta_c}{\partial \Pi_d} < 1; \frac{\partial^2 \beta_c}{\partial \Pi_d \partial \gamma} \leq 1 \tag{10.58}$$

where
C_p are the member's average bandwidth costs and hardware costs for distributing one unit of content in a secondary purchase
γ is the expected minimum number of secondary downloads/purchases per primary purchase
ρ_{sd} is the probability of a secondary purchase/download
η is the number of network members

C_m is the owner's/distributor's per-unit cost of monitoring the network. **S** is a vector for geographical dispersion of the P2P network members that have already downloaded the digital content. $S \rightarrow 1$, as geographical dispersion increases. C_v is the costs incurred by the member when the member's computer contracts a virus because of participation in the P2P network—for example, repairs and new hard drive. ρ_v is the probability that the purchasing member will contract a virus in any sale *after the primary sale* and that the owner/distributor and/or the P2P software firm will be held partly liable for such viruses—probability given the occurrence of secondary sale and partial or full download of one unit of digital content. ρ_f is the probability that the member will be detected in an illegal P2P network and fined. C_f is the applicable fine for participating in IOF. F is the fee paid to the content owner by the distributor when the digital content is downloaded by a P2P network member. **R₁** is the average ratio of *first purchases* (distributor to member) to *second purchases* (member to member) in the P2P system. If one unit of digital content is downloaded from more than one node/peer, the calculation assumes that the download is from one node/peer. For any given unit of digital content, there can be more than one *first purchase* depending on the relative location and proximity of the owner's/distributor's servers and the nearest node that has the desired content. **R₁** is determined by historical performance of the same or comparable digital content. **R₂** is the average ratio of *second purchases* to all other subsequent derivative purchases in the system. **R₂** is determined by historical performance of the same or comparable digital content. P_{p2} is the price of one unit of digital content in a secondary sale.

For any given unit of digital content purchased by primary sale, and for a given probability of a secondary sale (ρ_{sd}), if the primary member knows about the incentives that will be provided in exchange for sharing digital content, then the primary member will want to realize at least γ secondary sales in order to mentally justify the cost of primary download. This justification process may not exist where incentives (for sharing) are not offered. ■

Theorem 10.4

For the defined legal monitored-closed P2P system, there are minimum quasi-stability *conditions for* primary purchases *that are also akin to optimal search and stopping points.*

Proof: A network member can have sufficient incentives to purchase a unit of digital content in a *primary purchase* in a legal monitored-closed P2P system, *iff* all of the following conditions exist simultaneously:

$$\text{Max}(0, P_{p2}) * h < (\beta_f * \gamma); \text{ where } 0 < h < 1 \tag{10.59}$$

and h measures the member's perception of price fairness. As $h \rightarrow 1$, prices are deemed to be more fair.

$$\frac{\partial R_2}{\partial R_1} > 0; \frac{\partial R_1}{\partial \eta} < 0 \tag{10.60}$$

$$\{\text{Max}(0, P_{p2}) * h\} \leq \{\beta_c - ((\beta_f - C_m) * \gamma)\}; \text{ where } 0 < h < 1 \tag{10.61}$$

$$[\{\text{Max}(0, P_{p2}) * h\} * (1 - \rho_f)] \leq \{\beta_c - ((\beta_f - C_m) * \gamma) - (\Pi_{ms} + \Pi_{mps} + \Pi_{ts}) - (\rho_v * C_v)\} \tag{10.62}$$

$$\text{Max}(0, P_{p2}) \leq \{(\Pi_{ms} + \Pi_{mps} + \Pi_{ts}) - (P_v * C_v)\} \tag{10.63}$$

$$\frac{\partial U_i}{\partial \beta_u} > 0, \quad \text{and} \quad \frac{\partial^2 U_i}{\partial \beta_c \partial \beta_f} \geq 0 \tag{10.64}$$

$$\frac{\partial^2 U_i}{\partial \Pi_{ms} \partial \Pi_{mps}} \leq 0 \tag{10.65}$$

$$\frac{\partial U_i}{\partial U_g} > 0, \quad \text{and} \quad \frac{\partial^2 U_i}{\partial \gamma \partial \Pi_{ts}} \geq 0 \tag{10.66}$$

$$\frac{\partial \beta_c}{\partial P_{p2}} \geq 0, \quad \text{and} \quad \frac{\partial^2 \beta_c}{\partial \Pi_{ms} \partial \Pi_{mps}} \geq 0 \tag{10.67}$$

$$\frac{\partial \beta_u}{\partial \beta_f} \geq 0, \quad \text{and} \quad \frac{\partial^3 \beta_f}{\partial U_g \partial n \partial S} \geq 0 \tag{10.68}$$

$$\left[\left\{ \text{Max}\left(0, P_{p2}\right) + \left(C_m * \gamma\right) + \Pi_{ms} + \Pi_{mps} + \left(P_v * C_v\right) \right\} * \left(1 - \rho_f\right) \right]$$

$$\leq \left[\left(\beta_f * \gamma\right) + U_i + \left(\frac{U_g}{\eta}\right) + \beta_u \right] \tag{10.69}$$

$$\left[\left\{ \text{Max}\left(0, P_{p2}\right) + \left(C_m * \gamma\right) + \Pi_{ms} + \Pi_{mps} + \left(\rho_v * C_v\right) \right\} \right] \leq \left[\left(\beta_f * \gamma\right) + U_i + \left(\frac{U_g}{\eta}\right) + \beta_u \right] \tag{10.70}$$

$$\left[\left(\rho_v * C_v\right) + \left(\rho_f * C_f\right) \right] \leq \left[P_{p2} - \left(\left(\beta_f - C_m\right) * \gamma\right) - \beta_c + \left(\rho_v + C_v\right) \right] \tag{10.71}$$

assuming that Π_{ms}, Π_{mps}, and Π_{ts} are the same for both legal and illegal P2P networks where P_{p2} is the price of one unit of digital content in a secondary sale.

These conditions can be weighted and transformed into scores (or an index) that can be calibrated to determine an *optimal stopping point*. Thus, the conditions are akin to conditions for *optimal search* and an *optimal stopping point*, (when such scores reach a certain magnitude) all of which are derived without use of stochastic calculus, which has been found to be deficient (see comments in Taleb (2009) about the misuse of stochastic calculus). ■

It may not be necessary to pay the secondary source any incentive benefits for tertiary purchases or any further sales because of the following reasons:

1. After the secondary purchase, the secondary purchaser expands both the size of the network and the number of nodes that have the content; hence, the value of the service provided by the primary purchaser's node immediately declines substantially—the magnitude of the decrease in value is a function of the size of the network and the location of the nodes that demand the content.
2. After the secondary purchase, the cost advantage of downloading from the primary purchaser (secondary source) declines substantially.

3. Continuing to pay B_f to the primary purchaser for all subsequent derivative downloads after the secondary purchase provides substantial incentives or basis for (1) *network collusion* in which network members will *knowingly cooperate* (only if they can guess or estimate each other's presence/membership in the network—for example, by their "usernames" or by the type/names of files that they make publicly available in their hard drives) and download only very few files directly from the distributor but share the files among themselves, such that for any one unit of content, the ratio of primary purchases to secondary purchases is very small (less than 1/100 or 0.001) and/or (2) *incentive failure*, in which network members will *unknowingly cooperate* and download only very few files directly from the distributor but share the files among themselves many times, such that for any one unit of content, the ratio of primary purchases to secondary purchases (R_1) is very small (less than 1/100 or 0.001).

4. Continuing to pay β_f to the primary purchaser for all subsequent derivative downloads after the secondary download provides a strong incentive for some members to withdraw downloaded content from the file-folder that is used for file sharing, because of fear of security breaches and also provides a strong incentive for network members to load extraneous materials (like spyware and adware) into the file-folder that is used for file sharing.

5. According to Golle et al. (2001), empirical evidence suggests that users strongly dislike micropayments: having to decide before each download if a file is worth a few cents imposes mental decision-costs.

6. If the mechanisms used to calculate prices and *fees* are not made completely transparent to the network members, then the P2P system is likely to have a high cost in terms of *user attention* and *complexity deficit* (in which the member's lack of knowledge and perceptions of complexity of the system preclude or reduce the participation rate in, and adoption rate of, the system).

10.2.4 Price of One Unit of Digital Content in a Monitored-Closed P2P System

The price of one unit of legal content in this type of legal P2P file sharing system is described as follows and can be construed as an optimization problem. There are necessarily different pricing models because there are different types of customers (can be segmented by age, location, etc.) and different types of digital products and because information-producer firms differ (sometimes substantially) in various dimensions—distribution channels, knowledge, emphasis on pricing, scope of anti-piracy efforts, industry, form of digital content and DRM, etc. The price for a primary purchase (P_{p1}) (download directly from the content distributor/owner) is the same as in a client–server model. The price for a *secondary purchase* (P_{p2} is price for download from another node) differs and is described in the following models. P_{p2} includes β_c, which can also be paid net of the price.

$$P_{p1} = \text{Max}\left[\left\{\left(U_i\left(e^{-tr}\right) + \left(\frac{U_g * e^{-tr}}{\pi}\right) - \left(C_v * \rho_v\right)\right\}; \left\{X + Y_p - \right\}\left(\Pi_{ms}\right) + \text{Max}\left(0, \text{Min}\left(\Lambda_p, \Pi_p\right)\right)\right.$$

$$\left. - \text{Max}\left(0, \Pi_{mps}\right) - \left(C_v * \rho_v\right) + \beta_c + \lambda + L + C_m + S_1\right\}, 0\right] \tag{10.72}$$

$$P_{p2} = Max\left[\left\{\left\{\left(U_i * e^{-tr}\right) + \left(\frac{\left(U_g * e^{-tr}\right)}{\pi}\right) - \left(C_v * \rho_v\right)\right\}; \left\{X + Y_p - \right\}\left(\Pi_{ms}\right)\right.\right.$$

$$+ Max\left(0, Min\left(\Lambda_p, \Pi_p\right)\right) - Max\left(0, \Pi_{mps}\right)$$

$$\left.\left. - \left(C_v * \rho_v\right) - \beta_c + \lambda + L + + C_m + S_1\right\}; 0\right] * Max\left[1, \left\{\left(\frac{\partial^2 \Pi_{mps}}{\left(\partial \Pi_{ts} \partial \Pi_{ms}\right)}\right)\right\}\right]\right] \quad (10.73)$$

$$P_{p2} = Max\left\{0, Min\left[\left\{\Pi_{ms} - Max\left(0, \Pi_{mps}\right) + C_m - \left(C_v * \rho_v\right) + \Pi_{ts}\right\};\right.\right.$$

$$\left\{\left(U_i * e^{-tr}\right) + \left(\frac{\left(U_g * e^{-tr}\right)}{\pi}\right) - \left(C_v * P_v\right)\right\}; \left\{X + Y_p + Max\left(0, Min\left(\Lambda_p, \Pi_p\right)\right)\right.$$

$$\left.\left. - Max\left(0, \Pi_{mps}\right) - \left(C_v * \rho_v\right) + \lambda - \beta_c + L + C_m + S_1\right\}\right]\right\} \quad (10.74)$$

$$P_{p2} = Max\left[\left\{X + Y_p - \Pi_{ms} + Max\left(0, Min\left(\Lambda_p, \Pi_p\right)\right) - Max\left(0, \Pi_{mps}\right)\right.\right.$$

$$\left. - \left(C_v * \rho_v\right) + \lambda - \beta_c + L + C_m + S_1\right\}, 0\right]$$

$$* Max\left[\left\{\left(\partial^2 S/\partial \Pi_{ts} \partial \Pi_{ms}\right) + \left(\partial L/\partial \Pi_{ts}\right) + \left(\partial S/\partial n\right)\right\}; 1\right] \quad (10.75)$$

$$P_{p2} = Max\left[\left[\left\{\left(U_i * e^{-nr}\right) + \left(\frac{\left(U_g * e^{-nr}\right)}{\pi}\right) - \left(C_v * \rho_v\right)\right\}; \left\{X + Y_p - \right\}\left(\Pi_{ms}\right)\right.\right.$$

$$+ Max\left(0, Min\left(\Lambda_p, \Pi_p\right)\right) - Max\left(0, \Pi_{mps}\right) - \left(C_v * \rho_v\right) + \lambda - C\beta_c + L + C_m + S_1\right\}; 0\right]$$

$$* Max\left[1, \left\{Max\left(0, \left(\frac{\partial^2 \Pi_{mps}}{\left(\partial \Pi_{ts} \partial \Pi_{ms}\right)}\right)\right)\right\}\right] \quad (10.76)$$

Subject to the following conditions:

$$\beta_f < \beta_u, \beta_c \quad (10.77)$$

$$\left(\Pi_d + C_m\right) > \beta_u, \beta_c, \text{ for } secondary \; purchases \quad (10.78)$$

$$\left[Min(\beta_c, \beta_u) - \left(C_p * \gamma\right)\right] \geq \left(\Pi_d + C_m\right) \quad (10.79)$$

$$\frac{\partial \beta_u}{\partial \beta_f} > 0, \text{ and } \frac{\partial^2 \beta_u}{\partial \beta_f^2} \geq 0, \text{ and } \frac{\partial^2 \beta_u}{\partial \beta_f \partial \beta_c} \geq 0 \quad (10.80)$$

$$0 < \frac{\partial^2 C_m}{\partial \eta \partial S} < 1 \quad (10.81)$$

$$\frac{\partial \rho_s}{\partial \eta} > 0, \quad \text{and} \quad \frac{\partial \rho_{sd}}{\partial C_p} < 1 \tag{10.82}$$

$$\frac{\partial^2 \rho_s}{\partial \gamma \partial \eta} \geq 0 \tag{10.83}$$

$$\frac{\partial^2 \rho_{sd}}{\partial \beta_c \partial \gamma} \geq 0, \quad \text{and} \quad \frac{\partial \rho_{sd}}{\partial \gamma} > 0; \text{ this implies that network effects are a requirement} \tag{10.84}$$

$$\frac{\partial C_m}{\partial \gamma} < 1, \quad \text{and} \quad \frac{\partial^2 C_m}{\partial \gamma \partial \eta} < 1 \tag{10.85}$$

$$\frac{\partial^2 \Pi_d}{\partial \gamma \partial n} \leq 1, \quad \text{and} \quad \frac{\partial \Pi_d}{\partial P_{sd}} > 0, \quad \text{and} \quad \frac{\partial^2 \Pi_d}{\partial P_{sd}^2} \geq 0, \quad \text{and} \quad \frac{\partial \Pi_d}{\partial C_m} < 1 \tag{10.86}$$

$$\frac{\partial \Pi_d}{\partial \beta_c} < 1, \quad \text{and} \quad \frac{\partial^2 \Pi_d}{\partial \beta_c \partial n} \leq 1 \tag{10.87}$$

$$\frac{\partial C_m}{\partial \gamma} < 1, \quad \text{and} \quad \frac{\partial^2 C_m}{\partial \gamma \partial n} \leq 1 \tag{10.88}$$

$$\frac{\partial^2 \beta_c}{\partial \gamma \partial n} \leq 1; \frac{\partial \beta_c}{\partial \Pi_d} < 1; \frac{\partial^2 \beta_c}{\partial \Pi_d \partial \gamma} \leq 1 \tag{10.89}$$

$$\Pi_{ms}, \Lambda_p, \Pi_p, \Pi_{mps}, \Pi_{ts}, \Pi_{ms}, \Pi_{ts} > 0 \tag{10.90}$$

$$-\infty < U_i, U_g < +\infty \tag{10.91}$$

The foregoing pricing models for digital content can be solved as optimization models and are self-explanatory. Jiang (2012), Yuan and Tsao (2010), Xu et al. (2007), Ekstrom and Lu (2011), Guo et al. (2006), Yong et al. (2012), Ghosh and Rao (2012), and Faigle et al. (1998) and other articles discussed optimization.[7] Also see Lin et al. (2010) (fuzzy sets).

10.2.5 Price of One Unit of Digital Content in a Legal Client–Server Distribution System

10.2.5.1 A New Form of Noncooperative Network Game

This section introduces a new type of cooperative network game named the *repeated intermediated anonymous multimatching noncooperative network* game (RIAMNN games).

Yang et al. (2005), Li et al. (May 2007), Yuan and Tsao (2010), Yu et al. (2006), Li and Shen (2012), Chen and Liu (2011), Zhang and Van Der Schaar (2012), Padhariya et al. (2013), Shen and Li (2015), Xiao and Yeh (2012), Tang et al.(2015), Xu and Van Der Schaar (2013), and Lin et al. (2010) and other articles[8] studied games and networks.

The following are the characteristics of the noncooperative client–server (C-S) system, and the RIAMNN game:

1. Data storage is a commodity for which supply is not limited.
2. Each customer downloads the digital content only from the distributor's/owner's servers (its a client-server network).

3. There is no communication between any two nodes/members, and there is no *direct* file sharing among network members. Each member-query is sent to the distributor's central server that then searches the hard drives of all network members to find the nearest available content, obtains the content, and sends it to the querying member. Each member can upload legally purchased files onto his or her hard drive to be available for indirect sharing.

4. All payments by members are made only to the distributor.

5. The content owner/distributor knows (or can reasonably estimate) the distribution of consumers' prior valuations of available similar digital content.

6. The content distributor–intermediary controls the file-folder in the network members' hard drives where the downloaded content is stored, and such content cannot be copied from the file-folder or processed on another device.

7. The content distributor–intermediary sets the price based on consumer's expected valuations and utility and on the volume of digital content sold to customers.

8. The content creator either assumes the dual roles of creator and distributor or contracts with a third-party distributor to distribute the content.

9. The consumer's *utility value* of the unit of digital content typically exceeds its monetary value, but the content owner/distributor cannot charge a price equal to the true utility value of the unit of digital content because in the realm of digital content, the consumer's marginal propensity to substitute is relatively high (compared to other products), the consumer's marginal cost of substitution is relatively low, and the consumer's search costs are relatively low.

10. The consumer does not know the content owner's or the distributor's true production and distribution costs.

11. The distributor's marketing costs have some effect on consumer choice and such effects vary across time, type of digital content, and consumer profiles.

12. The digital distributor is not a monopolist in the typical meaning of the word, and the same distributor typically uses other channels (record stores, retail stores, DVDs, CDs, mail order, etc.), and the consumer can choose to obtain illegal copies of the content from other sources.

13. Due to pirating, for any given unit of digital content, at any time, there are many suppliers/sellers.

14. Node-A cannot store any files in Node-B or any other node—it can only download files from other nodes. Legal file sharing is the distribution mode—illegal file sharing is not permitted in the network, and, regardless of the structure of the C-S system, the distributor's servers are the primary source for *first purchases* (a *first purchase* is the initial download of the digital content by any node in the C-S system).

15. The distributor controls the network.

16. There cannot be any direct coalitions among the network members—however, there are indirect, anonymous, involuntary, and temporary *intermediated* coalitions that depend on the geographic locations of the nodes/members and the permitted content that each node stores.

17. There is partial monitoring of each game, because the network members are anonymous and cannot monitor each other. The network distributor–intermediary monitors all network members—the network is centralized and each node is required to publish its capacity and content, only to the distributor–intermediary and to other nodes in the C-S system.

18. The game has many geographically dispersed heterogeneous players and is repeated each time a member searches for, uploads, or downloads content.

19. Bandwidth is a commodity with nonnegligible costs.

20. There is anonymous and simultaneous, multiple *indirect matching* in each game because (1) members do not know the identity of other members and (2) in each game, each member may anonymously and *indirectly* match (through the distributor that serves as an

intermediary) simultaneously with one or more members, depending on the geographical location of the nearest nodes. Indirect matching means that the distributor acts as an intermediary and matches a member that has specific content (a *holding member*) with a member that seeks such content (the *seeking member*) and obtains and transfers such content without any direct contact/communication between both members. *Simultaneous multiple matching* means that the distributor–intermediary can match one seeking member with two or more *holding members* and then simultaneously obtain the content from the holding members.

21. Each new member of the network can be admitted into the network by simply registering and agreeing to comply with the rules. Each member/node can upload files into the system/network only if (1) the member has obtained verifiable permission from the owner of the content (and the uploading member agrees to bear all liability, if any, for infringement) or (2) the distributor has entered into an agreement with the content owner to either allow the distributor to circulate a copy of the content in the system or allow persons who legally purchase a legal copy of the content to circulate such unit of content in the system.

22. The game is a noncooperative game because (1) the network members essentially compete for allocation of portions of the processing capacity of the distributor's servers (these servers have limited capacity); (2) the network members compete for the distributor's finite bandwidth, which has to be allocated to members that request for content (and depending on available bandwidth, for any two network members, allocation of bandwidth may be a zero-sum subgame); and (3) network members essentially compete based on the amount of content that they upload and make publicly available (in some of these networks and games, the more content that a member makes available, the greater his or her *relevance* [and the greater the amount of bandwidth and/or processing capacity that the distributor allocates to send–receive communications between the distributor and that member] and the more incentives he or she earns).

23. Any distribution of value (derived from existence of, membership of, and/or participation in the network) must be stable with respect to coalitional deviations.

24. The structure of the network determines the types and durations of intentional and unintentional coalitions that may be formed.

25. Each member can see the holdings of other members. Deviations and the formation of coalitions can be *intentional/knowing* (when members can guess or estimate each other's presence/membership based on their holdings of digital content or when members know each other's *user names*) or *unintentional*. Thus, the set of unintentional and intentional coalitions is limited.

26. The distributor sets prices that can be either (1) a periodic subscription fee or (2) a pay-per-use fee. The prices charged to each participant may differ from those charged to others. The distributor may decide to cap the prices charged to each member.

A similar new type of network game is characterized as follows and is named the *repeated TU intermediated anonymous multimatching noncooperative network* game (RTIAMNC games).

1. Data storage is a commodity for which supply is not limited.

2. Each customer downloads the digital content only from the distributor's/owner's servers (its a client-sever network).

3. There is no direct communication between any two nodes, and there is no direct file sharing among network members. Each member query is sent to the distributor's central server, which then searches the hard drives of all network members to find the nearest available content, obtains the content, and sends it to the querying member. Each member can upload

legally purchased files onto his or her hard drive to be available for indirect sharing. The content distributor/owner controls the file-folder in the network members' hard drives where the downloaded content is stored, and such content cannot be copied from the file-folder or processed on another device.

4. All payments by members are made to only the distributor–intermediary.

5. The content distributor–intermediary knows (or can reasonably estimate) the distribution of consumers' prior valuations of available similar digital content.

6. The content distributor–intermediary sets the price based on consumer's expected valuations and utility and based on the volume of digital content sold to customers.

7. The content creator either assumes the dual roles of creator and distributor or contracts with a third-party distributor to distribute the content.

8. The consumer's *utility value* of the unit of digital content typically exceeds its monetary value, but the content owner/distributor cannot charge a price equal to the true utility value of the unit of digital content because in the realm of digital content, the consumer's marginal propensity to substitute is relatively high (compared to other products), the consumer's marginal cost of substitution is relatively low, and the consumer's search costs are relatively low.

9. The consumer does not know the content owner's or the distributor's true production and distribution costs.

10. The distributor's marketing costs have some effect on consumer choice and such effects vary across time, type of digital content, and consumer profiles.

11. The digital distributor is not a monopolist in the typical meaning of the word—because the same distributor typically uses other channels (record stores, retail stores, DVDs, CDs, mail order, etc.), and the consumer can choose to obtain illegal copies of the content from other sources.

12. Due to pirating, for any given unit of digital content, at any time, there are many suppliers/sellers.

13. Node-A cannot store any files in Node-B or any other node—it can only download files from the client–server systems' central server. Legal file sharing is the distribution mode—illegal file sharing is not permitted in the C-S network, and, regardless of the structure of the C-S system, the distributor's servers are the primary source for *first purchases* (a *first purchase* is the initial download of the digital content by any node in the P2P system).

14. The distributor–intermediary controls the network.

15. There cannot be any direct coalitions among the network members—there are indirect, anonymous, involuntary, and temporary *intermediated* coalitions that depend on the geographic location of the nodes/members and the permitted content that each node stores.

16. There is partial monitoring of each game, because the network members are anonymous and cannot monitor each other. The network sponsor monitors all network members—the network is centralized and each node is required to publish its capacity and content, to other nodes in the P2P system.

17. The game has many geographically dispersed heterogeneous players and is repeated each time a member searches for, uploads, or downloads content.

18. Bandwidth is a commodity with nonnegligible costs.

19. There is anonymous and simultaneous, multiple *indirect matching* in each game because (1) members do not know the identity of other members and (2) in each game, each member may anonymously and *indirectly* match (through the distributor that serves

as an intermediary) simultaneously with one or more members, depending on the geographical location of the nearest nodes. Indirect matching means that the distributor acts as an intermediary and matches a member that has specific content (a *holding member*) with a member that seeks such content (the *seeking member*) and obtains and transfers such content without any direct contact/communication between both members. *Simultaneous multiple matching* means that the distributor–intermediary can match one *seeking member* with two or more *holding members* and then simultaneously obtain the content from the holding members.

20. Each new member of the network can be admitted into the network by simply registering and agreeing to comply with the rules. Each member/node can upload files into the system/network only if (1) the member has obtained verifiable permission from the owner of the content (and the uploading member agrees to bear all liability, if any, for infringement) or (2) the distributor has entered into an agreement with the content owner to either allow the distributor to circulate a copy of the content in the system or allow persons who legally purchase a legal copy of the content to circulate such unit of content in the system.

21. The game is a noncooperative game because (1) the network members essentially compete for allocation of portions of the processing capacity of the distributor's servers (these servers have limited capacity); (2) the network members compete for the distributor–intermediary's finite bandwidth, which is allocated to members that request for digital content (and depending on the amount of available bandwidth, for any two network members and for any coalition that is a subset of the total population of members, the allocation of the distributor–intermediary's bandwidth may be a zero-sum subgame); (3) network members essentially compete based on the amount of content that they upload and make publicly available (in some of these networks and games, the more content that a member makes available, the greater his or her *relevance* [and the greater the amount of bandwidth and/or processing capacity that the distributor allocates to send–receive communications between the distributor and that member] and the more incentives he or she earns).

22. The utility that each network member gains from each repeated game is *transferable* without the member incurring any losses because the players have common currencies that may be valued equally or are valued equally by all players during specific units of time—the common currencies are (1) the value of the time spent by the member on searching for digital content, (2) the member's opportunity cost of searching for digital content in the network, (3) the member's enjoyment of the actual unit digital content (separate from the monetary cost/value of the unit), (4) the member's ability to search the network for digital content and to see the holdings of other network members, and (5) the transfer of utility associated with one unit of digital content, which does not reduce the value/appeal/perception of that unit of content.

23. Any distribution of value (derived from existence of, membership of, and/or participation in the network) must be stable with respect to coalitional deviations.

24. The structure of the network determines the types and durations of intentional and unintentional coalitions that may be formed.

25. Each member can see the holdings of other members. Deviations and the formation of coalitions can be *intentional/knowing* (when members can guess or estimate each other's

presence/membership based on their holdings of digital content or when members know each other's *user names*) or *unintentional*.

26. The distributor sets prices that can be either (1) a periodic subscription fee or (2) a pay-per-use fee. The prices charged to each participant may differ from those charged to others. The distributor may decide to cap the prices charged to each member.

10.2.6 Price of a Unit of Digital Content in A Client–Server Network

Let

Λ_t is the total average cost (pre-reproduction) for creating one unit of the digital content, as calculated with respect to the estimated breakeven volume. Λ_t is $\Lambda_f + \Lambda_v$

Λ_f is the average fixed costs (pre-reproduction) for creating one unit of the digital content, as calculated with respect to the estimated breakeven volume (Λ_f declines as volume (V) increases. The fixed costs of producing the IP are the costs of writing a book, filming a movie, or researching and developing an innovation. In most circumstances, the marginal cost of producing units of the digital content is very low and is typically almost zero. Once the distributor/owner reaches the breakeven volume (including financing costs), Π_m becomes more relevant. Marginal cost pricing will not provide profitable cost recovery.)

Λ_v is the average variable costs (pre-reproduction) for creating one unit of the digital content, as calculated with respect to the estimated breakeven volume

Λ_d is the average costs for distributing and marketing one unit of digital content

Λ_p is the average cost of enforcement of IP laws and monitoring

L is the average service loss, which occurs when the network becomes congested (due to a large number of customers simultaneously downloading content), where some consumers abandon their purchases and request for refunds, which also creates other administrative expenses (Service loss is expressed as a multiple of the price of one unit of digital content. Service loss incorporates the probability of congestion, the number of visitors to the website, the lost sales of digital content, the number of members in the P2P network, etc.)

V is the volume of *reproduced* units of digital content

V_b is the breakeven volume of reproduced units of digital content, at which the content distributor has recovered all costs of creating the digital content (e.g., the costs of writing a book, filming a movie, or researching and developing an innovation) plus all associated financing costs

$V_b > 0$. $V_b \, \varepsilon \, V$.

X is a cost factor. X is Λ_t, *iff* $V < V_b$; and X is Π_r, *iff* $V \geq V_b$

Y is a cost factor. Y is Λ_d, *iff* $V < V_b$; and Y is Π_d, *iff* $V \geq V_b$

Y_p is a cost factor. Y_p is Λ_d, *iff* $V < V_b$; and Y_p is 0, *iff* $V \geq V_b$

π is the estimated number of individuals that will share the unit of digital content ($\pi \, \varepsilon \, N$)

λ is the content owner's/distributor's profit margin

η is the number of nodes/members in the network

S_l is the sampling loss (Assume that for each unit of digital content purchased, the probability that the customer [that would have otherwise purchased the content] declined to purchase the unit [at an average price equal to marginal cost Π_s, $(\Pi_d + \Pi_r$ is $\Pi_s)$] after sampling is P_s. Then S_l is $\Pi_s * P_s$.)

S_l is used only on websites that have sampling features. *Sampling effect* refers to loss or gain in sales revenues that is solely attributable to allowing consumers to sample digital content. Sampling loss occurs when consumer curiosity is satisfied by sampling, and the consumer does not purchase digital content that he or she would have otherwise purchased. Sampling gain occurs when consumer curiosity is increased by sampling of digital content, and the consumer purchases the unit of digital content because of the sampling. A sampling-neutral consumer is not affected by sampling digital content.

The various prices for one reproduced unit of digital content in a legal client–server model are as follows:

$$\text{Max} \, P_3 = \text{Max}\left[\left\{\left(U_i\left(e^{-tr}\right)\right) + \left(\frac{U_g * e^{-tr}}{\pi}\right)\right\};\right.$$

$$\left.\left\{X + Y - \left(\Pi_{ms}\right) + \text{Max}\left(0, \text{Min}\left(\Lambda_p, \Pi_p\right)\right) - \text{Max}\left(0, \Pi_{mps}\right) + \lambda + L + S_l\right\}, 0\right] \quad (10.92)$$

$$\text{Max} \, P_4 = \text{Max}\left[\left\{\left(U_i * e^{-tr}\right) + \left(\frac{\left(U_g * e^{-tr}\right)}{\pi}\right)\right\}; \left\{X + Y - \left(\Pi_{ms}\right)\right.\right.$$

$$\left. + \text{Max}\left(0, \text{Min}\left(\Lambda_p, \Pi_p\right)\right) - \text{Max}\left(0, \Pi_{mps}\right) + \lambda + L + S_l\right\}; 0\right]$$

$$* \text{Max}\left[1, \left\{\left(\frac{\partial^2 \Pi_d}{\partial \Pi_{mps}\partial \Pi_{ms}}\right) + \left(\frac{\partial^2 \Pi_{mps}}{\left(\partial \Pi_{ts}\partial \Pi_{ms}\right)}\right)\right\}\right] \quad (10.93)$$

$$\text{Max} \, P_5 = \text{Max}\left\{0, \text{Min}\left[\left\{\Pi_{ms} - \text{Max}\left(0, \Pi_{mps}\right) + \Pi_{ts}\right\}; \left\{\left(U_i * e^{-tr}\right) + \left(\frac{\left(U_g * e^{-tr}\right)}{\pi}\right)\right\};\right.\right.$$

$$\left.\left. \left\{X + Y + \text{Max}\left(0, \text{Min}\left(\Lambda_p, \Pi_p\right)\right) - \text{Max}\left(0, \Pi_{mps}\right) + \lambda + L + S_l\right\}\right]\right\} \quad (10.94)$$

$$\text{Max} \, P_6 = \text{Max}\left[\left\{X + Y - \Pi_{ms} + \text{Max}\left(0, \text{Min}\left(\Lambda_p, \Pi_p\right)\right) - \text{Max}\left(0, \Pi_{mps}\right) + \lambda + L + S_l\right\}, 0\right]$$

$$* \text{Max}\left[\left\{\left(\frac{\partial^2 \Pi_d}{\partial \Pi_{ms}\partial \Pi_{mps}}\right) + \left(\frac{\partial \pi}{\partial \lambda}\right) + \left(\frac{\partial \lambda}{\partial \Pi_d}\right)\right\}, 1\right] \quad (10.95)$$

Here, the term $\text{Max}[\{(\partial^2\Pi_d/\partial\Pi_{ms}\partial\Pi_{mps}) + (\partial\pi/\partial\lambda) + (\partial\lambda/\partial\Pi_d)\}, 1]$ adjusts the price upward, only if there are certain behavioral tendencies and cost anomalies.

$$\text{Max} \, P_7 = \text{Max}\left[\left\{\left(U_i * e^{-tr}\right) + \left(\frac{\left(U_g * e^{-tr}\right)}{\pi}\right)\right\}; \left\{X + Y - \left(\Pi_{ms}\right)\right.\right.$$

$$\left. + \text{Max}\left(0, \text{Min}\left(\Lambda_p, \Pi_p\right)\right) -\right) \text{Max}\left(0, \Pi_{mps}\right) + \lambda + L + S_l\right\}; 0\right]$$

$$* \text{Max}\left[1, \left\{\text{Max}\left(0; \frac{\partial^2 \Pi_d}{\partial \Pi_{mps}\partial \Pi_{ms}}\right) + \text{Max}\left(0, \left(\frac{\partial^2 \Pi_{mps}}{\left(\partial \Pi_{ts}\partial \Pi_{ms}\right)}\right)\right)\right\}\right] \quad (10.96)$$

subject to the following constraints:

1. $-\infty < U_i* < +\infty$
2. $-\infty < U_g < +\infty$
3. $\Pi_{ms}; \Lambda_p; \Pi_p; \Pi_{mps}; \Pi_d; \Pi_{mps}; \Pi_{ms}; \Pi_{mps}; \Pi_{ts}; \Pi_{ms} \geq 0$

There are different formulas for the price of one unit of digital content because there are different types of digital content (news, educational materials, music, videos, etc.) and different types of content formats (MP3, streaming, etc.), and various broadband speeds are available in different countries/cities. Also, there are various feasible pricing models because information-producer firms differ (sometimes substantially) in various dimensions—distribution channels, knowledge, emphasis on pricing, scope of antipiracy efforts, industry, form of digital content and DRM, etc. As with other pricing models introduced in earlier text, the foregoing pricing models can be solved as optimization models and are self-explanatory.

The use of marginal costs (and a profit margin) to derive the price is necessary because of the following reasons:

1. Using the average cost is likely to result in overpricing of digital content.
2. Consumers that participate in illegal file sharing are obviously very price-sensitive, and the distributor's objective should include finding the maximum price that minimizes or eliminates consumer price sensitivity and propensity to share content illegally.
3. Digital content is unique because of its relatively low marginal costs.
4. The issue of consumers' perceptions about fairness of prices is particularly relevant for digital content.

10.3 Search Costs and Optimization

Within the context of IOF, consumer search costs can differ dramatically in the following ways:

1. Different consumers may place different values on their time that is used for search.
2. The opportunity costs of search can differ among consumers.
3. The notions and definition of a successful online search can differ dramatically across consumers and over time for any one consumer.
4. The utility gains from a search or a series of online searches can differ dramatically among consumers and can differ over time for any one consumer.

Branco et al. (2012, 2015) and Ke et al. (2016) attempted to develop models of optimal search, optimal stopping point, and optimal prices but all of their models are wrong for the following reasons. For the same reasons stated in Taleb (2009), stochastic calculus cannot be used in, and is very inappropriate for, the analysis of optimal-search, optimal stopping, or optimal prices. The typical product price does not following specific known distributions. Consumer tastes change rapidly. In the Internet, search costs are relatively very low.

As mentioned, the foregoing pricing models for digital content can be solved as optimization models and are self-explanatory. Jiang (2012), Yuan and Tsao (2010), Xu et al. (2007), Ekstrom and Lu (2011), Guo et al. (2006), Yong et al. (2012), Ghosh and Rao (2012), and Faigle et al. (1998) and other articles[9] discussed optimization. On fuzzy sets, see Lin et al. (2010).

10.4 Pricing Models as Network-Allocation Rules

The formulas introduced earlier for the prices of digital content represent new *network-allocation rules* (in the same sense as, but different from Shapley value), because of the following reasons. Each of the foregoing pricing formulas has the general form $P = Max\{(P_i - A);0\}$, where P_i is the cost-based price (including a profit margin) and A is the sum total of allocated benefits/disutilities that accrue from membership of and/or participation in the network. This approach assumes that prices must be zero or greater, but, in some situations, prices can be negative—that is, the content distributor pays the member when the member searches for and downloads content where, for example, (1) the distributor earns ancillary revenues (e.g., online advertising and sponsorship revenues, revenues from online loyalty programs) when the member joins or actively searches in the network or (2) the member earns some incentives for uploading files into the system/network. The prices of the unit of digital content incorporate the benefits of the network (cost savings, more efficient search, etc.) and inherently reallocate such benefits to the network members/nodes based on their location, proximity to the distributor's servers, etc. Thus, in the foregoing formulas, the prices of digital content are partly based on network topology—the distance between each node (including the distributor's servers) affects delivery costs, and bandwidth savings can be passed on to members. Some of the network storage costs and some computer processing costs are shifted to nodes, and this reduces the distributor's average and marginal costs of providing the content. Enforcement and prosecution costs can be almost zero because the network is legal. Each member's search costs can be reduced due to ready access to content. The content distributor's allocation of network access to each member often reduces the overall average and marginal access costs for all members. Thus, the distributor essentially allocates network access and prices in order to increase or maintain stability in the system. Here, *stability* can be defined in the following ways: (1) members have low incentive to deviate (e.g. leave the network); (2) members have low incentive to knowingly collude even when there is no anonymity; and (3) the *upload/download* ratio for each network member is similar and *valuable free riders* are allowed to participate in the network and incentives for bandwidth usage and uploads function.

Within this context, the distributor can cap prices charged to each member and can personalize prices based on location, etc. See Jackson (2005), Bateni et al. (2010), Lou and Hwang (2009), Hosanagar et al. (2008), and Christin et al. (2008), and note that the pricing formulas introduced herein also overcome many of the difficulties and limitations inherent in the use of Shapley value analysis and Stackelberg analysis in network pricing and allocation, which are explained in other chapters of this book.

Zhang et al. (2012; algorithms), Zhang et al. (2011, 2012; leasing), Yang et al. (2012; leasing), Ekstrom and Lu (2011), Yu et al. (2006), Kannan et al. (2008), and Xu et al. (2007; lease or buy decision) presented other approaches to the pricing of depreciable goods.

10.5 Conclusion

IOF and content control remain major problems with economic, technological, legal, and policy ramifications. These problems can be solved by development and implementation of appropriate pricing strategies that minimize losses for owners/distributors, reduce illegal copyright infringement, and incorporate the limitations of available technologies and Internet protocols.

Notes

1 Varian (2005) stated in part:

> …Here is a brief list of business models that might work in a world without effective copyright.
> *Make original cheaper than copy:*…
> *Make copy more expensive than original:*…
> *Sell physical complements:*…
> *Sell information complements:*
> One can give away the product (e.g., Red Hat Linux) and sell support contracts…
> *Subscriptions:*…
> *Sell personalized version:*
> One can sell a highly personalized version of a product so that copies made available to others would not be valuable.…
> *Advertise yourself:*
> A downloaded song can be an advertisement for a personal appearance…
> *Advertise other things:*
> Broadcast TV and radio give away content in order to sell advertisements…
> *Monitoring:*…
> *Site licenses:*…
> *Media tax:*.…
> *Ransom*:
> Allow potential readers to bid for content…
> *Pure public provision:*
> Artists and other creators of intellectual property are paid by the state, financed out of general revenues…
> *Prizes, awards, and commissions:*
> Wealthy individuals, businesses, or countries could commission works…
> All of these business models have their problems, of course, and none is likely to yield any sort of social optimum. On the other hand, it should be kept in mind that copyright is a second-best solution to intellectual property provision as well…

2 Hachez (2003) states the following in part:

> …Suppose that an entity needs n copies of the same software item. This entity can either buy (for cost 'C_b') the item or illegally obtain it. The first step in that case is to hack the protection mechanism (cost 'C_h'), then make n copies (of value C_c) of the item. The law intervenes in this model as the entity can get caught (probability 'P_l') and face fines (cost 'C_l'). Usually, those last values ('P_l' and 'C_l') may depend on n. The reality, actually, is unfortunately that:
> $\{n * C_b\} >> [C_h + \{n * C_c\} + \{P_l(n) * C_l(n)\}]$
> …The objective is therefore to modify the balance so that most people will have a strong incentive to buy the software items.… The rogue software company can rewrite the component (cost 'C_{rw}'), steal a component (cost 'C_s'), or reverse engineer a component (cost 'C_e')…

3 Sundararajan (2004) states the following in part:

> …It is shown that the seller's optimal pricing schedule can be characterized as a simple combination of two contracts—the optimal pricing schedule in the absence of piracy (termed the zero-piracy pricing schedule), and a piracy-indifferent pricing schedule, which makes all customers indifferent between legal usage and piracy. An increase in the quality of pirated goods lowers prices and profits; however, there may be social benefits from piracy realized through the expansion of the fraction of legal users and the volume of legal usage…

4 See Golle et al. (2001), Lang and Vragov (2005), and Buchegger and Le Boudec (June 2004).
5 See Romero et al. (2010), Faigle et al. (1998), Maschler and Peleg (1975), Meinhardt (2006), Faigle et al. (1998), and Oncan et al. (2009).
6 See Golle et al. (2001), Lang and Vragov (2005), and Anagnostakis and Greenwald (2006).
7 See Romero et al. (2010), Faigle et al. (1998), Maschler and Peleg (1975), Meinhardt (2006), and Oncan et al. (2009).
8 See Golle et al. (2001), Lang and Vragov (2005), Sun et al. (December 2005), Anagnostakis and Greenwald (2006), Despotovic and Aberer (2005), and Buchegger and Le Boudec (June 2004).
9 See Romero et al. (2010), Faigle et al. (1998), Maschler and Peleg (1975), Meinhardt (2006), and Oncan et al. (2009).

Chapter 11

Shapley Value Cannot Be Used in Network Access Pricing, Network Cost Allocation, the Pricing of Digital Content, or Analysis of Electricity Distribution Networks

Although game theory principles have been used extensively in developing analytical models for access pricing in Internet networks, transmission pricing in electric power networks, and access pricing in telephone/cable networks, most of the existing literature omits the effects of illegal online file sharing. This chapter explains why Shapley value analysis is generally inaccurate for most situations and why Shapley value analysis cannot be used for network access pricing, network cost allocation, the pricing of digital content, and analysis of electricity distribution networks.

11.1 Existing Literature

Borkotokey and Sarangi (2011) critiqued the Myerson value, the position value (for communication games only), and Jackson's flexible network values and stated that these rules do not take into account simultaneous multilateral interactions and do not consider the notion of simultaneous multilateral interaction in a network.

Some authors/researchers have attempted to apply the Shapley value (and related theories) to access pricing and to allocation of revenues/costs in networks—in articles such as Ma et al. (2010), Cao et al. (2002), Kattuman et al. (2004), Jia and Yokoyama (2003), Bakos and Nault (1997), Morais and Lima (2007), Angel et al. (2006), and Altman and Wynter (2004).

Ganesh et al. (2007), Yaiparoj et al. (2008), Bei et al. (2011), Pechersky and Sobolev (1995), Kawasaki (2000), Soltys and Wilson (2011), Noh and Rieger (2004), and Reka and Barabási (2002) provided other perspectives on networks, games, and Shapley value.

Several authors/researchers have explained the inaccuracies and problems inherent in the Shapley value function and related theories. Tick et al. (1999) stated that the Shapley value algorithms do not relate to the constraint space, but rather are based only on the coalition payoffs; thus, Shapley value type analysis can produce an allocation even for an inconsistent problem without any rational agreement point. Fatima et al. (2008) stated that (1) the problem of determining the Shapley value is #P-complete and (2) the Shapley value provides an allocation only with a limited degree of certainty (there is an *uncertainty* problem). Roth (1977) showed that a game's Shapley value is equal to its utility if and only if the players' preferences are neutral to (not affected by) both *ordinary risk* and *strategic risk*; otherwise, the Shapley value is not an accurate allocation tool or decision-making tool. Sastre and Trannoy (2001) found that the Shapley value rules do not satisfy the principle of independence of the aggregation level (the marginal contribution of a player depends on how other components of the allocated resource are treated). Kirman et al. (2007) found various problems inherent in the Shapley value function. Lima et al. (2008) concluded that were no feasible cores in cooperative games for allocation of costs in networks. Roth and Verrecchia (1979) explained the limitations and inconsistencies inherent in the original Shapley value theory and stated that Shapley value analysis does not account for *fairness*, and then they introduced a new explanation of Shapley value theory. Bakos and Nault (1997) explained the conditions under which ISPs and certain coalitions will invest in network infrastructure—their analysis is critical to understanding the need for and potential success of coalitions among ISPs. Biczok et al. (2008) showed that Shapley value analysis does not account for brand loyalty and quality of service (QoS).

Korillis et al. (1997) and Shakkotai and Srikant (2006) attempted to use Stackelberg bargaining analysis for network pricing. Most of the critiques and weaknesses of Shapley value analysis also apply to Stackelberg game analysis; thus, the inaccuracies and problems summarized in earlier text in Tick et al. (1999), Fatima et al. (2008), Roth (1977), Sastre and Trannoy (2001), Kirman et al. (2007), Lima et al. (2008), Roth and Verrecchia (1979), Bakos and Nault (1997), and Biczok et al. (2008) also apply to Stackelberg bargaining analysis (He et al., 2007). On the *conceptual model for decomposing value for the customer* (CMDVC), see Nicola et al. (2012). On alternative methods for network pricing and cost allocations, see Su (2011), Xu (2011), and Fu et al. (2007).

Fanelli et al. (2015) and Bilò et al. (2010) analyzed cost-sharing algorithms and games in networks. Disser et al. (2015) and Bilò et al. (2013) analyzed Shapley games. Canavoi et al. (2014), Moroshko and Crammer (2014), and other articles[1] analyzed *equilibria* in network games. However, the theories introduced in this chapter contradict many of the theories in these foregoing articles.

Troquard et al. (2011), Ågotnes et al. (2009), and Wolter and Wooldridge (2011) studied logic and the aggregation of preferences and judgment in games. Michalak et al. (2014) analyzed *generalized characteristic function games and Shapley value*. Fatima et al. (2007), Michalak et al. (2013), and Michalak et al. (2015) studied *Shapley value*.

11.2 Mechanism Design Theory Is Inaccurate

Shapley value function and Stackelberg bargaining as applied to interconnection pricing are essentially mechanism design theory (MDT). As explained in Nwogugu (2012), traditional MDT is generally inaccurate and impractical. MDT is the body of theory pertaining to economic mechanisms that are often defined by rules, norms, time, medium, and location. The literature on MDT has some major gaps and inaccuracies, some of which are explained as follows and in Myerson (1983, 2008), Friedman and Oren (1994), and Larson and Sandholm (July 2005).

MDT does not account for differences in agents' information-processing capabilities. MDT erroneously assumes that each mechanism is monolithic and static in time, space, and expense—in reality and on the contrary, some mechanisms are dispersed in space (various locations), time (requires participation, revisions of knowledge, and various disclosures at various times), and expenses (the costs of participation in the mechanism vary across time and participants).

Bergemann and Morris (2005) noted the following about MDT:

1. A common criticism of MDT is that the optimal mechanisms solving the well-defined planner's problem seem unreasonably complicated. As a result, researchers have often focused on mechanisms that are *more robust* or less sensitive to the assumed structure of the environment.
2. Mechanism design involves too many implicit common-knowledge assumptions in the description of the planner's problem. The more efficient modeling strategy is to first make explicit the implicit common-knowledge assumptions and then weaken them.
3. In mechanism design, the smallest type space that planners/researchers can work on is the *payoff type space*, where the possible types of each agent are assumed to be equal to the set of payoff types and assumed to have common knowledge prior to this type space. The largest type space that planners/researchers can work on is the union of all possible type spaces that could have arisen from the payoff environment. This is equivalent to working with a *universal type space*, in the sense of Mertens and Zamir (1985). There are many interesting type spaces in between the payoff type space and the universal type space.
4. MDT sometimes does not consider instances when ex post implementation is equivalent to interim (or Bayesian) implementation for all possible type spaces. The equivalence holds in the case of separable environments; examples of separable environments arise (1) when the planner is implementing a social choice function (not correspondence) and (2) in a quasilinear environment with no restrictions on transfers. The equivalence fails in general, including in some quasilinear environments with budget balance. In private value environments, ex post implementation is equivalent to dominant strategies implementation.
5. Hurwicz (1972, 1973) discussed the need for *nonparametric* mechanisms (independent of parameters of the model).
6. If a social choice correspondence (SCC) is ex post implementable, then it is clearly interim implementable on every type space, since the payoff type direct mechanism can be used to implement the SCC—but the converse is not always true. The gap arises because the planner may have the equilibrium outcome dependent on the agents' higher-order belief types, as well as their realized payoff type. The planner has no intrinsic interest in conditioning on nonpayoff relevant aspects of agents' types, but he or she is able to introduce slack in incentive constraints by doing so.

Glachant (1998) noted the following about MDT:

1. The normative power of mechanism design is significantly weakened by an implicit assumption of zero communication costs.
2. MDT assumes that administrative costs of public intervention are nil.

3. MDT makes unrealistic assumptions about the truthfulness of disclosures by market participants. Communication between agents is subject to strategic manipulation if (1) the objectives sought by the emitter and the receptor differ and (2) the receptor's decisions influence emitter's gains.
4. One key property of mechanism design is that the budget neutrality constraint at the level of the regulator cannot hold. Thus, the sum of all the payments or subsidies of firms is always negative. The fact that the use of mechanisms always results in public deficits is the sign of the informational rents enjoyed by the firms in their interactions with the regulator. As a result, mechanisms are only second-best optimal.
5. The principle of mechanisms is to make each firm pay for the consequences of information reported to the regulator.
6. Menus and side payments can suppress information asymmetry between regulators and firms.

11.3 Interconnection Fees Can Be Irrelevant in Network Design

The existing literature on network access pricing unnecessarily focuses on interconnection fees (peering fees and transiting fees) as the main element for the improvement of networks. The main method of analysis has been game theory, which has been shown to have major weaknesses.

Peering involves carrying the other ISP's traffic and the mutual *termination* of packets originating from each of the peer networks to the domain of the other. However, peering results in some costs/fees when there is traffic asymmetry. Peering requires adjacency of the network that is a significant limitation in the management of interconnection agreements for the approximately 35,000 Autonomous Systems or internet service providers (ASes) existing.

Johnson (Variety) (February 26, 2015)[2] noted that the US Federal Communications Commission (FCC) had approved the regulation of the Internet in the United States as a utility. *The Economic Times* (India) (January 9, 2015)[3] commented on cost allocation among Indian telecomm companies. Reuters (December 29, 2014; Mexico)[4] commented on regulator's rate setting for interconnection fees between competing networks in Mexico. *This Day* newspaper (Nigeria) (2013)[5] noted that the Nigerian Communications Commission was considering the choice between symmetric and asymmetric interconnection models for voice services. The reality is that in many countries, governments regulate interconnection fees for networks.[6] Many governments have experimented with *symmetric* and *asymmetric* pricing models and combinations of both (such as in Mexico and Nigeria).

The general consensus in the literature has been that peering is economically feasible only if the cost of the traffic exchange between two networks exceeds the sunk costs of building the interconnection infrastructure and the operation, administration and maintenance (OPM) costs for maintaining it. This consensus is wrong because it does not consider opportunity costs, and it does not consider the *reputation* of telecomm companies—interconnection has a symbiotic relationship with *reputation*.

Walrand (2008), Buccirossi et al. (2005), Cremer et al. (2000), Baake and Wichmann (1999), and Laffont et al. (2003) developed various models to compute the sometimes nonnegligible interconnection costs and other transaction costs that can affect network pricing, network design, regulators' decisions about mergers among ISPs, network exchanges, and ISPs' decisions about acceptance of traffic from various types of networks. The significant growth of Internet traffic volume (and why many ISPs throttle or reject certain types of traffic) can result in high packet transfer costs and, thus, nonnegligible interconnection costs (despite the fact that the transit prices have been declining quickly).

Furthermore, the opportunity costs of allocating ports of the racks at the Internet exchanges to the settlement-free peering interfaces as opposed to the value-generating transit contracts are also often nonnegligible.

Under established principles of game theory and dynamical systems analysis, the *interconnection fee* can be irrelevant or almost irrelevant, *if* any of the following conditions exist:

1. The interconnection fee is a very small component of the total average per-packet (per-unit) end-to-end cost of transmitting packets in the ISP's network or in the combined coalition members' network.
2. For purposes of financial reporting, network transmission costs (amortization, deprecation of network infrastructure, interconnection fees, and bandwidth) must be expensed in the period incurred.
3. The market is protected or regulated, for example, by government regulations. The government may also decide to fix, reduce, or limit interconnection fees in order to promote competition.[7]
4. Antitrust laws prohibit the direct or indirect formation of coalitions (especially of the types envisaged in the Shapley value function or Stackelberg games).
5. ISPs can cancel peering/interconnection agreements at will or with minimal cancellation costs, or ISPs can reject some types of Internet traffic at will.
6. For any distance d in the network in any given region r, ISPs can quickly and cheaply reconfigure their physical networks (routers, switches, etc.).
7. The cost of building wireless networks is lower than the cost of land-based networks.
8. There is no required minimum *contribution* (e.g., the minimum size of an ISP's network) to a coalition of ISPs by an ISP member—in such cases, an ISP with minimal or no physical network will be able to obtain a share of the coalition's revenues from the transmission of its packets.
9. Quality of Service (QoS) is a primary/dominant factor in an ISP's decisions about interconnection agreements.
10. In most markets, of the two types of interconnection agreements (peering and transiting agreements), peering agreements account for a substantial percentage (e.g., more than 70%) of all interconnection agreements and do not result in any additional costs for the ISP (each ISP agrees to carry the other ISP's traffic for free).
11. The Internet is a basic necessity and ISPs can pass on all their costs to consumers, and consumers are essentially *Price-takers* with quasi-inelastic demand (a steep and upwardly sloping demand curve).

Note that interconnection fees are only one component of the ISP's costs, and other cost components include (1) the nontransmission costs such as administration, marketing, compliance; (2) physical infrastructure maintenance costs; (3) the allocated amortized cost of building the physical network; (4) the opportunity costs of using no-fee peering versus paid interconnection; (5) costs of congestion; (6) capital expenses (network infrastructure costs); (7) variable transmission costs (bandwidth, professional staff, interconnection fees); and (8) compliance costs, etc. Thus, interconnection fees may be a nonmaterial component of the ISP's cost structure.

11.4 The Shapley Value Is Inaccurate and Cannot Be Used in the Analysis of Access Pricing or for the Allocation of Revenues/Costs in Networks

Within the context of interconnection agreements, the Shapley value can be accurate and relevant if and only if certain conditions exist—the following are the conditions required for Shapley value analysis to be valid and why these conditions are false and do not exist.

Condition 11.1

The physical structure of the Internet is never constant.

In reality, although the physical connections of ISP's networks may remain fixed in time and space, the true structure of the network (the actual transmission pathways, and hence the *network*) is not constant and changes instantaneously, depending on the locations of the sender–receiver pairs. In almost all instances, each packet has more than one feasible path. Furthermore, in land-based networks, the cable used in transporting packets typically has more than one section of wires so that for each distance d in any cable, there is more than one feasible transmission pathway. Similarly, in any wireless network, for any two points in distance d, there are many possible transmission paths.

Theorem 11.1

For any transmission, even if the originating ISP knows the cost structure and payoff of every other ISP that is required to transport any given packet, optimal allocation of costs or revenues among cooperating ISPs is never feasible.

Proof: The Shapley value analysis erroneously assumes that each ISP knows the cost structure and payoff patterns of every other ISP that is a member of the coalition. In reality, statutes prevent public disclosure of cost and pricing information of ISPs and also prevent ISPs from sharing information among themselves. Active competition among ISPs will almost always preclude their voluntary disclosure of their cost/price data to each other. ISPs can guess about their competitor's cost/price information and can recruit their competitors' staff in order to give them such information. However, network transmission costs are constantly changing because of not only the variations in the number and quality of feasible transmission paths, differences between full costing and variable costing, and the dynamic nature of wireless portions of networks but also the following factors: (1) entrance and exit of ISPs into markets, (2) inflation, (3) calculation of depreciation, (4) changes in capital expenditures, and (5) changes in marketing costs.

Assume a *second best-case* scenario where the competitors' cost/price data are fully observable to the originating ISP (O-ISP), and there is a coalition, but coalition members do not coordinate/unify their routing systems/protocols. The O-ISP can calculate a rough estimate of costs from point P_1 to point P_2, but O-ISP cannot dictate to other network members about when and how to route the packet and to which *third* ISP to transmit the packet; thus, each network member will typically be selfish despite coalition agreements. This state is henceforth referred to as *coordination-control neutrality*, and it prevents any optimal allocations. Assume a *first best-case* scenario, where all ISPs in the network cooperate to try and determine the most efficient routing path and also disclose their cost/price data to each other. As mentioned, such cooperation will be deemed illegal in most jurisdictions. Even if such cooperation is feasible, there can never be an optimal allocation because of the time frame of the required decisions. Assume that the transmission goes through several ISPs (Λ; Ω; Φ; Ψ; E; F;...; N) sequentially and over physical distances d_1, d_2, d_3, d_4,..., d_n in matching time intervals t_1, t_2, t_3, t_4,..., t_n, respectively. Note that Λ represents the set of all feasible ISPs that can handle the transmission over d_i in t_1 and Ω represents the set of all feasible ISPs that can handle the transmission over d_2 during t_2, and so on for all subsequent transmissions. The time intervals t_1, t_2,..., t_n are stochastic and unknown in prior periods, and the choices Λ, Ω, Φ,..., N are also unknown because of the changing nature and time of arrival of cost/price *pairs* of information. For efficient cooperative allocations, each transmitting ISP (Λ; Ω; Φ; Ψ; E; F;...; N) will have to provide instantaneous cost/price *pairs* of data ($\Psi_{cp(n)}$; $\Lambda_{cp(n)}$; $\Omega_{cp(n)}$; $\Phi_{cp(n)}$;...; $N_{cp(n)}$) over each distance d_1, d_2, d_3,..., d_n. Hence, for Λ to transmit to Ω during time t_2, Λ must have at least $\Lambda_{cp(2)}$ and $\Omega_{cp(2)}$, and $\Phi_{cp(2)}$ at the beginning of t_2, and for Ω to transmit to Φ during time t_3, Ω must have at least $\Omega_{cp(3)}$ and $\Phi_{cp(3)}$, and $\Psi_{cp(3)}$ at the beginning of t_3, and so on for subsequent transmissions. By the time the packet moves from Ω to Φ, $\Psi_{cp(n)}$, $E_{cp(n)}$, and $F_{cp(n)}$ have changed and a new allocation must be made. The sensitivity of the *optimality-of-allocations* to changes in the cost/price *pairs* is very high because of the nature and volumes of the transmission of packets (the components of each ISP's total transmission costs (TTCs) and prices can vary dramatically across different ISPs and are explained earlier). Because these TTCs and prices are difficult to calculate and the micro-time (per-millisecond) cost/price data required to calculate them are available infrequently (at best, on a daily or hourly basis), there is sufficient accurate data for determining any optimal allocation of costs or revenues among a cooperative network of ISPs. Second, because some ISP interconnections are free, introducing the voluntary or mandatory exchange of cost/price data among ISPs is likely to create substantial disagreements over fairness of allocations and/or will also affect (reduce) each ISP's willingness to invest capital to build physical or wireless networks. This is because each ISP calculates its return-on-capital and marketing return on investment (ROI) differently. Such disclosure-influenced free riding can, in turn, limit the growth of the coalition's overall network coverage and preclude or reduce any efficiency of the allocations of costs/revenues among the ISPs. ■

Theorem 11.2

For every packet and for each time interval t, and for any distance d in the coalition's combined network, each ISP (originating ISP or transmitting ISP) cannot choose an optimal path.

Proof: An ISP cannot control the routing choices of other ISPs. In reality, the selected path for each packet is determined by preestablished automated algorithms of each ISP, and these algorithms do not always adapt to changes in the network physical structure or transmission path(s), which was referred earlier as *coordination-control neutrality*. Furthermore, because each ISP is not able to obtain very accurate information about historical or future packet loss, it is impossible for the ISP to plot an *optimal transmission path*. It is highly unlikely that any ISP will permit other ISPs to control or overly influence its routing algorithms even in a cooperative network. Antitrust laws will almost surely prevent such coordination. Routing algorithms are complex and are sensitive to changes in network characteristics and the level of human input. The only feasible way that ISPs in a cooperative network can safely influence each other's routing algorithm is if they all use the same commercially available routing algorithm, which is highly unlikely. The second-best alternative is to provide a system of cash incentives to convince each ISP to allow other ISPs to influence their routing algorithms. The properties of any such incentive mechanism (Q) are as follows:

1. *Consistency–invariance and time-invariance*: The ISP cannot deviate from the incentive mechanism Q.
2. *Scope limitation*: Q is limited only to participating ISPs. This can present a substantial problem because coalition members cannot control the growth of nonmember ISPs. In some markets, coalition members must connect with nonmembers of the coalition in order to complete transmissions.
3. *Equivalency*: $\int_0^t Q_i \, dt > \int_0^t \Sigma O_i \, dt$, where O_i is the value of the ISP's opportunity costs of complying with the incentive mechanism in every transmission. Q_i is the value of the incentive mechanism for the ISP for transmission i.
4. *Additivity*: For any transmission over d_i.

Because any given ISP cannot *choose* an optimal path in the network, Shapley value analysis is not applicable to network access pricing or to cost allocation in networks. ■

Theorem 11.3

For any transmission over any distance (d), the ISP's share of revenues (or share of transmission costs) generated by the coalition is not always nonnegative (can be negative).

Proof: The Shapley value function erroneously assumes that the ISP's share of revenues generated by the coalition is always nonnegative and that the ISP's share of costs generated by the coalition transmission is always nonnegative. On the contrary, there are some instances where the ISP's share of total transmission revenues generated by the coalition is negative (less than zero) or should be negative, and these include the following:

1. When the ISP's transmission results in excessive packet loss such that the entire information unit has to be re-transmitted.
2. Where the ISP earns non-coalition third-party benefits for carrying the packet but is effectively subsidized indirectly by coalition members.
3. Where given specific transmission algorithms (and congestion control algorithms) that are implemented by coalition member ISPs, ISP-A's transmission of a packet increases the probability that certain other types of packets will be sent by both coalition members and nonmembers to and transmitted through ISP-A's network.
4. Where transmitting a certain packet through the ISP's network exponentially increases each subsequent coalition member's costs of carrying the same packet to its destination.
5. Where transmission by an ISP results in addition of data to the packet, which then increases the required minimum bandwidth and costs for further transmission by all other coalition members. ■

Observation 11.1

For any time interval t, and for any distance d in the coalition's networks, the marginal contribution of each coalition member ISP is not always directly proportional to (1) distance or (2) bandwidth consumed.

The Shapley function erroneously implies that for any time interval t, and for any distance d in the coalition's networks, the marginal contribution of each coalition member ISP is directly proportional to (1) distance and (2) bandwidth consumed. This is not always true. For example, with regard to distance, the marginal contribution of a coalition member ISP that transports a packet for 100 meters in an extremely high-density city block with significant Internet congestion is greater than the marginal contribution of an ISP that transports a similar packet for 1000 m in a low-density rural area with no Internet congestion.

Theorem 11.4

For any time interval t and for any distance d in the coalition's networks, the number of coalition members is not always nonnegative.

Proof: The Shapley function erroneously implies that for any time interval t and for any distance d in the coalition's networks, the number of coalition members is always nonnegative. An ISP can be deemed a *negative* member of a coalition when any of the following conditions exist:

1. X% of the ISP's network is physically proximate to the networks of coalition members even though the ISP is not a coalition member, and such proximity can significantly reduce the coalition's transportation burden by, for example, Q% > 85%.
2. The ISP (is a coalition member but) has no physical networks or wireless networks and enters into interconnection agreements with coalition members.
3. The ISP is a coalition member but routing traffic through that ISP's network for distance d increases overall transmission costs substantially, and there are other available and *cheaper* routes through other coalition members' networks. ■

Observation 11.2

For any time interval t, and for any distance d in the coalition members' networks, the marginal rate of transmission of packets (R_t) (the distance that the packet travels for each additional unit of bandwidth consumed) does not remain constant.

The *marginal rate of transmission of packets* varies constantly in most networks for various reasons, including traffic/congestion, size/diameter of the network cable, physical obstructions in wireless networks, type of protocol, and type of digital content. With such varying R_t, each coalition member's contribution cannot be measured by any standard unit, and hence, given the Shapley value function, any allocation will not be fair or stable. Thus, the Shapley value function is inapplicable to access pricing and cost allocation in networks.

Observation 11.3

For any time interval t, and for any distance d in the coalition members' networks, the marginal utility of substituting an ISP in the transmission path (the increase in utility gained from substituting an ISP in the transmission path) does not remain constant.

Clearly, both the originating ISP's marginal utility and the consumer's marginal utility of substituting any ISP in the transmission path (path between the sender and receiver) change instantaneously due to (1) changes in traffic and volume, (2) the size of the pipe, (3) the absolute efficiency and relative efficiency of each ISP's network, (4) timing, (5) transmission fees and terms of payment of such fees (nature of the contracts), etc. As explained before, the physical network may be constant but differs from transmission paths within it. Thus, Shapley value function is not applicable to access pricing.

Theorem 11.5

Shapley value function is inapplicable to access pricing and cost allocation in networks because for each packet, and for any time interval t, and for any distance d in the coalition members' networks, the end-to-end total interconnection fee is a small or insignificant component of the per-packet total transmission cost, and the Shapley value allocations of cost and/or revenues to coalition members will be unfeasible when costs and/or revenues exceed or fall below certain thresholds.

Proof: In most instances, the interconnection fees are not a main component of the TTC incurred by the ISP. For any time interval t and for any distance d in the coalition's network, if the ISP's average end-to-end TTC (R_a) or marginal end-to-end TTC (R_m) is below a certain dollar threshold (Y_r), the ISP may not care much about interconnection fees and a Shapley value allocation of cost and will not have adequate incentives to remain in any coalition of ISPs. Moreover, if R_a and R_m are above a certain dollar threshold (X_r), the ISP will face an increasing risk of operating losses, financial distress, and exit from the industry, and, hence, the ISP will not have sufficient incentive to remain in any coalition—the ISP will most probably shift its focus and resources to reducing its nontransmission costs and will probably attempt to create other coalitions with third parties. In general, participation in these coalitions is not mandatory and ISPs can negotiate with various coalitions for membership or exit, subject to terms of peering agreements. Hence, the following three states are possible: (1) $X_r > Y_r$; (2) $Y_r > X_r$; and (3) $X_r = Y_r$. However, if $X_r > Y_r$, and R_a, R_m ε (X_r, Y_r), the average coalition member will have some incentives to remain in the coalition, but such a member can improve its position by negotiating with other nonmember ISPs for peering agreements or by expanding its own physical infrastructure or by joining third-party coalitions. Even where membership in a coalition is mandatory for all or part of the time period, coalition member ISPs can still improve their payoffs by expanding their own physical networks.

Similarly, for any time interval t and for any distance d in the coalition's network, if the average per-unit interconnection fee (P_a) or marginal per-unit interconnection fee (P_m) (for transporting a unit of bandwidth or packet) is below a certain dollar threshold (Y_p), the ISP may not care much about interconnection fees and will not have adequate incentives to remain in any coalition of ISPs. Moreover, if P_a and P_m are above a certain dollar threshold (X_p), the ISP will have strong incentives to leave the coalition and expand its own physical network or strong incentives to reduce its physical network and enter into more peering/interconnection agreements with noncoalition ISPs. In general, participation in these coalitions is not mandatory and ISPs can negotiate with various coalitions for membership or exit, subject to terms of peering agreements. Hence, the following three states are possible: (1) $X_p > Y_p$; (2) $Y_p > X_p$; and (3) $X_p = Y_p$. However, if $X_p > Y_p$, and P_a, P_m ε (X_p; Y_p), the average coalition member will have some incentives to remain in the coalition, but such a member can improve its position by negotiating with other nonmember ISPs or by expanding its own physical infrastructure or by reducing its physical network infrastructure or by joining third-party coalitions. Even where membership in a coalition is mandatory for all or part of the time period, coalition member ISPs can still improve their payoffs by expanding their own physical networks. Thus, there can never be any Nash equilibrium or Shapley value equilibrium or Stackelberg equilibrium for such coalitions of transporting ISPs.

Similarly, for any time interval t and for any distance d in the coalition's network, if the average per-unit revenue (F_a) or marginal per-unit revenue (F_m) (for transporting a unit of bandwidth or packet) is below a certain dollar threshold (Y_f), the ISP will not have adequate incentives to remain in any coalition of ISPs, primarily because the ISP will face financial distress and possible exit from the market. Moreover, if F_a and F_m are above a certain dollar threshold (X_f), the ISP will have (1) strong incentives to leave the coalition and expand its own physical network; (2) substantial incentives to remain in the coalition but vary the size of its network, and hence the amount of its payoff; or (3) substantial incentives to reduce the size of its physical network and enter into more peering/interconnection agreements with both coalition member ISPs and/or noncoalition ISPs. In general, participation in these coalitions is not mandatory and ISPs can negotiate with various coalitions for membership or exit, subject to terms of interconnection/peering agreements. Hence, the following three states are possible: (1) $X_f > Y_f$; (2) $Y_f > X_f$; and (3) $X_f = Y_f$. However, if $X_f > Y_f$, and F_a, F_m ε (X_f, Y_f), the average coalition member will have some incentives to remain in the coalition, but such a member can improve its position by negotiating with other nonmember ISPs or by expanding its own physical infrastructure or by reducing its physical network infrastructure or by joining third-party coalitions. Even where membership in a coalition is mandatory for all or part of the time period, coalition member ISPs can still improve their payoffs by expanding their own physical networks. Thus, there can never be any Nash equilibrium or Shapley value equilibrium for such coalitions of transporting ISPs. ■

Observation 11.4

The Shapley value allocation is inefficient and unfeasible because the Shapley value function erroneously assumes that the resources of all coalition members are fixed for any time interval t, and each coalition member's contribution to the mechanism is limited/finite.

Each coalition member has different resources that vary in terms of availability and size; coalition members can vary their contribution to the Shapley value mechanism (e.g., increase the physical size of their network or change their routing algorithms). Furthermore, each coalition member's contribution to the mechanism can be infinite and unlimited, for example, each coalition member may be able to build a network that covers the subjection city or region and maintain the network on a 24/7 basis indefinitely.

Theorem 11.6

For any coalition S, there are certain conditions that must exist before there can be a feasible application of the Shapley value function to allocations in networks; but all such conditions are individually and collectively unfeasible.

Proof: These conditions are related to the nature of networks and are all unfeasible and are as follows (the proof of the unfeasibility of each condition is straightforward):

Condition 6(i): *In the Shapley value formula, N (total number of ISPs in the market/region) and s (number of ISPs in the coalition) are constant for all time periods t and for any region r.* This condition is not feasible because ISPs will enter and exit the coalition over time.

Condition 6(ii): *The marginal contribution of a coalition member (ISP1) is equally likely to occur as the marginal contribution of any other coalition member during any time interval t.* This condition is not feasible because different ISPs have very different resources, network architectures, and commitment to the coalition.

Condition 6(iii): *The terms of the coalition agreement (resource allocation formula) remain constant for any time interval t.*

Condition 6(iv): *In any coalition S, and for any time interval t, utilities are always transferable among any two pairs of ISPs.* This condition is not feasible because different ISPs have very different resources, network architectures, and commitment to the coalition. In this context, utility is in the form of transmission and brand equity, furthermore, the physical layout.

Condition 6(v): *For any time interval t, and for any number of ISPs in a market denoted by n, and for any distance d in the coalition members' network, in the Shapley value formula for calculating payoffs, as s → 0 (as the number of coalition members approaches zero), the absolute effect/contribution of each coalition member–ISP remains at least constant but increases and is proportional to the ISP's network size.*

Condition 6(vi): *For any time interval t, and for any distance d in the coalition members' network, in the Shapley value formula for calculating payoffs, as s → n (as the number of coalition members approaches the total number of ISPs in the market), the effect/contribution of each coalition member–ISP remains at least constant and is proportional to the ISP's network size.*

Condition 6(vii): *The governance structure of the coalition does not matter and does not affect the contributions and payoffs of coalition members.* This condition is not feasible. The peering/interconnection agreement may determine the nature of the governance of the coalition, or subcoalitions within the coalition. The coalition can be in the form of (1) separate agreements among ISPs at various times, (2) uncoordinated and separate strategic alliances among ISPs, (3) coordinated strategic alliances among ISPs that anticipate entry/exit of alliance members, (4) uncoordinated joint ventures among ISPs, (5) coordinated joint ventures among ISPs that anticipate entry/exit of alliance members, and (6) government-mandated interconnection agreements. The governance includes determination of costs and revenues, collection and sharing of revenues, and dispute resolution methods.

Condition 6(viii): *All interconnection agreements (peering agreements and transiting agreements) are the same.*

Condition 6(ix): *Illegal online file sharing does not affect ISP's profitability and cost structure.* This condition is not feasible because illegal online file sharing affects the profitability and Quality of Service (QoS) of ISPs. Most of the existing literature on network access-pricing analysis explicitly omits any analysis of the effects of illegal online file sharing.

Condition 6(x): *QoS concerns do not affect the probability of formation of coalitions.* This condition is not feasible in most instances, because more ISPs are becoming more concerned about QoS and are using QoS as a basis to differentiate and/or segment their services (to offer different tiers of Internet access).

Condition 6(xi): *Antitrust laws do not matter.* On the contrary, antitrust laws preclude the types of coalitions that are envisioned or implied by Shapley value analysis, Owen value, and Stackelberg games.

Condition 6(xii): *All coalition members contribute a minimum amount of resources (i.e., have a physical network).* Shapley value analysis may be accurate only if all coalition members contribute some minimum level of resources to the mechanism/game. The Shapley value formula for calculating the payoffs fails if one or more coalition members do not contribute any resources (e.g., physical network, bandwidth) to the game. On the contrary, some ISPs can be only marketing companies that do not own or lease any physical networks but use peering/interconnection agreements to transport data and thus earn revenues.

Condition 6(xiii): *The probabilities of formation of each coalition are equal.* Shapley value analysis (and related methods) erroneously assumes that the probability of each possible coalition is the same (and that the probability of each member's entry into the coalition is the same).

Condition 6(xiv): *Each coalition member's effort is equal to its contribution, which in turn is equal to an equivalent amount of utility.* The Shapley value function is not applicable to coalition analysis because each coalition member's effort is not always or necessarily equal to its *contribution*, which in turn is not equal to an equivalent amount of utility.

Condition 6(xv): *The utility created by any interconnection agreement in the coalition is constant for any packet-size and over any time period t, and such utility benefits only the two contracting ISPs.*

Condition 6(xvi): *Each ISP's contribution to the coalition is measured primarily by its geographic coverage and its connections to other ISPs.*

Observation 11.5

The Shapley value allocation is not feasible for revenue/cost allocation in networks because Shapley value function (for profit sharing) does not account for differences in sources of demand among coalition members (i.e., share of customers).

The Shapley value does not account for differences in sources of demand for the coalition's services and products and erroneously assumes that demand is uniform and equal for all coalition members—the sharing mechanism does not account for the number of customers delivered to the coalition by any ISP. To be accurate, the sharing mechanism should reward members for the volume of business and the quality of business (e.g., long-term vs. short-term customers, high-credit-quality vs. low-credit-quality, high-bandwidth vs. low-bandwidth transmissions) that they bring to the coalition.

Observation 11.6

The network transmission (and revenue sharing) game is not a cooperative game.

Network access transmission (cost allocation) and revenue allocation are not cooperative games or semicooperative games. The fact that ISPs enter into interconnection agreements does not make any revenue allocation or cost-allocation system a *cooperative* game. Network access (and any implicit revenue allocation or cost sharing) is a noncooperative game because of the following. In any given market, most ISPs are fierce competitors, and each ISP spends substantial amounts of money on advertising, promotions and marketing, and network infrastructure. Each ISP spends substantial amounts of capital (cash, human capital, intellectual capital) on building its own physical network, with the intent of providing as much geographical coverage as possible. If ISPs built their networks with the objective of minimizing the size of their physical networks (and obtaining as much coverage as possible through interconnection agreements), then it could be inferred that the ISPs seek and heavily depend on *cooperation*, although the result would likely be suboptimal, and there would probably be insufficient geographical coverage of each ISP's network or of the combined networks. Thus, it can be reasonably inferred that ISPs enter into interconnection agreements as a matter of convenience and to accommodate their customers' needs (if and when the ISP identifies certain traffic patterns). Furthermore, of the two types of interconnection agreements, peering agreements account for more than 70% of all interconnection agreements and usually do not result in any additional costs for the ISP (each ISP agrees to carry the other ISP's traffic for free). In most markets, most consumers have only one or two ISPs and one Internet access point. Hence, the consumer's choice of one ISP results in an automatic economic loss for other ISPs in the same market. This economic loss occurs because of the sunk costs (physical infrastructure, advertising costs, administrative costs) and infrastructure-leasing costs incurred by ISPs. Each time that an ISP (ISP1) transmits a packet for another coalition member (ISP2), ISP1 loses brand equity and ISP2 gains brand equity because ISP2 is completing service. Interconnection fees often do not compensate ISPs for such loss of brand equity. Therefore, Shapley value function is not applicable to network access pricing.

11.5 Properties of an Allocation Mechanism That Were Stated in Ma et al. (2010) Are Wrong

Those *properties* are wrong because of the following reasons:

1. *Symmetry*: The definition of *symmetry* in Ma et al. (2010) is not an accurate definition of *symmetry* within and outside the context of networks, and it erroneously assumes that any two ASes (Autonomous Systems) (internet service providers) that have the same *contribution* are in the same circumstances and/or have the same cost structure and generate the same utility. Note that an ISP's *contribution* does not necessarily result in a change in *utility* or *marginal utility*.
2. *Dummy*: As defined in Ma et al. (2010), this property ignores the economic value of flexibility. A *dummy* Autonomous System (AS) that provides utility in some but not all transactions should receive some share of the profits. Even *completely dummy* ASes can have value because they provide flexibility in case of emergencies.
3. *Strong monotonicity*: This property is not valid in all circumstances because *contribution* does not necessarily equate to added utility, and there may be *decreasing returns to scale* wherein the utility created by the ISP's efforts declines as efforts increase.
4. *Additivity*: This is not a valid property in all circumstances because there may be *increasing returns to contribution* or *decreasing returns to contribution* for some members, each member, or all members of the coalition.

See the definition of *fuzzy logic congestion controllers* (FLCCs) in Jammeh et al. (2009) and in Mendel (2007). Furthermore, note that the Shapley value function models in Ma et al. (2010) can be deemed to be forms of FLCCs.[8] Zhang and Wei (2014), Murofushi (1992), and Fan-Yong and Wang (2012) made some useful comments. Consider a subgame in which there is a market and there are six ISPs in the market (ISP$_1$,..., ISP$_6$) and an average of D% of total traffic has to pass through some part of each ISP's network in order to complete the transmission. It is in the best interest of all six ISPs to minimize D%, and any such process will most probably require individual or joint monitoring of each ISP's network expansion plans, and more probably, some level of collusion in network design or network expansion planning. Such collusion or collaboration is likely to be illegal under antitrust laws of most countries. Furthermore, assume that each ISP has its own FLCC (A_n), and so there are $A_1,\ldots, A_6$ FLCCs. The degree of similarity and/or goal congruence between any two pairs of FLCC algorithms is henceforth referred to as the *congruency index* (CI), which increases as the two FLCCs' objectives and criteria are more similar. For traffic to flow adequately, there must be at least B% of CI among different combinations of pairs of $A_1,\ldots, A_6$ FLCCs. If CI is below B%, then there is substantial risk of packet delay or packet loss, and as B% tends to 100%, the probability of successful transmission tends to one. FLCCs are typically highly proprietary algorithms. While technology companies typically meet in order to set industry standards, such standards are almost always for nonproprietary equipment, rules, and/or processes. However, there must be some minimum amount of collusion or collaboration among ISPs in order to ensure that there is the minimum *CI* percentage (B%); and such collusion is most probably illegal under the antitrust laws of most jurisdictions. Similarly, the coordination and collusion required to implement Shapley value functions in Internet networks will most probably be illegal under the antitrust laws of most jurisdictions.

11.6 The Shapley Value Function Cannot Be Used for Allocating Electricity Transmission Costs

For the same and similar reasons stated in this chapter and in Roth and Verrecchia (1979), and contrary to Lima et al. (2008), Chun et al. (2016), Rhymend and Uthariaraj (2016), Kim (2016), Calvo and Gutiérrez (2013), Jia and Yokoyama (2003), and Kattuman et al. (2004), the Shapley value function (and similar approaches such as the Owen value) cannot be used for allocating electricity transmission costs.

11.7 The Shapley Value Function Cannot Be Used for Discovering Influential Nodes in Social Networks

For the same and similar reasons stated in this chapter, and contrary to Narayanam and Narahari (2011), Chen and Teng (2016), Flores et al. (2016), and Suri and Narahari (2010), the Shapley value function and similar approaches (such as the Owen value) cannot be used for discovering influential nodes in social networks.

11.8 Conclusion

The Shapley value and related theories are clearly not applicable to Internet network pricing analysis, cost allocation in networks, or analysis of electricity distribution networks. The elimination or relaxation of some of the assumptions and prerequisite constraints implicit in Shapley value analysis will render the results meaningless. Antitrust laws also preclude applicability of Shapley value solutions in some circumstances. Thus, most of the theories introduced in Cao et al. (2002), Ma et al. (2010), Zhou et al. (2016), Kim (2016), and Perez-Castrillo and Wettstein (2001) are wrong.

Notes

1 See Hoefer et al. (2011); Bandyapadhyay et al. (2014); Bilò and Flammini (2011); Berenbrink and Schulte (2010); Azar et al. (2005); Anshelevich and Caskurlu (2011); and Blum et al. (2010).

2 See Johnson, T. (2015). This article stated the following in part:

> …The FCC approved robust rules of the road for the Internet on Thursday, a move that supporters believe will prevent conglomerates from consolidating control over the flow of online content, but that critics characterize as a huge regulatory overreach. The FCC's approach is one favored by many public interest groups, Hollywood content creators, and a large number of web companies including Netflix and Twitter: It is reclassifying Internet service as a Title-II telecommunications service, a regulatory designation akin to that of a utility. The move is intended to give the FCC solid authority to impose rules over Internet service. The new rules prohibit ISPs from blocking or throttling content, as well as from collecting payments from content providers for speedier access to their subscribers. The latter has been commonly referred to as the notion that ISPs would eventually create Internet 'fast lanes'….

3 See *The Economic Times* (India) (2015). This article stated the following in part:

> …Telecom operators spoke in different voices today as the regulator TRAI called them for an open house to discuss network connection charges that impacts mobile rates…. Telecoms were split based on *Bill-and-Keep* (BAK), *Long-Run Incremental Cost* (LRIC), and *Fully Allocated Cost* (FAC) methods for calculating mobile termination costs. State-run BSNL and Reliance Communication were in favor of using BAK for calculations. Bharti Airtel said that the fully allocated cost (FAC) model assures recovery of full cost, including historical costs, as it relies on actual data furnished by operators. On the other hand, Vodafone said that a cost-based approach on the work done principle is the most appropriate method. Under BAK, a service provider does not have to pay termination charges to its interconnecting operator and the service provider bills its own customers for outgoing traffic. While LRIC involves determining the incremental cost of providing an additional unit of service over current levels and over a defined future period of time. FAC involves allocation of all historical costs incurred to date for individual services based on a set of criteria such as relative capacity utilisation, minutes of usage, or proportional revenue generated. It considers costs that are both forward-looking and incremental, which would generate a credible charge that reflects real economic cost for providing interconnection. However, in its consultation paper on IUC, TRAI said: "Cost-based IUC have a strong economic rationale; however, there is no single, simple way to estimate the interconnection cost. Determination of cost-based charges is a complex exercise….

4 See Reuters (Mexico) (2014). This article stated the following in part:

> …The Mexican telecom regulators on Monday set the 2015 rates for interconnection fees between competing networks as part of measures to open up its historically hidebound sector dominated by Carlos Slim's America Movil. The Federal Institute of Telecommunications (IFT) said America Movil SAB de CV, which is trying to downsize to avoid tougher regulation, will be able to charge companies that use its network between 0.005162 pesos and 0.006246 pesos. Companies such as Telefonica and Nextel, which are exempted from the measures imposed on America Movil because of their smaller market shares, will be able to charge 0.2505 pesos. The government completed a major reform in 2014 designed to loosen Slim's hold on the market he has dominated for years. Next year could also see the arrival of the U.S. company AT&T Inc to compete with the billionaire. Earlier this month, the IFT approved AT&T's $1.7 billion purchase of Iusacell, Mexico's third-biggest mobile operator, which lags far behind America Movil. Slim's company has around 70 percent of the mobile market in Mexico….

5 See *This Day* newspaper (Nigeria) (2013). This article stated the following in part:

…Last month when Nigerian Communications Commission (NCC) made known its intention to carry out its routine review on the existing interconnection rate model and allowed operators to make inputs, the big players such as MTN, Airtel, and Globacom argued strongly that NCC should consider the symmetric model, which allows for equal termination rate, since it had in the past implemented the asymmetric model, which appeared not favorable to the bigger operators, since they pay higher termination rates, based on the large volume of calls generated on their networks and terminated on other networks. Contrary to their argument, the smaller operators of the Global System for Mobile Communication (GSM), and that of the Code Division Multiple Access (CDMA), insisted that NCC should continue with the asymmetric model until a time in the future when the smaller operators such as Etisalat, Visafone, Starcomms, and Multilinks were big enough to compete favorably with the bigger GSM operators. In spite of the argument put forward by the big players, NCC last week came up with an entirely new model, which is a combination of asymmetric and symmetric interconnection models, and it became a shocker to the big players who had thought that the NCC was going to consider the symmetric model, having fully deployed the asymmetric model in the past…. Presently, operators pay between N8.20 and N10 for interconnection rates, and this is a typical asymmetric model, whose rates depend largely on the volume of calls that is generated from one network and terminated on another network. Operators with larger volume of terminating calls pay higher rate. With the new interconnection rate model, NCC allowed differential payments (asymmetric) for a period of 2 years, and equal payments (symmetric) for the third year. The new interconnection rates will last for 3 years, before the next review will take place, since it is the tradition of NCC to review interconnection rates every 3 years. Announcing the new rates and model, Director, Public Affairs at NCC, Mr. Tony Ojobo, said the new set of interconnection rates determination for voice services will take effect from April 1, 2013. '… The new determination rates, which significantly reviewed prices downwards, are informed by the depth of competition in the industry while taken into consideration the position of new entrants and small operators, …' Ojobo said. Giving details of the mixture of asymmetric and symmetric models adopted by the NCC, Ojobo said the termination rates for voice services provided by new entrants and small operators in Nigeria irrespective of the originating network shall be N6.40 from April 1, 2013; N5.20 from April 1, 2014; and N3.90 from April 1, 2015. He also said that the termination rates for voice services provided by other operators in Nigeria irrespective of the originating network shall be N4.90 from April 1, 2013; N4.40 from April 1, 2014; and N3.90 from April 1, 2015. What this means is that in the first year, which will run from April 1, 2013, to March 31, 2014, the termination rate for small operators and new entrants will be N6.40 kobo, while that of the bigger operators will be N4.90 kobo, which clearly means that while smaller operators will pay the big operators N4.90 kobo for every call generated from the network of smaller operators but terminated on the network of big operators, while the bigger operators will pay the smaller operators N6.40 kobo for every call generated from their networks but terminated on the network of the smaller operators. Then from April 1, 2014 to March 31, 2015, operators will also pay differential rates but reduced from that of the previous years, with the smaller operators paying N4.40 kobo while bigger operators will pay N5.20 kobo. In the third year, all operators will pay an equal (symmetric) rate of N3.90 kobo, irrespective of the volume of calls generated and terminated. 'This determination shall take effect from April 1, 2013 and remain valid and binding on licensees for the next 3 years until further reviewed by the commission,…' Ojobo said. Clarifying the criteria used in measuring small and big operators, Ojobo defined a new entrant as a newly licensed operator entering an existing or new market within 0–3 years and defined a small operator for the purpose of the determination as an existing operator with a market share of 0 to 7.5% in terms of subscriber base. Anything above the listed range automatically defines the bid operator category. The current interconnection rate regulation was implemented through the commission's interconnection rate determination (IRD) issued on December 21, 2009, which clearly differentiates the smaller operators from the big operators in terms of their size and years of experience. 'Since then, the Nigerian communications market has seen tremendous growth in both subscriber numbers as well as traffic volumes and available technologies... Ojobo said.

6 See Spangler (2015). Spangler (March 4, 2015) stated in part:

> ...The FCC on February 26 approved new network neutrality rules, by a 3-2 vote, that will treat broadband services like traditional phone services under Title II, although those will restrict the commission from imposing rate regulation, tariffs, or limits on bundling. Big ISPs like Comcast and Verizon had argued strenuously against such a reclassification....

See *MTN may take ICASA to court over USD0.25 interconnect fee* (March 31, 2015; South Africa). Available at: https://www.telegeography.com/products/commsupdate/articles/2015/03/31/mtn-may-take-icasa-to-court-over-usd0-25-interconnect-fee/.

7 See Wireless Federation (January 2007). Romanian mobile operators challenge interconnection fees. Available at: http://wirelessfederation.com/news/5212-romanian-mobile-operators-challenge-interconnection-fees/.

8 Researchers have noted that (1) Shapley value weights calculated for fuzzy measures estimate the importance of each *singleton* (for additive fuzzy measures, the Shapley value will be the same as each *singleton*); (2) for a given fuzzy measure g, and $|\mathbf{X}| = n$, the Shapley index for every $i,..., n \in X$ is

$$\phi(i) = \sum_{E \subseteq X \setminus \{i\}} \frac{(n-|E|-1)!\,|E|!}{n!} [g(E \cup \{i\}) - g(E)];$$

and (3) the *Shapley value* is the vector $\phi(g) = (\psi(1),..., \psi(n))$.

Chapter 12

Stackelberg Analysis Cannot Be Used in Network Access Pricing, Network Cost Allocation, or Pricing of Digital Content

Game theory principles have been used extensively in developing analytical models for access pricing in Internet networks, transmission pricing in electric power networks, and access pricing in telephone/cable networks. This chapter shows that (1) Stackelberg analysis is inappropriate for most situations; (2) Stackelberg analysis is not applicable to network analysis, partly because of the constant evolution of networks; (3) the existing literature on network analysis and pricing contains major omissions and gaps; and (4) the effects of illegal online file sharing on the pricing of network access has been substantially omitted in most literature on network analysis.

12.1 Existing Literature

Fanelli et al. (2015) and Bilò et al. (2010) studied cost-allocation algorithms and games within the context of networks. Azar et al. (2005), Bilò and Flammini (2011), Bandyapadhyay et al. (2014), Anshelevich and Caskurlu (2011), and Canavoi et al. (2014) studied *equilibria* within networks. Bilò et al. (2015) and Kaporis and Spirakis (2009) analyzed Stackelberg games. However, the theories introduced in this chapter contradict many of the theories in the foregoing articles.

Troquard et al. (2011), Ågotnes et al. (2009), and Wolter and Wooldridge (2011) studied logic and the aggregation of preferences and judgment in games.

12.1.1 Most of the Weaknesses of the Shapley Value Function Also Apply to Stackelberg Game Analysis[1]

Most of the critiques and weaknesses of Shapley value function, also apply to Stackelberg games, and thus the inaccuracies and problems summarized (see endnotes) in Tick et al. (1999), Fatima et al. (2008), Roth (1977), Sastre and Trannoy (2001), Kirman et al. (2007), Lima et al. (2008), Roth and Verrecchia (1979), Bakos and Nault (1997), and Biczok et al. (2008) also apply to Stackelberg games.

12.1.2 Stackelberg Games and Related Approaches

Some authors have unsuccessfully attempted to use Stackelberg bargaining analysis for network pricing, and these authors include Korillis et al. (1997) and Shakkotai and Srikant (2006). For more details on the *Conceptual Model for Decomposing Value for the Customer*, see Nicola et al. (2012). For alternative methods for network pricing and cost allocations, see Su (2011), Xu (2011), and Fu et al. (2007).

Borkotokey and Sarangi (2011) critiqued the *Myerson value*, the *position value* (for communication games only), and *Jackson's flexible network values* and stated that these rules do not take into account simultaneous multilateral interactions and do not consider the notion of simultaneous multilateral interaction in a network. Baslam et al. (2012) noted that in telecommunications markets, the interactions between market participants that have different powers and different valuations of time cannot be analyzed by simple games.

The main difference among the models studied in the literature on network access prices (such as Basar et al., 2002; Roch et al., 2005; Briest et al., 2012) is the set of assumptions considered. However, the underlying assumptions for all forms of Stackelberg games are unrealistic.

Fanelli et al. (2015) and Bilò et al. (2010) studied cost-allocation algorithms and games within networks. Azar et al. (2005), Bilò and Flammini (2011), Bandyapadhyay et al. (2014), Anshelevich and Caskurlu (2011), and Canavoi et al. (2014) studied *equilibria* within networks. Bilò et al. (2015), Briest et al. (2012), and Kaporis and Spirakis (2009) analyzed Stackelberg games. However, the theories introduced in this Chapter contradict many of the theories in the foregoing articles.

12.2 Interconnection Fees Can Be Irrelevant in Network Design

As mentioned in the preceding chapter on Shapley value analysis, interconnection fees (peering fees and transiting fees) can be irrelevant in network design.

12.3 Properties of an Allocation Mechanism That Are Described in Ma et al. (2010) Are Not Valid

As explained in the preceding chapter, the four *properties* of the allocation mechanism (*symmetry*, *dummy*, *strong monotonicity*, and *additivity*) that are described in Ma et al. (2010) are not valid.

12.4 Stackelberg Game Analysis and Related Theories Are Inaccurate and Cannot Be Used in the Analysis of Access Pricing or for the Allocation of Revenues/Costs in Networks (i.e., Internet Networks, Power/Electricity Networks)

Many of the conditions mentioned earlier for the feasibility and validity of Shapley value analysis (explained in the preceding chapter) also apply to Stackelberg analysis, and since none of those conditions are feasible, Stackelberg analysis is inaccurate and cannot be used in network access-pricing or for the allocation of revenues/costs.

In reality, although the physical connections of ISP's networks may remain fixed in time and space, the true structure of the network (the actual transmission pathways, and hence the *network*) is not constant, and changes instantaneously, depending on the locations of the sender–receiver pairs. In almost all instances in a network, each packet has more than one feasible path. Furthermore, in land-based networks, the cable used in transporting packets typically has more than one section of wires so that for each distance d in any cable, there is more than one feasible transmission pathway. Similarly, in any wireless network, for any two points in distance d, there are many possible transmission paths. Stackelberg analysis erroneously assumes that the physical structure of the Internet is constant.

Theorem 12.1

For any transmission, even if the originating-ISP knows the cost structure and payoff of every other ISP that is required to transport any given packet, optimal allocation of costs or revenues among cooperating ISPs is never feasible.

Proof: The Stackelberg analysis erroneously assumes that each ISP knows the cost structure and payoff patterns of every other ISP that is a member of the coalition. In reality, statutes prevent public disclosure of cost and pricing information of ISPs; and statutes/regulations also prevent ISP from sharing information among themselves. Active competition among ISPs will almost always preclude their voluntary disclosure of their cost/price data to each other. ISPs can guess about their competitor's cost/price information and can recruit their competitors' staff in order to give them such information. However, network transmission costs are constantly changing not only because of the variations in the number and quality of feasible transmission paths, the differences between full costing and variable costing, and the dynamic nature of wireless portions of networks but also because of the following factors: (1) entrance and exits of ISPs into markets; (2) inflation; (3) calculation of depreciation; (4) changes in capital expenditures; and (5) changes in marketing costs.

Assume a *second best-case* scenario where the competitors' cost/price data are fully observable to the originating ISP (O-ISP), and there is a coalition, but coalition members do not coordinate/unify their routing systems/protocols. The O-ISP can calculate a rough estimate of costs from point P_1 to point P_2, but O-ISP cannot dictate to other network members about when and how to route the packet and to which *third*-ISP to transmit the packet—and thus, each network member will typically be selfish despite coalition agreements. This state is referred to as *coordination-control neutrality* and it prevents any optimal allocations. Assume a *first best-case* scenario, where all ISPs in the network cooperate to try and determine the most efficient routing path, and also disclose their cost/price data to each other. As mentioned, such cooperation will be deemed illegal in most jurisdictions. Even if such cooperation is feasible, there can never be an optimal allocation because of the time frame of the required decisions. Assume that the transmission goes through several ISPs (O, A, B, C, D, ..., N) sequentially, for distances d_1, d_2, d_3, d_4, ..., d_n in time intervals t_1, t_2, t_3, t_4, ..., t_n. Note that A represents the set of all feasible ISPs that can handle the transmission over di_2 in $t1_2$, and B represents the set of all feasible ISPs that can handle the transmission over d_2 during t_2 and so on for all subsequent transmissions. Hence, the time intervals t_1, t_2, ..., t_n are stochastic and unknown in prior periods, and the choices A, B, C, ..., N are also unknown because of the changing nature of cost/price pairs of information. For efficient cooperative allocations, each transmitting ISP (O, A, B, C, ..., N) will have to provide instantaneous cost/price pairs of data (O_{cp}, A_{cp}, B_{cp}, C_{cp}, ..., N_{cp}), for each distance d_1, d_2, d_3, ..., d_n. Hence for A to transmit to B during time t_2, A must have at least A_{cp} and B_{cp} and C_{cp} at the beginning of t_2, and for B to transmit to C during time t_3, B must have at least B_{cp} and C_{cp}, D_{cp} at the beginning of t_3, and so on for subsequent transmissions. By the time the packet moves from B to C, D_{cp} and E_{cp} and F_{cp} have changed, and a new allocation must be made. The sensitivity of the optimality of allocations to changes in the cost/price pairs is very high because of the nature and volumes of the transmission of packets (the components of each ISPs total transmission costs (TTCs) and prices can vary dramatically across different ISPs and are explained earlier). First, because these TTCs and prices are difficult to calculate and the microtime (per millisecond) cost data required to calculate them are available infrequently (at best, on a daily or hourly basis), there is sufficient accurate data for determining any optimal allocation of costs or revenues among a cooperative network of ISPs. Second, because most ISP interconnections are free, introducing the voluntary or mandatory exchange of cost/price data among ISPs is likely to create substantial disagreements over fairness of allocations and or will also affect (reduce) each ISP's willingness to invest capital to build physical or wireless networks. This is because each ISP calculates or is very likely to calculate its return on capital and marketing ROI differently. Such disclosure-influenced free riding will, in turn, limit the growth of the coalition's overall network and preclude or eliminate any efficiency of the allocations of costs/revenues among the ISPs. ■

Theorem 12.2

For every packet and for each time interval t, and for any distance d in the coalition's combined network, each ISP (O-ISP or transmitting ISP) cannot choose an optimal path.

Proof: An ISP cannot control the routing choices of other ISPs. In reality the selected path for each packet is determined by preestablished automated algorithms of each ISP, and these algorithms do not always adapt to changes in the network physical structure or transmission path(s)—which is hereby referred to as *coordination-control neutrality*. Furthermore, because each ISP is not able to obtain very accurate information about historical or future packet loss, it is impossible for the ISP to plot an *optimal transmission path*. It is highly unlikely that any ISP will permit other ISPs to control or overly influence its routing algorithms even in a cooperative network. Antitrust laws will almost surely prevent such coordination. Routing algorithms are complex and are sensitive to changes in network characteristics and the level of human input. The only feasible way that ISPs in a cooperative network can safely influence each other's routing algorithm is if they all use the same commercially available routing algorithm—which is highly unlikely. The second-best alternative is to provide a system of cash incentives to convince each ISP to allow other ISPs to influence their routing algorithms. The properties of any such incentive (Q) are as follows:

1. *Consistency and time invariance*: The ISP cannot deviate from the incentive mechanism Q.
2. *Scope limitation*: Q is limited only to participating ISPs. This presents a huge problem because coalition members cannot control the growth of nonmember ISPs. In some markets, coalition members must connect with nonmembers of the coalition, in order to complete transmissions.
3. *Equivalency*: $\int_0^\tau Q_i \, dt > \int_0^\tau \Sigma O_i \, dt$, where O_i is the value of the ISP's opportunity costs of complying with the incentive mechanism in every transmission. Q_i is the value of the incentive mechanism for the ISP for transmission i.
4. *Additivity*: For any transmission over d_i.

Because any given ISP cannot *choose* an optimal path in the network, Stackelberg analysis is not applicable to network access-pricing or revenue allocation or cost allocation in networks. ■

Theorem 12.3

For any network transmission over any distance (d), the ISP's share of revenues (or share of transmission costs) generated by the coalition is not always nonnegative (can be negative).

Proof: The Stackelberg analysis function erroneously assumes that the ISP's share of revenues generated by the coalition is always nonnegative and that the ISP's share of costs generated by the coalition transmission is always nonnegative. On the contrary, there are some instances where the ISP's share of total transmission revenues generated by the coalition is negative (less than zero) or should be negative, and these include the following:

1. When the ISP's transmission results in excessive packet loss such that the entire information unit has to be retransmitted.
2. Where the ISP earns noncoalition third-party benefits for carrying the packet, but is effectively subsidized indirectly by coalition members.
3. Where given specific transmission algorithms (and congestion control algorithms) that are implemented by coalition-member ISPs, ISP-A's transmission of a packet increases the probability that certain other types of packets will be sent by both coalition member and nonmembers and transmitted through ISP-A's network.
4. Where transmitting a certain packet through the ISP's network exponentially increases each subsequent coalition member's costs of carrying the same packet to its destination.
5. Where transmission by an ISP results in addition of data to the packet that then increases the required minimum bandwidth and costs for further transmission by all other coalition members.

Given the foregoing, Stackelberg analysis is not applicable to network access pricing or cost allocation (or revenue allocation) in networks. ■

Observation 12.1

For any time interval t, and for any distance d in the coalition's networks, the marginal contribution of each coalition-member ISP is not always directly proportional to (1) distance or (2) bandwidth consumed.

Stackelberg analysis erroneously implies that for any time interval t, and for any distance d in the coalition's networks, the marginal contribution of each coalition-member ISP is directly proportional to (1) distance and (2) bandwidth consumed. This is not always true. For example, with regard to distance, the marginal contribution of a coalition-member ISP that transports a packet for 100 meters in an extremely high-density city block with significant Internet congestion is or can be greater than the marginal contribution of an ISP that transports a similar packet for 1000 m in a low-density rural area with no Internet congestion.

Theorem 12.4

For any time interval t and for any distance d in the coalition's networks, the number of coalition members is not always nonnegative.

Proof: An ISP can be deemed a *negative* member of a coalition when any of the following conditions exist:

1. X% of the ISP's network is physically proximate to the networks of coalition members even though the ISP is not a coalition member, and such proximity can reduce the coalition's transportation burden by Q%.
2. The ISP has no physical networks or wireless networks but enters into interconnection agreements with coalition members (or the ISP has minimal physical networks—about 5% of the average network size).

Stackelberg analysis erroneously implies that for any time interval t and for any distance d in the Coalition's networks, the number of coalition members is not always nonnegative, and hence, Stackelberg analysis is not applicable to network access pricing or to cost allocation in networks. ■

Observation 12.2

For any time interval t and for any distance d in the coalition members' networks, the marginal rate of transmission of packets (R_t) (the distance that the packet travels for each additional unit of bandwidth consumed) does not remain constant, and thus, Stackelberg analysis is not applicable to network access pricing or cost allocation in networks.

The *marginal rate of transmission* of packets varies or can vary constantly in most networks for various reasons including traffic/congestion, size/diameter of the network cable, physical obstructions in wireless networks, type of protocol, and type of digital content. With such varying R_t, each coalition member's contribution cannot be measured by any standard unit, and hence given the Stackelberg theory and formula, any allocation will not be fair or stable. Thus, Stackelberg analysis is inapplicable to access pricing.

Theorem 12.5

For any time interval t, and for any distance d in the coalition members' networks, the marginal utility of substituting an ISP in the transmission path (the increase in utility gained from substituting an ISP in the transmission path) does not remain constant, and Stackelberg analysis is not applicable to network pricing.

Proof: Clearly, both the O-ISP's and the consumer's marginal utility of substituting any ISP in the transmission path (path between sender and receiver) changes instantaneously due to (1) changes in traffic and volume, (2) the size of the pipe, (3) the absolute efficiency and relative efficiency of each ISP's network, (4) timing, (5) transmission fees and terms of payment of such fees (nature of the contracts), and (6) physical barriers (for wireless networks), etc. As explained before, the physical network may be constant but differs from transmission paths within it. Thus, Stackelberg analysis is not applicable to access pricing or cost allocation in networks. ■

Theorem 12.6

The Stackelberg analysis is inapplicable because for each packet, and for any time interval t, and for any distance d in the coalition members' networks, the end-to-end total interconnection fee is a small or insignificant component of the per-packet TTC, and the Stackelberg analysis allocations of cost and/or revenues to coalition members will be unfeasible when costs and/or revenues exceed or fall below certain thresholds.

Proof: In most instances, the interconnection fees are not a main component of the TTC incurred by the ISP. For any time interval t and for any distance d in the coalition's network, if the ISP's *average end-to-end TTC* (R_a) or *marginal end-to-end TTC* (R_m) is below a certain dollar threshold (Y_r), the ISP may not care much about interconnection fees and will not have adequate incentives to remain in any coalition of ISPs. Also, if R_a and R_m are above a certain dollar threshold (X_r), the ISP will face an increasing risk of operating losses, financial distress, and exit, and hence, the ISP will not have sufficient incentive to remain in any coalition—the ISP will most probably shift its focus and resources to reducing its nontransmission costs and will probably attempt to create other coalitions with third parties. In general, participation in these coalitions is not mandatory and ISPs can negotiate with various coalitions for membership or exit, subject to terms of peering agreements. Hence, there are three possible states, which are as follows: (1) $X_r > Y_r$, (2) $Y_r > X_r$, and (3) $X_r = Y_r$. However, if $X_r > Y_r$, and R_a, $R_m \in (X_r, Y_r)$, the average coalition member will have some incentives to remain in the coalition, but such member can improve its position by negotiating with other nonmember ISPs for peering agreements or by expanding its own physical infrastructure or by joining third-party coalitions. Even where membership in a coalition is mandatory for all or part of the time period, coalition-member ISPs can still improve their payoffs by expanding their own physical networks.

Similarly, for any time interval t and for any distance d in the coalition's network, if the *average per-unit interconnection fee* (P_a) or *marginal per-unit interconnection fee* (P_m) (for transporting a unit of bandwidth or packet) is below a certain dollar threshold (Y_p), the ISP may not care much about interconnection fees and will not have adequate incentives to remain in any coalition of ISPs. Also, if P_a and P_m are above a certain dollar threshold (X_p), the ISP will have strong incentives to leave the coalition and expand its own physical network or strong incentives to reduce its physical network and enter into more peering/interconnection agreements with noncoalition ISPs. In general, participation in these coalitions is not mandatory and ISPs can negotiate with various coalitions for membership or exit, subject to terms of peering agreements. Hence, there are three possible states, which are as follows: (1) $X_p > Y_p$, (2) $Y_p > X_p$, and (3) $X_p = Y_p$. However, if $X_p > Y_p$, and P_a, $P_m \in (X_p; Y_p)$, the average coalition member will have some incentives to remain in the coalition, but such member can improve its position by negotiating with other nonmember ISPs or by expanding its own physical infrastructure or by reducing its physical network infrastructure or by joining third-party coalitions. Even where membership in a coalition is mandatory for all or part of the time period, coalition-member ISPs can still improve their payoffs by expanding their own physical networks. Thus, there can never be any Nash equilibrium or Stackelberg equilibrium for such coalitions of transporting ISPs.

Similarly, for any time interval t and for any distance d in the coalition's network, if the average per-unit revenue (F_a) or marginal per-unit revenue (F_m) (for transporting a unit of bandwidth or packet) is below a certain dollar threshold (Y_f), the ISP will not have adequate incentives to remain in any coalition of ISPs, primarily because the ISP will face financial distress and possible exit from the market. Also, if F_a and F_m are above a certain dollar threshold (X_f), the ISP will have (1) strong incentives to leave the coalition and expand its own physical network; or (2) substantial incentives to remain in the coalition but vary the size of its network, and hence, the amount of its payoff; or (3) substantial incentives to reduce the size of its physical network and enter into more peering/interconnection agreements with both coalition-member ISPs and or noncoalition ISPs. In general, participation in these coalitions is not mandatory and ISPs can negotiate with various coalitions for membership or exit, subject to terms of interconnection/peering agreements. Hence, there are three possible states, which are as follows: (1) $X_f > Y_f$, (2) $Y_f > X_f$, and (3) $X_f = Y_f$. However, if $X_f > Y_f$, and F_a, $F_m \in (X_f, Y_f)$, the average coalition member will have some incentives to remain in the coalition, but such member can improve its position by negotiating with other nonmember ISPs or by expanding its own physical infrastructure or by reducing its physical network infra- structure or by joining third-party coalitions. Even where membership in a coalition is mandatory for all or part of the time period, coalition-member ISPs can still improve their payoffs by expand- ing their own physical networks. Thus, there can never be any Nash equilibrium or Stackelberg equilibrium for such coalitions of transporting ISPs. ■

Observation 12.3

The Stackelberg analysis allocation is inefficient and unfeasible because Stackelberg analysis erroneously assumes that the resources of all coalition members are fixed for any time interval t, and each coalition member's contribution to the mechanism is limited/finite.

Each coalition member has different resources that vary in terms of availability and size, and coalition members can vary their contribution to the mechanism (e.g., increase the physical size of their network or change their routing algorithms). Furthermore, each coalition mem- ber's contribution to the mechanism can be infinite and unlimited—for example, each coalition member may be able to build a network that covers the subjection city or region and maintain the network on a 24/7 basis indefinitely.

Theorem 12.7

For any coalition S, there are certain conditions that must exist before there can be a feasible appli- cation of the Shapley value to allocations in networks, but all such conditions are individually and collectively unfeasible.

Proof: These conditions are related to the nature of networks and are all unfeasible and are as follows (the proof of the unfeasibility of each condition is straightforward):

Condition 7(i): *In Stackelberg analysis, N (total number of ISPs in the market/region) and s (number of ISPs in the coalition) are constant for all time periods t and for any region r.* This condition is not feasible because ISPs will enter and exit the coalition over time.

Condition 7(ii): *The marginal contribution of coalition member (ISP1) is equally likely to occur as the marginal contribution of any other coalition member during any time interval t.* This condition is not feasible because different ISPs have very different resources, network architectures, and commitment to the coalition.

Condition 7(iii): *The terms of the coalition agreement (resource allocation formula) remains constant for any time interval t.*

Condition 7(iv): *In any coalition S, and for any time interval t, utilities are always transferable among any two pairs of ISPs.* This condition is not feasible because different ISPs have very different resources, network architectures, and commitment to the coalition. In this context, utility is in the form of transmission and brand equity. Furthermore, the physical layout.

Condition 7(v): *For any time interval t, and for any number of ISPs in a market denoted by n, and for any distance d in the coalition members' network, in the Shapley value formula for calculating payoffs, as s → 0 (as the number of coalition members approaches zero), the absolute effect/contribution of each coalition-member ISP remains at least constant but increases and is proportional to the ISP's network size.*

Condition 7(vi): *For any time interval t, and for any distance d in the coalition members' network, in The Shapley value formula for calculating payoffs, as s → n (as the number of coalition members approaches the total number of ISPs in the market), the effect/contribution of each coalition-member ISP remains at least constant and is proportional to the ISP's network size.*

Condition 7(vii): *The governance structure of the coalition does not matter and does not affect the contributions and payoffs of coalition members.* This condition is not feasible. The peering/interconnection agreement may determine the nature of the governance of the coalition or subcoalitions within the coalition. The coalition can be in the form of (1) separate agreements among ISPs at various times, (2) uncoordinated and separate strategic alliances among ISPs, (3) coordinated strategic alliances among ISPs that anticipate entry/exit of alliance members, (4) uncoordinated joint ventures among ISPs, (5) coordinated joint ventures among ISPs that anticipate entry/exit of alliance members, and (6) government-mandated interconnection agreements. The governance includes (1) determination of costs and revenues, (2) collection and sharing of revenues, and (3) dispute resolution methods.

Condition 7(viii): *All interconnection agreements (peering agreements and transiting agreements) are the same.*

Condition 7(ix): *Illegal online file sharing does not affect ISP's profitability and cost structure.* This condition is not feasible because illegal online file sharing affects the profitability and QoS of ISPs. Most of the existing literature on network pricing analysis explicitly omits any analysis of the effects of illegal online file sharing.

Condition 7(x): *QoS concerns do not affect the probability of formation of coalitions.* This condition is not feasible in most instances, because more ISPs are becoming more concerned about QoS and are using QoS as a basis to segment their services (to offer different tiers of Internet access).

Condition 7(xi): *Antitrust laws do not matter.* On the contrary, antitrust laws preclude the types of coalitions that are envisioned or implied by Shapley value analysis and Stackelberg games.

Condition 7(xii): *All coalition members contribute a minimum amount of resources (i.e., have a physical network)*. Shapley value analysis may be accurate only if all coalition members contribute some minimum level of resources to the mechanism/game. The Shapley value formula for calculating the payoffs fails if one or more coalition members do not contribute any resources (e.g., physical network, bandwidth) to the game. On the contrary, some ISPs can be only marketing companies that do not have any physical networks but use peering/interconnection agreements to transport data and, thus, earn revenues.

Condition 7(xiii): *The probabilities of formation of each coalition are equal*. Shapley value analysis erroneously assumes that the probability of each possible coalition (and probability of each member's entry into the coalition) is the same.

Condition 7(xiv): *Each coalition member's effort is equal to its contribution that in turn is equal to an equivalent amount of utility*. On the contrary, each coalition member's effort is not equal to its *contribution* that in turn is not equal to an equivalent amount of utility.

Condition 7(xv): *The utility created by any interconnection agreement in the coalition is constant for any packet size and over any time period t, and such utility benefits only the two contracting ISPs*.

Condition 7(xvi): *Each ISPs contribution to the coalition is measured primarily by its geographic coverage and its connections to other ISPs*.

Condition 7(xvii): *In any coalition S, and for any time interval t, utilities are transferable among any two pairs of ISPs*. This condition is clearly false.

Condition 7(xviii): *There must be a leader and followers*. In the context of ISPs, there really is not a *leader* because any peering agreement or interconnection agreement must be signed by two ISPs.

Condition 7(xix): *The first mover must know that the follower must not have any means of committing to a future non-Stackelberg follower action*. This condition does not exist in the context of networks. Follower ISPs (ISPs that enter into interconnection or peering agreements after other ISPs have done so) can and do have resources to commit to non-Stackelberg follower actions, and other ISPs (in the same local market and or in other markets) may not know of these resources (such as human capital, business relationships, borrowing capacity, intellectual property).

Condition 7(xx): *There must be permanence in the first-mover's (Stackelberg Leader's) commitment, and the first-mover must derive some advantage from being the first-mover (the Stackelberg leader cannot change/re-negotiate his/her commitment, and the Stackelberg follower must know the details of the Stackelberg leader's commitment before the follower takes any action)*. On the contrary, for any market m and for any time interval t, the first ISP to enter into a peering/interconnection agreement is not required to (and typically does not) make any commitment except those stated in specific agreements with other ISPs. The leader can terminate or breach such agreements, sometimes without any penalty (and thus, there is no permanence of commitment). Also, in any market m, and for any time interval t, the two "first-mover" ISPs do not always gain any competitive advantage from being the first-movers given the nature of Internet networks—the power and effectiveness of such Internet network typically grows as it expands.

Condition 7(xxi): *For all types of networks and for any segment of a network, in order for Stackelberg analysis to be applicable to access pricing, the leader (first mover) must know ex ante that the follower observes his or her action*. However, this condition does not exist or rarely exists in most markets, because some interconnection agreements have confidentiality clauses and ISPs in the same area/market do not necessarily know all the actions of other local ISPs with regard to peering/interconnection agreements. ◼

Observation 12.4

The Stackelberg allocation is not feasible for revenue/cost allocation in networks because the Stackelberg mechanism (for profit sharing) does not account for differences in sources of demand among coalition members (i.e., share of customers).

The Stackelberg mechanism does not account for differences in sources of demand for the coalition's services and products and erroneously assumes that demand is uniform and equal for all coalition members—the Sharing mechanism does not account for the number of customers delivered to the coalition by any ISP. To be accurate and to prevent jealousy and defections, the sharing mechanism must reward ISP members for the volume of business (completed paid transmissions) and the quality of business (e.g., long-term vs. short-term customers, high-bandwidth vs. low-bandwidth transmissions) that they bring to the coalition.

Observation 12.5

The network transmission (and revenue sharing) game is not a cooperative game.

Network access transmission and revenue allocation is not a cooperative game or semicooperative game. The fact that ISPs enter into interconnection agreements does not make any revenue allocation system a *cooperative* game. Network access (and any implicit revenue allocation or cost sharing) is a noncooperative game because of the following:

1. In any given market, most ISPs are fierce competitors, and each ISP spends substantial amounts of money on advertising, promotions, and marketing.
2. Each ISP spends substantial amounts of capital (cash, human capital, intellectual capital) on building its own physical network, with the intent of providing as much geographical coverage as possible. If ISPs built their networks with the objective of minimizing the size of their physical networks (and obtaining as much coverage as possible through interconnection agreements), then it could be inferred that the ISPs seek and heavily depend on *cooperation* although the result would likely be suboptimal and insufficient geographical coverage of each ISP's network or of the combined networks. Thus, it can be reasonably inferred that ISPs enter into interconnection agreements as a matter of convenience and to accommodate their customers' needs (if and when the ISP identifies certain traffic patterns). Furthermore, of the two types of interconnection agreements, peering agreements) account for more than 70% of all interconnection agreements, and peering agreements do not result in any additional costs for the ISP (each ISP agrees to carry the other ISP's traffic for free).
3. In most markets, most consumers have only one or two ISPs, and one Internet access point. Hence, the consumer's choice of one ISP results in an automatic economic loss for other ISPs in the same market. This economic loss occurs because of the sunk costs (physical infrastructure, advertising costs, administrative costs) incurred by ISPs.
4. Each time that an ISP (ISP1) transits a packet for another coalition member (ISP2), ISP1 losses brand equity and ISP2 gains brand equity because ISP2 is completing service. Interconnection fees often do not compensate ISPs for such loss of brand equity.

Therefore, Stackelberg analysis is not applicable to network access pricing.

Observation 12.6

The entry of each ISP into the coalition is not sequential, and the nature of such sequence affects the payoffs of coalition members and renders Stackelberg analysis inapplicable.

In reality, the formation of peering agreements is typically random. ISPs typically negotiate interconnection agreements only in pairs and at specific points in time. There may be negotiations between two or more pairs at exactly the same time, or in any number of sequences, depending on the unique circumstances of each pair of ISPs. ISPs are not usually required to enter into interconnection agreements and can terminate such peering agreements. Furthermore, in certain instances, the sequence of entry into the coalition may not always affect the payoffs of coalition members, because (1) the packets are a commodity good and are easily produced, (2) in most markets there are relatively few ISPs, (3) some ISPs can combine wireless networks and land-based networks, and (4) the opportunities created by a new member may be equal to or less than the opportunity created by the entry of another new member or may be easily and quickly replicated by the expansion of an existing member's network (such that the coalition's net revenues and profits are same or better).

12.5 Stackelberg Analysis Cannot Be Used for Allocating Electricity Transmission Costs, Allocating Costs in Networks, or Allocating Network Revenues

For the same and similar reasons stated herein, and contrary to Lima et al. (2008), Jia and Yokoyama (2003), Haddadi et al. (2016), Somjit et al. (2016), Roughgarden (2012), Bhaskar et al. (2015), Fanelli et al. (2013), Liao et al. (2013), Briest et al. (2012), and Kattuman et al. (2004), Stackelberg analysis cannot be used for allocating electricity transmission costs or for allocating network revenues and cannot be used for allocating costs in networks (see comments in Roth and Verrecchia, 1979).

12.6 Relaxation of Assumptions Implicit in Stackelberg Analysis and the Effects of Regulation, Antitrust Concerns, and the Structure of Peering Agreements Render Stackelberg Analysis Meaningless

The effects of regulation, antitrust concerns and the structure of peering agreements, and thus the optimal number of ISPs in any region can be substantial and can also render Stackelberg analysis meaningless. The elimination or relaxation of some of the prerequisite constraints implicit in Stackelberg game analysis and related approaches will render the results meaningless.

Thus, most of the theories introduced in Cao et al. (2002), Ma et al. (2010), He et al. (2007), Korillis et al. (1997), Elias et al. (2011), Yang et al. (2007), Nie (2012), Ferreira and Bode (2013), Bei et al. (2011), Anshelevich et al. (2011), Roughgarden (2012), Bhaskar, et al. (2015), Fanelli et al. (2013), Briest et al. (2012), and Arcaute et al. (2013) are wrong.

12.7 Conclusion

Stackelberg games and related approaches are clearly not applicable to Internet network pricing analysis, allocation of costs in networks, and analysis of electricity distribution networks.

Note

1 Some authors/researchers have unsuccessfully attempted to apply the Shapley value (and related theories) to access pricing and to allocation of revenues/costs in networks. These include Ma et al. (2010), Cao et al. (2002), Zhou et al. (2016), Kim (2016), Kattuman et al. (2004), Jia and Yokoyama (2003), Bakos and Nault (1997), Morais and Lima (2007), Angel et al. (2006), and Altman and Wynter (2004). Also see He et al. (2007).

Chapter 13

Illegal File Sharing and Network-Access Pricing

Internet network-access pricing remains a controversial issue that is of concern to government regulators, consumers, and ISPs, given the growing prevalence of the Internet in daily transactions around the world. This chapter (1) develops model of network-access pricing, which reduces or can reduce the information producers' losses from copyright infringement and improves social welfare and the efficiency of computer networks; (2) develops optimal conditions for such pricing scheme, which will incorporate the effects of congestion, social welfare, copyright infringements, evolution of networks, and variations in usage; and (3) analyzes some of the main pricing issues and illustrates how the present mispricing of Internet access contributes to network congestion and illegal online file sharing (IOF). The models developed in this chapter are also applicable to providers of virtual private networks in various industries such as consumer health care, financial services, education, entertainment, etc.

IOF affects the economics, profitability, and business models of companies in many industries such as entertainment, education, travel, investments/finance, and any business where knowledge has value. The pricing of Internet network access is a form of dynamical game because (1) the setting of optimal prices is a series of repeated games among the ISPs and regulators and network members; (2) the optimal access prices are not constant, but change over time, and also depend on the location/topology of network nodes; (3) there are various elements that change constantly (i.e., time, network topology, wealth of ISPs, network congestion, illegal file sharing, magnitude of enforcement, consumers' preferences, consumers' wealth, etc.).

13.1 Existing Literature

Kawase and Makino (2013) introduced the concepts of *potential-optimal price of anarchy* (POPoA) and *potential-optimal price of stability* (POPoS), where "POPoA" is the ratio between the worst cost of Nash equilibrium with optimal potential and the minimum social cost, and "POPoS" is the ratio between the best cost of Nash equilibrium with optimal potential and the minimum social cost. Gassner et al. (2009), Fotakis et al. (2009, 2014), Bilò et al. (2013), Fanelli et al. (2015), Berenbrink and Schulte (2010), Hoefer et al. (2011), Blum et al. (2010), Fiat and Saia (2007), Azar et al. (2005), and Fotakis and Tzamos (2013) studied network routing and congestion games.

Some authors/researchers have attempted to apply the Shapley value (and related theories) to network access pricing and to the allocation of revenues/costs in networks—and these include Ma et al. (2010), Biczok et al. (2008), Morais and Lima (2007), He et al. (2007), Angel et al. (2006), and other articles.[1] As explained in this book, such models are inappropriate. See the critique of the Shapley value in Tick et al. (1999), Fatima et al. (2008), Roth (1977), Sastre and Trannoy (2001), Kirman et al. (2007), Lima et al. (2008), Roth and Verrecchia (1979), and Biczok et al. (2008).

Some authors have attempted to use Stackelberg bargaining analysis for network pricing (see Korillis et al., 1997; Shakkotai and Srikant, 2006). Most of the critiques and weaknesses of Shapley value analysis also apply to Stackelberg game analysis; and thus the inaccuracies and problems summarized in Tick et al. (1999), Fatima et al. (2008), Roth (1977), Sastre and Trannoy (2001), Kirman et al. (2007), Lima et al. (2008), Roth and Verrecchia (1979), Bakos and Nault (1997), and Biczok et al. (2008) also apply to Stackelberg bargaining analysis (He et al., 2007). As explained in this book, Shapley value function and related analysis and Stackelberg games cannot be used in the analysis of network-access pricing.

The *marginal cost controversy* and *net neutrality* were discussed in Chapter 7.

The general literature on Internet access pricing is extensive and includes Sundararajan (2004), Fjell et al. (2010), de Rus and Socorro (2014), Di Pillo et al. (2010), Kao et al. (2014), Inderst & Peitz (2012), Do et al. (2016), Al-Manthari et al. (2011), McClure (2007), Sidak (2006), Yuksel et al. (2007), Clark and Easaw (2007), Guthrie et al. (2006), Kotakorpi (2006), Fjell and Foros (2008), and other articles.[2] However, there are gaps and omissions in the literature, which are described as follows.

Most network-access pricing models in the literature do not consider deterrence (illegal file sharing) and monitoring/enforcement costs imposed on ISPs by courts and government agencies. The models do not incorporate the irrelevance of sunk cost effects. Networks typically need maintenance and have to be upgraded. The pricing models do not consider full costs. Most network-access pricing models do not incorporate incentives—incentives for networks to increase efficient routing and incentives for users to limit their use and hence reduce congestion. The pricing of access and transmission in Internet networks within the context of IOF remains a critical issue that has not been addressed in the existing literature.

13.1.1 A Critique of Sundararajan (2004)

Sundararajan (2004) introduced a pricing scheme for Internet services and provided solutions for pricing based on fixed-fee contracts and consumption-based contracts. Sundararajan (2004) is notable because it is one of the few articles to recognize the dynamics of costs (fixed, variable, and average costs) and volume, consumption, and time changes and to make assumptions about different classes of Internet users.

The problems and limitations in the Sundararajan (2004) analysis are as follows:

1. Sundararajan (2004) erroneously assumes that the opportunity costs of choosing a fixed-fee contract is measurable in the same dimensions/factors (time, value of consumer's time, bandwidth speed, type of digital content, monitoring costs, compliance costs, etc.) as the opportunity costs of choosing a usage-based contract. Sundararajan (2004) does not account for the economic costs of IOF and the compliance costs, monitoring costs, intellectual

property enforcement costs, and secondary liability costs (see Chapters 1 and 2) that have been imposed on ISPs by court rulings in the United States and many other countries.

2. Sundararajan (2004) erroneously assumes that the marginal cost of providing a unit of access is zero. This is false, because (1) there are IP enforcement costs and compliance costs and (2) the marginal cost of providing Internet service varies directly with the size and type of the digital content, the distance between the source server and destination, and the success rate of transmission/transfer (in most file transmissions, any failed transfers are repeated).

3. Contrary to Sundararajan (2004), regardless of the type of contract chosen by the consumer, the *consumer surplus* is meaningful and is a basis of choice only within certain domains of access prices. Below a certain access-price threshold (P_L), any *consumer surplus* that results from choosing either a fixed-fee or usage-based contract is not a major decision factor for the consumer simply because the access price is very low relative to other expenses—in such instances there is significant divergence between *actual consumer surplus* and *perceived consumer surplus* (which is the lower and more relevant of the two). Above a certain access-price threshold (P_h), *consumer surplus* and access price become more of a concern and a major decision factor because the access price is high relative to other household expenses or operating expenses. In such instances, there is much less divergence between *perceived consumer surplus* and *actual consumer surplus* (which is the lower and more relevant of the two), and the *consumer surplus* is capped/limited primarily by the consumer's wealth and budget. The *perceived consumer surplus* is conjectured here to have both monetary and nonmonetary (emotions, satisfaction, value, peace of mind, perceived savings) components.

4. Contrary to Sundararajan (2004), regardless of the type of contract chosen by the consumer, the consumer surplus is meaningful and is a major basis for choice only within certain domains of expected cumulative usage. Below a certain expected cumulative usage threshold, any consumer surplus that results from choosing either a fixed-fee or usage-based contract is not a major decision factor for the consumer simply because the expected usage is very low—in such instances there is significant divergence between actual-consumer-surplus and perceived consumer surplus (which is the lower and more relevant of the two). Above a certain cumulative usage threshold, consumer surplus becomes more of a concern and a major decision factor because of the frequency of use, psychological effects of dependency on the Internet—in such instances, there is much less divergence between perceived consumer surplus and actual consumer surplus (which is the lower and less relevant of the two), and the actual consumer surplus is capped/limited primarily by the consumer's wealth and budget. The perceived consumer surplus has monetary and nonmonetary (emotions, satisfaction, value, peace of mind, perceived savings) components. However, most consumers are not conscious of consumer surplus when they make decisions.

5. Contrary to Sundararajan (2004), the consumer surplus also has an absolute monetary limit regardless of whether the consumer chooses a fixed-fee, usage-based fee, or hybrid contract. This limit depends on total household expenditures (or company operating expenses), the periodic budgeting process, available alternatives to Internet use, the amount and changes in consumer leisure time, the absolute amount of transactions that must be executed through the Internet, etc.

6. The definition and use of *consumer surplus* in the models and equations in Sundararajan (2004) completely neglect the effect of demand and scarcity of various classes of Internet access (i.e., narrowband vs. broadband, wireless vs. fixed line). In effect, where scarcity and

demand for Internet access are very high, the consumer surplus is the most irrelevant factor in consumer choice models.

7. The models and proofs in Sundararajan (2004) omitted the fact that the *consumer surplus* is highly dependent on the class of access (narrowband vs. broadband), the type of delivery (wireless vs. fixed line), and the types of device (cell phone vs. desktop vs. laptop vs. hand-held device). Hence, the analysis in Sundararajan (2004) is an over-generalization; and the *consumer surplus* was not evaluated relative to consumer's expectations about either cumulative usage or expected usage per period.

8. The models in Sundararajan (2004) erroneously assume that there are only two types of consumers and assigns certain characteristics to these two types. The models in Sundararajan (2004) do not account for the economic and psychological costs of switching between a fixed-fee and a usage-based contract. The models erroneously assume that when presented with a choice between a fixed-fee and usage-based contract from one ISP, the consumer will not also consider services provided by other ISPs. In reality, at the time of choice, the consumer's opportunity set also includes (1) other ISPs, (2) the choice of eliminating all Internet access, and (3) the choice of shorter contracts or month-to-month contracts.

9. The models in Sundararajan (2004) erroneously assume that if transaction costs are nonzero (i.e., if C(q) > 0 for q > 0), then it is always profit-improving for the seller of an information good to offer a fixed-fee contract. That proposition erroneously ignores the following: (1) the probability that the consumer will switch to another ISP; (2) the magnitude of the costs incurred by the consumer to switching between a fixed-fee contract and a usage-based contract or to switch to another ISP; (3) the magnitude of the transaction costs; (4) the magnitude of the variable costs of access (which, as described earlier, can vary significantly); (5) a consumer that is an active member of several P2P file sharing networks and regularly downloads bandwidth-intensive digital content from other servers will be an unprofitable customer under a fixed-fee contract but will be a profitable customer under a usage-based contract; and (6) the usage-based contract offered by another ISP may have a periodic cap or may have lower per-unit fees than the contract offered by the subject ISP.

10. Sundararajan (2004) stated in part the following:

> ...The transaction cost-function C(q) is assumed to take the following form:
>
> $$C(q) = 0, \text{ for } q = 0;$$
>
> $$C(q) = \{K + c(q)\}, \text{ for } q > 0,$$
>
> where $K \geq 0$, $c_1(q) \geq 0$ (non-decreasing variable costs), and variable costs are 'not too concave'....

Those assumptions are erroneous. In most instances, when consumption is zero (q = 0), there are certain minimal transaction costs (setup costs, interconnection fees, administrative fees, amortized hardware costs, etc.). There are instances where consumption is negative (q < 0) as in (1) where the ISP gives the consumer a price rebate/discount or (2) where the file-transfer mechanism/protocol actually increases available bandwidth that is attributable to the ISP under trading rules in bandwidth markets (for forward contracts, futures contracts, and spot transactions); or (3) where all attempted file transfers to and from the consumer failed; or

(4) where the billing system is such that all the network costs of the transmission is billed only to the ISP that services the consumer that initiated the transmission. In instances where the transfer/transmission is done by streaming rather than traditional file transfer, the cost function will be different from Sundararajan's (2004) assumption. Furthermore, there are *spot* and *forward* bandwidth markets, and the ISPs' forward contracts may be lower than spot prices for bandwidth, in which case the cost functions will be different from Sundararajan's (2004) assumption.

11. The *hybrid* contract proposed by Sundararajan (2004) is, at best, vague. Sundararajan (2004) describes a usage-based contract that has a "...nonlinear two-part tariff, which a minimum fee of $\{\tau*(\theta K)\}$ for a usage level between 0 and a prespecified upper limit $\{q*(\theta K)\}$, and additional variable payments for usage above $\{q*(\theta K)\}$. Moreover, the function p(q) is strictly concave, indicating an increasing level of volume discounts with usage...." The vagueness arises because the *minimum fee* (the fixed part of the two-part fee) is not based on the ISP's costs or the ISP's capabilities and positions in bandwidth markets but is based only on a certain level of consumption by the consumer (which is not a sufficient condition for efficient cost recovery by the ISP).

12. The models and pricing schemes introduced in Sundararajan (2004) do not consider Internet congestion and associated effects.

13. Sundararajan (2004) proposes that the optimal usage-based pricing schedule in the presence of an unlimited-usage fixed-fee contract is independent of the value of the fixed-fee contract. This proposition does not consider (1) consumer perceptions of the relative fairness of the fixed fee and the usage-based fee and (2) consumers' budgeting processes.

13.1.2 A Critique of Jammeh et al. (2009): The Myth of Intelligent Congestion Control Using Fuzzy Logic Congestion Controllers

Some researchers have developed and supposedly tested various algorithms for the control of congestion in Internet networks—see Jammeh et al. (2009), Rezaei et al. (2008), and Barrett and Woodall (1997). If feasible and accurate, congestion controllers have the potential to drastically change the parameters of network-access pricing because network congestion has a significant effect on network efficiency, bandwidth costs, and maintenance costs.

The most popular congestion controllers are the Type 1 and Type 2 *fuzzy logic congestion controllers* (FLCCs), which are described in Jammeh et al. (2009) and in Mendel (2007). FLCCs are based on *fuzzy logic*. However, Barrett and Woodall (1997), Wolkenhauer and Edmunds (1997), and Brock et al. (2009) explained the weaknesses and computational problems inherent in *fuzzy logic*. Such Type 2 FLCCs are not feasible or accurate because of the following reasons:

1. There may be unforeseen traffic scenarios for which the FLCC fuzzy logic was not designed. The assumption that the FLCC's fuzzy logic covers all possible known and unknown traffic scenarios/patterns is false. Furthermore, most FLCCs are not designed as learning algorithms.

2. The FLCC is only valid within the ISP's networks, but since there are peering agreements, even if the FLCC works, its effectiveness is limited.

3. The IT2 FLCC supposedly extends the *footprint of uncertainty* (FOU) of the membership function, but there is an underlying and erroneous assumption that the variation/variance is constant with the FOU.

4. Since a network path's available bandwidth is *volatile* and difficult to predict, algorithm-based controllers (and FLCCs) are unsuitable and inaccurate.

5. The FLCCs cannot handle streaming video because parts of the transmission come from various nodes/sources. FLCCs work best when the transmission comes from only one source (unidirectional).

As mentioned in Chapter 11, consider a subgame in which there is a market and there are six ISPs in the market ($ISP_1,\ldots, ISP_6$); and an average of D% of total traffic has to pass through some parts of each ISP's network in order to complete the transmission. It is in the best interest of all six ISPs to minimize D%, and any such process will most probably require individual or joint monitoring of each ISP's network expansion plans and, more probably, some level of collusion in network design or network expansion planning. Such collusion or collaboration is likely to be illegal under antitrust laws of most countries. Also assume that each ISP has its own FLCC (A_i) and so the FLCCs are A_1, A_2, A_3, A_4, A_5, and A_6. The degree of similarity and/or goal congruence between any two pairs of FLCC algorithms is henceforth referred to as the *congruence index* (CI), which increases as the two FLCC's objectives and criteria are more similar. For traffic to flow adequately, there must be at least B% of CI among different combinations of pairs of FLCC's A_1, A_2, A_3, A_4, A_5, and A_6. If CI is less than B%, then there is substantial risk of packet delay or packet loss; and as B% tends to 100%, the probability of successful transmission tends to one. FLCCs are typically highly proprietary algorithms. While technology companies typically meet to set industry standards, such standards are almost always for nonproprietary equipment, rules, and/or processes and that there must be some minimum amount of collusion or collaboration among ISPs in order to ensure that there is the minimum *CI* percentage (B%)—such collusion is most probably illegal under the antitrust laws of most jurisdictions.

13.2 Issues in Internet Access Pricing

IOF not only robs content owners of profits but also causes network congestion, uses excessive bandwidth, and has high opportunity cost (the value of information that would have otherwise been transmitted in a timely manner over the Internet). The growth of legal and illegal P2P traffic has been substantially enhanced by the present pricing systems for routing traffic through the Internet. Under the present system of peering agreements and customer agreements, many customers pay a fixed fee for Internet access, and there are no termination charges (as in telephone exchanges). Thus, Internet transmission costs are being misallocated, and such customers do not have any incentive to limit their Internet/bandwidth use. It is conceivable that a different pricing system will make it prohibitively expensive for end customers to engage in illegal P2P file sharing, while legal P2P file sharing will be facilitated by forming agreements (and/or strategic alliances and distribution agreements) between content owners/sellers and ISPs or Internet backbone providers (IBPs).

Some of the main issues in Internet access pricing are as follows:

■ Users typically do not monitor the cost of their Internet usage. Typically, Internet users cannot see the size of their bandwidth usage. Some researchers have proposed systems in which users will be shown their actual bandwidth usage, and the bandwidth that they demand when they request to download or upload information. It is most likely that such systems will have negative impact on users, will slow down and interrupt people's use of the Internet, and hence potentially hinder creative and constructive work, and thus will not be useful or popular.

■ Users should pay more for use of bandwidth in high-congestion periods. When there is network congestion, ISPs sometimes have to purchase additional bandwidth (plus necessary equipment), and users bear some of the increased costs in the form of delays.

■ The user's intensity of Internet use (usage costs—the number of bits transmitted for the whole time spent on the Internet) and the number of hours that the user spends on the Internet (access costs) should be incorporated into the pricing scheme. Both elements can be captured by existing accounting/billing systems—in kilobits per second.

■ *Net neutrality* remains a major controversy.

■ The ISP incurs various types of costs in order to transmit content to customers, and these costs are (1) administrative costs, (2) marketing costs, (3) infrastructure maintenance costs, (4) capital expenses (network infrastructure costs), (5) variable transmission costs (bandwidth, professional staff, interconnection fees), and (6) compliance costs.

There are substantial differences among the following: (1) cost of providing bandwidth x to consumer, (2) price paid by consumer for bandwidth x, (3) utility to consumer from consuming bandwidth x, and (4) cost of Internet congestion caused by consumer. These differences are not considered in the literature when developing access-pricing models.

Substitutability of IBPs and ISPs remains a major issue. Similarly, predictability of prices (from consumers' perspective) is a major concern to users—users will prefer predictable Internet access/usage prices.

The ISP's cost of providing Internet access consists of at least two groups of costs:

1. *Access costs*: Installation costs, interconnection costs (interconnection with other ISPs), consumer activation costs, maintenance costs.
2. *Usage costs*: Current load of network, volume of packets actually transferred, retransmission of dropped packets, cost of providing additional bandwidth (to solve congestion), maintenance costs, network load costs (delays).

13.3 New Network-Access-Pricing Scheme That Can Reduce IOF

The following is an Internet access pricing scheme for Internet access that seeks to incorporate Internet usage, online copyright infringement, congestion costs, and the ISP's costs of providing service. This pricing scheme assumes the following. There will be two tiers of traffic: (1) level one (the IBPs) and (2) level two (the ISPs). There will be termination charges per user, only if the user exceeds a prespecified bandwidth threshold per month. The customer's monthly access fee will consist of two components: (1) a flat fee for Internet access and use of a certain amount of bandwidth per month, and if the customer uses more than a certain amount of bandwidth in any month, then the second level will apply; and (2) the second level is a fixed fee per unit of bandwidth over and above a prespecified amount of bandwidth—this fee can be capped for each period (monthly or quarterly or semiannually or annually). Consumers' and company's choices about access pricing fees are based on household wealth or company assets, budgets, and the relative price and utility of Internet access compared to other expenses. The ISP incurs several types of costs in order to provide services such as general and administrative costs, direct transmission costs (interconnection fees, bandwidth, labor, depreciation of equipment), marketing costs, capital expenditures (Internet infrastructure, buildings, equipment, etc.), and compliance and regulatory costs.

Let:

C_n is the connection cost—this is the cost of connecting a user to the network. C_n is more significant in wireless networks.

Φ_{nt} is the cost of usage of bandwidth in *normal* use in time t, expressed as units of bandwidth per second. The cost of bandwidth is usually expressed as x units per second. Hence Φ_{nt} captures both the amount of bandwidth used and duration of use.

Φ_{ht} is the cost of usage of bandwidth in *high-congestion* use in time t, per consumer per month, expressed as dollars per units of bandwidth per second, $\Phi_{ht} > \Phi_{nt}$.

Φ_{st} is the average cost of usage of bandwidth per consumer per month. Hence, for illegal online file sharers, $\Phi_t > \Phi_{st}$ where Φ_t is the actual cost of usage in time t.

P is the price charged to subscriber per month for Internet access.

P_{min} is the minimum price paid by all subscribers per month. This price will typically be sufficient to cover the ISP's access costs, $P_{min} \geq Max\{0, (F + \upsilon + C_n + (\pi * \rho))\}$.

P_{max} is the maximum price paid by all subscribers per month.

F is the ISP's fixed costs per unit of bandwidth (1 kbs) provided per second.

υ is the ISP's variable costs per unit of bandwidth (1 kbs) provided per second.

α is the average number of units of bandwidth consumed by each subscriber each month (in kbs).

ρ is the probability of Internet congestion in time t.

π is the average potential costs of congestion caused by one consumer's use of one unit of bandwidth (kbs) provided per second in time t. π is f (incremental bandwidth used up in congestion period, total congestion period costs, frequency of occurrence of congestion, etc.).

Ω is the total demand for bandwidth.

λ is the average usage of bandwidth in normal times (in kbs).

β is the price for one unit of bandwidth (I kb) per second for normal use.

Ψ is the number of seconds consumed per user (time).

Hence, the ISP's objective function will be:

$$Min\ P = Min[P_{max}; P_{min}; \{Max(P_{min}, (C + \Phi_{nt} + \Phi_{ht}))|((C + \Phi_{ht} + \Phi_{nt}) \cong P_{min})\}] \quad (13.1)$$

so that

$$P_{min} \geq (C + \Phi_{st}) > 0 \quad (13.2)$$

$$P_{min} \geq [\alpha(F + \upsilon + \pi) + C] \quad (13.3)$$

$$\Phi_{ht} = \left\{ \left(\frac{\Omega}{\lambda} \right) * \beta * \Psi \right\} \quad (13.4)$$

(the formula for determining Internet access pricing for congestion periods)

The aforementioned ISP's objective function is a minimization function because Internet access is a commoditized service; it is often difficult to create any competitive advantage based on perceived quality; and the main basis for competition in the access market is price. Consumers are highly sensitive to price, and hence selling Internet access at the minimum price that ensures a profit should be a major objective.

The ideal Internet access price should be capped because consumers are price sensitive; consumers and most companies rely on budgets and constantly assess the relative prices of various necessities; and consumers' perceptions of *value* are significantly affected by changes in periodic fees and any major variances from budgeted amounts.

Thus, the ISP will likely choose to raise prices when all the following conditions exist:

$$\frac{\partial \alpha}{\partial v} \geq 1; \quad \text{and} \quad \frac{\partial^2 \alpha}{\partial v^2} > 0 \tag{13.5}$$

$$\frac{\partial \rho}{\partial \alpha} \geq 1; \quad \text{and} \quad \frac{\partial^2 \rho}{\partial \alpha^2} > 0 \tag{13.6}$$

$$\frac{\partial \pi}{\partial \Omega} \geq 1; \quad \text{and} \quad \frac{\partial^2 \pi}{\partial \Omega^2} > 0 \tag{13.7}$$

$$\frac{\partial F}{\partial \Omega} \geq 1; \quad \text{and} \quad \frac{\partial^2 F}{\partial \Omega^2} > 0 \tag{13.8}$$

13.4 Effects of Internet Protocols

Internet protocols have a substantial effect on peering and transmissions and hence on the file sharing problem. Blundo et al. (2005), Sicker and Stuka (2004), Amah et al (2016), Qadir et al. (2014), López et al. (2010) discussed relevant issues. Some companies have developed proprietary protocols for file sharing, but most protocols are related to the four most common protocols (SMTP, IP, FTP, HTTP), although file sharers also use Hotline, IRC, Usenet, and ICQ protocols. The key issues are as follows. There is no dominant standard protocol, and companies can and will always develop new protocols for downloading files. At present, there are no coordination mechanisms among Internet protocols, online payment systems, and downloading processes at content owners' websites and storage systems. The major IP backbones do not regulate protocols. The cost of creating and implementing new protocols is relatively low. The knowledge for creating new protocols is easily understandable and can be acquired by a large number of people.

As long as individuals can create protocols, and IP backbones do not regulate the type of protocols they carry, illegal file sharing is likely to continue. Possible solutions include but are not limited to the following:

1. Designing and encrypting media files such that they can be transported in the Internet using only one type of proprietary protocol that will be controlled only by the content owner/distributor and such that the file will be locatable wherever it is in the Internet.
2. Having all ISPs and IP backbones limit the number of permitted protocols and develop standard protocols for different purposes (by limiting and standardizing protocols, content owners will be better able to monitor and control file sharing).
3. Making it mandatory for ISPs to identify and report Internet users who consume substantial bandwidth.

13.5 Conclusion

The often symbiotic relationship between IOF and content control can have significant adverse effects on the accuracy and efficiency of the pricing of Internet access, which in turn has economic, technological, legal, and policy ramifications. IOF problems can be solved by the development of appropriate access-pricing mechanisms that minimize losses for owners/distributors (through effective cost recovery and cost matching), reduce illegal copyright infringement (by charging for excessive usage and suspect usage), and incorporate the limitations of available technologies and Internet protocols.

Notes

1　See Cao et al. (2002), Kattuman et al. (2004), Jia and Yokoyama (2003), and Altman and Wynter (2004).

2　See Sarmento and Brandao (2007), Valletti (2003), Peitz (2005), and Federal Communications Commission (2007).

Chapter 14

Conclusion*

Although illegal online file sharing (IOF) is based on modern technology, much of the debate about enforcement of intellectual property (IP) rights and even file sharing technology revolves around applicable IP statutes in each country and cross-country collaboration by law enforcement agencies, industry trade groups, and private companies that want to enforce IP laws. Presently, there are no unified sets of laws, clear standards of behavior, standards of evidence, or *efficient* laws that function with respect to the sociological patterns of IOF. IOF and inadequate content control remain major problems with significant economic, technological, and policy ramifications. These problems have not been fully addressed by existing laws and evidentiary standards. In the United States, the controlling U.S. Supreme Court decision did not provide required guidance in various aspects (discovery, evidentiary standards, intent, and conduct), and it potentially creates liability for parties not mentioned or analyzed in the case (such as Internet service providers [ISPs]) and places substantial technological burdens on some companies that seek to distribute content. The recent court rulings in various countries have made some (but not adequate) progress in terms of standards for conduct and intent.

14.1 Reduction of the Economic Value of Digital Content

Existing copyright laws in many jurisdictions reduce the economic value of digital content in many ways.

1. In many jurisdictions, existing copyright laws can increase (and do not always reduce) the costs of investigation and enforcement. Existing copyright laws do not provide (e.g., through taxation, permits, licenses, etc.) for the funding of investigation and enforcement of copyright laws. In some jurisdictions, there are no cost-effective special proceedings and/or summary proceedings for adjudication of infringement cases. Copyright laws have not fully incorporated Internet operations, and existing Internet operation standards do not facilitate

---

* This chapter contains excerpts from an article that was written by Michael Nwogugu and is cited as: Nwogugu, M. (2006). Corporate governance and the economics of digital content: Some legal issues. *Computer and Telecommunications Law Review*, 12(1), 5–13.

monitoring, investigation, and enforcement of copyright laws. However, according to Pearce (February 20, 2015), ISPs have developed a draft antipiracy scheme under which notices will be issued to ISP customers who are accused of online piracy.

2. In many countries/jurisdictions, copying of portions of copyrighted work is legal. This is improper and amounts to economic misappropriation because even the small portion copied may have significant use value and emotional value that translates into monetary value, depending on the content.[1] Perhaps one solution is that limits on third party's copying of portions of copyrighted works should depend on the nature of the content that is being copied (see the comments in Handler, 2003).

3. In some jurisdictions and copyright statutes, there is or there can be a wide divergence between copyright laws on one hand, and social norms, modes of socialization and group activities on the other hand. Menard (1998) reviewed the maladaptation of statutes to organizations. Most existing copyright laws are oriented toward *structured environments, organized firms,* identifiable individuals, and time-dependent situations and hence are inadequate (do not suit many hybrid organization forms). It is imperative that the methods of investigation, evidence, enforcement, and regulation embodied in copyright laws be based on traditional, nontraditional, and anticipated modes of online and off-line communication and socialization and be adaptable to unstructured situations and hybrid organizational forms. Bechtold (2003), and Lethin (2003) addressed some of these issues. For example, IOF grew out of online *communities,* and thus, investigations and enforcement should be geared toward identifying infringing groups, punishing groups (within online and off-line contexts), and/or banning groups that make the software. IOF is partly the result of socialization that occurs off-line and is subsequently manifested in online activities.

4. In many jurisdictions, statutes and common law have created divergences in ownership between the actual works (i.e., a sheet of music) and ownership of the performed work (i.e., the taped concert or performance). Under these regimes, it is possible for a creator of work to lose all rights in the work depending on how it is performed/produced. There is no substantial or meaningful economic or legal basis for such divergences in ownership.

5. In many jurisdictions, the monetary and nonmonetary punishments for infringement are not effective and do not provide sufficient deterrence effects.

6. The recent rulings (Australian courts) in copyright disputes may encourage violations of privacy of Internet users by ISPs—where, for example, ISPs monitor e-mails and files sent by Internet users.

7. The evidentiary standards (for copyright infringements) are often not codified. Even with special subpoenas, the cost of the required monitoring and/or discovery can be substantial. Broucek et al. (2005) analyzed evidentiary issue encountered by Australian computer forensic experts. There are almost no internationally accepted laws and litigation standards for copyright and infringement. The concept of *fair use* provides many loopholes for infringement. Klein et al. (2002) analyzed fair use.

8. Similarly, the *staple article of commerce doctrine* from patent law has been rendered meaningless by the advent of illegal file sharing, primarily because of the ease of conversion from noninfringing to infringing uses. Under the *staple article of commerce* doctrine, the maker/distributor of a product is not liable for patent infringement by its customers if the product is suited for any commercial noninfringing use. Arkenbout et al. (2004) analyzed IP strategies.

9. The U.S. Supreme Court held that the maker/distributor of a dual-use (infringing and noninfringing uses) technology may be liable for the infringing activities of third parties where the maker/distributor actively seeks to advance the infringement. This U.S. Supreme Court's holding is actually insufficient and does not provide enough protection because substantial

economic damage can still occur without the maker/distributor's active or passive inducement. Hence, some key issues are the prevention of manufacture of potentially infringing devices and imposition of some duty to prevent infringement and a duty to incorporate filtering/control mechanisms in such technologies.

10. Most copyright laws in most jurisdictions do not provide any specific standards for Internet backbones, web-hosting companies, manufacturers of storage devices and ISPs—these entities control or can control the largest portion of transmission of IP—and downloads of music, software, academic materials, patented data, etc.

11. The applicability of copyright laws in some jurisdictions is somewhat reduced due to the high activity thresholds required in order to prosecute people. Furthermore, in some jurisdictions, the evidentiary standards required for obtaining search warrants and/or for prosecution increase the costs of prosecution.

12. The *substantial noninfringing use* concept (typical in copyright and IP statutes) has been rendered meaningless by the advent of file sharing, because where the device maker has not advertised to, or advised or induced perpetrators, it is difficult to determine and/or establish noninfringing use. P2P systems can be used for perfectly legal purposes, and within these perfectly legal contexts, there can still be illegal file sharing that may not be identifiable by existing technologies. Whether or not a significant number of potential uses of the device are noninfringing has become a moot question, primarily because of the ease of conversion from noninfringing to infringing uses.

14.2 Incentives to Innovate

Another major issue is whether the incentives to innovate provided to entrepreneurs and companies by the U.S. Supreme Court's ruling in *Grokster* and in *Sony* (and similar rulings in terminal courts in other countries) outweigh the need for copyright and patent protection. Garoupa (2003, 2004) studied crime and deterrence. U.S. Department of Justice (October 2004) and U.S. Congress (2004) discussed copyright laws. Such incentives include protection from unauthorized copying and assurance of earning monetary profits from their work, rights to their work, and mechanisms to control ownership transfer and trading of their works. Several key factors are worth noting. In today's world, intellectual property (IP) accounts for more than 30% of the total market values of companies in most developed countries. This proportion will likely continue to increase as the global economy shifts to a knowledge-based economy. During the last 20 years, the pace of innovation in digital rights management systems (DRMSs) has been slower than the rate of growth of the volume (dollar value and physical count) of intellectual capital, despite all the incentives and protection provided by *Sony* (and similar court rulings in various countries). From R&D and product development perspectives, the incremental costs to device makers to include content control and filtering mechanisms in DRM system mechanisms may be significant. However, the benefits of including such control and filtering mechanisms far outweigh any associated incremental costs; such mechanisms can exponentially increase the efficiency of DRM management.

Nowak et al. (2000) and Balasko and Shell (1980) studied moneyless markets and the modeling of behaviors. The existing problems in investigation and prosecution may cause creators/distributors to change their business models. Without the psychological comfort provided by copyright, very few musicians and almost no distributor will engage in dissemination of digital content. Copyright forms the foundation for property rights, specific identification, and transferability, all of which are useful in trading/transferring digital content in all types of markets—even if the musician decided to give away music for free, these elements will still be required. Distinctions have to be made:

- Between zero willingness-to-pay and gifts.
- Between intrinsic value of a unit of digital content and, on the other hand, money paid for value/utility received.
- Between property rights and transfer rights (which are a subset of property rights.

The incentives to produce digital content can be disaggregated into the following components:

- Emotion, devoid of monetary pursuit
- Habit
- Human need for recognition and community
- Human need for property and associated rights
- Human need for money and ability to exchange/trade for goods
- Knowledge that there are some forms of legal protection for materials produced
- Knowledge that there are methods of distribution that provide protection for digital content and recognition for the author.

Hence, contrary to Ku (2002) and similar articles in the literature, it is impractical for authors of digital content to profit while completely eliminating copyright in all instances—only a very small percentage of authors/artists who have certain levels of international name brand recognition and stable audience may be able to earn revenues from alternative sources such as live concerts. Ku's (2002) analysis is an overgeneralization because the trends it discussed, even if true, apply only to a very small percentage of players in the music industry and not to all other industries/sectors that produce/distribute/store digital content. The taxation regimes suggested in Ku (2002) and similar articles are not feasible, do not provide adequate incentives for the production of content (in fact, they discourage creativity), and do not adequately reward authors because the basis of taxation (number of copying devices, number of blank digital audio tapes, etc.) can be manipulated (e.g., reported incorrectly; some items are sold off the books), and the rate of growth of the volume of such items is substantially different from, and lower than, the rate of growth of the volume of illegal and legal online file sharing. Any formula for sharing such tax revenues will probably be debatable and deemed unfair by some people.

Except for the development and introduction of legal Internet file sharing systems, particularly for university students, content distribution business models have not evolved significantly during the last decade. This can be attributed to (1) the actual and perceived protection provided by appellate court decisions (such as the U.S. Supreme Court's decision in *Sony* and similar court rulings in other countries); (2) technological limitations; (3) reluctance to try new business models due to fear of loss of sales; (4) availability of capital for R&D, administrative costs, and marketing; (5) actual and perceived uncertainty associated with possible changes in regulation and the impact of political lobbyists who influence government legislators; (6) limitations imposed by current industry and Internet standards; and (7) lack of creativity.

Furthermore, the nature of the existing contracts between ISPs (Internet access providers) and Internet users does not shift liability to users for their activities. This has been the case in many countries as explained by McKay (2005); Vaccaro and Cohn (2004); and Engel (1999). Some of these contracts expressly place restrictions on transmission of pornographic and copyrighted materials. But the recent rulings by the U.S. Supreme Court and Australian courts effectively create a duty for ISPs (and hence a shift of liability to ISPs) to go beyond mere warnings, disclaimers, and agreements—which is what is required to prevent copyright infringement. Hence many of such agreements have been rendered partially void as a matter of law.

14.3 Increase in Transaction Costs

The existing copyright laws increase transaction costs in the management of digital rights. These costs arise from the following:

1. *Investigating suspicious activity*: (a) The standards of proof required for obtaining search warrants, subpoenas, and evidence are relatively high, and (b) the time delays involved in litigating these cases are relatively substantial, thus increasing costs—many of these copyright laws do not contain any expedited or special procedures that can be used to reduce the time and expense required for investigation.
2. *Enforcement costs*: The cost of prosecution by government officers.

14.4 Deterrence Effect of Copyright Laws

The deterrence effect of these copyright and IP laws have been weak, as exemplified in the United States, where despite prosecution and criminal sanctions and substantial publicity, many people still participate in illegal file sharing.

14.5 Information Leaks

Many of the existing copyright laws do not have any provisions for limiting or expanding the flow of information about investigations into copyright violations, related judicial proceedings, details of specific acts and perpetrators, and the role of various parties involved. This inherent lack of control over the flow of information increases information costs, investigation costs, and prosecution costs, and can reduce the deterrence effect.

Note

1 See *TCN Channel Nine Pty Ltd vs. Network Ten Ltd.*, FCAFC 146, 2002 (Australian Federal Court).

References

Chapter 1

Adermon, A. and Liang, C. (2014). Piracy and music sales: The effects of an anti-piracy law. *Journal of Economic Behavior & Organization*, 105, 90–106.

Anonymous (2011). IP addresses alone cannot be used to identify individuals, US judge says. Available at: http://www.out-law.com/page-11901. Accessed on July 30, 2016.

Arias, J. and Ellis, C. (2013). The decreasing excludability of digital music: Implications for copyrights law. *American Economist*, 58, 124–133.

Barr, K. et al. (2003). Intellectual property crimes. *The American Criminal Law Review*, 40, 789–792.

Bateman, C.R. et al. (2013). Ethical decision making in a peer-to-peer file sharing situation: The role of moral absolutes and social consensus. *Journal of Business Ethics*, 115, 229–240.

BEC Crew (August 28, 2015). Scientists tried to replicate 100 psychology experiments and 64% failed. http://www.sciencealert.com/scientists-tried-to-replicate-100-psychology-experiments-and-64-failed. Accessed on July 30, 2016.

Benkler, Y. (2002). Intellectual property and the organization of information production. *International Review of Law & Economics*, 22, 81–107.

Bohannon, J. (August 28, 2015). Many psychology papers fail replication test. *Science*, 349(6251), 910–911.

Boyle, J. and Jenkins, J. (2014). *Intellectual Property Law and the Information Society: Cases & Materials*, 1st edn. Duke Law School. http://web.law.duke.edu/cspd/pdf/IPCasebook2014.pdf. Accessed on July 30, 2016.

Buettel, R. (2010). Australian voluntary code of conduct for ISPs. In *OECD Workshop—The Role of Internet Intermediaries in Advancing Public Policy Objectives*. http://www.oecd.org/sti/ieconomy/45509366.pdf. Accessed on July 30, 2016.

Carter, A. and Perry, J. (2004). Computer crimes. *The American Criminal Law Review*, 41(2), 313–365.

Chan, R.Y.K. and Lai, J.W.M. (2011). Does ethical ideology affect software piracy attitude and behavior? An empirical investigation of computer users in china. *European Journal of Information Systems*, 20, 659–673.

Clayton, R. (2012). Online traceability: Who did that? (Consumer Focus version), pp. 30, 35. Available at: http://www.consumerfocus.org.uk/publications/online-traceability-who-did-that-technical-expert-report-on-collecting-robust-evidence-of-copyright-infringement-through-peer-to-peer-filesharing. Accessed on July 30, 2016.

Coluccio, G. (2013). Terry and the pirates: A first hand account of the continuing struggle against piracy. *The SAIS Review of International Affairs*, 33, 151–154.

Denegri-Knott, J. and Taylor, J. (2005). The labeling game: A conceptual exploration of deviance on the internet. *Social Science Computer Review*, 23(4), 93–107.

Dimita, G. (2010). Copyright and shared networking technologies. PhD thesis, Queen Mary, University of London, London, U.K.

Dolinski, J. (2012). Legal boundaries between internet piracy and a legal exchange of files through the internet. *Internal Security*, 4(1), 165–180.

EDRI (2012). Finland: Open WiFi owners are not liable for copyright infringement. Available at: http://www.edri.org/edrigram/number10.10/open-wifi-not-liable-copyright-infringement. Accessed on July 30, 2016.

Edwards, L. (2009). Should ISPs be compelled to become copyright cops? Available at: http://www.icyte.com/system/snapshots/fs1/3/b/9/6/3b961a19a7bb43d198b34b194af3f1460ac1fbf1/index.html. Accessed on July 30, 2016.

Eivazi, K. (2012). Is termination of internet users' accounts by an ISP a proportionate response to copyright infringement? *Computer Law & Security Review*, 28(4), 458–467.

European Publishers Council (2011). European commission recognises importance of copyright for content creators in key new proposals. Available at: http://www.epceurope.org/presscentre/archive/european-commission-recognisesimportance-of-copyright-for-content-creators-in-key-new-proposals.shtml. Accessed on July 30, 2016.

Gavaldà-Mirallesa, A. et al. (2014). Impact of heterogeneity and socioeconomic factors on individual behavior in decentralized sharing ecosystems. *Proceedings of the National Academy of Sciences of the USA*, 111(43), 15322–15327.

Geiger, C. (2007). The New French Law on copyright and neighbouring rights of 1 August 2006—An adaptation to the needs of the information society? *IIC*, 38(4), 401–428.

Geiger, C. (2011). Honourable attempt but (ultimately) disproportionately offensive against peer-to-peer on the internet (HADOPI)—A critical analysis of the recent anti-file-sharing legislation in France. *IIC*, 42(4), 457–472.

Guibault, L. et al. (2007). Study on the implementation and effect in member states' Laws of Directive 2001/29/EC on the harmonisation of certain aspects of copyright and related rights in the information society. Report to the European Commission, DG Internal Market.

Hinduja, S. (2012). General strain, self-control, and music piracy. *International Journal of Cyber Criminology*, 6, 951–967.

Interdonato, R. and Tagarelli, A. (2015). Ranking silent nodes in information networks: A quantitative approach and applications. *Physics Procedia*, 62, 36–41.

Ioannidis, J.P.A. (2005). Why most published research findings are false. *PLoS Medicine*, 2(8), e124.

Just, M. (July 4, 2003). Internet file sharing and the liability of intermediaries for copyright infringement: A need for international concensus. *Journal of Information Technology Law*, 1.

Kennedy, G. and Doyle, S. (2007). A snapshot of legal developments and industry issues relevant to information technology, media and telecommunications in key jurisdictions across the Asia Pacific—Co-ordinated by Lovells and contributed to by other leading law firms in the region. *Computer Law & Security Review*, 23(2), 148–155.

Kigerl, A.C. (2013). Infringing nations: Predicting software piracy rates, bit-torrent tracker hosting, and p2p file sharing client downloads between countries. *International Journal of Cyber Criminology*, 7(1), 62.

Lefranc, D. (2010). The metamorphosis of contrefaçon in French copyright law. In Bently, L., Davis, J., and Ginsburg, J.C., eds. *Copyright and Piracy—An Interdisciplinary Critique*. Cambridge Intellectual Property and Information Law (No. 13).

Lovejoy, N. (January 2011). Procedural concerns with the HADOPI graduated response model. *JOLT Digest*. Available at: http://jolt.law.harvard.edu/digest/copyright/procedural-concerns-with-the-hadopi-graduated-response-model. Accessed on July 30, 2016.

Man, W. et al. (2013). Combatting peer-to-peer file sharing of copyrighted material via anti-piracy laws: Issues, trends, and solutions. *Computer Law & Security Review*, 29(4), 382–402.

Manta, I. (2011).The puzzle of criminal sanctions for intellectual property infringement. *Harvard Journal of Law & Technology*, 24(2), 469–518.

Meyer, T. and Van Audenhove, L. (2010). Graduated response and the emergence of a European surveillance society. *Info—The Journal of Policy, Regulation and Strategy for Telecommunications*, 12(6), 69–79.

Miles, E. (2004). *In Re Aimster*; and *MGM Inc. v. Grokster Ltd.*: Peer-to-peer and the Sony doctrine. *Berkeley Technology Law Journal*, 19(1), 21–57.

Mlcakova, A. and Whitley, E. (2004). Configuring peer-to-peer software: An empirical study of how users react to the regulatory features of software. *European Journal of Information Systems*, 13(2), 95–102.

Moiny, J.F. (2011). Are Internet protocol addresses personal data? The fight against online copyright infringement. *Computer Law & Security Review*, 27(4), 348–361.

Oguer, F. (2011). The Hadopi act vs. the global license as a psychological game. *Review of European Studies*, 3(1), 79–84.

Open Science Collaboration (August 28, 2015). Estimating the reproducibility of psychological science. *Science*, 349(6251), 943–945.

Pearce, R. (February 20, 2015). ISPs unveil draft anti-piracy scheme—Draft code will see notices issued to ISP customers accused of online piracy. *Computerworld*. Available at: http://www.computerworld.com.au/article/568620/isps-unveil-proposed-notice-scheme-copyright-infringement/. Accessed on July 30, 2016.

Rayna, T. and Barbier, L. (2010). Fighting consumer piracy with graduated response: An evaluation of the French and British implementations. *International Journal of Foresight and Innovation Policy*, 6(4), 294–314.

RIAA (2015). Scope of the problem. Available at: https://www.riaa.com/physicalpiracy.php?content_selector=piracy-online-scope-of-the-problem. Accessed on July 30, 2016.

Risen, T. (September 18, 2013). Online piracy grows, reflecting consumer trends-netflix, Amazon downloads did not slow online piracy, study found. Available at: http://www.usnews.com/news/articles/2013/09/18/online-piracy-grows-reflecting-consumer-trends. Accessed on July 30, 2016.

Sang, Y. et al. (2015). Understanding the intentions behind illegal downloading: A comparative study of American and Korean college students. *Telematics and Informatics*, 32(2), 333–343.

Scholes, W. (January 14, 2014). Piracy's ripple effect on the global economy. Available at: http://www.diplomaticourier.com/piracy-s-ripple-effect-on-the-global-economy/. Accessed on July 30, 2016.

Sinha, R. and Mandel, N. (2008). Preventing digital music piracy: The carrot or the stick? *Journal of Marketing*, 72, 1–15.

Stalla-Bourdillon, S. et al. (2014). From porn to cybersecurity passing by copyright: How mass surveillance technologies are gaining legitimacy—The case of deep packet inspection technologies. *Computer Law & Security Review*, 30(6), 670–686.

Strahilevitz, L. (2003). Charismatic code, social norms, and the emergence of cooperation on the file-swapping networks. *Virginia Law Review*, 89(3), 505–595.

Strowel, A. (2010). The 'Graduated Response' in France: Is it the good reply to online copyright infringements? In Stamatoudi, I.A., ed. *Copyright Enforcement and the Internet*. Kluwer Law International, Alphen aan den Rijn, the Netherlands.

Suzor, N. (2014). Free-riding, cooperation, and 'peaceful revolutions' in copyright. *Harvard Journal of Law & Technology*.

Synodinou, T. (2015). Intermediaries' liability for online copyright infringement in the EU: Evolutions and confusions. *Computer Law & Security Review*, 31(1), 57–67.

Tamberlin, J. (July 14, 2005). *Universal Music Australia Pty vs. Cooper, FCA 972*. http://austlii.edu.au/cases/cth/federal_ct/2005/972.html. Accessed on July 30, 2016.

TERA (Paris) (2010). Building a digital economy: The importance of saving jobs in the EU's creative industries. TERA Consultants, Paris, France.

Wade, J. (2004). The music industry's war on piracy. *Risk Management*, 51(2), 10–15.

Werkers, E. (2011). Intermediaries in the eye of the copyright storm—A comparative analysis of the three strike approach within the European Union. ICRI Working Paper No. 4/2011. Available at SSRN: http://ssrn.com/abstract=1920271 or http://dx.doi.org/10.2139/ssrn.1920271. Accessed on July 30, 2016.

Wilcox, J. (September 5, 2005). *Universal Music Australia Pty Ltd v. Sharman License Holdings Ltd, FCA 1241*. http://www.austlii.edu.au/cases/cth/federal_ct/2005/1242.html. Accessed on July 30, 2016.

Wohlers, A.E. (2012). Digital piracy: An integrated theoretical approach. *Choice*, 49(10), 19–66.

Wu, T. et al. (2014). Incentive mechanism for P2P file sharing based on social network and game theory. *Journal of Network and Computer Applications*, 41, 47–55.

Wu, W. and Yang, H. (2013). A comparative study of college students' ethical perception concerning internet piracy. *Quality and Quantity*, 47, 111–120.

Yoon, C. (2011). Theory of planned behavior and ethics theory in digital piracy: An integrated model. *Journal of Business Ethics*, 100, 405–417.

Yoon, K. (2002). The optimal level of copyright protection. *Information Economics and Policy*, 14, 327–348.

Yu, S. (2014). Fear of cyber crime among college students in the United States: An exploratory study. *International Journal of Cyber Criminology*, 8(1), 36–46.

Chapter 2

Aaltonen, M. and Salmi, V. (2013). Versatile delinquents or specialized pirates? A comparison of correlates of illegal downloading and traditional juvenile crime. *Journal of Scandinavian Studies in Criminology and Crime Prevention*, 14(2), 188–193.

Amiroso, D. and Case, T. (2007). Music sharing in Russia: Understanding behavioral intention and use of music downloading. In *Proceedings of AMCIS 2007*.

Aoki, M. and Yoshikawa, H. (2009). The nature of equilibrium in macroeconomics: A critique of equilibrium search theory. *Economics: The Open-Access, Open-Assessment E-Journal*, 3, 2009–2037.

Argan, M. et al. (2013). A study of motivational factors associated with peer-to-peer (P2P) file-sharing. *Procedia—Social and Behavioral Sciences*, 99(6), 180–188.

Ariely, D. and Silva, J. (August 2002). Payment methods design: Psychological and economic aspects of payments. Paper #196. Center for e-Business, MIT, Cambridge, MA.

Asvanund, A. et al. (2004). An empirical analysis of network externalities in peer-to-peer music-sharing networks. *Information Systems Research*, 15(2), 155–174.

Atsushi, I. (2002). Production function and efficiency analysis for public library services. *Annals of Japan Society of Library Science*, 48(2), 49–72.

Baier, S. et al. (2002). How important are capital and total factor productivity for economics growth? Working Paper #2002-2a, Federal Reserve Bank of Atlanta, Atlanta, GA.

Bajari, P. and Hortacsu, A. (2004). Economic insights from internet auctions. *Journal of Economic Literature*, 42(2), 457–486.

Baker, B. (1998). *An Inductive Approach to Production-Function Modeling: A Comparison of Group Method of Data Handling (GMDH) and Other Neural Network Methods*. Annual Meeting of the American Education Finance Association, Mobile, March 13. AL.

Balasko, Y. and Shell, K. (1980). The overlapping generations model, I: The case of pure exchange without money. *Journal of Economic Theory*, 23, 281–306.

Battese, G. and Coelli, T. (1988). Prediction of firm level technical efficiencies with a generalized frontier production function and panel data. *Journal of Econometrics*, 38(3), 387–399.

Battese, G. and Coelli, T. (1995). A model for technical inefficiency effects in a stochastic frontier production function for panel data. *Empirical Economics*, 20(2), 325–332.

Beck, M. et al. (2010). Measuring search efficiency in complex visual search tasks: Global and local clutter. *Journal of Experimental Psychology: Applied*, 16(3), 238–250.

Beckenback, F. (2000). Multiagent modeling of resource systems and markets. *Advances in Complex Systems*, 3, 231–243.

Becker, G. (1973). A theory of marriage, Part I. *Journal of Political Economy*, 81, 813–846.

Becker, J. and Clement, M. (2006). Dynamics of illegal participation in peer-to-peer networks—Why do people illegally share media files? *Journal of Media Economics*, 19(1), 7–32.

Bernard, L. (1926a). Primary and derivative groups, Chapter 26. In *An Introduction to Social Psychology*. Henry Holt & Co., New York, pp. 411–425. http://www.brocku.ca/MeadProject/Bernard/1926/1926_26.html. Accessed on July 30, 2016.

Bernard, L. (1926b). Primary and derivative attitudes and ideals, Chapter 27. In *An Introduction to Social Psychology*. Henry Holt & Co., New York, pp. 425–437. Available at: https://www.brocku.ca/MeadProject/Bernard/1926/1926_27.html. Accessed on July 30, 2016.

Bernard, L. (1936). The conflict between primary group attitudes and derivative group ideals in modern society. *American Journal of Sociology*, 41(5), 611–623.

Bhattacharjee, S. et al. (2002). Digital music and online sharing: Software piracy 2.0? *Communications of the ACM*, 46(7), 107–111.

Bhattacharjee, S. et al. (2006). Impact of legal threats on online music sharing activity: An analysis of music industry legal actions. *Journal of Law and Economics*, XLIX(1), 91–114.

Bolton, L.E. et al. (2003). Consumer perceptions of price (un)fairness. *Journal of Consumer Research*, 29(4), 474–492.

Bolton, R. N. et al. (2004). The theoretical underpinnings of customer asset management: A framework and propositions for future research. *Journal of the Academic of Marketing Science*, 32(3), 1–20.

Borja, K. et al. (2015). The effect of music streaming services on music piracy among college students. *Computers in Human Behavior*, 45, 69–76.

Branco, F. et al. (2012). Optimal search for product information. *Management Science*, 58(11), 2037–2056.

Branco, F. et al. (2015). Too much information? information provision and search costs. *Marketing Science*.

Brockett, P. et al. (2005). Financial intermediary versus production approach to efficiency of marketing distribution systems and organizational structure of insurance companies. *Journal of Risk and Insurance*, 72(3), 393–412.

Bromiley, P. et al. (1989). On using event study methodology in strategic management research. In Burton, R.M., Forsyth, J., and Obel, B., eds. *Organizational Responses to the New Business Conditions: An Empirical Perspective*. Amsterdam: Elsevier Science, pp. 25–40.

Burdett, K. and Mortensen, D. (1998). Equilibrium wage differentials and employer size. *International Economic Review*, 39(2), 257–274.

Butterfield, K. D. et al. (2000). Moral awareness in business organizations: Influences of issue-related and social context factors. *Human Relations*, 53, 981–1018.

Chen, F. (2005). Monotonic matching in search equilibrium. *Journal of Mathematical Economics*, 41(6), 705–721.

Chi, W. (2008). Does file sharing crowd out copyrighted goods? Evidence from the music recording industry. Working Paper, Department of Economics, Johns Hopkins University, Baltimore, MD. Available at: http://www.econ.sinica.edu.tw/upload/file/0224-3.pdf. Accessed on July 30, 2016.

Cho, H., Chung, S., and Filippova, A. (2015). Perceptions of social norms surrounding digital piracy: The effect of social projection and communication exposure on injunctive and descriptive social norms. *Computers in Human Behavior*, 48, 506–515.

Ciccarelli, G. and Lo Cigno, R. (2011). Collusion in peer-to-peer systems. *Computer Networks*, 55(15), 3517–3532.

Clement, M. et al. (February 2010). Consumer responses to a legal alternative to filesharing. Working Paper.

Cooper, D.C. et al. (2003). Compatibility of land SAR procedures with search theory. Working Paper. Available at: http://www.uscg.mil/hq/cg5/cg534/nsarc/LandSearchMethodsReview.pdf. Accessed on July 30, 2016.

Cooper, M. (January 2006). The economics of collaborative production: A framework for analyzing the emerging mode of digital production. Working Paper, Center for Internet and Society, Stanford University, Stanford, CA. Prepared for presentation at *The Economics of Open Content: A Commercial-Noncommercial Forum*, January 23–24, 2006, Massachusetts Institute of Technology, Cambridge, MA.

Cox, J. and Collins, A. (2014). Sailing in the same ship? Differences in factors motivating piracy of music and movie content. *Journal of Behavioral and Experimental Economics*, 50, 70–76.

Cox, J. et al. (2010). Seeders, leechers and social norms: Evidence from the market for illicit digital downloading. *Information Economics and Policy*, 22(4), 299–305.

Coyle, J.R. et al. (2009). "To buy or to pirate": The matrix of music consumers' acquisition-mode decision-making. *Journal of Business Research*, 62(10), 1031–1037.

Curien, N. and Moreau, F. (2009). The music industry in the digital era: Toward new contracts. *Journal of Media Economics*, 22(2), 102–113.

D'Astous, A. et al. (2005). Music piracy on the web—How effective are anti-piracy arguments? Evidence from the theory of planned behavior. *Journal of Consumer Policy*, 28(3), 289–310.

Deck, C. and Schlesinger, H. (2014). Consistency of higher order risk preferences. *Econometrica*, 82(5), 1913–1943.

Dellnitz, M. and Junge, O. (1999). On the approximation of complicated dynamical behavior. *SIAM Journal on Numerical Analysis*, 36(2), 491–515.

Diamond, P. (1971). A model of price adjustment. *Journal of Economic Theory*, 3(2), 156–168.

Diamond, P. (1982a). *A Search Equilibrium Approach to the Micro Foundations of Macroeconomics*, Wicksell Lectures. MIT Press, Cambridge, MA, 1984.

Diamond, P. (1982b). Aggregate demand management in search equilibrium. *Journal of Political Economy*, 90(5), 881–894.

Diamond, P. (1982c). Wage determination and efficiency in search equilibrium. *Review of Economic Studies*, XLIX, 217–227.

Diamond, P. (1984). Money in search equilibrium. *Econometrica*, 52(1), 1–20.

Diamond, P. (1987a). Consumer differences and prices in a search model. *Quarterly Journal of Economics*, 102(2), 429–436.

Diamond, P. (1987b). Credit in search equilibrium. In *Symposium on Monetary Theory*, Institute of Economics, Academia Sinica, revised version in Kohn, M. and Tsiang, S.-C., eds. *Finance Constraints, Expectations, and Macroeconomics*. Oxford University Press, Oxford, U.K., 1988, pp. 95–119.

Diamond, P. (1993). Search, sticky prices and inflation. *Review of Economic Studies*, 60, 53–68.

Diamond, P. et al. (1964). Stationary utility and time perspective. *Econometrica*, 32(1/2), 82–100.

Diamond, P. and Maskin, E. (1981). An equilibrium analysis of search and breach of contract II: A non-steady state example. *Journal of Economic Theory*, 25(2), 165–195.

Diamond, P. and Yellin, J. (1987). Pricing and the distribution of money holdings in a search economy, II. In Barnett, W. and Singleton, K., eds. *New Approaches to Monetary Economics*. Cambridge University Press, Cambridge, pp. 311–324.

Diehl, K. et al. (2003). Smart Agents: When lower search costs for quality information increase price sensitivity. *Journal of Consumer Research*, 30, 56–60.

Ernst, E. and Semmler, W. (2010). Global dynamics in a model with search and matching in labor and capital markets. *Journal of Economic Dynamics and Control*, 34(9), 1651–1679.

Faulk, G.K. et al. (2005). The effects of changing technology and government policy on the commercialization of music. *Journal of Nonprofit & Public Sector Marketing*, 13(1), 75–90.

Felipe, J. et al. (2008). Correcting for biases when estimating production functions: An illusion of the laws of algebra? *Cambridge Journal of Economics*, 32(3), 441–459.

Fioretti, G. (2007). The production function. *Physica A: Statistical Mechanics and Its Applications*, 374(2), 707–714.

Freeman, E. (2005). Corporate liability for illegal downloading of copyrighted music. *EDPACS: The EDP Audit, Control, and Security Newsletter*, 32(9), 13–20.

Gandolfo, G. (2008). Comment on "C.E.S. production functions in the light of the Cambridge critique". *Journal of Macroeconomics*, 30(2), 798–800.

Garcia-Perez, J. (2002). Equilibrium search models: The role of the assumptions. *Investigaciones Economicas*, 26(2), 255–284.

Golle, P. et al. (2001). Incentives for sharing in peer-to-peer networks. In Goos, G., Hartmanis, J. and Van Leeuwen, J., eds. *Electronic Commerce*, Lecture Notes in Computer Science, Springer, Germany Vol. 2232, pp. 75–87.

Gopal, R. et al. (2002). A behavioral model of digital music piracy. *Journal of Organizational Computing and Electronic Commerce*, 14(2), 89–105.

Gopal, R. et al. (2004). A behavioral model of digital music piracy. *Journal of Organizational Computing and Electronic Commerce*, 14(2), 89–105.

Growiec, J. (2008). Production functions and distributions of unit factor productivities: Uncovering the link. *Economics Letters*, 101(1), 87–90.

Gurbaxani, V. et al. (2000). The production of information services: a firm-level analysis of information systems budgets. *Information Systems Research*, 11(2), 159–176.

Hall, R.E. (2005). Employment fluctuations with equilibrium wage stickiness. *The American Economic Review*, 95(1), 50–65.

Hanoch, G. and Rothschild, M. (1972). Testing the assumptions of production theory: A non-parametric approach. *Journal of Political Economy*, 80(2), 256–275.

Harrison, J. et al. (February 2005). Event studies and the importance of longer-term measures in assessing the performance outcomes of complex events. Working Paper.

Higgins, G.E. et al. (2006). Digital piracy: Assessing the contributions of an integrated self-control theory and social learning theory using structural equation modeling. *Criminal Justice Studies: A Critical Journal of Crime, Law and Society*, 19(1), 3–22.

Higgins, G.E. et al. (2008). Digital piracy: An examination of three measurements of self-control. *Deviant Behavior*, 29(5), 440–460.

Hinduja, S. (2006). A critical examination of the digital music phenomenon. *Critical Criminology*, 14, 387–409.

Hinduja, S. (2012). General strain, self-control, and music piracy. *International Journal of Cyber Criminology*, 6, 951–967.

Holt, T.J. and Copes, H. (2010). Transferring sub-cultural knowledge on-line: Practices and beliefs of persistent digital pirates. *Deviant Behavior*, 31(7), 625–654.

Hosmer, D. et al. (1991). The importance of assessing the fit of logistic regression models. *American Journal of Public Health*, 81(12), 1630–1635.

Hughes, D. et al. (2006). Peer-to-peer: Is deviant behavior the norm on P2P filesharing networks? *IEEE Distributed Systems Online*, 7(2), 1–3.

Hulleman, J. (2010). Inhibitory tagging in visual search: Only in difficult search are items tagged individually. *Vision Research*, 50(20), 2069–2079.

Inman, J.J. and Zeelenberg, M. (2002). Regret in repeat purchase versus switching decisions: The attenuating role of decision justifiability. *Journal of Consumer Research*, 29(1), 116–128.

Ireland, N.J. (1994). On limiting the market for status signals. *Journal of public Economics*, 53(1), 91–110.

Iwamura, T. and Takefuji, Y. (2000). An artificial market based on agents with fluid attitude toward risks and returns. *Advances in Complex Systems*, 3, 385-397. http://dx.doi.org/10.1142/S0219525900000273. Accessed on July 30, 2016.

Jacobs, R. et al. (2012). Digital movie piracy: A perspective on downloading behavior through social cognitive theory. *Computers in Human Behavior*, 28(3), 958–967.

Jaisingh, J. (2007). Piracy on file-sharing networks: Strategies for recording companies. *Journal of Organizational Computing and Electronic Commerce*, 17(4), 329–348.

Jambon, M. and Smetana, J. (2012). College students' moral evaluations of illegal music downloading. *Journal of Applied Developmental Psychology*, 33(1), 31–39.

Janssen, M.A. and Jager, W. (2000). The human actor in ecological-economic models: Preface. *Ecological Economics*, 35(3), 307–310.

Jenny, A. et al. (2006). Psychological factors determining individual compliance with rules for common pool resource management: The case of a Cuban community sharing a solar energy system. *Human Ecology*, 35, 239–250.

Johnson, M. et al. (2009). Laissez-Faire file sharing: Access control designed for individuals at the endpoints. In *NSPW 2009*, Oxford, U.K., September 2009.

Jones, R. (2005). Entertaining code: Filesharing, digital rights management regimes, and criminological theories of compliance. *International Review of Law, Computers & Technology*, 19(3), 287–303.

Ke, T.T. et al. (2016). Search for information on multiple products. *Management Science*.

Khalil, O. and Wang, S. (2002). Information technology enabled meta-management for virtual organizations. *International Journal of Production Economics*, 75(1–2), 127–134.

Kigerl, A.C. (2013). Infringing nations: Predicting software piracy rates, bit-torrent tracker hosting, and p2p file sharing client downloads between countries. *International Journal of Cyber Criminology*, 7(1), 62.

Klampanos, I. and Jose, J. (2012). Searching in peer-to-peer networks. *Computer Science Review*, 6(4), 161–183.

Kleinsteuber, H. (2005). The internet between regulation and governance. Working Paper. Available at: http://www.osce.org/fom/13844?download=true. Accessed on July 30, 2016.

Koopman, B.O. (1946). Search and screening (OEG report no. 56, The Summary Reports Group of the Columbia University Division of War Research). Center for Naval Analyses, Alexandria, VA.

Koopman, B.O. (1980). *Search and Screening: General Principles with Historical Applications*. Pergamon Press, New York.

Krajbich, I. et al. (2010). Visual fixations and the computation and comparison of value in simple choice. *Nature neuroscience*, 13(10), 1292–1298.

Krajbich, I. and Rangel, A. (2011). Multialternative drift-diffusion model predicts the relationship between visual fixations and choice in value-based decisions. *Proceedings of the National Academy of Sciences*, 108(33), 13852–13857.

Kultti, K. (2000). A model of random matching and price formation. *European Economic Review*, 44(10), 1841–1856.

Lebowitz, S. (2006). Filesharing: Creative destruction or just plain destruction? *Journal of Law and Economics*, XLIX(1), 1–20.

Lee, F.S. and Keen, S. (2004). The incoherent emperor: a heterodox critique of neoclassical microeconomic theory. *Review of Social Economy*, 62(2), 169–199.

Lence, S.H. and Miller, D. (1998). Estimation of multi-output production functions with incomplete data: A generalised maximum entropy approach. *European Review of Agricultural Economics*, 25, 188–209.

Lester, B. (2010). Directed search with multi-vacancy firms. *Journal of Economic Theory*, 145(6), 2108–2132.

Lindenberger, D. (2003). Service production functions. *Journal of Economics*, 80(2), 127–142.

Liu, L. and Dukes, A. (2013). Consideration set formation with multiproduct firms: The case of within-firm and across-firm evaluation costs. *Management Science*, 59(8), 1871–1886.

Lubatkin, M. and Shrieves, R. (1986). Towards reconciliation of market performance measures to strategic management research. *Academy of Management Review*, 11, 497–512.

Lucas, R.E. and Prescott, E. C.(1974). Equilibrium search and unemployment. *Journal of Economic Theory*, 7, 188–209.

Lurie, N.H. 2004. Decision making in information-rich environments: The role of information structure. *Journal of Consumer Research*, 30(4), 473–486.

MacKinley, A. (1997). Event studies in economics and finance. *Journal of Economic Literature*, 35(1), 13–39.

McCombie, J. and Dixon, R. (1991). Estimating technical change in aggregate production functions: A critique. *International Review of Applied Economics*, 5(1), 24–46.

McWilliams, A. and Siegel, D. (1999). Issues in the use of the event study methodology: A critical analysis of corporate social responsibility studies. *Organizational Research Methods*, 2, 340–365.

Menzio, G. and Shi, S. (2010). Block recursive equilibria for stochastic models of search on the job. *Journal of Economic Theory*, 145(4), 1453–1494.

Merlone, U. (2002). Incentives and computing systems for team based organizations: A mathematical and economic analysis. *Organization Science*, 13(6), 734–736.

Merz, M. (1995). Search in the labor market and the real business cycle. *Journal of Monetary Economics*, 36(2), 269–300.

Miklashevich, I. (2003). Mathematical representation of social systems: Uncertainty and optimization of social system evolution. *Nonlinear Phenomena in Complex Systems*, 6(2), 678–686.

Miller, R. (2001). Firms' cost functions: A reconstruction. *Review of Industrial Organization*, 18, 183–200.

Moore, R. and McMullan, E. (2004). Perceptions of peer-to-peer file sharing among university students. *Journal of Criminal Justice and Popular Culture*, 11(1), 1–9.

Morris, R.G. et al. (2009). The role of gender in predicting the willingness to engage in digital piracy among college students. *Criminal Justice Studies: A Critical Journal of Crime, Law and Society*, 22(4), 393–404.

Mortensen, D. (1982). The matching process as a non-cooperative/bargaining game. In McCall, J., ed. *The Economics of Information and Uncertainty*. NBER. ISBN: 0226555593.

Mortensen, D. and Pissarides, C. (1994). Job creation and job destruction in the theory of unemployment. *Review of Economic Studies*, 61, 397–415.

Mortensen, D. and Pissarides, C. (1999). New developments in models of search in the labor market. CEPR Discussion Paper No. 2053. Also Published in Ashenfelter, O. and Card, D., *Handbook of Labor Economics*, Vol. 3. Elsevier Science, Amsterdam, the Netherlands, pp. 2567–2627.

Mortensen, D. and Wright, R. (2002). Competitive pricing and efficiency in search equilibrium. *International Economic Review*, 43(1), 1–20.

Mosca, S. and Viscolani, B. (2004). Optimal goodwill path to introduce a new product. *Journal of Optimization Theory and Applications*, 123(1), 149–162.

Moscarini, G. and Smith, L. (2001). The optimal level of experimentation. *Econometrica*, 69(6), 1629–1644.

Moss, M., Wellman, A., and Cotsonis, G. (2003). An appraisal of multivariable logistic models in the pulmonary and critical care literature. *Chest*, 123(3), 923–928.

Nami, M. et al. (2007). A preliminary formal specification of virtual organization creation with RAISE specification language. In *Fifth ACIS International Conference on Software Engineering Research, Management & Applications (SERA 2007)*, Busan, Korea, pp. 227–232.

Neill, J. (2003). Production and production functions: Some implications of a refinement to process analysis. *Journal of Economic Behavior & Organization*, 51(4), 507–521.

Netanel, N. (2003). Impose a commercial use levy to allow free peer-to-peer file sharing. *Harvard Journal of Law & Technology*, 17, 1–20.

Noussair, C.N. et al. (2013). Higher order risk attitudes, demographics and saving. *Review of Economic Studies*, 81(1), 325–355.

Nwogugu, M. (2006/2013). Economic psychology issues inherent in illegal online filesharing by individuals and institutions; and illegal online filesharing as production systems. Working Paper. Available at: www.ssrn.com. Accessed on July 30, 2016.

Nwogugu, M. (2009). Illegal online filesharing: Information producers' strategies. *International Journal of Mathematics, Game Theory and Algebra*, 17(5/6), 329–342.

Ozmutlu, S. et al. (2003a). *Multitasking Web searching: implications for design.* In ASIST-03: Annual Meeting of the American Society for Information Science and Technology, October 18–22, 40(1), 416–421. Long Beach, CA.

Ozmutlu, S. et al. (2003b). Multimedia web searching trends: 1997–2001. *Information Processing & Management*, 39(4), 611–621.

Pavlov, O. and Saeed, K. (2004). A resource-based analysis of peer-to-peer technology. *System Dynamics Review*, 20(3), 237–262.

Pessach, G. (2008). [Networked] Memory Institutions: Social Remembering, Privatization And its Discontents. *Cardozo Arts & Entertainment Law Journal*, 26, 71–80.

Peters, M. (1992). On the efficiency of ex-ante and ex-post pricing institutions. *Economic Theory*, 2, 85–101.

Pickard, L., Kitchenham, B., and Jones, P. (1999). Comments on: Evaluating alternative software production functions. *Transactions on Software Engineering*, 25(2), 282–285.

Pissarides, C. (1979). Job matchings with state employment agencies and random search. *Economic Journal*, 89, 818–833.

Pissarides, C.A. (1985). Short-run equilibrium dynamics of unemployment, vacancies, and real wages. *American Economic Review*, 75(4), 676–690.

Pissarides, C.A. (2000). *Equilibrium unemployment theory*, 2nd edn. MIT Press, Cambridge, MA.

Podoshen, J. (2008). Why take tunes? An exploratory multinational look at student downloading. *Journal of Internet Commerce*, 7(2), 180–202.

Postmes, T. and Brunsting S. (2002) Collective action in the age of the Internet: mass communication and online mobilization. *Social Science Computer Review*, 20(3), 290–301.

Quiring, O. et al. (2008). Decentralized electronic markets: Exploring the effects of revenue splitting inside file sharing systems. *Electronic Markets*, 18(2), 175–186.

Ratchford, B.T. et al. (2003). On the Efficiency of Internet markets for consumer goods. *Journal of Public Policy & Marketing*, 22(1), 4–16.

Reagan, J. (1998). Building a set of standards for use of regression. *Journal of Broadcasting & Electronic Media*, 42, 535–539.

Richmond, A. et al. (2007). Valuing ecosystem services: A shadow price for net primary production. *Ecological Economics*, 64(2), 454–462.

Rob, R. and Waldfogel, J. (2006). Piracy on the high C's: Music downloading, sales displacement and social welfare in a sample of college students. *Journal of Law and Economics*, XLIX(1), 29–62.

Roberts, K. and Weitzman, M. (1981). Funding criteria for research, development, and exploration projects. *Econometrica*, 49(5), 1261–1288.

Roberts, R. et al. (2005). Request based virtual organizations (RBVO): An implementation scenario. http://epubs.cclrc.ac.uk/bitstream/695/PROVE-05-Roberts-Svirskas-Matthews-v21.pdf. Accessed on July 30, 2016.

Rothschild, M. (1974). Searching for the lowest price when the distribution of prices is unknown. *The Journal of Political Economy*, 82(4), 689–711.

Sandulli, F.D. and Martín-Barbero, S. (2008). 99 Cents per song: A fair price for digital music? The effects of music industry strategies to raise the willingness to pay by P2P users. *Journal of Website Promotion*, 2(3), 3–15.

Sang, Y. et al. (2015). Understanding the intentions behind illegal downloading: A comparative study of American and Korean college students. *Telematics and Informatics*, 32(2), 333–343.

Santin, D. (2008). On the approximation of production functions: A comparison of artificial neural networks frontiers and efficiency techniques. *Applied Economics Letters*, 15(8), 597–600.

Schwab, R.M. and Zampelli, E.M. (1987). Disentangling the demand function from the production function for local public services: The case of public safety. *Journal of Public Economics*, 33(2), 245–260.

Shaikh, A. (2005). Nonlinear dynamics and pseudo-production functions. *Eastern Economic Journal*, 31(3), 417–422.

Shimer, R. (2005). The cyclical behavior of equilibrium unemployment and vacancies. *American Economic Review*, 95(1), 25–49.

Shimer, R. and Smith, L. (2000). Assortative matching and search. *Econometrica*, 68, 343–369.

Sigismondi, P. (2009). Hollywood piracy in China: An accidental case of US public diplomacy in the globalization age? *Chinese Journal of Communication*, 2(3), 273–287.

Sonntag, A. (2015). Search costs and adaptive consumers: Short time delays do not affect choice quality. *Journal of Economic Behavior & Organization*, 113, 64–79.

Steinmetz, K. and Tunnell, K. (2013). Under the pixelated jolly roger: A study of on-line pirates. *Deviant Behavior*, 34(1), 53–67.

Stone, L.D. (1989). *Theory of Optimal Search*, 2nd edn. ORSA Books, Arlington, VA.

Stone, L.D. (1992). Search for the SS central America: Mathematical treasure hunting. *Interfaces*, 22, 32–54.

Sumita, U. and Zuo, J. (2010). The impact of mobile access to the internet on information search completion time and customer conversion. *Electronic Commerce Research and Applications*, 9(5), 410–417.

Svensson, M. and Larsson, S. (2009). Social norms and intellectual property: Online norms and the European legal development. Working Paper, Lund University, Lund, Sweden.

Trafimow, D. (2003). Hypothesis testing and theory evaluation at the boundaries: Surprising insights from Baye's theorem. *Psychological Review*, 110, 526–530.

Tsiros, M. and Mittal, V. (2000). Regret: A model of its antecedents and consequences in consumer decision making. *Journal of Consumer Research*, 26(4), 401–417.

Tu, Y. et al. (2005). Problems of correlations between explanatory variables in multiple regression analysis in the dental literature. *British Dentistry Journal*, 199(7), 457–461.

U.S. Federal Trade Commission (June 2005). Peer-to-peer filesharing technology: Consumer protection and competition issues. Staff report of the U.S. Federal Trade Commission.

Ulieru, M. (2002). A fuzzy mathematics approach to modelling holonic structures. http://www.cs.unb.ca/~ulieru/Publications/PubWeb/Romania-paper-Last.doc. Accessed on July 30, 2016.

Vaccaro, V. and Cohn, D. (2004). The evolution of business models and marketing strategies in the music industry. *International Journal on Media Management*, 6(1/2), 46–58.

Van den Berg, G.J. and van Vuuren, A. (2002), Using firm data to assess the performance of equilibrium search models of the labor market. *Annals of Economics and Statistics*, 67/68, 227–256.

Virag, G. (2011). High profit equilibria in directed search models. *Games and Economic Behavior*, 71(1), 224–234.

Von Lohmann, F. (2004). Voluntary collective licensing for music file sharing. *Communications of the ACM*, 47(10), 21–24.

Wagner, H. and Weitzel, T. (2007). Towards an IT production function: Understanding routines as fundamental for IT value creation. *Journal of Enterprise Information Management*, 20(4), 380–395.

Wall, R. (1998). An empirical investigation of the production function of the family firm. *Journal of Small Business Management*, 36(2), 24–32.

Wang, X. and McClung, S. (2012). The immorality of illegal downloading: The role of anticipated guilt and general emotions. *Computers in Human Behavior*, 28(1), 153–159.

Watanabe, M. (2008). Inflation, price competition, and consumer search technology. *Journal of Economic Dynamics and Control*, 32(12), 3780–3806.

Weber, E.U. et al. 2004. Predicting risk sensitivity in humans and lower animals: risk as variance or coefficient of variation. *Psychological review*, 111, 430–445.

Weitzman, M. (1979). Optimal search for the best alternative. *Econometrica*, 47(3), 641–654.

Wilson, M. and Schraefel, M.C. (2010). Evaluating collaborative information-seeking interfaces with a search-oriented inspection method and re-framed information seeking theory. *Information Processing & Management*, 46(6), 718–732.

Wingrove, T. et al. (2009). Why were millions of people not obeying the law? Motivational influences on non-compliance with the law in the case of music piracy. *Psychology, Crime & Law*, 17, 261–276.

Wong, S., Altman, E., and Rojas-Mora, J. (2011). Internet access: Where law, economy, culture and technology meet. *Computer Networks*, 55(2), 470–479.

Xiaohe, L. (2006). On P2P filesharing: A major problem—A Chinese perspective. *Journal of Business Ethics*, 63, 63–73.

Yen, A. (May 2009). Torts and the construction of inducement and contributory liability in Amazon and Visa. Working Paper #179, Boston College Law School, Newton, MA.

Yu, S. (2014). Fear of cyber crime among college students in the United States: An exploratory study. *International Journal of Cyber Criminology*, 8(1), 36–46.

Zentner, A. (2006). Measuring the effect of filesharing on music purchases. *Journal of Law & Economics*, XLIX(1), 63–90.

Zimmerman G.L. et al. (2000). A 'stages of change' approach to helping patients change behavior [American Academy of Family Physicians Web site], 61(5), 1409–1416.

Chapter 3

Adermon, A. and Liang, C. (2014). Piracy and music sales: The effects of an anti-piracy law. *Journal of Economic Behavior & Organization*, 105, 90–106.

Anshelevich, E. and Caskurlu, B. (2011). Exact and approximate equilibria for optimal group network formation. *Theoretical Computer Science*, 412(39), 5298–5314.

Appleyard, M. (2015). Corporate responses to online music piracy: Strategic lessons for the challenge of additive manufacturing. *Business Horizons*, 58(1), 69–76.

Aron, R., Sundararajan, A., and Viswanathan, S. (2006). Intelligent agents in electronic markets for information goods: Customization, preference revelation and pricing. *Decision Support Systems*, 41(4), 764–786.

Bae, S. and Choi, J.P. (2006). A model of piracy. *Information Economics and Policy*, 18(3), 303–320.

Bai, J. and Waldfogel, J. (2012). Movie piracy and sales displacement in two samples of Chinese consumers. *Information Economics and Policy*, 24(3–4), 187–196.

Banerjee, D. (2003). Software piracy: A strategic analysis and policy instruments. *International Journal of Industrial Organization*, 21(1), 97–127.

Bei, X. et al. (2011). A bounded budget betweenness centrality game for strategic network formations. *Theoretical Computer Science*, 412(52), 7147–7168.

Benkler, Y. (2002). Intellectual property and the organization of information production. *International Review of Law & Economics*, 22, 81–107.

Benkler, Y. (2004). Sharing nicely: On sharable goods and the emergence of sharing as a modality of economic production. *Yale Law Journal*, 114, 273–343.

Bhattacharjee, S. et al. (2006a). Consumer search and retailer strategies in the presence of online music sharing. *Journal of Management Information Systems*, 23(1), 129–159.

Bhattacharjee, S. et al. (2006b). Impact of legal threats on individual behavior: An analysis of music industry actions and online music sharing. *Journal of Law and Economics*, 49(1), 91–114.

Boldrin, M. and Levine, D. (2002). The case against intellectual property. Working Paper. Available at: http://levine.sscnet.ucla.edu/papers/intellectual.pdf. Accessed on July 30, 2016.

Boldrin, M. and Levine, D. (2005). The economics of ideas and intellectual property. *Proceedings of the National Academy of Sciences of the United States of America*, 102(4), 1252–1256.

Boldrin, M. and Levine, D. (2012). *The Case Against Patents*. Working Paper Series, Federal Reserve Bank Of St. Louis, St. Louis, MO.

Cao, Z. and Yang, X. (2014). The fashion game: Network extension of matching pennies. *Theoretical Computer Science*, 540–541, 169–181.

Cevik, B. and Ozertan, G. (2008). Pricing strategies and protection of digital products under presence of piracy. *Journal of Artificial Societies and Social Simulation*, 11(4), 1–4.

Choi, D.Y. and Perez, A. (2007). Online piracy, innovation, and legitimate business models. *Technovation*, 27(4), 168–178.

Coleman, P. et al. (2007). Intractable conflict as an attractor a dynamical systems approach to conflict escalation and intractability. *American Behavioral Scientist*, 50(11), 1454–1475.

Cook, D. and Wang, W. (2004). Neutralizing the piracy of motion pictures: Reengineering the industry's supply chain. *Technology in Society*, 26(4), 567–583.

Danaher, B. and Smith, M. (2014). Gone in 60 seconds: The impact of the megaupload shutdown on movie sales. *International Journal of Industrial Organization*, 33, 1–8.

Douglas, D. et al. (2007). Equity perceptions as a deterrent to software piracy behavior. *Information & Management*, 44(5), 503–512.

Eliasson, G. and Wihlborg, C. (2003). On the macroeconomic effects of establishing tradability in weak property rights. *Journal of Evolutionary Economics*, 13(5), 607–632.

Fazli, M. et al. (2014). On non-progressive spread of influence through social networks. *Theoretical Computer Science*, 550, 36–50.

Gale, D. and Rosenthal, R. (Winter 1994). Price and quality cycles for experience goods. *RAND Journal of Economics*, 25, 590–607.

Georgiou, K. et al. (2014). Social exchange networks with distant bargaining. *Theoretical Computer Science*, 554, 263–274.

Gillespie, T. (2006). Designed to 'effectively frustrate': Copyright, technology and the agency of users. *New Media & Society*, 8, 651–669.

Gong, J., Smith, M., and Telang, R. (2015). Substitution or promotion? The impact of price discounts on cross-channel sales of digital movies. *Journal of Retailing*, 91(2), 343–357.

Gopal, R. and Bhattacharjee, S. (2003). No more shadow boxing with online music piracy: Strategic business models to enhance revenues. In *Proceedings of the 36th Hawaii International Conference on Systems Sciences*, HI.

Gopal, R. et al. (2002). A behavioral model of digital music piracy. *Journal of Organizational Computing and Electronic Commerce*, 14(2), 89–105.

Grewal, D. et al. (2010). Strategic online and offline retail pricing: A review and research agenda. *Journal of Interactive Marketing*, 24(2), 138–154.

Halbheer, D. et al. (2014). Choosing a digital content strategy: How much should be free? *International Journal of Research in Marketing*, 31(2), 192–206.

Hanks, F. (2004). Intellectual property and price discrimination: A challenge for Australian Competition Law. *Information Economics and Policy*, 16(1), 113–134.

Hinduja, S. (2006). A critical examination of the digital music phenomenon. *Critical Criminology*, 14, 387–409.

Hui, W. et al. (2008). Economics of shareware: How do uncertainty and piracy affect shareware quality and brand premium? *Decision Support Systems*, 44(3), 580–594.

Jaisingh, J. (2007). Piracy on file-sharing networks: Strategies for recording companies. *Journal of Organizational Computing and Electronic Commerce*, 17(4), 329–348.

Jeong, B. et al. (2012). The impacts of piracy and supply chain contracts on digital music channel performance. *Decision Support Systems*, 52(3), 590–603.

Kempe, D. et al. (2013). Maximizing the spread of influence through a social network. *Theory of Computing*, 11, 105–147.

Kim, J. (2007). Strategic use of copyright protection to deter entry. *Topics in Economic Analysis & Policy*, 7(1), 1765.

Kim, M. and Lee, B. (2015). Analysis of an advertisement based business model under technological advancements in fair use personal recording services. *Electronic Commerce Research and Applications*, 14(3), 169–180.

Kramer, A. et al. (2015). Experimental evidence of massive-scale emotional contagion through social networks. *Proceedings of the National Academy of Sciences of the United States of America*, 111(24), 8788–8790.

Krämer, J. et al. (2013). Net neutrality: A progress report. *Telecommunications Policy*, 37(9), 794–813.

Kwan, S. et al. (2008). Risk of using pirated software and its impact on software protection strategies. *Decision Support Systems*, 45(3), 504–516.

Lang, K. et al. (2009). Designing markets for co-production of digital culture goods. *Decision Support Systems*, 48(1), 33–45.

Lebowitz, S. (2006). Filesharing: Creative destruction or just plain destruction? *Journal of Law and Economics*, XLIX(1), 1–20.

Liu, Y. (2009). Optimal software strategies in the presence of network externalities. PhD thesis, University of Florida, Gainesville, FL. Available at: http://ufdcimages.uflib.ufl.edu/UF/E0/02/48/31/00001/liu_y.pdf. Accessed on July 30, 2016.

Ma, H. et al. (2014). Mining hidden links in social networks to achieve equilibrium. *Theoretical Computer Science*, 556, 13–24.

Mansell, R. and Steinmueller, E. (2013). Copyright infringement online: The case of the Digital Economy Act judicial review in the United Kingdom. *New Media & Society*, 15, 1–6.

Melnik, S. et al. (2013). Multi-stage complex contagions. *Chaos*, 23, 013124.

Netanel, N. (2003). Impose a commercial use levy to allow free peer-to-peer file sharing. *Harvard Journal of Law & Technology*, 17, 1–20.

Peitz, M. and Waelbroeck, P. (2006). Piracy of digital products: A critical review of the theoretical literature. *Information Economics and Policy*, 18(4), 449–476.

Perritt, H. (2007a). New architectures for music: Law should get out of the way. *Hastings Communications and Entertainment Law Journal*, 29(3), 320–360.

Perritt, H. (2007b). Music markets and myths. *Seton Hall Journal of Sports and Entertainment Law*, 21(1), 61–103.

Piolatto, A. and Schuett, F. (2012). Music piracy: A case of "The Rich Get Richer and the Poor Get Poorer". *Information Economics and Policy*, 24(1), 30–39.

Quiring, O. et al. (2008). Can filesharers be triggered by economic incentives? Results of an experiment. *New Media & Society*, 10(3), 433–453.

U.S. Federal Trade Commission (June 2005). Peer-to-peer filesharing technology: Consumer protection and competition issues. Staff report of the U.S. Federal Trade Commission.

Vaccaro, V. and Cohn, D. (2004). The evolution of business models and marketing strategies in the music industry. *International Journal on Media Management*, 6(1/2), 46–58.

Varian, H. (March 2005). Copying and copyright. *Journal of Economic Perspectives*, 19(2), 121–138.

Von Lohmann, F. (2004). Voluntary collective licensing for music file sharing. *Communications of the ACM*, 47(10), 21–24.

Warr, R. and Goode, M. (2011). Is the music industry stuck between rock and a hard place? The role of the Internet and three possible scenarios. *Journal of Retailing and Consumer Services*, 18(2), 126–131.

Wulandari, H. (2014). Economy and technology as influential factors for digital piracy sustainability: An Indonesian case. *Procedia—Social and Behavioral Sciences*, 164, 112–117.

Xiao, B. and Feng, Y. (2005). Uncertain switching costs and purchase decisions in electronic markets. *Annals of Operations Research*, 135, 179–196.

Yoon, K. (2002). The optimal level of copyright protection. *Information Economics and Policy*, 14, 327–348.

Zentner, A. (2005). File sharing and international sales of copyrighted music: An empirical analysis with a panel of countries. *B.E. Journal of Economic Analysis & Policy*, 5(1), 1452–1455.

Zentner, A. (2006). Measuring the effect of file sharing on music purchases. *Journal of Law and Economics*, XLIX(1), 63–90.

Chapter 4

Aaltonen, M. and Salmi, V. (2013). Versatile delinquents or specialized pirates? A comparison of correlates of illegal downloading and traditional juvenile crime. *Journal of Scandinavian Studies in Criminology and Crime Prevention*, 14(2), 188–193.

Adermon, A. and Liang, C. (2014). Piracy and music sales: The effects of an anti-piracy law. *Journal of Economic Behavior & Organization*, 105, 90–106.

Ågotnes, T. et al. (2010). Robust normative systems and a logic of norm compliance. *Logic Journal of IGPL*, 18(1), 4–30.

Ågotnes, T. and Wooldridge, M. (2010). Optimal social laws. In *Proceedings of the Ninth International Conference on Autonomous Agents and Multi-Agent Systems (AAMAS-2010)*, Toronto, Ontario, Canada, May 2010.

Andrighetto, G. and Conte, R. (2012). Cognitive dynamics of norm compliance. From norm adoption to flexible automated conformity. *Artificial Intelligence and Law*, 20(4), 359–381.

Anshelevich, E. and Caskurlu, B. (2011). Exact and approximate equilibria for optimal group network formation. *Theoretical Computer Science*, 412(39), 5298–5314.

Antunes, A. et al. (2008). The effect of financial repression and enforcement on entrepreneurship and economic development. *Journal of Monetary Economics*, 55(2), 278–297.

Arai, Y. (2011). Civil and criminal penalties for copyright infringement. *Information Economics and Policy*, 23(3–4), 270–280.

Argan, M., Argan, M., Ozer, A., and Kose, H. (2013). A study of motivational factors associated with peer-to-peer (P2P) file-sharing. *Procedia—Social and Behavioral Sciences*, 99(6), 180–188.

Arthur, W.B. (1999). Complexity and the economy. *Science*, 284, 107–109.

Avraham, R. and Liu, Z. (2012). Private information and the option to not sue: A reevaluation of contract remedies. *Journal of Economics & Organization*, 28(1), 77–102.

Bachrach, Y. et al. (2013). Proof systems and transformation games. *Annals of Mathematics and Artificial Intelligence*, 67(1), 1–30.

Baker, S. and Mezzetti, C. (2001). Prosecutorial resources, plea bargaining, and the decision to go to trial. *Journal of Economics & Organization*, 17(1), 149–167.

Bakker, P. (2005). File sharing—Fight, ignore or compete. Paid download services vs. P2P-networks. *Telematics and Informatics*, 22, 41–55.

Banerjee, D. (2003). Software piracy: A strategic analysis and policy instruments. *International Journal of Industrial Organization*, 21(1), 97–127.

Banerjee, D.S. (2006). Enforcement sharing and commercial piracy. *Review of Economic Research on Copyright Issues*, 3, 53–69.

Bar-Gill, O. (2005). Pricing legal options: A behavioral perspective. *Review of Law & Economics*, 1, 203–223.

Barnett, T. (2011). Obtaining a fair arbitration outcome. *Law, Probability and Risk*, 10(2), 123–131.

Barr, K. et al. (2003). Intellectual property crimes. *The American Criminal Law Review*, 40(2), 771–823.

Becker, J. and Clement, M. (2006). Dynamics of illegal participation in peer-to-peer networks—Why do people illegally share media files? *Journal of Media Economics*, 19(1), 7–32.

Bednar, J. (2006). Is full compliance possible? Conditions for shirking with imperfect monitoring and continuous action spaces. *Journal of Theoretical Politics*, 18, 347–375.

Beesley, J. (2010). Organized chaos: Seeing with new eyes. *Current Issues in Criminal Justice*, 21(3), 343–364.

Bhattacharjee, S. et al. (2006). Impact of legal threats on online music sharing activity: An analysis of music industry legal actions. *Journal of Law and Economics*, XLIX(1), 91–114.

Bhole, B. and Wagner, J. (2008). The joint use of regulation and strict liability with multidimensional care and uncertain conviction. *International Review of Law & Economics*, 28(2), 123–132.

Bilò, V. et al. (2013). Social context congestion games. *Theoretical Computer Science*, 514, 21–35.

Bodenhuasen, G. et al. (2003). Social cognition. In Weiner, I., Million, T., and Lerner, M.J., eds. *Handbook of Psychology: Personality and Social Psychology*, Vol. 5. John Wiley & Sons, NJ.

Bonadio, E. (2008). Remedies and sanctions for the infringement of Intellectual Property Rights under EC law. *European Intellectual Property Review*, 8, 320–335.

Borja, K. et al. (2015). The effect of music streaming services on music piracy among college students. *Computers in Human Behavior*, 45, 69–76.

Boyd, C. and Hoffman, D. (2013). Litigating toward settlement. *Journal of Law, Economic & Organization*, 29(4), 898–929.

Burgemeestre, B. et al. (2011). Value-based argumentation for justifying compliance. *Artificial Intelligence and Law*, 19(2–3), 149–186.

Cárdenas, E.J. (September 6, 2012). Globalization of securities enforcement: A shift toward enhanced regulatory intensity in Brazil's capital market? *Brooklyn Journal of International Law*, 37(3), 807–810.

Chapman, B. (2013). Incommensurability, proportionality and defeasibility. *Law, Probability & Risk*, 12(3–4), 259–274.

Chen, K. and Wang, J. (2007). Fee-shifting rules in litigation with contingency fees. *Journal of Law, Economic & Organization*, 23(3), 519–546.

Cho, H. et al. (2015). Perceptions of social norms surrounding digital piracy: The effect of social projection and communication exposure on injunctive and descriptive social norms. *Computers in Human Behavior*, 48, 506–515.

Chopard, B. et al. (2010). Trial and settlement negotiations between asymmetrically skilled parties. *International Review of Law & Economics*, 30(1), 18–27.

Christodoulou, G. et al. (2012). Convergence and approximation in potential games. *Theoretical Computer Science*, 438, 13–27.

Clark, B. (2007). Illegal downloads: Sharing out online liability: Sharing files, sharing risks. *Journal of Intellectual Property Law & Practice*, 2(6), 402–418.

Cornell, B. (1990). The incentive to sue: An option-pricing approach. *Journal of Legal Studies*, 19(1), 173–87.

Cox, J. and Collins, A. (2014). Sailing in the same ship? Differences in factors motivating piracy of music and movie content. *Journal of Behavioral and Experimental Economics*, 50, 70–76.

Cox, J., Collins, A., and Drinkwater, S. (2010). Seeders, leechers and social norms: Evidence from the market for illicit digital downloading. *Information Economics and Policy*, 22(4), 299–305.

Coyle, J.R. et al. (2009). "To buy or to pirate": The matrix of music consumers' acquisition-mode decision-making. *Journal of Business Research*, 62(10), 1031–1037.

Daughety, A. and Reinganum, J. (2010). Population-based liability determination, mass torts, and the incentives for suit, settlement, and trial. *Journal of Economics & Organization*, 26(3), 460–492.

De Mesquita, E. and Stephenson, M. (2006). Legal institutions and informal networks. *Journal of Theoretical Politics*, 18, 40–67.

De Dreu, C. et al. (2006). Motivated information processing, strategic choice and the quality of negotiated agreement. *Journal of Personality and Social Psychology*, 90, 927–943.

Demolombe, R. (2011). Relationships between obligations and actions in the context of institutional agents, human agents or software agents. *Artificial Intelligence and Law*, 19(2–3), 99–115.

Edwards, L. (2008). Should ISPs be compelled to become copyright cops? File-sharing, the music industry and enforcement online. *Journal of the Society for Computers and Law*, 19(6).

Eivazi, K. (2012). Is termination of internet users' accounts by an ISP a proportionate response to copyright infringement? *Computer Law & Security Review*, 28(4), 458–467.

Emek, Y. and Feldman, M. (2012). Computing optimal contracts in combinatorial agencies. *Theoretical Computer Science*, 452, 56–74.

Farmera, A. and Pecorino, P. (2002). Pretrial bargaining with self-serving bias and asymmetric information. *Journal of Economic Behavior & Organization*, 48(2), 163–176.

Fehr, E. et al. (2002). Strong reciprocity, human cooperation, and the enforcement of social norms. *Human Nature*, 13(1), 1–25.

Fellner, G. et al. (2013). Testing enforcement strategies in the field: Threat, moral appeal and social information. *Journal of the European Economic Association*, 3, 634–660.

Fiat, A. and Saia, J. (2007). Censorship resistant peer-to-peer networks. *Theory of Computing*, 3, 1–23.

Friedman, D. and Wittman, D. (2007). Litigation with symmetric bargaining and two-sided incomplete information. *Journal of Law, Economic & Organization*, 23(1), 98–126.

Friedman, E. and Wickelgren, A.L. (2010). Chilling, settlement, and the accuracy of the legal process. *Journal of Economics & Organization*, 26(1), 144–157.

Friehe, T. (2008). Optimal sanctions and endogeneity of differences in detection probabilities. *International Review of Law & Economics*, 28(2), 89–156.

Gabarró, J., García, A., and Serna, M. (2011). The complexity of game isomorphism. *Theoretical Computer Science*, 412(48), 6675–6695.

Gill, R.A. (1996). An integrated social fabric matrix/system dynamics approach to policy analysis. *System Dynamics Review*, 12(3), 167–181.

Grant, J. et al. (2014). Manipulating games by sharing information. *Studia Logica*, 102, 267–295.

Grüsser, S.M. et al. (2007). Excessive computer game playing: Evidence for addiction and aggression? *Cyberpsychology and Behavior*, 10, 290–292.

Gunn, M. (2015). Peer-to-peer file sharing as user rights activism. *University of Western Ontario Journal of Legal studies*, 5(3). http://ir.lib.uwo.ca/uwojls/vol5/iss3/3. Accessed on July 30, 2016.

Hegde, N., Massoulié, L., and Viennot, L. (2015). Self-organizing flows in social networks. *Theoretical Computer Science*, 584, 3–18.

Helbing, D. and Johansson, A. (2010a). Evolutionary dynamics of populations with conflicting interactions: Classification and analytical treatment considering asymmetry and power. *Physical Review E*, 81, 016112.

Helbing, D. and Johansson, A. (2010b). Cooperation, norms, and revolutions: A unified game-theoretical approach. *PLoS ONE*, 5(10), e12530.

Helbing, D. et al. (2010a). Defector-accelerated cooperativeness and punishment in public goods games with mutations. *Physical Review E*, 81(5), 057104.

Helbing, D. et al. (2010b). Punish, but not too hard: How costly punishment spreads in the spatial public goods game. *New Journal of Physics*, 12, 083005.

Hennig-Thurau, T. et al. (2007). Consumer file sharing of motion pictures. *Journal of Marketing*, 71, 1–18.

Henrich, J. and Boyd, R. (2001). Why people punish defectors: Weak conformist transmission can stabilize costly enforcement of norms in cooperative dilemmas. *Journal of Theoretical Biology*, 208, 79–89.

Heyes, A. et al. (2004). Legal expenses insurance, risk aversion and litigation. *International Review of Law & Economics*, 24, 107–119.

Howson, N.C. (2012). Enforcement without foundation? Insider trading and China's administrative law crisis. *American Journal of Comparative Law*, 60(4), 955–1002.

Huang, D. et al. (2007). A survey of factors influencing people's perception of information security. In Jacko, J., ed. *Human–Computer Interaction. HCI Applications and Services*. Lecture Notes in Computer Science, Springer, Vol. 4553, pp. 906–915.

Hylton, K. (2002). An asymmetric-information model of litigation. *International Review of Law & Economics*, 22, 153–175.

Hylton, K. (2008). When should a case be dismissed? The economics of pleading and summary judgment standards. *Supreme Court Economic Review*, 16, 39–49.

Hylton, K.N. and Lin, H. (2009). Trial selection theory and evidence: A review. In Sanchirico, C., ed. *Encyclopedia of Law and Economics: Procedural Law and Economics*, Vol. X. Edward Elgar Publishing, Boston University School of Law Working Paper No. 09-27. Available at SSRN: http://ssrn.com/abstract=1407557. Accessed on July 30, 2016.

Jacobs, R. et al. (2012). Digital movie piracy: A perspective on downloading behavior through social cognitive theory. *Computers in Human Behavior*, 28(3), 958–967.

Jain, S.K. and Kundu, R.P. (2006). Characterization of efficient simple liability rules with multiple tortfeasors. *International Review of Law & Economics*, 26(3), 410–427.

Jambon, M. and Smetana, J. (2012). College students' moral evaluations of illegal music downloading. *Journal of Applied Developmental Psychology*, 33(1), 31–39.

Jeong, B. and Khouja, M. (2013). Analysis of the effectiveness of preventive and deterrent piracy control strategies: Agent-based modeling approach. *Computers in Human Behavior*, 29(6), 2744–2755.

Kacsuk, Z. (2011). The mathematics of patent claim analysis. *Artificial Intelligence and Law*, 19(4), 263–289.

Kiel, D. and Elliott, E. (1997). *Chaos Theory in the Social Sciences: Foundations and Applications*. University of Michigan Press, Ann Arbor, MI.

Kim, C. (2014). Adversarial and inquisitorial procedures with information acquisition. *Journal of Economics & Organization*, 30(4), 767–803.

Kim, M. and Lee, B. (2015). Analysis of an advertisement based business model under technological advancements in fair use personal recording services. *Electronic Commerce Research and Applications*, 14(3), 169–180.

Kleinman, M.A.R. (1993). Enforcement swamping: A positive feedback mechanism in rates of illicit activity. *Mathematical and Computer Modeling*, 17, 65–75.

Klement, A. and Neeman, Z. (2005). Against compromise: A mechanism design approach. *Journal of Economics & Organization*, 21(2), 285–314.

Knoblich, G. and Sebanz, N. (2008). Evolving intentions for social interaction: From entrainment to joint action. *Philosophical Transactions of the Royal Society B*, 363(1499), 2021–2031.

Kuhlman, C. and Mortveit, H. (2014). Attractor stability in non-uniform Boolean networks. *Theoretical Computer Science*, 559, 20–33.

Lang, M. and Wambach, A. (2013). The fog of fraud—Mitigating fraud by strategic ambiguity. *Games & Economic Behavior*, 8(1), 255–275.

Lea, S. and Webley, P. (2006). Money as tool, money as drug: The biological psychology of a strong incentive. *Behavioral and Brain Sciences*, 29, 161–209.

Leclerc, F. et al. (1995). Waiting time and decision making: Is time like money? *Journal of Consumer Research*, 22, 110–119.

Lemley, M. and Weiser, P. (2007). Should property or liability rules govern information? *Texas Law Review*, 85, 783–793.

Leong, S. and Saw, C. (2007). Copyright infringement in a borderless world—Does territoriality matter? Society of Composers, Authors and Music Publishers of Canada v Canadian Association of Internet Providers [2004] 2 SCR 427. *International Journal of Law & Information Technology*, 15, 38–53.

Leshem, S. and Tabach, A. (2012). Commitment versus flexibility in enforcement games. *B.E. Journal of Theoretical Economics*, 12(1), 1–42.

LoPucki, L.M. (1997). The systems approach to law. *Cornell Law Review*, 82, 479–483.

Losada, M. and Heaphy, E. (2004). The role of positivity and connectivity in the performance of business teams: A nonlinear dynamics model. *American Behavioral Scientist*, 47(6), 740–765.

Marco, T. (2005). The option value of patent litigation: Theory and evidence. *Review of Financial Economics*, 14, 323–351.

Melnik, S. et al. (2013). Multi-stage complex contagions. *Chaos*, 23, 013124.

Miklashevich, I. (2003). Mathematical representation of social systems: Uncertainty and optimization of social system evolution. *Nonlinear Phenomena in Complex Systems*, 6(2), 678–686.

Miles, E. (2004). *In Re Aimster*; and *MGM Inc. v. Grokster Ltd.*: Peer-to-peer and the Sony doctrine. *Berkeley Technology Law Journal*, 19(1), 21–57.

Miller, C. (2012). A comment on Saks and Neufeld: 'Convergent evolution in law and science: The structure of decision making under uncertainty'. *Law, Probability & Risk*, 11(1), 101–104.

Miller, D. and Watson, J. (2013). A theory of disagreement in repeated games with bargaining. *Econometrica*, 81(6), 2303–2350.

Mogilner, C. and Aaker, J. (2009). 'The Time vs. Money Effect': Shifting product attitudes and decisions through personal connection. *Journal of Consumer Research*, 36(2), 277–291.

Mogy, R. and Pruitt, D. (1974). Effects of a threatener's enforcement costs on threat credibility and compliance. *Journal of Personality and Social Psychology*, 29(2), 173–180.

Nwogugu, M. (Updated in 2013). Complexity and optimal sanctions for illegal online filesharing, under un-constrained transferable utility and unknown demand. Available at: www.ssrn.com. Accessed on July 30, 2016.

Ohtsubo, Y. et al. (2010). Dishonesty invites costly third-party punishment. *Evolution & Human Behavior*, 31(4), 259–262.

Okada, E. and Hoch, S. (2004). Spending time versus spending money. *Journal of Consumer Research*, 31, 313–323.

Ong, R. (2015). Liability of Internet intermediaries for user-generated content: An examination of *Oriental Press Group Ltd vs. Fevaworks Solutions Ltd*. *Computer Law & Security Review*, 31(1), 131–138.

Pavlov, O.V. (2005). Dynamic analysis of an institutional conflict: Copyright owners against online file sharing. *Journal of Economic Issues*, 39(3), 633–663.

Peguera, M. (2008). "I Just Know That I (Actually) Know Nothing": Actual knowledge and other problems in ISP liability case law in Spain. *European Intellectual Property Review*, 7, 280–285.

Perc, M. et al. (2013). Understanding recurrent crime as system-immanent collective behavior. *PLoS ONE*, 8(10), e76063.

Perritt, H. (2007a). New architectures for music: Law should get out of the way. *Hastings Communications and Entertainment Law Journal*, 29(3), 320–360.

Perritt, H. (2007b). Music markets and myths. *Seton Hall Journal of Sports and Entertainment Law*, 21(1), 61–103.

Piercey, M.D. (2009). Motivated reasoning versus numerical probability assessment: Evidence from an accounting context. *Organizational Behavior and Human Decision Processes*, 108(2), 330–341.

Podoshen, J. (2008). Why take tunes? An exploratory multinational look at student downloading. *Journal of Internet Commerce*, 7(2), 180–202.

Post, D.G. and Eisen, M. (2000). How long is the coastline of the law? Thoughts on the fractal nature of legal systems. *Journal of Legal Studies*, 29, 545–555.

Prakken, H. (2008). Formalizing ordinary legal disputes: A case study. *Artificial Intelligence and Law*, 16(4), 333–359.

Radzicki, M.J. and Tauheed, L. (2009). In defense of system dynamics: A response to Professor Hayden. *Journal of Economic Issues*, 43(4), 1043–1061.

Rincke, J. and Traxler, C. (2011). Enforcement spillovers. *Review of Economics and Statistics*, 93(4), 1224–1234.

Rouillon, S. (2008). Safety regulation vs. liability with heterogeneous probabilities of suit. *International Review of Law & Economics*, 28(2), 133–139.

Ruhl, J.B. and Ruhl, H. (1997). The arrow of the law in modern administrative states: Using complexity theory to reveal the diminishing returns and increasing risks the burgeoning of law poses to society. *University of California Davis Law Review*, 30, 405–426 (explaining the various kinds of attractors).

Saini, R. and Ashwani, M. (2008). How I decide depends on what I spend: Use of heuristics is greater for time than for money. *Journal of Consumer Research*, 34, 914–922.

Samuelson, W.F. (1998). Settlements out of court: Efficiency and equity. *Group Decision and Negotiation*, 7(2), 157–177.

Sang, Y. et al. (2015). Understanding the intentions behind illegal downloading: A comparative study of American and Korean college students. *Telematics and Informatics*, 32(2), 333–343.

Scholz, J. (1991). Cooperative regulatory enforcement and the politics of administrative effectiveness. *American Political Science Review*, 85(1), 115–136.

Short, M. et al. (2010). Dissipation and displacement of hotspots in reaction–diffusion models of crime. *Proceedings of the National Academy of Sciences of the United States of America*, 107, 3961–3965.

Soman, D. (2001). The mental accounting of sunk time costs: Why time is not like money. *Journal of Behavioral Decision Making*, 14, 169–185.

Steinmetz, K. and Tunnell, K. (2013). Under the pixelated jolly roger: A study of on-line pirates. *Journal: Deviant Behavior*, 34(1), 53–67.

Sterman, J.D. (1989). Deterministic chaos in an experimental economic system. *Journal of Economic Behavior & Organization*, 12, 1–28.

Sugden, P. (2008). You can click but you can't hide: Copyright pirates and crime—The "Drink or Die" prosecutions. *European Intellectual Property Review*, 30(6), 222–228.

Synodinou, T. (2015). Intermediaries' liability for online copyright infringement in the EU: Evolutions and confusions. *Computer Law & Security Review*, 31(1), 57–67.

Tang, G. (2010). Is administrative enforcement the answer? Copyright protection in the digital era. *Computer Law & Security Review*, 26(4), 406–417.

Tetlock, P.E. (2002). Social functionalist frameworks for judgment and choice: Intuitive politicians, theologians and prosecutors. *Psychological Review*, 109(3), 451–471.

Tsebelis, G. (1993). Penalty and crime: Further theoretical considerations and empirical evidence. *Journal of Theoretical Politics*, 5, 349–374.

Tussey, D. (2005). Music at the edge of chaos: A complex systems perspective on file sharing. *Loyola University Chicago Law Journal*, 37, 101–120.

Urpelainen, J. (2011). The enforcement–exploitation trade-off in international cooperation between weak and powerful states. *European Journal of International Relations*, 17(4), 631–653.

Van Boven, L. and Ashworth, L. (2007). Looking forward, looking back: Anticipation is more evocative than retrospection. *Journal of Experimental Psychology: General*, 136, 289–300.

Van Gennip, Y. et al. (2013). Community detection using spectral clustering on sparse geosocial data. *SIAM Journal of Applied Mathematics*, 73(1), 67–83.

Van Otterloo, S. et al. (2006). Knowledge condition games. *Journal of Logic, Language, and Information*, 15(4), 425–452.

Vincents, O.B. (2007). When rights clash online: The tracking of P2P copyright infringements vs. the EC personal data directive. *International Journal of Law and Information Technology*,16,270–296.

Vincents, O.B. (2008). Secondary liability for copyright infringement in the BitTorrent platform: Placing the blame where it belongs. *European Intellectual Property Review*, 30(1), 4–8.

Waldfogel, J. (1998). Reconciling asymmetric information and divergent expectations theories of litigation. *Journal of Law and Economics*, 41, 451–476.

Wang, G. et al. (1994). Litigation and pretrial negotiation under incomplete information. *Journal of Law, Economics & Organization*, 10, 187–200.

Wang, X. and McClung, S. (2012). The immorality of illegal downloading: The role of anticipated guilt and general emotions. *Computers in Human Behavior*, 28(1), 153–159.

Weenig, M.W.H. and Maarleveld, M. (2002). The impact of time constraint on information search strategies in complex choice tasks. *Journal of Economic Psychology*, 23, 689–702.

Williams, C. and Arrigo, B.A. (2002). *Law Psychology and Justice: Chaos Theory and New (Dis)Order*. State University of New York Press, Albany, NY.

Wooldridge, M. et al. (2013). Incentive engineering for Boolean Games. *Artificial Intelligence*, 195, 418–439.

Yeung, D. et al. (2010). Dynamic game of offending and law enforcement: A stochastic extension. *International Game Theory Review*, 12(4), 471–481.

Young, T. (1997). The ABCs of crime: Attractors, bifurcations and chaotic dynamics. In Milanovic, D., ed. *Chaos, Criminology and Social Justice: The New Orderly (Dis)Order*. Praeger Publishers, Westport, CT.

Zauberman, G. and Lynch, J. (2005). Resource slack and propensity to discount delayed investments of time versus money. *Journal of Experimental Psychology: General*, 134, 23–37.

Zhang, J. et al. (2012). Bank risk taking, efficiency and law enforcement: Evidence from Chinese city commercial banks. *China Economic Review*, 23(2), 284–295.

Zhang, N. and Walton, D. (2010). Recent trends in evidence law in China and the new evidence scholarship. *Law, Probability & Risk*, 9(2), 103–129.

Chapter 5

Adkinson, W. (March 2004). Liability of P2P file-sharing systems for copyright infringement by their users. Progress and Freedom Foundation, USA, Progress on Point # 117.

Avinadav, T. et al. (2014). Analysis of protection and pricing strategies for digital products under uncertain demand. *International Journal of Production Economics*, 158, 54–64.

Bakker, P. (2005). File sharing—Fight, ignore or compete. Paid download services vs. P2P-networks. *Telematics and Informatics*, 22, 41–55.

Beekhuyzen, J. et al. (2015). Illuminating the underground: The reality of un-authorised file sharing. *Information Systems Journal*, 25(3), 171–192.

Blum, A. et al. (2010). Routing without regret: On convergence to Nash equilibria of regret-minimizing algorithms in routing games. *Theory of Computing*, 6, 179–199.

Chen, T. and Horng, G. (2007). A lightweight and anonymous copyright-protection protocol. *Computer Standards & Interfaces*, 29(2), 229–237.

Choi, B.H. (2006). The Grokster dead-end. *Harvard Journal of Law & Technology*, 19(2), 393–411.

Depoorter, B. and Parisi, F. (2002). Fair use and copyright protection: A price theory explanation. *International Review of Law & Economics*, 21, 453–473.

Feige, U. and Vondrak, J. (2010). The submodular welfare problem with demand queries. *Theoretical Computer Science*, 6, 247–290.

Fetscherin, M. and Knolmayer, G. (2004). Business models for content delivery: An empirical analysis of the newspaper and magazines industry. *The International Journal on Media Management*, 6(1-2), 4-11. Available at: www.mediajournal.org/modules/pub/view.php/mediajournal-178. Accessed on July 30, 2016.

Gavalda-Miralles, A. et al. (2014). Impact of heterogeneity and socioeconomic factors on individual behavior in decentralized sharing ecosystems. *Proceedings of the National Academy of Sciences of the United States of America*, 111, 15322–15327.

Golle, P., Leyton-Brown, K. et al. (2001). Incentives for sharing in peer-to-peer networks. In Goos,G., Hartmanis, J. and Van Leeuwen, J., eds. *Proceedings of the Second International Workshop on Electronic Commerce*. Lecture Notes in Computer Science, Springer, Vol. 2232.

Kolpakov, R. and Raffinot, M. (2008). New algorithms for text fingerprinting. *Journal of Discrete Algorithms*, 6(2), 243–255.

Landes, W. and Lichtman, D. (2003). Indirect liability for copyright infringement: Napster and beyond. *Journal of Economic Perspectives*, 17(2), 113–124.

Lemley, M.A. and Reese, R.A. (2004). Reducing digital copyright infringement without restricting innovation. *Stanford Law Review*, 1345–1434.

Lin, Y. and Wu, J. (2008). Content adaptive watermarking for multimedia fingerprinting. *Computer Standards & Interfaces*, 30(5), 271–287.

Meisel, B. (2008). Entry into the market for online distribution of digital content: Economic and legal ramifications. *SCRIPTed: A Journal of Law, Technology & Society*, 5(1), 50–60.

Mertzios, G., Nikoletseas, S., Raptopoulos, C., and Spirakis, P. (2013). Natural models for evolution on networks. *Theoretical Computer Science*, 477, 76–95.

Samuelson, P. (2005). Did MGM really win the *Grokster* case? *Communications of the ACM*, 48(10), 24–34.

Shao, M. (2007). A privacy-preserving buyer-seller watermarking protocol with semi-trust third party. In In Fischer-Hübner,S., Lambrinoudakis, C. and Pernul, G., eds. *Trust, Privacy and Security in Digital Business*. Lecture Notes in Computer Science. Springer.

Steinmetz, R. and Wehrle, K., eds. (September 2005). *Peer-to-Peer Systems and Applications*. Lecture Notes in Computer Science, Vol. 3485. ISBN: 3-540-29192-X.

Stutzbach, D. et al. (2008). Characterizing unstructured overlay topologies in modern P2P file-sharing systems. *IEEE/ACM Transactions on Networking*, 16(2), 267–280.

Swangmuang, S. and Krishnamurthy, P. (2008). An effective location fingerprint model for wireless indoor localization. *Pervasive and Mobile Computing*, in press, available online April 26, 2008.

Von Lohmann, F. (2003). What peer-to-peer developers need to know about copyright law. *Electronic Frontier Foundation*, 3. Available from: http://www.eff.org/IP/P2P/p2p_copyright_wp.php. Accessed on July 30, 2016.

Wu, Y. and Pang, H. (2008). A lightweight buyer–seller watermarking protocol. Available at: http://www.hindawi.com/RecentlyAcceptedArticlePDF.aspx?journal=AM&number=905065. Accessed on July 30, 2016.

Ye, Z. et al. (2005). Trusted paths for browsers. *ACM Transactions on Information and Systems Security*, 8(2), 153–186.

Chapter 6

Adlakha, S. et al. (2015). Equilibria of dynamic games with many players: Existence, approximation, and market structure. *Journal of Economic Theory*, 156, 269–316.

Anshelevich, E. and Caskurlu, B. (2011). Exact and approximate equilibria for optimal group network formation. *Theoretical Computer Science*, 412(39), 5298–5314.

Azar, Y. et al. (2005). Combining online algorithms for acceptance and rejection. *Theory of Computing*, 1, 105–117.

Ballester, L.C. and Seigneur, J. (2015). Extending trust management with cooperation incentives: a fully decentralized framework for user-centric network environments. *Journal of Trust Management*, Vol. 2.

Bei, X. et al. (2011). A bounded budget betweenness centrality game for strategic network formations. *Theoretical Computer Science*, 412(52), 7147–7168.

Bloch, F. and Quérou, N. (2013). Pricing in social networks. *Games and economic behavior*, 80, 243–261.

Blum, A. et al. (2010). Routing without regret: On convergence to Nash equilibria of regret-minimizing algorithms in routing games. *Theory of Computing*, 6, 179–199.

Candogan, O. et al. (2012). Optimal pricing in networks with externalities. *Operations Research*, 60(4), 883–905.

Chen, H. et al. (2012). Incentive mechanisms for P2P network nodes based on repeated game. *Journal of Networks*, 7(2), 385–395.

Coleman, P. et al. (2007). Intractable conflict as an attractor: A dynamical systems approach to conflict escalation and intractability. *American Behavioral Scientist*, 50(11), 1454–1475.

Dembo, A. and Zeitouni, O. (1998). Large deviations techniques and applications. In *Applications of Mathematics*. Springer.

Diederich, A. and Busemeyer, J. (1999). Conflict and the stochastic-dominance principle of decision making. *Psychological Science*, 10(4), 353–359.

Fainmesser, I. P. and Galeotti, A. (2015). Pricing network effects. *Review of Economic Studies*, forthcoming.

Feige, U. and Vondrak, J. (2010). The submodular welfare problem with demand queries. *Theoretical Computer Science*, 6, 247–290.

Feldman, M. et al. (2004). Robust incentive techniques for peer-to-peer networks. In *Proceedings of the 5th ACM conference on Electronic commerce*, New York, 102–111.

Feldman, M. et al. (2006). Freeriding and whitewashing in peer-to-peer systems. *IEEE Journal on Selected Areas in Communications*, 24(5), 1010–1019.

Fiat, A. and Saia, J. (2007). Censorship resistant peer-to-peer networks. *Theory of Computing*, 3, 1–23.

Galeotti, A. et al. (2010). Network games. *Review of Economic Studies*, 77, 218–244.

Giotis, I. and Guruswami, V. (2006). Correlation clustering with a fixed number of clusters. *Theory of Computing*, 2, 249–266.

Gradwohl, R. and Reingold, O. (2010). Partial exposure in large games. *Games and Economic Behavior*, 68(2), 602–613.

Hamida, E. et al. (2008). Neighbor discovery in multi-hop wireless networks: Evaluation and dimensioning with interferences considerations. *Discrete Mathematics and Theoretical Computer Science*, 10(2), 87–114.

Hua, J. et al. (2012). A dynamic game theory approach to solve the free riding problem in the peer-to-peer networks. *Journal of Simulation*, 6, 43–55.

Huo, Y. (2011). Adopting game theory to inhibit free-riding in P2P network. *Journal of Computational Information Systems*, 7(2), 645–653.

Kets, W. et al. (2011). Inequality and network structure. *Games and Economic Behavior*, 73(1), 215–226.

Lou, X. and Hwang, K. (2009). Collusive piracy prevention in P2P content delivery networks. *IEEE Transactions on Computers*, 58(7), 970–983.

Nisgav, A. and Patt-Shamir, B. (2011). Finding similar users in social networks. *Theory of Computing Systems*, 49(4), 720–737.

Pavlov, O.V. (2005). Dynamic analysis of an institutional conflict: Copyright owners against online file sharing. *Journal of Economic Issues*, 39(3), 633–663.

Ramaswamy, V., et al. (2012). Incentives for P2P-assisted content distribution: If you can't beat'em, join'em. In *Communication, Control, and Computing (Allerton), 50th Annual Allerton Conference on IEEE*, 1409–1416.

Schmeidler, D. (1973). Equilibrium points of non-atomic games. *Journal of Statistical Physics*, 17(4), 295–300.

Sherman, A. et al. (2012). FairTorrent: A deficit-based distributed algorithm to ensure fairness in P2P systems. *IEEE/ACM Transactions on Networking*, 20(5), 1361–1369.

Tseng, Y.M. and Chen, F.G. (2011). A free-rider aware reputation system for peer-to-peer file-sharing networks. *Expert Systems and Applications*, 38(3), 2432–2440.

Chapter 7

Andersen, D.G. (February 2005). Improving end-to-end availability using overlay networks, PhD thesis, Massachusetts Institute of Technology, Cambridge, MA.

Aron, R. et al. (2006). Intelligent agents in electronic markets for information goods: Customization, preference revelation and pricing. *Decision Support Systems*, 41(4), 764–786.

Asvanund, A. et al. (2004). An empirical analysis of network externalities in peer-to-peer music-sharing networks. *Information Systems Research*, 15(2), 155–174.

Bakos, Y. and Brynjolfsson, E. (1999). Bundling information goods: Pricing, profits and efficiency. *Management Science*, 45(12), 1613–1619.

Barnett, T. (U.S. Department of Justice) (September 2006). Interoperability between antitrust and intellectual property. In Presentation to the George Mason University School of Law Symposium *Managing Antitrust Issues in a Global Marketplace*, Washington, DC.

Bauer, J. and Obar, J. (2014). Reconciling political and economic goals in the net neutrality debate. *Information Policy*, 30(1), 1–19.

Bei, X. et al. (2011). A bounded budget betweenness centrality game for strategic network formations. *Theoretical Computer Science*, 412(52), 7147–7168.

Belleflamme, P. and Picard, P.M. (2007). Piracy and competition. *Journal of Economics & Management Strategy*, 16(2), 351–383.

Benkler, Y. (2002). Intellectual property and the organization of information production. *International Review of Law & Economics*, 22, 81–107.

Benkler, Y. (2004). Sharing nicely: On sharable goods and the emergence of sharing as a modality of economic production. *Yale Law Journal*, 114, 273–343.

Bhargava, H. and Choudhary, V. (2008). Research note—When is versioning optimal for information goods? *Management Science*, 54, 1029–1035.

Bilò, V. et al. (2010). When ignorance helps: Graphical multicast cost sharing games. *Theoretical Computer Science*, 411(3), 660–671.

Bockstedt, J. et al. (2005). The move to artist-led online music distribution: Explaining structural changes in the digital music market. In Sprague, R.H., Jr., ed. *Proceedings of the 38th Annual Hawaii International Conference on System Sciences*, Vols. 3–6, January 2005.

Boldrin, M. and Levine, D. (2002). The case against intellectual property. Working Paper.

Boldrin, M. and Levine, D. (2005). The economics of ideas and intellectual property. *Proceedings of the National Academy of Sciences of the United States of America*, 102(4), 1252–1256.

Boldrin, M. and Levine, D. (2012). The case against patents. Research Division Federal Reserve Bank of St. Louis—Working paper series. Working Paper 2012-035A, US Federal Reserve Bank of St. Louis, USA. http://research.stlouisfed.org/wp/2012/2012-035.pdf. Accessed on July 30, 2016.

Brynjolfsson, E. et al. (2011). Goodbye Pareto principle, hello long tail: The effect of search costs on the concentration of product sales. *Management Science*, 57, 1373–1386.

Campbell, D. and Picciotto, S. (2006). The acceptable face of intervention: Intellectual property in Posnerian law and economics. *Social & Legal Studies*, 15(3), 435–452.

Cao, X. et al. (2002). Internet pricing with a game theoretical approach: Concepts and examples. *IEEE/ACM Transactions on Networking*, 10(2), 208–216.

Cao, Z. and Yang, X. (2014). The fashion game: Network extension of matching pennies. *Theoretical Computer Science*, 540–541, 169–181.

Cerf, V. et al. (2014). Internet governance is our shared responsibility. *I/S: A Journal of Law and Policy for the Information Society*, 10(1), 1–42.

Chen, Y. and Savage, S.J. (2011). The effects of competition on the price for cable modem internet access. *Review of Economics and Statistics*, 93, 201–217.

Cheng, H.K. et al. (2011). The debate on net neutrality: A policy perspective. *Information Systems Research*, 22, 60–82.

Choi, D. and Perez, A. (2007). Online piracy, innovation, and legitimate business models. *Technovation*, 27(4), 168–178.

Choi, J.P. and Kim, B.C. (2010). Net neutrality and investment incentives. *RAND Journal of Economics*, 41, 446–471.

Clement, M. et al. (2012). Consumer responses to legal music download services that compete with illegal alternatives. *Service Science*, 4, 4–23.

Conner, K. and Rumelt, R. (1991). Software piracy: An analysis of protection strategies. *Management Science*, 37(2), 125–139.

Cook, D. and Wang, W. (2004). Neutralizing the piracy of motion pictures: Reengineering the industry's supply chain. *Technology in Society*, 26(4), 567–583.

Danaher, B. et al. (2010). Converting pirates without cannibalizing purchasers: The impact of digital distribution on physical sales and internet piracy. *Marketing Science*, 29, 1138–1151.

Danay, R. (Autumn 2005). Copyright vs. free expression: The case of peer-to-peer filesharing of music in the UK. *Yale Journal of Law and Technology*, 8(1).

DeCastro, J. et al. (2008). Can entrepreneurial firms benefit from product piracy? *Journal of Business Venturing*, 23(1), 75–90.

Delgado, A. (2003). Confessions of a tennis-shoe pirate—Can proper pricing of factors of production deter copyright infringment? *Journal of Technology Law & Policy*, 8(2), 179–210.

Domon, K. (2006). Price discrimination of digital content. *Economics Letters*, 93, 421–426.

Duffy, J. (2004). The marginal cost controversy in intellectual property. *University of Chicago Law Review*, 71(1), 37–56.

Economides, N. (2008). Net neutrality, non-discrimination and digital distribution of content through the internet. I/S: *A Journal of Law and Policy for the Information Society*, 4, 209–233. Available at: http://www.stern.nyu.edu/networks/Economides_Net_Neutrality.pdf. Accessed on July 30, 2016.

Economides, N. and Hermalin, B. (2012). The economics of network neutrality. *RAND Journal of Economics*, 43(4),602–629.

Economides, N. and Tag, J. (2012). Network neutrality on the Internet: A two-sided market analysis. *Information Economics and Policy*, 24, 91–104.

Ewing, J. (September 13, 2003). The orthodoxy of open access. *Nature*.

Fazli, M. et al. (2014). On non-progressive spread of influence through social networks. *Theoretical Computer Science*, 550, 36–50.

Fiat, A. and Saia, J. (2007). Censorship resistant peer-to-peer networks. *Theory of Computing*, 3, 1–23.

Gabarró, J., García, A., and Serna, M. (2011). The complexity of game isomorphism. *Theoretical Computer Science*, 412(48), 6675–6695.

Gandhi, R. (April 8, 2015). Net neutrality: Why Internet is in danger of being shackled. *The Economic Times*. Available at: http://articles.economictimes.indiatimes.com/2015-04-08/news/60943272_1_net-neutrality-telecom-operators-viber. Accessed on July 30, 2016.

Georgiou, K. et al. (2014). Social exchange networks with distant bargaining. *Theoretical Computer Science*, 554, 263–274.

Ghosh, S. (2006). The intellectual property incentive: Not so natural as to warrant strong exclusivity. *SCRIPTed*, 3(2), 96–106.

Gong, J. et al. (2015). Substitution or promotion? The impact of price discounts on cross-channel sales of digital movies. *Journal of Retailing*, 91(2), 343–357.

Gopal, R. et al. (2006). Do artists benefit from online music sharing? *Journal of Business*, 79(3), 1503–1513.

Greenhalgh, C. and Rogers, M. (2007). The value of intellectual property rights to firms and society. *Oxford Review of Economic Policy*, 23, 541–567.

Grewal, D. et al. (2010). Strategic online and offline retail pricing: A review and research agenda. *Journal of Interactive Marketing*, 24(2), 138–154.

Gupta, A. et al. (2006). Pricing of risk for loss guaranteed intradomain internet service contracts. *Computer Networks*, 50, 2787–2804.

Gupta, A. and Zhang, L. (2008). Pricing for end to end assured bandwidth services. *International Journal of Information Technology & Decision Making*, 7(2), 361–389.

Hagiu, A. (2009). Two-Sided Platforms: Product Variety and Pricing Structures. *Journal of Economics & Management Strategy*, 18(4), 1011–1043.

Halbheer, D. et al. (2014). Choosing a digital content strategy: How much should be free? *International Journal of Research in Marketing*, 31(2), 192–206.

Hegde, N. et al. (2015). Self-organizing flows in social networks. *Theoretical Computer Science*, 584, 3–18.

Hennig-Thurau, T. et al. (2007). Consumer file sharing of motion pictures. *Journal of Marketing*, 71, 1–18.

Hitt, L. and Chen, P. (2005). Bundling with customer self-selection: A simple approach to bundling low-marginal-cost goods. *Management Science*, 51(10), 1481–1493.

Hogendorn, C. (2007). Broadband internet: net neutrality versus open access. *International Economics and Economic Policy*, 4, 185–208.

Horan, A. et al. (Office of Industries—U.S. International Trade Commission) (October 2005). Foreign infringement of intellectual property rights: Implications for selected US industries. Working Paper, U.S. International Trade Commission, Washington, DC.

Jaisingh, J. (2007). Piracy on file-sharing networks: Strategies for recording companies. *Journal of Organizational Computing and Electronic Commerce*, 17(4), 329–348.

Jeong, B. et al. (2012). The impacts of piracy and supply chain contracts on digital music channel performance. *Decision Support Systems*, 52(3), 590–603.

Jin, G. and Kato, A. (2007). Dividing online and offline: A case study. *Review of Economic Studies*, 74(3), 981–1004.

Johnson, T. (Variety) (February 26, 2015). Net neutrality: FCC approves new rules of the road for internet service. Available at: http://variety.com/2015/biz/news/net-neutrality-rules-fcc-reclassifies-internet-1201440638/. Accessed on July 30, 2016.

Kannan, P. et al. (2009). Pricing product lines of digital content: A model using online choice experiment. *Marketing Science*, 28(4), 620–636.

Karp, L. (1996). Depreciation erodes the coase conjecture. *European Economic Review*, 40(2), 473–490.

Kempe, D. et al. (2013). Maximizing the spread of influence through a social network. *Theory of Computing*, 11, 105–147.

Khong, D. (2006). Copyright failure and the protection for tables and compilation. *SCRIPTed: A Journal of Law, Technology & Society*, 3(2), 153–160.

Khouja, M. et al. (2007). Applications of agent-based modeling to pricing of reproducible information goods. *Decision Support Systems*, 44(3), 725–739.

Khouja, M. and Smith, M.A. (2007). Optimal pricing for information goods with piracy and saturation effect. *European Journal of Operational Research*, 176(1), 482–497.

King, S. and Lampe, R. (2003). Network externalities, price discrimination and profitable piracy. *Information Economics and Policy*, 15(3), 271–290.

Kodialam, M. and Venkateswaran, V. (2003). Bandwidth allocation in multicast trees with QoS constraints. *International Journal of Information Technology & Decision Making*, 2(4), 619–624.

Kramer, A. et al. (2015). Experimental evidence of massive-scale emotional contagion through social networks. *Proceedings of the National Academy of Sciences of the United States of America*, 111(24), 8788–8790.

Krämer, J. et al. (2013). Net neutrality: A progress report. *Telecommunications Policy*, 37(9), 794–813.

Ku, R. (2002). The creative destruction of copyright: Napster and the new economics of digital technology. *University of Chicago Law Review*, 69(1), 263–324.

Lang, K. et al. (2009). Designing markets for co-production of digital culture goods. *Decision Support Systems*, 48(1), 33–45.

Latcovich, S. and Smith, H. (2001). Pricing, sunk costs, and market structure online: Evidence from book retailing. *Oxford Review of Economic Policy*, 17(2), 217–234.

Liebowitz, S. (2005). Pitfalls in measuring the impact of filesharing on the sound recording market. *CESifo Economic Studies*, 51(2–3), 439–477.

Liebowitz, S.J. (2008). Testing file-sharing's impact by examining record sales in cities. *Management Science*, 54(4), 852–859.

Liebowitz, S.J. (2007). *How reliable is the Oberholzer-Gee and Strumpf paper on file-sharing?* Available at: http://dx.doi.org/10.2139/ssrn.1014399. Accessed on July 30, 2016.

Madrigal, A.C. and LaFrance, A. (April 25, 2014). Net neutrality: A guide to (and history of) a contested idea. Available at: http://www.theatlantic.com/technology/archive/2014/04/the-best-writing-on-net-neutrality/361237/. Accessed on July 30, 2016.

Mari, A. (March 26, 2014). Brazil passes groundbreaking Internet governance bill. *ZDNet*. Available at: http://www.zdnet.com/brazil-passes-groundbreaking-internet-governance-bill-7000027740/. Accessed on July 30, 2016.

Melnik, S. et al. (2013). Multi-stage complex contagions. *Chaos*, 23, 013124.

Michel, N. (2005). Digital file sharing and the music industry: Was there a substitution effect? *Review of Economic Research on Copyright Issues*, 2(2), 41–52.

Musacchio, J. et al. (2009). A two-sided market analysis of provider investment incentives with an application to the net-neutrality issue. *Review of Network Economics*, 8(1), 22–28.

Netanel, N. (2003). Impose a commercial use levy to allow free peer-to-peer file sharing. *Harvard Journal of Law & Technology*, 17, 1–20.

Newman, L. (January 21, 2014). Net neutrality is already in trouble in the developing world. *Slate*.

Nwogugu, M. (2006). Corporate governance and the economics of digital content: Some legal issues. *Computer & Telecommunications Law Review*, 12(1), 5–13.

Oberholzer-Gee, F. and Strumpf, K. (2007). The effect of filesharing on record sales: An empirical analysis. *Journal of Political Economy*, 115, 1–42.

Ouellet, J.F. (2007). The purchase versus illegal download of music by consumers: The influence of consumer response towards the artist and music. *Canadian Journal of Administrative Sciences*, 24(2), 107–119.

Ouma, M. (2006). Optimal enforcement of music copyright in sub-Saharan Africa: Reality or myth? *Journal of World Intellectual Property*, 9(5), 592–627.

Picard, R. (2004). A note on economic losses due to theft, infringement, and piracy of protected works. *Journal of Media Economics*, 17(3), 207–217.

Ramello, G. and Silva, F. (2007). New directions in copyright law and economics. *Review of Law & Economics*, 3(3), 643–647.

Ruiz, R.R. and Lohr, S. (February 26, 2015). In net neutrality victory, F.C.C. classifies broadband internet service as a public utility. *New York Times*.

Sag, M. (2006). Piracy: Twelve year-olds, grandmothers, and other good targets for the recording industry. *Northwestern Journal of Technology and Intellectual Property*, 4(2), 2–12.

Schmidt, A. (2006). Multilevel markets and incentives for information goods. *Information Economics and Policy*, 18(2), 125–138.

Singleton, S. (December 2007). Jargonomics: Intellectual property prices and marginal cost. Progress & Freedom Foundation, USA, Progress & Freedom Foundation Progress on Point Paper No. 14.24.

Singh, S. (April 8, 2015). Politicos slam TRAI's stance on net neutrality. *India Today*. Available at: http://indiatoday.intoday.in/technology/story/politicos-raise-concern-over-trais-threatening-consultation-on-net-neutrality/1/429135.html. Accessed on July 30, 2016.

Sinha, R.K. et al. (2010). Don't think twice, it's all right: Music piracy and pricing in a DRM-free environment. *Journal of Marketing*, 74(2), 40–54.

Spangler, T. (March 4, 2015). Updated: Netflix CFO says pressing FCC for Title II broadband regs was not its preferred option.

Subirana, B. (2000). Zero entry barriers in a computationally complex world: Transaction streams and the complexity of the digital trade of intangible goods. *Journal of Organizational and End User Computing*, 12(2), 43–55.

Von Lohmann, F. (2004). Voluntary collective licensing for music file sharing. *Communications of the ACM*, 47(10), 21–24.

Weyl, G. (2010). A price theory of multi-sided platforms. *American Economic Review*, 100, 1642–1672.

Wu, S. et al. (2008). Customized bundle pricing for information goods: A nonlinear mixed-integer programming approach. *Management Science*, 54(3), 608–622.

Yoo, C. (Fall 2005). Beyond net neutrality. *Harvard Journal of Law & Technology*, 19(1), 1–77.

Yoon, K. (2002). The optimal level of copyright protection. *Information Economics and Policy*, 14, 327–348.

Yuan, M. (2006). A better copyright system? Comparing welfare of indefinitely renewable copyright versus fixed-length copyright. *Economics of Innovation and New Technology*, 15(6), 519–542.

Zenter, A. (2006). Measuring the effect of file sharing on music purchases. *Journal of Law and Economics*, 49(1), 63–90.

Zhang, M. (2003). Stardom, peer-to-peer and the socially optimal distribution of music. Working Paper, MIT, Cambridge, MA. Available at: http://web.mit.edu/zxq/www/mit/15575/p2p.pdf. Accessed on July 30, 2016.

Chapter 8

Aaberge, R. and Mogstad, M. (February 2010). Robust inequality comparisons. IZA DP No. 4769. Institute for the Study of Labor, Bonn, Germany.

Ågotnes, T. et al. (2009b). On the logic of preference and judgment aggregation. *Autonomous Agents and Multi-Agent Systems*, 22, 4–30.

Baucells, M. and Heukamp, F.H. (2006). Stochastic dominance and cumulative prospect theory. *Management Science*, 52(9), 1409–1423.

Bergemann, D. and Morris, S. (2005). Robust mechanism design. *Econometrica*, 73(6), 1771–1813.

Bernard, L. (1926a). Primary and derivative groups, Chapter 26. In Bernard, L.L., ed. *An Introduction to Social Psychology*. Henry Holt & Co., New York, pp. 411–425.

Bernard, L. (1926b). Primary and derivative attitudes and ideals, Chapter 27. In Bernard, L.L., ed. *An Introduction to Social Psychology*. Henry Holt & Co., New York, pp. 425–437.

Bernard, L. (1936). The conflict between primary group attitudes and derivative group ideals in modern society. *American Journal of Sociology*, 41(5), 611–623.

Birnbaum, M. (2005a). Three new tests of independence that differentiate models of risky decision making. *Management Science*, 51, 1346–1358.

Birnbaum, M. (2005b). A comparison of five models that predict violations of first-order stochastic dominance in risky decision making. *Journal of Risk and Uncertainty*, 31(3), 263–287.

Biswas, T. (2012). Stochastic dominance and comparative risk aversion. *Review of Economic Analysis*, 4, 105–122. Originally published in Banerjee, D., eds. *Essays in Economic Analysis and Policy*. Oxford University Press, Oxford, U.K., pp. 113–130.

Blavatskyy, P. (2006). Violations of betweenness or random errors? *Economic Letters*, 91, 34–38.

Blavatskyy, P. (2008). Stochastic utility theorem. *Journal of Mathematical Economics*, 44, 1049–1056.

Blavatskyy, P. (2012). Probabilistic choice and stochastic dominance. *Economic Theory*, 50(1), 59–83.

Boujelben, M. et al. (2009). The first belief dominance: A new approach in evidence theory for comparing basic belief assignments. *Lecture Notes in Computer Science*, 5783, 272–283.

Castellano, R. and Cerqueti, R. (2012). Roots and effects of financial misperception in a stochastic dominance framework. *Quality & Quantity*, 47(6), 3371–3389.

Chen, H. et al. (2012). Incentive mechanisms for P2P network nodes based on repeated game. *Journal of Networks*, 7(2), 385–395.

Coleman, P. et al. (2007). Intractable conflict as an attractor: A dynamical systems approach to conflict escalation and intractability. *American Behavioral Scientist*, 50(11), 1454–1475.

Crainich, D. et al. (2013). Even (mixed) risk lovers are prudent. *American Economic Review*, 103, 1529–1535.

Davidson, R. (2008). Stochastic dominance. In Durlauf, S. and Blume, L., eds. *New Palgrave Dictionary of Economics*, 2nd edn. Palgrave Macmillan.

De, M.R.G. et al. (2011). Expected utility theory, prospect theory and regret theory compared for prediction of route choice behavior. *Transportation Research Record*, 223, 9–28.

Deck, C. and Schlesinger, H. (2014). Consistency of higher order risk preferences. *Econometrica*, 82(5), 1913–1943.

Diederich, A. and Busemeyer, J. (1999). Conflict and the stochastic-dominance principle of decision making. *Psychological Science*, 10(4), 353–359.

Ebert, S. (2013). Even (mixed) risk lovers are prudent: Comment. *American Economic Review*, 103, 1536–1537.

Eeckhoudt, L. et al. (2009). Apportioning of risks via stochastic dominance. *Journal of Economic Theory*, 144, 994–1003.

Feldman, M. et al. (2006). Freeriding and whitewashing in peer-to-peer systems. *IEEE Journal on Selected Areas in Communications*, 24(5), 1010–1019.

Fong, W. et al. (2008). Stochastic dominance and behavior towards risk: The market for Internet stocks. *Journal of Economic Behavior & Organization*, 68(1), 194–208.

Gao, S. et al. (2010). Adaptive route choice in risky traffic networks: A prospect theory approach. *Transportation Research Part C: Emerging Technologies*, 18, 727–740.

Gollier, C. and Muermann, A. (2010). Optimal choice and beliefs with ex-ante savoring and ex-post disappointment. *Management Science*, 56(8), 1272–1284.

Gradwohl, R. and Reingold, O. (2010). Partial exposure in large games. *Games and Economic Behavior*, 68(2), 602–613.

Guo, Z. (March 2012). Stochastic dominance and its applications in portfolio management. Working Paper.

Heathcote, A. et al. (2010). Distribution-free tests of stochastic dominance for small samples. *Journal of Mathematical Psychology*, 54, 454–463.

Hjorth, K. and Fosgerau, M. (2012). Using prospect theory to investigate the low marginal value of travel time for small time changes. *Transportation Research Part B: Methodological*, 46, 917–932.

Jou, R.C. and Chen, K.H. (2013). An application of cumulative prospect theory to freeway drivers' route choice behaviours. *Transportation Research Part A: Policy and Practice*, 49, 123–131.

Lamberson, P.J. (2009). Linking network structure and diffusion through stochastic dominance. Working Paper, MIT Sloan Research Paper No. 4760-09, MIT Sloan School of Management, Cambridge, MA.

Li, Q.S. et al. (2012). Stochastic VIKOR method based on prospect theory. *Computer Engineering and Applications*, 48, 1–4.

Li, T. and Mandayam, N. (2014). When users interfere with protocols: Prospect theory in wireless networks using random access and data pricing as an example. *IEEE Transactions on Wireless Communications*, 13(4), 1888–1907.

Li, X. et al. (2015). Multi-objective optimization of urban bus network using cumulative prospect theory. *Journal of Systems Science and Complexity*, 28(3), 661–678.

Loomes, G. et al. (2002). A microeconomic test of alternative stochastic theories of risky choice. *Journal of Risk and Uncertainty*, 24, 103–130.

Mellers, B.A. et al. (1992). Violations of dominance in pricing judgments. *Journal of Risk and Uncertainty*, 5, 73–90.

Nisgav, A. and Patt-Shamir, B. (2011). Finding similar users in social networks. *Theory of Computing Systems*, 49(4), 720–737.

Noussair, C.N. et al. (2013). Higher order risk attitudes, demographics and saving. *Review of Economic Studies*, 81(1), 325–355.

Nwogugu, M. (2005a). Towards multifactor models of decision making and risk: Critique of prospect theory and related approaches, part one. *Journal of Risk Finance*, 6(2), 150–162.

Nwogugu, M. (2005b). Towards multifactor models of decision making and risk: Critique of prospect theory and related approaches, part two. *Journal of Risk Finance*, 6(2), 163–173.

Nwogugu, M. (2005c). Towards multifactor models of decision making and risk: Critique of prospect theory and related approaches, part three. *Journal of Risk Finance*, 6(3), 267–276.

Nwogugu, M. (2006a). A further critique of cumulative prospect theory and related approaches. *Applied Mathematics & Computation*, 179(2), 451–465.

Nwogugu, M. (2006b). Regret minimization, willingness-to-accept-losses and framing. *Applied Mathematics & Computation*, 179(2), 440–450.

Nwogugu, M. (2012). *Risk in Global Real Estate Market*. John Wiley & Sons, NJ.

Nwogugu, M. (2013). Decision-making, sub-additive recursive "matching" noise and biases in risk-weighted index calculation methods in in-complete markets with partially observable multi-attribute preferences. *Discrete Mathematics, Algorithms and Applications*, 5(3), 1350020.

Ogryczak, W. and Ruszczynski, A. (1999). From stochastic dominance to mean-risk models: Semi-deviations as risk measures. *European Journal of Operational Research*, 116, 33–50.

Pavlov, O.V. (2005). Dynamic analysis of an institutional conflict: Copyright owners against online file sharing. *Journal of Economic Issues*, 39(3), 633–663.

Post, T. and Kopa, M. (2013). General linear formulations of stochastic dominance criteria. *European Journal of Operational Research*, 230(2), 321–332.

Sherman, A. et al. (2012). FairTorrent: A deficit-based distributed algorithm to ensure fairness in P2P systems. *IEEE/ACM Transactions on Networking*, 20(5), 1361–1369.

Stein, W. and Pfaffenberger, R.C. (1987). Some problems in the analysis of stochastic dominance. *Mathematical Modelling*, 8, 209–211.

Troquard, N. et al. (2011). Reasoning about social choice functions. *Journal of Philosophical Logic*, 40, 473–498.

Wang, Z.X. et al. (2010). Multi-index grey relational decision-making based on cumulative prospect theory. *Control and Decision*, 25, 232–236.

Wolter, F. and Wooldridge, M. (2011). Temporal and dynamic logic. *Journal of Indian Council of Philosophical Research*, XXVII(1), 249–276.

Wu, L. and Yang, L.C. (2013). Prospect theory-based route choice model in dynamic route guidance system. *Control Theory & Applications*, 30, 916–921.

Wu, X. and Nie, Y. (2011). Modeling heterogeneous risk-taking behavior in route choice: A stochastic dominance approach. *Procedia—Social and Behavioral Sciences*, 17, 82–404.

Xia, J.J. et al. (2012). Travel routing behaviors based on prospect theory. *Journal of Highway and Transportation Research and Development*, 29, 126–130.

Zhang, W. and He, R. (2014). Dynamic route choice based on prospect theory. *Procedia—Social and Behavioral Sciences*, 138, 159–167.

Zhao, L. and Zhang, X.C. (2007). A traveler route choice model based on prospect theory and case study. *China Civil Engineering Journal*, 40, 82–86.

Chapter 9

Aoki, M. and Yoshikawa, H. (2009). The nature of equilibrium in macroeconomics: A critique of equilibrium search theory. *Economics: The Open-Access, Open-Assessment E-Journal*, 3, 2009–2037.

Aumann, R.J. and Dreze, J.H. (2008). Rational expectations in games. *American Economic Review*, 98, 72–86.

Bernheim, D. (1984). Rationalizable strategic behavior. *Econometrica*, 52, 1007–1028.

Daskalakis, C. (2008). The complexity of Nash equilibria. PhD thesis, Department of Computer Science, University of California, Berkeley, CA.

Golle, P. et al. (2001). Incentives for sharing in peer-to-peer networks. In Goos,G., Hartmanis, J. and Van Leeuwen, J., eds. *Electronic Commerce*, Lecture Notes in Computer Science, Springer, Germany Vol. 2232, pp. 75–87.

Goodman, J. and Porter, P. (1988). Theory of competitive regulatory equilibrium. *Public Choice*, 59(1), 51–66.

Govindan, S. and Wilson, R. (2006). Sufficient conditions for stable equilibria. *Theoretical Economics*, 1, 167–206.

Klein, B. et al. (2002). The economics of copyright "fair use" in a networked world. *American Economic Review*, 92(2), 205–208.

Kohlberg, E. and Mertens, J. (1986). On the strategic stability of equilibria. *Econometrica*, 54, 1003–1037.

Krishnan, R. et al. (2003). The economics of peer-to-peer networks. *Journal of Information Technology Theory and Application*, 5(3), 31–44.

Pearce, D. (1984). Rationalizable strategic behavior and the problem of perfection. *Econometrica*, 52, 1029–1050.

Risse, M. (2000). What is rational about Nash equilibria? *Synthese*, 124(3), 361–384.

Virag, G. (2011). High profit equilibria in directed search models. *Games and Economic Behavior*, 71(1), 224–234.

Chapter 10

Ågotnes, T. et al. (2009a). Logics for qualitative coalitional games. *Logic Journal of IGPL*, 17(3), 299–321.

Ågotnes, T. et al. (2009b). Reasoning about coalitional games. *Artificial Intelligence*, 173(1), 45–79.

AhmadiPourAnari, N. et al. (2013). Equilibrium pricing with positive externalities. *Theoretical Computer Science*, 476, 1–15.

Albert, R. and Barabási, A. (2002). Statistical mechanics of complex networks. *Review of Modern Physics*, 74, 47–97.

Anagnostakis, K.G. and Greenwald, M.B. (2006). Exchange-based incentive mechanisms for peer-to-peer file sharing. Working Paper, University of Pennsylvania, Philadelphia, PA.

Anderson, N. (2007). Peer-to-peer poisoners: A tour of media-defender. *Ars Technica*, September 2007.

Anshelevich, E. and Caskurlu, B. (2011). Exact and approximate equilibria for optimal group network formation. *Theoretical Computer Science*, 412(39), 5298–5314.

Antos, A. et al. (2013). Toward a classification of finite partial-monitoring games. *Theoretical Computer Science*, 473, 77–99.

Asvanund, A. et al. (2004). An empirical analysis of network externalities in peer-to-peer music-sharing networks. *Information Systems Research*, 15(2), 155–174.

Avinadav, T. et al. (2014). Analysis of protection and pricing strategies for digital products under uncertain demand. *International Journal of Production Economics*, 158, 54–64.

Bachrach, Y. et al. (2013). Proof systems and transformation games. *Annals of Mathematics and Artificial Intelligence*, 67(1), 1–30.

Balcan, M. and Blumm, A. (2007). Approximation algorithms and online mechanisms for item pricing. *Theory of Computing*, 3, 179–195.

Basu, S. et al. (2015). Pricing cloud services—The impact of broadband quality. *Omega*, 50, 96–114.

Bateni, M. et al. (2010). The cooperative game theory foundations of network bargaining games. Working Paper, Department of Computer Science, Princeton University, Princeton, NJ.

Beekhuyzen, J. et al. (2015). Illuminating the underground: The reality of un-authorised file sharing. *Information Systems Journal*, 25(3), 171–192.

Bei, X. et al. (2011). A bounded budget betweenness centrality game for strategic network formations. *Theoretical Computer Science*, 412(52), 7147–7168.

Bilò, V. et al. (2006). Sharing the cost of multicast transmissions in wireless networks. *Theoretical Computer Science*, 369(1–3), 269–284.

Bilò, V. et al. (2010). When ignorance helps: Graphical multicast cost sharing games. *Theoretical Computer Science*, 411(3), 660–671.

Bilò, V. et al. (2013). Social context congestion games. *Theoretical Computer Science*, 514, 21–35.

Branco, F. et al. (2012). Optimal search for product information. *Management Science*, 58(11), 2037–2056.

Branco, F. et al. (2015). Too much information? Information provision and search costs. *Marketing Science*.

Brynjolfsson, E., Hu, Y., and Simester, D. (2011). Goodbye Pareto principle, hello long tail: The effect of search costs on the concentration of product sales. *Management Science*, 57, 1373–1386.

Buchegger, S. and Le Boudec, J.-Y. (June 2004). A robust reputation system for P2P and mobile ad-hoc networks. In *Proceedings of P2PEcon2004*, Harvard University, Cambridge, MA.

Cao, Z. and Yang, X. (2013). Complementary cooperation, minimal winning coalitions, and power indices. *Theoretical Computer Science*, 470, 53–92.

Chellappa, R. and Shivendu, S. (2005). Managing piracy: Pricing and sampling strategies for digital experience goods in vertically segmented markets. *Information Systems Research*, 16, 400–417.

Chen, J. and Chang, C. (2013). Dynamic pricing for new and remanufactured products in a closed-loop supply chain. *International Journal of Production Economics*, 146(1), 153–160.

Chen, P. and Hitt, L.M. (2002). Measuring switching costs and the determinants of customer retention in internet-enabled businesses: A study of the online brokerage industry. *Information Systems Research*, 13, 255–274.

Chen, Y. and Liu, K. (2011). Indirect reciprocity game modelling for cooperation stimulation in cognitive networks. *IEEE Transactions on Communications*, 59(1), 159–168.

Cheng, H.K., Bandyopadhyay, S., and Guo, H. (2011). The debate on net neutrality: A policy perspective. *Information Systems Research*, 22, 60–82.

Chin, F. et al. (2015). Competitive algorithms for unbounded one-way trading. *Theoretical Computer Science*, 572, 66–82.

Christin, N. et al. (August 2008). Economics-informed design of content delivery networks. In Buyya, R., Pathan, A., and Vakali, A., eds. *Content Delivery Networks: Principles and Paradigms*. Springer-Verlag, Germany.

Clement, M. et al. (2012). Consumer responses to legal music download services that compete with illegal alternatives. *Service Science*, 4, 4–23.

Danaher, B. et al. (2010). Converting pirates without cannibalizing purchasers: The impact of digital distribution on physical sales and internet piracy. *Marketing Science*, 29, 1138–1151.

Despotovic, Z. and Aberer, K. (2005). Probabilistic prediction of peers' performance in P2P networks. *Engineering Applications of Artificial Intelligence*, 18(7), 771–780.

Devanbu, P. and Stubblebine, S. (2002). Stack and queue integrity on hostile platforms. *IEEE Transactions on Software Engineering*, 28(1), 100–108.

Dunne, P. et al. (2010). Solving coalitional resource games. *Artificial Intelligence*, 174, 20–50.

Dunne, P. et al. (2007). A logical characterisation of qualitative coalitional games. *Journal of Applied Non-Classical Logics*, 17(4), 477–509.

Eger, K. and Killat, U. (2008). Bandwidth trading in bittorrent-like P2P networks for content distribution. *Computer Communications*, 31(2), 201–211.

Ekstrom, E. and Lu, B. (2011). Optimal selling of an asset under incomplete information. *International Journal of Stochastic Analysis*, 2011, 1–17.

Faigle, U. et al. (1998). The nucleon of cooperative games and an algorithm for matching games. *Mathematical Programming*, 83, 195–211.

Fiat, A. and Saia, J. (2007). Censorship resistant peer-to-peer networks. *Theory of Computing*, 3, 1–23.

Fotakis, D. et al. (2009). The structure and complexity of Nash equilibria for a selfish routing game. *Theoretical Computer Science*, 410(36), 3305–3326.

Gans, J. (2012). Mobile application pricing. *Information Economics and Policy*, 24(1), 52–59.

Gavalda-Miralles, A. et al. (2014). Impact of heterogeneity and socioeconomic factors on individual behavior in decentralized sharing ecosystems. *Proceedings of the National Academy of Sciences of the United States of America*, 111, 15322–15327.

Ghosh, M.K. and Rao, K.S.M. (2012). Existence of value in stochastic differential games of mixed type. *Stochastic Analysis and Applications*, 30, 895–905.

Golle, P. et al. (2001). Incentives for sharing in peer-to-peer networks. In Goos,G., Hartmanis, J. and Van Leeuwen, J., eds. *Electronic Commerce*. Lecture Notes in Computer Science, Springer, Germany, Vol. 2232, pp. 75–87.

Grant, J. et al. (2014). Manipulating games by sharing information. *Studia Logica*, 102, 267–295.

Grüner, S. et al. (2013). Connectivity games over dynamic networks. *Theoretical Computer Science*, 493, 46–65.

Guo, Z. et al. (2006). Application of stochastic approximation to digital knowledge products pricing in electronic commerce. In *Proceedings of the Sixth World Congress on Intelligent Control and Automation (WCICA)*, Dalian, China, Vol. 1, pp. 1626–1630.

Hachez, G. (2003). A comparative study of software protection tools suited for e-commerce with contributions to software watermarking and smart cards. PhD thesis, Facultes Sciences Appliquees Laboratoire de Micro´electronique, Catholic University of Louvain, Leuven, Belgium. Available at: http://citeseerx.ist.psu.edu/viewdoc/download;jsessionid=91BB6B1FF2336BEF7BDDCDF3612A9789?doi=10.1.1.13.6076&rep=rep1&type=pdf. Accessed on July 30, 2016.

Hegde, N. et al. (2015). Self-organizing flows in social networks. *Theoretical Computer Science*, 584, 3–18.

Hosanagar, K. et al. (2008). Service adoption and pricing of content delivery network (CDN) services. *Management Science*, 54(9), 1579–1593.

Iamnitchi, A. et al. (2011). The small world of file sharing. *IEEE Transactions on Parallel and Distributed Systems*, 22(7), 1120–1134.

Jackson, M. (2005). Allocation rules for network games. *Games and Economic Behavior*, 51, 128–154.

Jena, S. and Sarmah, S. (2014). Optimal acquisition price management in a remanufacturing system. *International Journal of Sustainable Engineering*, 7(2), 154–170.

Jiang, Y. (2012). Optimization of online promotion: A profit maximizing model integrating price discount and product recommendation. *International Journal of Information Technology & Decision Making*, 11, 961–967.

Kangasharju, J. (April 2002). Internet content distribution. PhD thesis, L'Universite de Nice-Sophia Antipolis, Nice, France.

Kannan, P. et al. (2008). Pricing product lines of digital content: A model using online choice experiment. *In Hawaii International Conference on System Sciences, Proceedings of the 41st Annual, IEEE, 300*. Available at: http://csdl.computer.org/comp/proceedings/hicss/2008/3075/00/30750300.pdf. Accessed on July 30, 2016.

Kannan, P. et al. (2009). Pricing product lines of digital content: A model using online choice experiment. *Marketing Science*, 28(4), 620–636.

Kannan, P.K. (2013). Designing and pricing digital content products and services: A research review. In Malhotra, N.K., ed. *Review of Marketing Research*, Vol. 10. Emerald Group Publishing Limited, Bingley, U.K., p. 97.

Kawase, Y. and Makino, K. (2013). Nash equilibria with minimum potential in undirected broadcast games. *Theoretical Computer Science*, 482, 33–47.

Ke, T.T., Shen, Z.J.M., and Villas-Boas, J.M. (2016). Search for information on multiple products. *Management Science*.

Kets, W., Iyengar, G., Sethi, R., and Bowles, S. (2011). Inequality and network structure. *Games and Economic Behavior*, 73(1), 215–226.

Khouja, M., Hadzikadic, M., Rajagopalan, H.K., and Tsay, L.S. (2007). Applications of agent-based modeling to pricing of reproducible information goods. *Decision Support Systems*, 44(3), 725–739.

Kogan, K. et al. (2013). Containing piracy with product pricing, updating and protection investments. *International Journal of Production Economics*, 144(2), 468–478.

Kumar, C. et al. (2011). A mechanism for pricing and resource allocation in peer-to-peer networks. *Electronic Commerce Research and Applications*, 10(1), 26–37.

Lang, K. and Vragov, R. (2005). A pricing mechanism for digital content distribution over computer networks. *Journal of Management Information Systems*, 22(2), 121–139.

Li, C. et al. (May 2007). An incentive mechanism for message relaying in unstructured peer-to-peer systems. In *Proceedings of the Sixth International Joint Conference on Autonomous Agents and Multi-Agent Systems (AAMAS'07)*, Honolulu, HI, May 14–18, 2007. Available at http://www.cs.cmu.edu/~softagents/papers/cuihongLi_message_relaying_aamas2007.pdf. Accessed on July 30, 2016.

Li, Y. (2010). Pricing digital content distribution over heterogeneous channels. *Decision Support Systems*, 50(1), 243–257.

Li, Y. et al. (2009). Collection pricing decision in a remanufacturing system considering random yield and random demand. *Systems Engineering–Theory & Practice*, 29(8), 19–27.

Li, Z. and Shen, H. (2012). Game-theoretic analysis of cooperation incentive strategies in mobile ad hoc networks. *IEEE Transactions on Mobile Computing*, 11(8), 1287–1303.

Lin, C. et al. (2010). Fuzzy group decision making in pursuit of a competitive marketing strategy. *International Journal of Information Technology & Decision Making*, 9(2), 281–300.

Liu, G. et al. (2015). An efficient and trustworthy P2P and social network integrated file sharing system. *IEEE Transactions on Computers*, 64(1), 54–70.

Liu, Y. et al. (2011). Optimal software pricing in the presence of piracy and word-of-mouth effect. *Decision Support Systems*, 51(1), 99–107.

Lou, X. and Hwang, K. (2009). Collusive piracy prevention in P2P content delivery networks. *IEEE Transactions on Computers*, 58(7), 970–983.

Maschler, M. and Peleg, B. (1975). Stable sets and stable points of set valued dynamic systems with applications to game theory. *SIAM Journal of Control and Optimization*, 14, 985–995.

Matsuda, Y. et al. (2010). Evolutionary game theory-based evaluation of P2P file-sharing systems in heterogeneous environments. *International Journal of Digital Multimedia Broadcasting*, 2010, 1–12.

Matsumoto, A. (2003). Let it be: Chaotic price instability can be beneficial. *Chaos, Solitons and Fractals*, 18(4), 745–758.

Meinhardt, H. (2006). An LP approach to compute the pre-kernel for cooperative games. *Computers & Operations Research*, 33, 535–557.

Mertzios, G. et al. (2013). Natural models for evolution on networks. *Theoretical Computer Science*, 477, 76–95.

Nikoletseas, S. et al. (2015). On the structure of equilibria in basic network formation. *Theoretical Computer Science*, 590, 96–105.

Nisgav, A. and Patt-Shamir, B. (2011). Finding similar users in social networks. *Theory of Computing Systems*, 49(4), 720–737.

Nwogugu, M. (2012). A survey of digital piracy and content pricing. Working Paper.

Nwogugu, M. (2012/2014a). Shapley value analysis cannot be used in network access pricing. Working Paper.

Nwogugu, M. (2012/2014b). Stackelberg analysis cannot be used in network access pricing. Working Paper. Available at: www.ssrn.com. Accessed on July 30, 2016.

Oberholzer-Gee, F. and Strumpf, K. (2007). The effect of filesharing on record sales: An empirical analysis. *Journal of Political Economy*, 115, 1–42.

OECD (2008). *The Economic Impact of Counterfeiting and Piracy*. OECD, Paris, France.

Oncan, T. et al. (2009). A comparative analysis of several asymmetric traveling salesman problem formulations. *Computers & Operations Research*, 36(3), 637–654.

Ouellet, J.F. (2007). The purchase versus illegal download of music by consumers: The influence of consumer response towards the artist and music. *Canadian Journal of Administrative Sciences*, 24(2), 107–119.

Padhariya, N. et al. (2013). Economic incentive-based brokerage schemes for improving data availability in mobile-P2P networks. *Computer Communications*, 36(8), 861–874.

Pal, R. and Hui, P. (2013). Economic models for cloud service markets: Pricing and capacity planning. *Theoretical Computer Science*, 496, 113–124.

Perritt, H. (2007a). New architectures for music: Law should get out of the way. *Hastings Communications and Entertainment Law Journal*, 29(3), 320–360.

Perritt, H. (2007b). Music markets and myths. *Seton Hall Journal of Sports and Entertainment Law*, 21(1), 61–103.

Phelps, S. and Wooldridge, M. (2013). Game theory and evolution. *IEEE Intelligent Systems*, 28(4), 76–81.

Qiaolun, G. et al. (2008). Pricing management for a closed-loop supply chain. *Journal of Revenue and Pricing Management*, 7, 45–60.

Rahwan, T. et al. (2012). Towards anytime coalition structure generation in multi-agent systems with positive or negative externalities. *Artificial Intelligence*, 186, 95–122.

Romero, P. et al. (2010). A cooperative network game efficiently solved via an ant colony optimization approach. In Dorigo, M., Birattari, M., and Di Caro, G., eds. *Swarm Intelligence*. Lecture Notes in Computer Science, Vol. 6234. Springer, Germany, pp. 336–343.

Shen, H. and Li, Z. (2015). A hierarchical account-aided reputation management system for MANETs. *IEEE/ACM Transactions on Networking* (*TON*), 23(1), 70–84.

Sinha, R.K. et al. (2010). Don't think twice, it's all right: Music piracy and pricing in a DRM-free environment. *Journal of Marketing*, 74(2), 40–54.

Stutzbach, D. et al. (2008). Characterizing unstructured overlay topologies in modern P2P file-sharing systems. *IEEE/ACM Transactions on Networking*, 16(2), 267–280.

Sundararajan, A. (2004). Managing digital piracy: Pricing and protection. *Information Systems Research*, 15, 287–308.

Taleb, N.N. (2009). Finiteness of variance is irrelevant in the practice of quantitative finance. *Complexity*, 14(3), 66–76.

Tang, C. et al. (2015). When reputation enforces evolutionary cooperation in unreliable MANETs. *IEEE transactions on cybernetics*, 45(10), 2190–2201.

Tauhiduzzaman, M. and Wang, M. (2015). Fighting pollution attacks in P2P streaming. *Computer Networks*, 79, 39–52.

Thatcher, M. and Pingry, D. (2004). An economic model of product quality and IT value. *Information Systems Research*, 15, 268–286.

Ting, H. and Xiang, X. (2015). Online pricing for multi-type of items. *Theoretical Computer Science*, 572, 66–82.

U.S. Federal Trade Commission (June 2005). Peer-to-peer filesharing technology: Consumer protection and competition issues. Staff report of the U.S. Federal Trade Commission, US FTC.

Vadde, S. et al. (2011). Pricing decisions in a multi-criteria setting for product recovery facilities. *Omega*, 39(2), 186–193.

Van Otterloo, S. et al. (2006). Knowledge condition games. *Journal of Logic, Language, and Information*, 15(4), 425–452.

Varian, H. (March 2005). Copying and copyright. *Journal of Economic Perspectives*, 19(2), 121–138.

Wang, H. and Tung, C. (2011). Construction of a model towards EOQ and pricing strategy for gradually obsolescent products. *Applied Mathematics & Computation*, 217(16), 6926–6933.

Watts, D. and Strogatz, S. (1998). Collective dynamics of 'small-world' networks. *Nature*, 393, 440–442.

Wei, J. and Zhao, J. (2011). Pricing decisions with retail competition in a fuzzy closed-loop supply chain. *Expert Systems & Application*, 38(9), 11209–11216.

Weyl, G. (2010). A price theory of multi-sided platforms. *American Economic Review*, 100, 1642–1672.

Wingrove, T. et al. (2009). Why were millions of people not obeying the law? Motivational influences on non-compliance with the law in the case of music piracy. *Psychology, Crime & Law*, 17, 261–276.

Wooldridge, M. (2012). Does game theory work? *IEEE Intelligent Systems*, 27(6), 76–80.

Wooldridge, M., Endriss, U., Kraus, S., and Lang, J. (2013). Incentive engineering for Boolean Games. *Artificial Intelligence*, 195, 418–439.

Xiao, H. and Yeh, E.M. (2012). The impact of incomplete information on games in parallel relay networks. *IEEE Journal on Selected Areas in Communications*, 30(1), 176–187.

Xiong, Y. et al. (2014). Dynamic pricing models for used products in remanufacturing with lost-sales and uncertain quality. *International Journal of Production Economics*, 147, 678–688.

Xu, M. and Van Der Schaar, M. (2013). Token system design for autonomic wireless relay networks. *IEEE Transactions on Communications*, 61(7), 2924–2935.

Xu, Y. et al. (2007). On the on-line rent-or-buy problem in probabilistic environments. *Journal of Global Optimization*, 38(1), 1–20.

Yang, B. et al. (2005). Addressing the non-cooperation problem in competitive P2P systems. Working Paper, Stanford University, Stanford, CA. Available at: http://infolab.stanford.edu/~byang/pubs/rtr.pdf. Accessed on July 30, 2016.

Yang, X. et al. (2012). Optimal randomized algorithm for a generalized ski-rental with interest rate. *Information Processing Letters*, 112(13), 548–551.

Yong, Z. et al. (2012). Competitive algorithms for online pricing. *Discrete Mathematics, Algorithms and Applications*, 4(2). Available at: http://dx.doi.org/10.1142/S1793830912500152. Accessed on July 30, 2016.

Yu, A. et al. (2011). Pricing strategies for tied digital contents and devices. *Decision Support Systems*, 51(3), 405–412.

Yu, H. et al. (2006). Game theoretical analysis of buy-it-now price auctions. *International Journal of Information Technology & Decision Making*, 5(3), 557–581.

Yuan, S. and Tsao, J. (2010). An incentive mechanism for ad-hoc wireless content service: Contextualized micro pricing. *International Journal of Information Technology & Decision Making*, 9(1), 81–113.

Zhang, Y. and van der Schaar, M. (2012). Peer-to-peer multimedia sharing based on social norms. *Signal Processing: Image Communication*, 27(5), 383–400.

Zhang, Y. et al. (2012). Competitive algorithms for online pricing. *Discrete Mathematics, Algorithms and Applications*, 4(2).

Zhang, Y. et al. (2011). Competitive strategy for on-line leasing of depreciable equipment. *Mathematical and Computer Modelling*, 54(1–2), 466–476.

Zhang, Y. et al. (2012). Risk-reward models for on-line leasing of depreciable equipment. *Computers & Mathematics with Applications*, 63(1), 167–174.

Chapter 11

Ågotnes, T. et al. (2009). On the logic of preference and judgment aggregation. *Autonomous Agents and Multi-Agent Systems*, 22, 4–30.

Altman, E. and Wynter, L. (2004). Equilibrium games and pricing in transportation and telecommunication networks. *Networks and Spatial Economics*, 4(1), 7–21.

Angel, E. et al. (2006). Fair cost-sharing methods for the minimum spanning tree game. *Information Processing Letters*, 100(1), 29–35.

Anshelevich, E. and Caskurlu, B. (2011). Exact and approximate equilibria for optimal group network formation. *Theoretical Computer Science*, 412(39), 5298–5314.

Azar, Y. et al. (2005). Combining online algorithms for acceptance and rejection. *Theory of Computing*, 1, 105–117.

Baake, P. and Wichmann, T. (1999). On the economics of internet peering. *Netnomics*, 1(1), 89–105.

Bakos, Y. and Nault, B. (1997). Ownership and investment in electronic networks. *Information Systems Research*, 8(4), 321–341.

Bandyapadhyay, S. et al. (2014). Voronoi game on graphs. *Theoretical Computer Science*, 562, 270–282.

Bei, X. et al. (2011). A bounded budget betweenness centrality game for strategic network formations. *Theoretical Computer Science*, 412(52), 7147–7168.

Berenbrink, P. and Schulte, O. (2010). Evolutionary equilibrium in Bayesian routing games: Specialization and niche formation. *Theoretical Computer Science*, 411(7–9), 1054–1074.

Bergemann, D. and Morris, S. (2005). Robust mechanism design. *Econometrica*, 73(6), 1771–1813.

Biczok, G. et al. (2008). Pricing internet access for disloyal users: A game theoretic analysis. In *Proceedings of NetEcon 2008*, Seattle, WA, August 22, 2008.

Bilò, V. et al. (2013). Social context congestion games. *Theoretical Computer Science*, 514, 21–35.

Bilò, V. et al. (2010). When ignorance helps: Graphical multicast cost sharing games. *Theoretical Computer Science*, 411(3), 660–671.

Bilò, V. and Flammini, M. (2011). Extending the notion of rationality of selfish agents: Second order Nash equilibria. *Theoretical Computer Science*, 412(22), 2296–2311.

Blum, A. et al. (2010). Routing without regret: On convergence to Nash equilibria of regret-minimizing algorithms in routing games. *Theory of Computing*, 6, 179–199.

Borkotokey, S. and Sarangi, S. (2011). *Allocation rules for fixed and flexible networks: the role of players and their Links*. Working Paper.

Buccirossi, P. et al. (2005). Competition in the internet backbone market. *World Competition*, 28(2), 235–254.

Canavoi, F. et al. (2014). The discrete strategy improvement algorithm for parity games and complexity measures for directed graphs. *Theoretical Computer Science*, 560, 235–250.

Cao, X. et al. (2002). Internet pricing with a game theoretical approach: Concepts and examples. *IEEE/ACM Transactions on Networking*, 10(2), 208–216.

Calvo, E. and Gutiérrez, E. (2013). The Shapley-solidarity value for games with a coalition structure. *International Game Theory Review*, 15(1).

Chen, W. and Teng, S.H. (2016). *Interplay between Social Influence and Network Centrality: Shapley Values and Scalable Algorithms*. http://arxiv.org/pdf/1602.03780v2.pdf. Accessed on July 30, 2016.

Chun, Y. et al. (2016). A Strategic Implementation of the Shapley Value for the Nested Cost-Sharing Problem. *Journal of Public Economic Theory*, forthcoming.

Clark, J.A. and Tsiaparas, A. (2002). Bandwidth-on-demand networks—A solution to peer-to-peer file sharing. *BT Technology Journal*, 20(1), 53–55.

Cremer, J. et al. (2000). Connectivity in the commercial internet. *The Journal of Industrial Economics*, 48(4), 433–472.

Disser, Y. et al. (2015). Improving the image-bound on the price of stability in undirected Shapley network design games. *Theoretical Computer Science*, 562, 557–564.

Fanelli, A. et al. (2015). The ring design game with fair cost allocation. *Theoretical Computer Science*, 562, 90–100.

Fan-Yong, M. and Wang, Y. (2012). The Shapley value for fuzzy games on vague sets. *WSEAS Transactions on Information Science and Applications*, 9(2), 47–50.

Fatima, S. et al. (September 2008). A linear approximation method for the Shapley value. *Artificial Intelligence*, 172(14), 1673–1699.

Flores, R. et al. (2016). Assessment of groups in a network organization based on the Shapley group value. *Decision Support Systems*, 83, 97–105.

Friedman, E. and Oren, S. (1994). The complexity of resource allocation and price mechanisms under bounded rationality. *Economic Theory*, 6(2), 1432–1479.

Fu, G. et al. (2007). Multicriteria analysis on the strategies to open Taiwan's mobile virtual network operators services. *International Journal of Information Technology & Decision Making*, 6(1), 85–112.

Ganesh, A. et al. (2007). Congestion pricing and noncooperative games in communication networks. *Operations Research*, 55(3), 430–438.

Glachant, M. (1998). The use of regulatory mechanism design in environmental policy: A theoretical critique. In Duchin, F., Faucheux, S., Gowdy, J., and Nicolai, I., eds. *Firms and Sustainability*. Edward Elgar Publishers Northampton, MA.

Golle, P. et al. (2001). Incentives for sharing in peer-to-peer networks. In Goos,G., Hartmanis, J. and Van Leeuwen, J., eds. *Electronic Commerce*, Lecture Notes in Computer Science, Springer, Germany Vol. 2232, pp. 75–87.

He, X. et al. (2007). A survey of Stackelberg differential game models in supply and marketing channels. *Journal of Systems Science and Systems Engineering (JSSE)*, 16(4), 385–413.

Hoefer, M. et al. (2011). Competitive routing over time. *Theoretical Computer Science*, 412(39), 5420–5432.

Hurwicz, L. (1972). *On Informationally Decentralized Systems*. In C. B. McGuire and R. Radner, eds. Decision and organization: A volume in honor of Jacob Marschak. North Holland, Amsterdam, the Netherlands.

Hurwicz, L. (1973). The design of mechanisms for resource allocations. *American Economic Review*, 63(2), 1–30.

Jammeh, W. et al. (2009). Interval type-2 fussy logic congestion control of video streaming. *IEEE Transactions on Networks*, 17(5), 1123–1142.

Jia, N. and Yokoyama, R. (2003). Profit allocation of independent power producers based on cooperative game theory. *International Journal of Electrical Power & Energy Systems*, 25(8), 633–641.

Johnson, T. (Variety) (February 26, 2015). Net neutrality: FCC approves new rules of the road for internet service. Available at: http://variety.com/2015/biz/news/net-neutrality-rules-fcc-reclassifies-internet-1201440638/. Accessed on July 30, 2016.

Kattuman, P. et al. (2004). Allocating electricity transmission costs through tracing: A game-theoretic rationale. *Operations Research Letters*, 32(2), 114–120.

Kawasaki, H. (2000). Conjugate points for a nonlinear programming problem with constraints. *Journal of Nonlinear and Convex Analysis*, 1(2000), 87–293.

Kim, S. (2016). Asymptotic shapley value based resource allocation scheme for IoT services. *Computer Networks*, 100, 55–63.

Kirman, A. et al. (2007). Marginal contribution, reciprocity and equity in segregated groups: Bounded rationality and self organization in social networks. *Journal of Economic Dynamics and Control*, 31(6), 2085–2107.

Korillis, Y. et al. (1997). Achieving network optima using Stackelberg routing strategies. *IEEE/ACM Transactions on Networking*, 5, 161–172.

Laffont, J. et al. (2003). Internet interconnection and the off-net cost pricing principle. *RAND Journal of Economics*, 34(2), 370–390.

Lima, D. et al. (2008). A cooperative game theory analysis for transmission loss allocation. *Electric Power Systems Research*, 78(2), 264–275.

Larson, K. and Sandholm, T. (2005). Mechanism design and deliberative agents. In *Proceedings of the fourth international joint conference on Autonomous agents and multiagent systems (AAMAS)*, 650–656.

Ma, R. et al. (2010). Internet economics: The use of Shapley value for ISP settlement. *IEEE Transactions on Networking*,18(3), 75–787.

Mendel, J. (February 2007). Type-2 fuzzy sets and systems: An overview. *IEEE Computational Intelligence Magazine*, 2(1), 20–29.

Merten, J. and Zamir, S. (1985). Formulation of Bayesian analysis for games with incomplete information. *International Journal of Game Theory*, 14(1), 1–29.

Michalak, P. et al. (2013). Efficient computation of the Shapley value for game-theoretic network centrality. *Journal of Artificial Intelligence Research*, 46, 607–650.

Michalak, T. et al. (2014). Implementation and computation of a value for generalized characteristic function games. *ACM Transactions on Economics & Computation*, 2(4).

Michalak, T. et al. (2015). Defeating terrorist networks with game theory. *IEEE Intelligent Systems*, 30(1), 53–61.

Morais, M. and Lima, J.W. (2007). Combined natural gas and electricity network pricing. *Electric Power Systems Research*, 77(5–6), 712–719.

Moroshko, E. and Crammer, K. (2014). Weighted last-step min–max algorithm with improved sub-logarithmic regret. *Theoretical Computer Science*, 559, 107–124.

Murofushi, T. (1992). A technique for reading fuzzy measures (i): The Shapley value with respect to a fuzzy measure. In *Second Fuzzy Workshop*, Nagaoka, Japan, October 1992, pp. 39–48.

Myerson, R. (1983). Mechanism design by an informed principal. *Econometrica*, 51(6), 1767–1797.

Myerson, R. (2008). Perspectives on mechanism design in economic theory. *American Economic Review*, 98(3), 586–603.

Narayanam, R. and Narahari, Y. (2011). A Shapley value-based approach to discover influential nodes in social networks. *IEEE Transactions on Automation Science and Engineering*, 8(1), 130–147.

Nicola, S. et al. (2012). A novel framework for modeling value for the customer: An essay on negotiation. *International Journal of Information Technology & Decision Making*, 11, 661–667.

Noh, J. and Rieger, H. (2004). Random walks on complex networks. *Physical Review Letters*, 92(11), 118701 (1–4).

Nwogugu, M. (2012). *Risk in Global Real Estate Market*. John Wiley & Sons, NJ.

Pechersky, S. and Sobolev, A. (1995). Set-valued nonlinear analogues of the Shapley value. *International Journal of Game Theory*, 24(1), 57–78.

Perez-Castrillo, D. and Wettstein, D. (2001). Bidding for the surplus: A non-cooperative approach to the Shapley value. *Journal of Economic Theory*, 100(2), 274–294.

Reka, A. and Barabási, A. (2002). Statistical mechanics of complex networks. *Reviews of Modern Physics*, 74, 47–97.

Reuters (Mexico) (Monday December 29, 2014). Mexico telecoms regulator sets 2015 interconnection fees. Available at: http://www.reuters.com/article/2014/12/29/mexico-telecoms-idUSL1N0UD1GX20141229. Accessed on July 30, 2016.

Rhymend, A. and Uthariaraj, V. (2016). Handling Misbehaving Nodes in Ad hoc Networks using Shapley Value. *Transylvannia Review*, 24(9).

Roth, A.E. (1977). The Shapley value as a von Neumann-Morgenstern utility. *Econometrica: Journal of the Econometric Society*, 657–664.

Roth, A. and Verrecchia, R. (1979). The Shapley value as applied to cost allocation: A re-interpretation. *Journal of Accounting Research*, 17(1), 295–304.

Sastre, M. and Trannoy, A. (2001). Shapley inequality decomposition by factor components. Working Paper.

Shakkotai, S. and Srikant, R. (2006). Economics of network pricing with multiple ISPs. *IEEE/ACM Transactions on Networking*, 14(6), 1233–1236.

Soltys, M. and Wilson, C. (2011). On the complexity of computing winning strategies for finite poset games. *Theory of Computing Systems*, 48(3), 680–692.

Spangler, T. (March 4, 2015). Updated: Netflix CFO says pressing FCC for title II broadband regs was not its preferred option. Available at: http://variety.com/2015/digital/news/netflix-cfo-pleased-with-fcc-title-ii-ruling-although-its-preference-would-have-been-no-broadband-regulation-1201446282/. Accessed on July 30, 2016.

Su, Z. (2011). A hybrid fuzzy approach to fuzzy multi-attribute group decision-making. *International Journal of Information Technology & Decision Making*, 10(4), 695–711.

Suri, N. and Narahari, Y. (2010). Shapley value based approach to discover influential nodes in social networks. *IEEE Transaction on Automation Science and Engineering*, 99, 1–18.

The Economic Times (India) (January 9, 2015). Telcos split over method for charging interconnect charges. http://articles.economictimes.indiatimes.com/2015-01-09/news/57883939_1_iuc-20-paise-interconnection. Accessed on July 30, 2016.

This Day Newspaper (Nigeria) (March 28, 2013). Between symmetric and asymmetric interconnection models for voice services. Available at: http://www.thisdaylive.com/articles/between-symmetric-and-asymmetric-interconnection-models-for-voice-services/143383. Accessed on July 30, 2016.

Tick, E. et al. (1999). Finding fair allocations for the coalition problem with constraints. In *Proceedings of the International Conference on Logic Programming*, MIT Press, pp. 530–544.

Troquard, N. et al. (2011). Reasoning about social choice functions. *Journal of Philosophical Logic*, 40, 473–498.

Walrand, J. (2008). Economic models of communication networks. Sigmetrics Tutorial, 2008, Chapter 3. In Liu, Z., Xia, C., Liu, Z., and Xia, C., eds. *Performance Modeling and Engineering*. Springer Publishing Company, Germany.

Wolter, F. and Wooldridge, M. (2011). Temporal and dynamic logic. *Journal of Indian Council of Philosophical Research*, XXVII(1), 249–276.

Xu, Z. (2011). Approaches to multi-stage multi-attribute group decision making. *International Journal of Information Technology & Decision Making*, 10(1), 121–146.

Yaiparoj, S. et al. (2008). On the economics of GPRS networks with Wi-Fi integration. *European Journal of Operational Research*, 187(3), 1459–1475.

Zhang, N. and Wei, G. (2014). A multiple criteria hesitant fuzzy decision making with Shapley value-based VIKOR method. *Journal of Intelligent & Fuzzy Systems: Applications in Engineering and Technology*, 26(2), 1065–1075.

Zhou, W. et al. (2016). Cooperative Interconnection Settlement among ISPs through NAP. *European Journal Of Operations Research*, forthcoming.

Chapter 12

Ågotnes, T. et al. (2009). On the logic of preference and judgment aggregation. *Autonomous Agents and Multi-Agent Systems*, 22, 4–30.

Altman, E. and Wynter, L. (2004). Equilibrium games and pricing in transportation and telecommunication networks. *Networks and Spatial Economics*, 4(1), 7–21.

Angel, E. et al. (2006). Fair cost-sharing methods for the minimum spanning tree game. *Information processing letters*, 100(1), 29–35.

Anshelevich, E. and Caskurlu, B. (2011). Exact and approximate equilibria for optimal group network formation. *Theoretical Computer Science*, 412(39), 5298–5314.

Anshelevich, E. et al. (2006). Strategic network formation through peering and service agreements. *Games and Economic Behavior*, 73(1), 17–38.

Arcaute, E. et al. (2013). Dynamics in tree formation games. *Games and Economic Behavior*, 79, 1–29.

Azar, Y. et al. (2005). Combining online algorithms for acceptance and rejection. *Theory of Computing*, 1, 105–117.

Bakos, Y. and Nault, B. (1997). Ownership and investment in electronic networks. *Information Systems Research*, 8(4), 321–341.

Bandyapadhyay, S. et al. (2014). Voronoi game on graphs. *Theoretical Computer Science*, 562, 270–282.

Basar, T. et al. (2002). A Stackelberg network game with a large number of followers. *Journal of Optimization Theory and Applications*, 115, 79–490.

Baslam, M. et al. (2012). New insights from a bounded rationality analysis for strategic price-QoS war. *VALUETOOLS*, 2012, 280–289.

Bei, X. et al. (2011). A bounded budget betweenness centrality game for strategic network formations. *Theoretical Computer Science*, 412(52), 7147–7168.

Bhaskar, U. et al. (2015). A Stackelberg strategy for routing flow over time. *Games & Economic Behavior*, 92, 232–247.

Biczok, G. et al. (2008). Pricing internet access for disloyal users: A game theoretic analysis. In *Proceedings of NetEcon 2008*, Seattle, WA, August 22, 2008.

Bilò, D. et al. (2015). Specializations and generalizations of the Stackelberg minimum spanning tree game. *Theoretical Computer Science*, 562, 643–657.

Bilò, V. et al. (2010). When ignorance helps: Graphical multicast cost sharing games. *Theoretical Computer Science*, 411(3), 660–671.

Bilò, V. and Flammini, M. (2011). Extending the notion of rationality of selfish agents: Second order Nash equilibria. *Theoretical Computer Science*, 412(22), 2296–2311.

Briest, P. et al. (2012). Stackelberg network pricing games. *Algorithmica*, 62(3–4), 733–753.

Canavoi, F. et al. (2014). The discrete strategy improvement algorithm for parity games and complexity measures for directed graphs. *Theoretical Computer Science*, 560, 235–250.

Cao, X. et al. (2002). Internet pricing with a game theoretical approach: Concepts and examples. *IEEE/ACM Transactions on Networking*, 10(2), 208–216.

Clark, J.A. and Tsiaparas, A. (2002). Bandwidth-on-demand networks—A solution to peer-to-peer file sharing. *BT Technology Journal*, 20(1), 53–55.

Elias, J. et al. (2011). A game theoretic analysis of network design with socially aware users. *Computer Networks*, 55(1), 106–118.

Fanelli, A. et al. (2013). Stackelberg strategies for network design games. *Internet Mathematics*, 9(4), 336–359.

Fanelli, A. et al. (2015). The ring design game with fair cost allocation. *Theoretical Computer Science*, 562, 90–100.

Fatima, S. et al. (2004). An agenda based framework for multi-issue negotiation. *Artificial Intelligence*, 152, 1–45.

Ferreira, F. and Bode, O. (2013). Licensing endogenous cost-reduction in a differentiated Stackelberg model. *Communications in Nonlinear Science and Numerical Simulation*, 18(2), 308–315.

Fu, G. et al. (2007). Multicriteria analysis on the strategies to open Taiwan's mobile virtual network operators services. *International Journal of Information Technology & Decision Making*, 6(1), 85–112.

Golle, P. et al. (2001). Incentives for sharing in peer-to-peer networks. In Goos,G., Hartmanis, J. and Van Leeuwen, J., eds. *Electronic Commerce*, Lecture Notes in Computer Science, Springer, Germany Vol. 2232, pp. 75–87.

Haddadi, S. et al. (2016). On the power allocation strategies in coordinated multi-cell networks using Stackelberg game. *EURASIP Journal on Wireless Communications and Networking*, 91. DOI: 10.1186/s13638-016-0579-3.

He, X. et al. (2007). A survey of Stackelberg differential game models in supply and marketing channels. *Journal of Systems Science and Systems Engineering* (*JSSSE*), 16(4), 385–413.

Jia, N. and Yokoyama, R. (2003). Profit allocation of independent power producers based on cooperative game theory. *International Journal of Electrical Power & Energy Systems*, 25(8), 633–641.

Kaporis, A. and Spirakis, A. (2009). The price of optimum in Stackelberg games on arbitrary single commodity networks and latency functions. *Theoretical Computer Science*, 410(8–10), 745–755.

Kattuman, P. et al. (2004). Allocating electricity transmission costs through tracing: A game-theoretic rationale. *Operations Research Letters*, 32(2), 114–120.

Kim, S. (2016). Asymptotic shapley value based resource allocation scheme for IoT services. *Computer Networks: The International Journal of Computer and Telecommunications Networking*, 100, 55–63.

Kirman, A. et al. (2007). Marginal contribution, reciprocity and equity in segregated groups: Bounded rationality and self organization in social networks. *Journal of Economic Dynamics and Control*, 31(6), 2085–2107.

Korillis, Y. et al. (1997). Achieving network optima using Stackelberg routing strategies. *IEEE/ACM Transactions on Networking*, 5, 161–172.

Liao, C. et al. (2013). The power distribution network expansion planning based on stackelberg minimum weight K-STAR game. *Journal of Circuits, Systems & Computers*, 22(06), 1350041.

Lima, D. et al. (2008). A cooperative game theory analysis for transmission loss allocation. *Electric Power Systems Research*, 78(2), 264–275.

Ma, R. et al. (2010). Internet economics: The use of Shapley value for ISP settlement. *IEEE Transactions on Networking*, 18(3), 75–787.

Morais, M. and Lima, J.W. (2007). Combined natural gas and electricity network pricing. *Electric Power Systems Research*, 77(5–6), 712–719.

Nicola, S. et al. (2012). A novel framework for modeling value for the customer: An essay on negotiation. *International Journal of Information Technology & Decision Making*, 11, 661–667.

Nie, P. (2012). A note on dynamic Stackelberg games with leaders in turn. *Nonlinear Analysis: Real World Applications*, 13(1), 85–90.

Roch, S. et al. (2005). Design and analysis of an approximation algorithm for Stackelberg network pricing. *Networks*, 46(1), 57–67.

Roth, A.E. (1977). The Shapley value as a von Neumann-Morgenstern utility. *Econometrica: Journal of the Econometric Society*, 657–664.

Roth, A. and Verrecchia, R. (1979). The Shapley value as applied to cost allocation: A re-interpretation. *Journal of Accounting Research*, 17(1), 295–304.

Roughgarden, T. (2004). Stackelberg scheduling strategies. *SIAM Journal on Computing*, 33(2), 332–350.

Sastre, M. and Trannoy, A. (2001). Shapley inequality decomposition by factor components. Working Paper.

Shakkotai, S. and Srikant, R. (2006). Economics of network pricing with multiple ISPs. *IEEE/ACM Transactions on Networking*, 14(6), 1233–1236.

Somjit, S. et al. (2016). KSBS Solution of Power Allocation in Multi-user Multi-relay Networks Using Stackelberg Game. In *Recent Advances in Information and Communication Technology* 2016, 267–276. Springer International Publishing.

Su, Z. (2011). A hybrid fuzzy approach to fuzzy multi-attribute group decision-making. *International Journal of Information Technology & Decision Making*, 10(4), 695–711.

Tick, E. et al. (1999). Finding fair allocations for the coalition problem with constraints. In De Schreye, D. ed. *ICLP*, MIT Press, Las Cruces, NM, November 29-December 4, pp. 530–544.

Troquard, N. et al. (2011). Reasoning about social choice functions. *Journal of Philosophical Logic*, 40, 473–498.

Wolter, F. and Wooldridge, M. (2011). Temporal and dynamic logic. *Journal of Indian Council of Philosophical Research*, XXVII(1), 249–276.

Xu, Z. (2011). Approaches to multi-stage multi-attribute group decision making. *International Journal of Information Technology & Decision Making*, 10(1), 121–146.

Yang, H. et al. (2007). Stackelberg games and multiple equilibrium behaviors on networks. *Transportation Research Part B: Methodological*, 41(8), 841–861.

Zhou, W. et al. (2016). Cooperative Interconnection Settlement among ISPs through NAP. *European Journal of Operational Research*, forthcoming.

Chapter 13

Al-Manthari, B. et al. (2011). Congestion prevention in broadband wireless access systems: An economic approach. *Journal of Network and Computer Applications*, 34(6), 1836–1847.

Amah, T. et al. (2016). Towards next-generation routing protocols for pocket switched networks. *Journal of Network and Computer Applications*, 70, 51–88.

Altman, E. and Wynter, L. (2004). Equilibrium games and pricing in transportation and telecommunication networks. *Networks and Spatial Economics*, 4(1), 7–21.

Angel, E. et al. (2006). Fair cost-sharing methods for the minimum spanning tree game. *Information Processing Letters*, 100(1), 29–35.

Azar, Y. et al. (2005). Combining online algorithms for acceptance and rejection. *Theory of Computing*, 1, 105–117.

Bakos, Y. and Nault, B. (1997). Ownership and investment in electronic networks. *Information Systems Research*, 8(4), 321–341.

Barrett, J.D. and Woodall, W.H. (1997). A probabilistic alternative to fuzzy logic controllers. *IIE Transactions on Quality and Reliability Engineering*, 29(6), 459–467.

Berenbrink, P. and Schulte, O. (2010). Evolutionary equilibrium in Bayesian routing games: Specialization and niche formation. *Theoretical Computer Science*, 411(7–9), 1054–1074.

Biczok, G. et al. (2008). Pricing internet access for disloyal users: A game theoretic analysis. In *Proceedings of NetEcon 2008*, Seattle, WA, August 22, 2008.

Bilò, V. et al. (2013). Social context congestion games. *Theoretical Computer Science*, 514, 21–35.

Blum, A. et al. (2010). Routing without regret: On convergence to Nash equilibria of regret-minimizing algorithms in routing games. *Theory of Computing*, 6, 179–199.

Blundo, C. et al. (2005). Secure e-coupons. *Electronic Commerce Research*, 5(1), 117–139.

Brock, G. et al. (2009). Fuzzy logic and related methods as a screening tool for detecting gene regulatory networks. *Information Fusion*, 10, 250–259.

Cao, X. et al. (2002). Internet pricing with a game theoretical approach: Concepts and examples. *IEEE/ACM Transactions on Networking*, 10(2), 208–216.

Clark, E. and Easaw, J. (2007). Optimal access pricing for natural monopoly networks when costs are sunk and revenues are uncertain. *European Journal of Operational Research*, 178(2), 595–602.

de Rus, G. and Socorro, M.P. (2014). Access pricing, infrastructure investment and intermodal competition. *Transportation Research Part E: Logistics and Transportation Review*, 70, 374–387.

Do, C. et al. (2016). Dynamics of service selection and provider pricing game in heterogeneous cloud market. *Journal of Network and Computer Applications*, 69, 152–165.

Di Pillo, F. et al. (2010). Asymmetry in mobile access charges: is it an effective regulatory measure? *Netnomics*, 11(3), 291–314.

Fanelli, A., Leniowski, D., Monaco, G., and Sankowski, P. (2015). The ring design game with fair cost allocation. *Theoretical Computer Science*, 562, 90–100.

Fatima, S. et al. (September 2008). A linear approximation method for the Shapley value. *Artificial Intelligence*, 172(14), 1673–1699.

Federal Communications Commission (2007). High-speed services for internet access. US FTC.

Fiat, A. and Saia, J. (2007). Censorship resistant peer-to-peer networks. *Theory of Computing*, 3, 1–23.

Fjell, K. and Foros, O. (2008). Access regulation and strategic transfer pricing. *Management Accounting Research*, 19(1), 18–31.

Fjell, K. et al. (2010). Endogenous average cost based access pricing. *Review of Industrial Organization*, 36(2), 149–162.

Fotakis, D. et al. (2009). The structure and complexity of Nash equilibria for a selfish routing game. *Theoretical Computer Science*, 410(36), 3305–3326.

Fotakis, D. et al. (2014). On the hardness of network design for bottleneck routing games. *Theoretical Computer Science*, 521, 107–122.

Fotakis, D. and Tzamos, C. (2013). Winner-imposing strategy proof mechanisms for multiple facility location games. *Theoretical Computer Science*, 472, 90–103.

Gassner, E. et al. (2009). How hard is it to find extreme Nash equilibria in network congestion games? *Theoretical Computer Science*, 410(47–49), 4989–4999.

Guthrie, G. et al. (2006). Pricing access: Forward-looking versus backward-looking cost rules. *European Economic Review*, 50(7), 1767–1789.

He, X. et al. (2007). A survey of Stackelberg differential game models in supply and marketing channels. *Journal of Systems Science and Systems Engineering (JSSSE)*, 16(4), 385–413.

Hoefer, M. et al. (2011). Competitive routing over time. *Theoretical Computer Science*, 412(39), 5420–5432.

Inderst, R. and Peitz, M. (2012). Network investment, access and competition. *Telecommunications Policy*, 36(5), 407–418.

Jammeh, W. et al. (2009). Interval type-2 fussy logic congestion control of video streaming. *IEEE Transactions on Networks*, 17(5), 1123–1142.

Kao, T. et al. (2014). Optimal access regulation with downstream competition. *Journal of Regulatory Economics*, 45(1), 75–93.

Kattuman, P. et al. (2004). Allocating electricity transmission costs through tracing: A game-theoretic rationale. *Operations Research Letters*, 32(2), 114–120.

Kawase, Y. and Makino, K. (2013). Nash equilibria with minimum potential in undirected broadcast games. *Theoretical Computer Science*, 482, 33–47.

Kirman, A. et al. (2007). Marginal contribution, reciprocity and equity in segregated groups: Bounded rationality and self organization in social networks. *Journal of Economic Dynamics and Control*, 31(6), 2085–2107.

Korillis, Y. et al. (1997). Achieving network optima using Stackelberg routing strategies. *IEEE/ACM Transactions on Networking*, 5, 161–172.

Kotakorpi, K. (2006). Access price regulation, investment and entry in telecommunications. *International Journal of Industrial Organization*, 24(5), 1013–1020.

Lima, D. et al. (2008). A cooperative game theory analysis for transmission loss allocation. *Electric Power Systems Research*, 78(2), 264–275.

López, P. et al. (2010). Moving routing protocols to the user space in MANET middleware. *Journal of Network and Computer Applications*, 33(5), 588–602.

Ma, R. et al. (2010). Internet economics: The use of Shapley value for ISP settlement. *IEEE Transactions on Networking*, 18(3), 75–787.

McClure, D. (May 1, 2007). The exabyte internet. U.S. Internet Industry Association. http://www.usiia.org/pubs/The%20Exabyte%20Internet.pdf. Accessed on July 30, 2016.

Mendel, J. (February 2007). Type-2 fuzzy sets and systems: An overview. *IEEE Computational Intelligence Magazine*, 2(1), 20–29.

Morais, M. and Lima, J.W. (2007). Combined natural gas and electricity network pricing. *Electric Power Systems Research*, 77(5–6), 712–719.

Nwogugu, M. (2006). Corporate governance and the economics of digital content: Some legal issues. *Computer & Telecommunications Law Review*, 12(1), 5–13.

Peitz, M. (2005). Asymmetric regulation of access and price discrimination in telecommunications. *Journal of Regulatory Economics*, 28(3), 327–343.

Qadir, J. et al. (2014). Multicasting in cognitive radio networks: Algorithms, techniques and protocols. *Journal of Network and Computer Applications*, 45, 44–61.

Rezaei, M. et al. (2008). Semi-fuzzy rate controller for variable bit rate video. *IEEE Transactions On Circuits and Systems for Video Technology*, 18(5), 633–645.

Roth, A. and Verrecchia, R. (1979). The Shapley value as applied to cost allocation: A re-interpretation. *Journal of Accounting Research*, 17(1), 295–304.

Sarmento, P. and Brandao, A. (2007). Access pricing: A comparison between full deregulation and two alternative instruments of access price regulation, cost-based and retail-minus. *Telecommunications Policy*, 31(5), 236–250.

Sastre, M. and Trannoy, A. (2001). Shapley inequality decomposition by factor components. Working Paper.

Shakkotai, S. and Srikant, R. (2006). Economics of network pricing with multiple ISPs. *IEEE/ACM Transactions on Networking*, 14(6), 1233–1236.

Sicker, D. and Stuka, M. (2004). An evaluation of VoIP traversal of firewalls and NATs within an enterprise environment. *Information Systems Frontiers*, 6(3), 219–228.

Sidak, J.G. (September 2006). A consumer-welfare approach to network neutrality regulation of the internet. *Journal of Competition Law and Economics*, 2(3), 349–474.

Sundararajan, A. (2004). Nonlinear pricing of information goods. *Management Science*, 50(12), 1660–1673.

Tick, E. et al. (1999). Finding fair allocations for the coalition problem with constraints. In *Proceedings of the International Conference on Logic Programming*, MIT Press, Cambridge, MA, pp. 530–544.

Valletti, T. (2003). The theory of access pricing and its linkage with investment incentives. *Telecommunications Policy*, 27(10–11), 659–675.

Wolkenhauer, O. and Edmunds, J.M. (1997). A critique of fuzzy logic in control. *International journal of electrical engineering education*, 34(3), 235–242.

Yuksel, M. et al. (2007). Value of supporting class of service in IP backbones. www.cse.unr.edu/yuksem/my-papers/iwqos07.pdf. Accessed on July 30, 2016.

Chapter 14

Arkenbout, E. et al. (2004). Copyright in the information society: Scenarios and strategies. *European Journal of Law and Economics*, 17(2), 237–242.

Balasko, Y. and Shell, K. (1980). The overlapping generations model, I: The case of pure exchange without money. *Journal of Economic Theory*, 23, 281–306.

Bechtold, S. (2003). The present and future of digital rights management—Musings on emerging legal problems. In Becker, E. et al., eds. *Digital Rights Management*. LNCS, Vol. 2770. Springer-Verlag, Berlin, Germany, pp. 597–654.

Broucek, V. et al. (2005). Music piracy, universities and the Australian Federal Court: Issues for forensic computing specialists. *Computer Law & Security Report*, 21(1), 30–37.

Engel, F. (1999). The role of service level agreements in the internet service provider industry. *International Journal of Network Management*, 9, 299–301.

Garoupa, N. (2003). Behavioral economic analysis of crime: A critical review. *European Journal of Law and Economics*, 15(1), 5–15.

Garoupa, N. (2005). Economics of business crime: Theory and public poly implications. *Security Journal*, 18(1), 29–41

Gervais, D. (2001). Transmissions of music on the internet: An analysis of the copyright laws of Canada, France, Germany, Japan, the United Kingdom and the United States. *Vanderbilt Journal of Transnational Law*, 34, 1363–1373.

Handler, M. (2003). A real pea souper: The panel case and the development of the fair dealing defences to copyright infringement in Australia. *Melbourne University Law Review*, 27, 381–390.

Klein, B. et al. (2002). The economics of copyright "fair use" in a networked world. *American Economic Review*, 92(2), 205–208.

Ku, R. (2002). The creative destruction of copyright: Napster and the new economics of digital technology. *University of Chicago Law Review*, 69(1), 263–324.

Lethin, R. (2003). Technical and social components of peer-to-peer computing. *Communications of the ACM*, 46(2), 30–32.

McKay, H. (2005). Development of the contractual relationship between an ISP and its customers—Is a fair deal in sight? *Computer Law & Security Law Report*, 21(3), 193–278.

Menard, C. (1998). Mal-adaptation of regulation to hybrid organizational forms. *International Review of Law & Economics*, 18, 403–417.

Nowak, N. et al. (2000). Modeling the temporal coordination of behavior and internal states. *Advances in Complex Systems*, 3, 67–86.

Pearce, R. (February 20, 2015). ISPs unveil draft anti-piracy scheme—Draft code will see notices issued to ISP customers accused of online piracy. *Computerworld*.

U.S. Congress (2004). HR 4077—To enhance criminal enforcement of the copyright laws, to educate the public about application of the copyright laws to the internet, and for other purposes, 108th congress, 2nd session.

U.S. Department of Justice (October 2004). Report of the Department of Justice's task force on intellectual property.

Vaccaro, V. and Cohn, D. (2004). The evolution of business models and marketing strategies in the music industry. *International Journal on Media Management*, 6(1/2), 46–58.

Index